Teaching K–6 Mathematics

Teaching K–6 Mathematics

Douglas K. Brumbaugh
David Rock
Linda S. Brumbaugh
Michelle L. Rock

LEA **LAWRENCE ERLBAUM ASSOCIATES, PUBLISHERS**
2003 Mahwah, New Jersey   London

Lawrence Erlbaum Associates, Inc., Publishers
10 Industrial Avenue
Mahwah, New Jersey 07430

Cover design by Kathryn Houghtaling

Library of Congress Cataloging-in-Publication Data

Teaching K–6 Mathematics, by Douglas K. Brumbaugh, David Rock,
Linda S. Brumbaugh, and Michelle L. Rock / (ISBN: 0-8058-3268-8: pbk.)

Cataloging-In-Publication Data for this volume can be obtained by
contacting the Library of Congress.

In loving memory of Pat and Web Brumbaugh, and J. Z. Schmidt

To Shawn, Mike, and Laura, Linda and Doug's kids

To Lucile "Grandma" Schmidt, Linda's mom

To Barbara and Jerry, David's parents

To Ruth and Ken, Michelle's parents

*To Carly, Kyle, and Katelyn, Michelle and David's kids who
keep us on our toes each and everyday*

To April, David's sister, and Mark and Chris, Michelle's brothers

*To Judy Rosenstock and Francis Duvall, the principals who
gave David and Michelle their first teaching positions*

To all our teachers

To all our students: past, present, and future

Contents in Brief

Contents

Preface

This book bucks the current trend of creating a mathematics methods book for grades K-8. We believe there are huge differences between elementary (grades K–5 or K–6) and middle school (grades 5–6 through 8–9).

The students are different:
• Developmentally (stages of abstract thought ability)
• Socially (hormones)

The teachers are different:

• Mathematical attitude
• Mathematical background

The demands are different:

• Many elementary teachers teach all subjects
• Middle school teachers specialize

The school atmosphere is different:

• Elementary students are learning to be on their own
• Middle schoolers are expected to function on their own

Mathematical preparation for certification is different in many states.

Elementary school certification typically requires:

• College Algebra or Finite Mathematics
• Mathematics content for Elementary Teachers

• Mathematics methods for Elementary Teachers

Middle school certification typically requires:

• 18 hours of mathematics that includes:
• Trigonometry or Calculus
• College Geometry
• Statistics

Given all of the listed differences, we believe that a textbook intended for students in both elementary and middle school mathematics methods courses short-changes both groups. Thus, we have chosen to limit the focus of this book to the elementary grades. We are aware that many elementary teachers "move up" to the middle school but our hope is that before doing so, they will take additional course work to develop the specific mathematical background needed for teaching at this level. In this text, we decided not to include topics appropriate only for middle school teachers of mathematics, because doing so will shortchange elementary education majors. Either the topics specific to teaching middle school mathematics will be skipped in the elementary mathematics methods class and thus a part of the book is not used, or it is covered, but the development of the fundamental approaches necessary for a good elementary program are glossed over. Either way, the student is not adequately prepared to deal with the considerable and specific challenges associated with the teaching of elementary school mathematics.

As a team, the authors bring to this book a lot of direct experience in the teaching of elementary mathematics. Linda and Michelle combine more than 30 years of experience in teaching elementary school. David and Doug combine more than 40 years of research and development in teaching elementary school mathematics, and each has spent extensive time teaching mathematics in elementary schools as well as elementary mathematics methods courses similar to those for which this text is intended.

TO THE STUDENTS

In this text we talk directly to you, the prospective teacher of elementary school mathematics. We want to help you see a multitude of ways you can help your future students learn to see the power, beauty, necessity, and usefulness of mathematics in the world. We want to assist you in delivering your students the message that without a working knowledge of mathematics, they are excluded from a majority of career opportunities. We want to give you ideas on how to entice your students into the fascinating world of recreational mathematics and its applications. We want to guide you through the many developmental aspects of teaching mathematics effectively so students will learn to use its power to make their own lives easier.

We have written this text in an informal style that we hope conveys our intention to have a discussion with you about how you can become an effective teacher of mathematics at the elementary school level, not telling you or lecturing to you. We envision you attempting to "pick our brains" as we talk, taking advantage of our many years of experience doing what

you are proposing to do. We want to share our backgrounds to help you miss pitfalls and become the best teacher of elementary school mathematics you can possibly be.

TO THE FACULTY

This text is different from many of those on the market. We do not want to presume to tell you how to operate in your course. You are the local authority. What we want to do is to present you with a developmentally sound, research-based, practical tool to blend with your approach to developing the best teachers of elementary school mathematics.

The text is divided into 11 parts, each of which is an outtake from the National Council of Teachers of Mathematics' Principles and Standards for School Mathematics (Standards 2000). Each chapter begins with a list of focal points that will be discussed. Part 1 deals with guiding principles that permeate the text while Parts 2 through 11 deal with the specific the standards for elementary mathematics education: Number and Operations; Algebra; Geometry; Measurement; Data Analysis and Probability; Problem Solving; Reasoning and Proof; Communication; Connections; Representation. Each part begins with a list of focal points it will address. The focal points for Part 1 are: beginnings, curriculum, planning, assessment, technology, and manipulatives. We start with these ideas because they are intertwined with each topic. We cannot perceive of an effective elementary mathematics program without planning, assessment, technology, and manipulatives. We discuss developmental stages children pass through and the types of things that can reasonably be expected of them while they are doing it. We deal with constructivism and its impact on the modern classroom.

UNIQUE FEATURES

Tricks, Activities, and Games (TAG)

We realize that not all mathematical learning can be fun. However, we provide a wealth of ideas that could be used to attract students to learning mathematics, often without their realizing that they are being enticed until it is too late. Each part has several TAG entries and many of them, with little or no variation, could be used in different levels of the K–6 curriculum.

Technology is an integral part of the book. Students are expected to do Internet searches to expand their horizons, investigate new sites appropriate for elementary students, sample new software that could be used in the classroom, and develop ways to blend calculators into the curriculum.

Manipulatives are essential for students to learn elementary mathematics concepts. Cuisenaire rods, base 10 blocks, chips, number lines, and geoboards, are all part of the manipulative landscape that is created in this text.

Careful attention is given to blending the appropriate amount of emphasis on rote work, developmental activities, fun, application, technology, manipulatives, assessment, and planning so the prospective teachers become accustomed to variable approaches and decision making as a curriculum is determined.

ACKNOWLEDGMENTS

The following people reviewed the manuscript and made invaluable suggestions: Sandra L. Canter, Ball State University; Bruce F. Godsave, State University of New York at Geneseo; Charles E. Lamb, Texas A & M University; Trena L. Wilkerson, Baylor University. Theirs was not an easy task and we appreciate the efforts they made to build this into a stronger book.

Our editor, Naomi Silverman, once again was invaluable as a motivator, resource, and friend. She had the vision and drive to get us started, keep us going, and provide direction along the way. Without her, this book would not exist.

Lori Hawver filled in the spaces for us. When Naomi gave us the big picture, Lori would provide the detailed assistance that made our development so much easier. When we had questions, Lori was a fountain of knowledge.

Eileen Engel, our Production Editor was an endless source of ideas, information, and quality touches.

People play a primary role in helping to mold us into who we are and what we become. Each person listed here is special. Our family and loved ones are obviously connected to us and have had a tremendous impact on us.

Beyond them are all those we have met in the classroom (teachers and students), too countless to name, and yet each has exerted some level of influence on us. To all of you, we say—THANX!

About the Authors

DOUGLAS K. BRUMBAUGH

I am a teacher. I have been teaching for nearly 40 years as I write this. I teach college, in-service, or K–12 almost daily. I received my BS from Adrian College and went on to the University of Georgia for my masters and doctorate in mathematics education. As I talk with others about teaching and learning in the K–12 environment, my immersion in teaching is beneficial. Students change, classroom environment changes, the curriculum changes—and I change. The thoughts and examples in this book are based on my experiences as a teacher working with garden-variety kids. Classroom-tested success stories are the ideas, materials, and situations you will read about and do. This text's problems and activities will stretch you while providing a beginning collection of classroom ideas. Learn, expand your horizons, teach, and treasure each day you are given!

LINDA S. BRUMBAUGH

I am beginning my 30th year of teaching in the elementary school as I write this. I have taught several years in each of third, fourth and fifth grades. I received my BS in elementary education from the University of Florida and my Masters in elementary education from the University of Central Florida. As I look back over my career, it is easy to see the excitement on the children's faces as they encountered new concepts, worked with a manipulative, learned a new piece of software, experienced some new application of mathematics, played a new mathematical game, or got caught up in some new mathematical trick. As they got excited about learning, so did I. Each day of each year brought some new learning opportunity for me and for the children. Many of the activities that occurred in my classes are presented throughout this text. You are about to embark on the most exciting career path imaginable. You will have the opportunity to work with open minds on a daily basis. Teach them to learn. Enjoy the experience.

DAVID ROCK

I wake up every morning with a desire to go to work! One of the greatest feelings is to see the look of math anxiety fade from a scared face, whether it is young or old. I teach children the power of mathematics and adults the excitement of mathematics education. Teachers must have an open mind and the eagerness to continue learning. As educators, we must be reflective: What can I do to effectively teach the learners around me? Kids come to school at a young age, eager and excited about learning. We must foster and nurture this desire to learn at all ages, especially in the elementary years. I was born in Richmond, VA but grew up in the Washington DC area. I received my BS degree from Vanderbilt University and Masters and Doctoral degrees from the University of Central Florida. I am currently at The University of Mississippi where I am an associate professor of mathematics education. I have a wonderful and supporting family. Michelle and I have been married for 10 years, and we are blessed with three beautiful children that love to learn.

MICHELLE L. ROCK

I have always wanted to be an elementary school teacher. In third grade, I told my teacher, Ms. Hofer, that I wanted to be just like her. She inspired me as a student and inspired me as an adult. She made me realize that a teacher touches a child's life forever. I was born Portland, OR but lived in Orlando, FL for 22 years. I received my BS degree in elementary education from the University of Central Florida, which enabled me to achieved my dream. I am married to David and have three precious children.

As a Teacher of Mathematics: An Introduction

As an elementary educator, you are expected to learn how to teach a variety of subject areas. Each of these areas is important to you and your career. In this text, the focus is on one of those areas—mathematics. Our task, along with your teacher, is to help you become an effective teacher of mathematics.

There is a difference between a mathematics teacher and a teacher of mathematics. A mathematics teacher likes mathematics and happens to be teaching. A teacher of mathematics likes teaching and happens to be teaching mathematics. We are looking at you as a teacher of mathematics.

WHAT MAKES AN EFFECTIVE TEACHER OF MATHEMATICS?

Who was your favorite teacher? What qualities keep the memory of that teacher with you? As a teacher of mathematics, you must have a desire to teach, and you must also have a command of the content. An effective teacher has to know the subject, know more than what is being covered, and teach from the overflow (J. Anthony, personal communication, May 26, 2000). That is why we cover content and methodology in this text.

If the teacher is not competent and confident with the subject matter, barriers to creating a positive experience best suited for each student could result. *You* must have the desire to learn mathematics. *You* must have the desire to learn how to educate the students. *You* must have the desire to learn how to supply the optimum educational environment for each student. An effective teacher of mathematics continues to investigate new mathematical concepts and teaching strategies in mathematics. As you do this, your thirst and excitement is easily seen by your students. If you do not know the answer to a question posed by one of your students, your thirst for knowledge should drive you to pursue the situation until you possess that information. At the same time, you can stimulate your students to make similar pursuits along the road to new knowledge, each at your own respective level and pace.

The effective teacher of mathematics must be devoted to the profession. A teacher must create a stimulating atmosphere conducive to learning. An effective teacher of mathematics wants to help erase the fear and anxiety felt by so many students. A true teacher is always willing to learn new methods and strategies for teaching mathematics.

So, let the adventure begin!

1
Guiding Principles for School Mathematics

BEGINNINGS

How wonderful it would be if we knew everything about kids, teaching, mathematics, and the teaching of mathematics. We could bottle it, sell it, become rich, and solve a lot of problems for everyone in the process. We all know there is no magic formula for teaching mathematics. Each of us struggles to find ways to reach students at levels appropriate for them. In the process of attempting to find keys, we often stumble and miss objectives, but we also learn a variety of things that can be catalogued and used at a later date in other settings. (Brumbaugh et al., 1997, p. 86)

As you continue your education and teaching career, you should compile a list of resources that helps your students develop the necessary skills to learn mathematics.

You, as a prospective teacher, should be aware of age level, developmental characteristics, and interaction dynamics of students. Each student needs to be understood as an individual. You also need to know mathematics. You should want to understand the foundations of the material you are teaching so you can provide explanations that make sense.

In addition to knowing mathematics, you need to know about teaching mathematics. Teaching a modern mathematics curriculum demands that you go beyond the statement, "Because I said so and I am the teacher." You have to know what sequence of presentation is most appropriate for your students (which might be different from that in your text or list of objectives for the year). What manipulative should be used in what capacity becomes a critical consideration as topics are introduced for the first time. How do you know when to move from the concrete stage? Another question to answer! We need to start.

Students' Opinions About Mathematics

Look at what kids say when responding to "Why Do We Study Math in School?"

"Because it's hard and we have to learn hard things at school. We learn easy stuff at home like manners." *Corrine, grade K*

"Because it always comes after reading." *Roger, grade 1*

"Because all the calculators might run out of batteries or something." *Thomas, grade 1*

"Because it's important. It's a law from President Clinton and it says so in the Bible on the first page." *Jolene, grade 2*

"Because you can drown if you don't." *Amy Beth, grade K*

"Because what would you do with your check from work when you grow up? *Brad, grade 1*

"Because you have to count if you want to be an astronaut. Like 10 . . . 9 . . . 8 . . . 7 . . . blast off!" *Michael, grade 1*

"Because you could never find the right page." *MaryAnn, grade 1*

"Because when you grow up you couldn't tell if you are rich or not." *Raji, grade 2*

"Because my teacher could get sued if we don't. That's what she said. Any subject we don't know—Wham! She gets sued. And she's already poor." *Corly, grade 3* (from a presentation in Philadelphia by Joseph Tate)

Prior to entering elementary school, children have a multitude of exposures to mathematics and are generally anxious to learn more about the subject. By the time they leave fifth grade, many of them are not nearly as excited about learning mathematics. Why? There are many factors, some of which are easy to identify and some of which are next to impossible to spot. Society plays an important role in students' perceptions of mathematics. If an adult says, "I don't like math," it is likely that others in the conversation will support the statement by saying, "Me, too." Students hear statements like that and soon conclude that mathematics is not a popular thing to know. Then they hear people say things like, "I never need math," and the value of the subject goes down another notch. That context provides a wonderful opportunity to share

The Math Curse (Scieszka, 1995) with your class. This book is a satire on different types of mathematics problems that have been posed to students. In the process, you will be integrating mathematics and literature and the class will learn about a student who realizes that mathematics is everywhere and, in the process, learns how to deal with it.

Society is not the only culprit in this discussion, however. Teachers, curriculum, tests, textbooks, and a number of other factors contribute to the negative attitudes that students develop about mathematics. You cannot dictate or control how your colleagues teach, but if you provide a dynamic, inviting mathematics class, they will hear about it from your students. You may be able to influence attitudes by being a member of a school mathematics committee and sharing ideas learned from conferences and workshops. Suppose, for example, the objective for your class is to add several two-digit numbers where regrouping is involved. You could assign several problems or you could present the following situation to them. (T represents a teacher comment and S shows a student comment.)

TRICK

T: "We are going to add five 2-digit numbers. You will pick two of them and I will pick three of them. When we are done, the sum will be 247. For now, do not repeat the digits within an addend."

Write 247 in "standard column addition format" so the students can see it.

T: "Pick a 2-digit number."
S: "35" (Write it above the ones and tens digits of the sum.)
T: "What is your second addend?"

S: "78" (Write it in the respective columns above the 35.)

T: "I pick 49, 21, and 64 (in any order)." (Write them in the respective columns above the 78.)

In almost all settings, the students will now add to see if you got the answer right. Generally, they want to know if you can do that all the time or how it works. Either way, they are asking you to do another problem and, in the process, they will practice more addition.

Another example that involves both addition and subtraction is "1,089." When this is done with a class, each student would do a different example. The numbers shown here are for explanation and clarification.

TRICK (1089)

T: "Write any 3-digit number." "Do not repeat the digits." (479)

T: "If I reverse the digits in my number, what do I get?"

S: "974."

T: "Which is larger, 479 or 974?"

S: "974."

T: "Subtract the smaller from the larger. If your subtraction answer is 99, write it as 099." (974 − 479 = 495)

T: "Take that answer and reverse its digits, adding it to its reversal. (495 + 594 = 1089)

S: "We all get the same answer!"

S: "Will that always work?"

T: "Try another one and see."

Here again the students are asking to do another problem. These problems are so intriguing for students that they eagerly strive to discover the "secret" and then tell others about it.

You often have limited control over the composition of your class, the basic objectives for the year, the textbook, and a multitude of other factors. These items are not necessarily barriers, but they can be challenges. You are the local professional in your classroom. It is your responsibility to devise ways to overcome resistances that occur as you go about providing your students with the best possible mathematics education.

Lynn Oberlin provides a list entitled "How to Teach Children to Hate Mathematics."

Children generally do not hate mathematics when they start school. This is a trait which they acquire as a part of their elementary school training. The feat of loathing mathematics can generally be accomplished if the teacher will use one or more of the following procedures.

1. Assign the same work to everyone in the class. This technique is effective with about two thirds of the class. The bottom third of the class will become frustrated from trying to do the impossible while the top third will hate the boredom. WARNING: This MAY NOT be effective with about the middle $\frac{1}{3}$ of the students.

2. Go through the book, problem by problem, page by page. In time, the drudgery and monotony is bound to get to them.

3. Assign written work every day. Before long, just the word "mathematics" will remove every smile in the room.

4. Be sure that each student has plenty of homework. This is especially important over the weekends and vacation periods.

5. Never correlate mathematics with life situations. A student might find

it useful and get to enjoy mathematics.

6. Insist there is ONLY one correct way to solve each problem. This is very important as some creative student might look for different ways to solve a problem. He could even grow to like math.

7. Assign mathematics as a punishment for misbehavior. The association works wonders. Soon math and punishment will take on the same meaning.

8. Be sure that ALL students complete ALL the review work in front of the textbook. This ought to last until Thanksgiving or Christmas, and is certain to kill off the interest of most students.

9. Use long drill type assignments with many examples of the same type problem. (for example: 30 long column addition problems) This type of assignment requires little teacher time and keeps the students occupied for a long time. The majority of the pupils are sure to dislike it.

10. Always insist that papers are prepared in a certain way. Name, date, page number, etc., must each be placed in a specific spot. If a student fails to follow this procedure, tear up his paper and let him start over again. Instant humiliation and despair are almost guaranteed.

11. Lastly, insist that EVERY problem worked incorrectly be reworked until it is correct. This procedure is most effective in promoting distaste for math and if followed very carefully, the student may even learn to detest his teacher as well. (Oberlin, 1985)

What we do, how we do it, what we say, and how we say it all influence how children learn mathematics. It is your responsibility to ensure that in your classroom each child develops a positive attitude about mathematics and its role in their lives. If we are lucky, this spills over into the home.

Exercises

1. Do each of the problems listed here (the left one first, the one to its right second, etc.). The italicized, bold numbers are those supplied by the student. A new hint is given as you move to the right in the problems. What is the secret to doing the trick?

24	73	65	16	33	00
46	52	23	*83*	*66*	*99*
73	14	*76*	36	11	44
75	*85*	*34*	63	88	*55*
+*53*	+*47*	+59	+62	+48	+93
271	271	257	260	246	291

2. Explain how the trick in Exercise 1 of this section works.

3. Do a trick similar to the one in Exercise 1 of this section using seven 4-digit addends. Describe the general answer and explain your conclusions.

4. Find another number trick that involves addition. Do the trick with a class of elementary students who have the appropriate background. Describe the reaction of the students.

Things to Do When You Have Three Minutes of Extra Time

One of the quickest ways to encounter problems with a class is to ask them to be quiet until the end of the period. They *will* find something to do, *honest*. You are best advised to have something to occupy their minds in situations like this, and games and tricks are wonderful items to use.

You could use something like a reprint of a problem-solving problem (see http://www.olemiss.edu/mathed/brain/). This could either be shown directly from the Web, copied and made into a transparency, or distributed to each student.

The problem-solving problems can be a part of your set of learning centers. You could color coordinate folders, with each color representing a different topic, concept, or operation. In each folder, place a game, trick, problem, or activity related to what you have covered during the year. During these few spare minutes, students could be directed to work in a folder of their choice, or you could assign a particular folder to a student or group. In a class that is working on addition facts and learning to use calculators, you could give a list of problem pairs like those in Table 1.1 and ask them to arrive at a conclusion.

Games can be used to fill those extra few minutes. Doing something like the "*I have-Who has?*" game can provide needed drill while teaching the value of paying attention. In the *I have-Who has?* game, each card contains two pieces of information: a question and the answer to a problem on another card. The cards are distributed to all students. One individual reads their problem and all the other players work it. The individual holding the card with the right answer reads the "I have" statement and then asks the question below it. Each answer within the set is unique. Table 1.2 shows some sample cards. There are many other productive things that can be done in those few extra minutes.

Exercises

5. Locate a Web site that lists problem-solving problems appropriate for elementary school students. Provide the name of the site, the address, and a brief description of the site.

6. Present an appropriate problem-solving problem you found on a Web site to a group of elementary students and describe their reactions.

7. Locate a Web site that lists games, tricks, activities, or technology appropriate for elementary school students. Pro-

TABLE 1.1

DIRECTIONS: Write the answer to each problem in the blank provided.

3 + 4 = _____
4 + 3 = _____

7 + 1 = _____
1 + 7 = _____

After you have done the problems, look at each pair like 3 + 4 and 4 + 3 or 6 + 5 and 5 + 6. Write what you notice about the answer in each pair in the space below.

2 + 9 = _____
9 + 2 = _____

5 + 6 = _____
6 + 5 = _____

_____

8 + 0 = _____
0 + 8 = _____

_____

TABLE 1.2

I have 8. Who has 7 − 6?	I have 1. Who has 9 + 3?	I have 12. Who has 3 × 5?	I have 15. Who has $\frac{24}{3}$?

vide the name of the site, the address, and a brief description of the site.

8. Present an appropriate game or trick you found on a Web site to a group of elementary students and describe their reactions.

What to Do With the Unusual Student

Look at people. We come in all sizes, shapes, and descriptions. Our physical similarities and differences are easy to spot. Differences pertaining to mental capabilities, interests, aptitudes, and attitudes are not as easy to determine.

Capable students are frequently overlooked in a heterogeneously grouped class, not intentionally, but mainly because the other students demand so much of the teacher's time. What do you do with a talented student in your classroom? A common solution involves the talented student helping a less capable student learn the concepts being covered. This can be tremendously beneficial for both parties. The talented student learns to explain and gains deeper understanding of the topics. The weaker student gets some extra help. In this scenario, interpersonal skills, communication abilities, and perhaps even a life-long friendship can be fostered. Using this as an exclusive approach for the talented students takes away from their opportunities to accept new academic challenges.

Some time should be spent promoting activities that stretch the mathematical capabilities of the talented student. For example, the entire class could be given the following problem: Form a magic triangle (place one value in each circle to get the same sum on each side of the triangle) using 23, 34, 45, 56, 67, and 78 (see Fig. 1.1). This provides an opportunity for all students to practice addition skills. The talented students can be asked to arrange the values so the largest possible sum is obtained and explain their method for determining that their choice is the largest sum.

The time spent with the less mathematically capable (weak) students probably involves more work with manipulatives. Perhaps there is a need to use a different manipulative than the one used with the class in the initial explanation because of the learning modality of the students involved. Maybe the same manipulative will be adequate if the concept is developed at a slower pace. A possible problem is that students sometimes resist returning to the beginning and re-creating the evolution. They want to do the abstraction. It is faster and easier. Often your students, weak or not, have been trained to use the

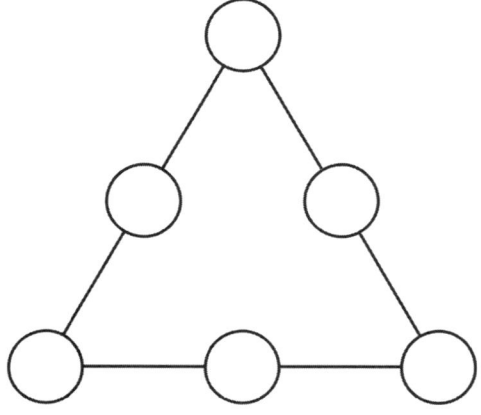

FIG. 1.1.

rules without benefit of manipulatives. That is not good. All students need to progress through the developmental learning stages from concrete to abstract.

Weak students, capable students, and students who have fallen behind because of absence, lack of attention, or emphasis in another subject area can also benefit from technology. There are pieces of software designed to develop fundamentals, create environments that introduce new topics, stimulate a desire to practice skills, or investigate extensions or applications of mastered material. Calculator books are available that can be used in a similar fashion. CDs, videotapes, movies, filmstrips, and selected TV programs can be used to meet the special needs of any student.

Exercises

9. Locate a resource that is appropriate for a student needing special assistance in learning mathematics. List the resource and briefly describe what "is claimed to be done" for the student who uses it. Reflect on the manufacturer's claim and state why you agree or disagree.

10. Locate a resource that is appropriate for a mathematically talented student. List the resource and briefly describe what "is claimed to be done" for the student who uses it. Reflect on the manufacturer's claim and state why you agree or disagree.

11. Is it feasible that a resource could be used for students of all ability levels? Why or why not? If possible, cite an example.

When to Change Pace

Your class is comprised of students with different ability levels, attention spans, backgrounds, preferences, and a whole multitude of other things that make each student an individual. A nationally known tutoring company has an advertisement that elaborates on the idea that a child learns at a pace and in a manner that is unique for that person. The advertisement continues with the idea that, once that child gets to the school environment, the expectation is that all children learn the same way, at the same pace, and with the same attitude. The advertisement continues, this is not the case and this learning center is willing to supplement the child's learning (for a fee, of course). There is some truth in the advertisement. Certainly not all children learn at the same rate.

How do you know when to change pace? If the last several concepts have been easy for the child, it is time to confront them with a more difficult learning task to avoid getting the idea that learning is always easy. However, if the last few concepts have provided extra challenges as the students attempted to learn, it is time to shift to something relatively easy so they do not become discouraged. Your objectives may not provide the answer. Your textbook may not provide the answer. You will have to determine what is best for the class based on your knowledge of your students, how much they can tolerate, and the curricular expectations for them for the year. You want the pace to allow the student to feel successful about the learning of mathematics.

Where Does the Textbook Fit in All of This?

Textbooks become the de-facto curriculum in many schools. (Begle, 1973; Fey, 1980; National Advisory Committee on Mathematics Education, 1975; Porter, Floden, Freeman, Schmidt, & Schwille,

1986). Often the material in a textbook is not new.

> James Flanders . . . surveyed four math series to see how much new material was added to books from one grade to the next. He found that only 40% of the material in a second-grader's book wasn't a repeat of first grade. . . .
>
> William Schmidt, an education professor at Michigan State University in East Lansing, studied 1,500 math textbooks from 50 Countries. His conclusion: U.S. math education is a mile wide and an inch deep, a failing that begins with textbooks.
>
> In his study of textbooks, Mr. Schmidt found that U.S. books covered up to 35 different math topics a year—that means teachers fly through them at a speed of one a week. (Kronholz, 1998)

What do you do? You have a textbook to work with. That does not mean you must follow it page by page, day after day. You are the local authority in your classroom. You know what your students are ready to do. You know the concepts they have mastered and the background they have experienced. You decide. You can skip around in the mathematics textbook. You can employ additional resources to enhance the lesson. Opportunities abound, and the textbook is only one of them.

Equity

The National Council of Teachers of Mathematics (NCTM) *Curriculum and Evaluation Standards for School Mathematics* (National Council of Teachers of Mathematics, 1989) presents the position that an effective teacher of mathematics is able to motivate **all** students to learn. These sentiments are repeated in *Principles and Standards for School Mathematics* (National Council of Teachers of Mathematics, 2000), making it a recurring theme in the

teaching and learning of mathematics. Why does the idea that all students need to be motivated to learn mathematics keep showing up? Mathematics is the key to many opportunities. It opens doors to careers, enables informed decisions, and helps us compete as a nation (Mathematical Sciences Education Board [MSEB], 1989). The only constant that today's students will face in their working lives is change. It is predicted that your students will change careers as many as five times. Changing a career implies major reeducation. If even a part of the statement about changing careers is accepted, teachers of mathematics have an awesome responsibility. We must teach our students to absorb new ideas, adapt to change, cope with ambiguity, perceive patterns, and solve unconventional problems (Mathematical Sciences Education Board, 1989). Without these abilities, today's students will have a difficult time in their working future. A large segment of our society is willing to make statements like:

"I hated math in school."

"Math; YUCK!"

"I did not do well in math."

These cannot continue to be acceptable statements. If an individual says "I cannot read," countless others express sorrow, perhaps pity, and then scurry to find ways to help that person learn to read. In contrast, if one hears "I can't do math," a common response is "I know, me too." How can that be? Why is there not a reaction similar to the one about reading? It is our commission to change the response that generates the needed help for the individual in question. Society's perception of mathematics can be seen at a social gathering. When asked your profession, you most likely state that you are an elementary teacher. When asked what subject you enjoy teaching the most, check their response when you say, "Math." A common response to your statement is, "I hated math in school. I still have trouble doing math!" If you said you favorite subject to teach was English, it is hard to imagine getting a response of, "I hated English. I still have trouble reading and writing."

Why is there such diversity in reactions to mathematics? If we believe that all children can learn meaningful mathematics and science, there are significant educational structures and contextual conditions that must be changed to reflect a system that is equitable for all students. When equity is a fundamental principle of the reform movement, it serves as a template for designing and implementing programs, practices, and policies. The perspectives on equity vary, but the following statements provide guidance for thinking about this concept:

> Equity has a variety of connotations, depending upon who is using it. It is used to mean equal access of all children to instruction, inclusion of all in the classroom, capacity building, diversity, or the offering of special services. Some, however, fear equity in any form.
>
> Equity is providing all that is needed to help students overcome the consequence of barriers, regardless of where we find them.
>
> Equity as diversity or multiculturalism is not the addition of materials or ideas from under represented cultures; rather it involves the integrated use of context and approaches of all cultural perspectives.
>
> Equity means equal distribution of resources, particularly with money. This implies that one school or district receives the same amount as another, usually in the same district or state. (Cummings, 1995, pp. 1–2)

The preceding statements illustrate how diverse the discussion on equity can be.

However, some common language emerges: inclusion, access, fairness, enabling, diversity, multiculturalism, capacity building, special services, and learning.

Equity issues in education have been a focal point in the study of students learning mathematics. Society often presents views that are not always conducive to good mathematics learning or instruction. Many times good performance in mathematics is viewed as the exception rather than the rule. Frequently, boys were expected to perform better than girls in mathematical settings. For years there was an unstated position that "nice girls" did not do mathematics. Thankfully that attitude has changed. There is still peer pressure in some segments of school society that places negative value on good performance in mathematics. Such perceptions can destroy some students' ambitions.

As a teacher of mathematics, it is your responsibility to "sell" the subject to all students. As an effective representative of your product, what do you do to create an appealing atmosphere? How do you convince *all* students in your classes they can succeed? Can you demonstrate applications of the concepts being learned? When a student says, "When will I ever use this junk?" (perhaps not in those words, but the message is that clear), what will you say? Students have become hardened to the learning of mathematics. Many of them are convinced there is no earthly value to the subject. We give them examples supposedly from everyday life. For some strange reason, the answers to our problems are almost always integers. Somehow students are aware that, in the real world, the answers are not always integers. We give them real-world problems to work with, but often these situations are not from their world and they are rarely aimed at girls. We should provide equity for all students who must be encouraged in all mathematical settings.

Exercise

12. Examine the problem sections of an elementary mathematics textbook. How many of the problems come from the world as viewed by a student? Of all the problems, how many are designed to appeal to girls?

CURRICULUM

Professor E. G. Begle said, "We have learned a lot about teaching better mathematics but not much about teaching mathematics better" (Crosswhite, 1986, p. 54). When perusing the history of teaching mathematics, it appears as if we constantly look for a magic method or strategy to serve all students. There is no enchanted formula that fits every learner. We need to realize that a variety of methods are necessary to meet the mathematical learning needs of all students. Our task, as teachers of mathematics, is to determine which method is most beneficial for each student and when these strategies are most effective. If a teacher uses a strategy with no positive result from the learner, at what point is that method abandoned in favor of another? The decision is most often influenced by our own background, training, experiences, bias, and current curriculum.

We assume you have had exposure to educational learning theories, curriculum, and methods of instruction in education classes. It is further assumed that you will investigate selected issues in greater depth as you see the need.

Constructivist's Base

The constructivist philosophy has evolved in the last 50 years. Adherents of constructivism support the notion that children learn effectively through interactions with experiences in their natural environment. Steffe and Killion (1986) stated that, from a constructivist perspective, "mathematics teaching consists primarily of the mathematical interactions between a teacher and children" (p. 207). This indirect approach to instruction allows the student to learn in the context of meaningful activities. Learning is a life-long process that results from interactions with a multitude of situations (Brown et al., 1989). The constructivist approach does not focus solely on the action of the teacher or learner, but on the interactions between the two. The teacher should make a conscious effort to see their own personal actions as well as the student's from the student's point of view (Cobb & Steffe, 1983).

Piaget believed in the importance of human interaction and physical manipulation as essential to the gaining of knowledge. The emphasis of the constructivist classroom begins with the student. The constructivist educator demonstrates a respect for the student.

Ideals of Modern Social Construcitivism

1. Learning is dependent on the prior conceptions the learner brings to the experience.
2. The learner must construct his or her own meaning.
3. Learning is contextual.
   Learning is dependent of the shared understandings learners negotiate with others.
4. Effective teaching involves understanding students' existing cognitive

structures and providing appropriate learning activities to assist them.

5. Teachers can utilize one or more key strategies to facilitate conceptual change, depending on the congruence of the concepts with student understanding and conceptualization.
6. The key elements of conceptual change can be addressed by specific teaching methods.
7. Greater emphasis should be placed on "learning how to learn" than accumulating facts. In terms of content, less is more.
(Anderson et al., 1994)

The following list goes hand in hand with the ideals above.

1. The teacher of mathematics must consider the prior conceptions the student brings into the classroom. You will need to alter your instructional strategies and materials depending on the student's prior experiences with mathematics and life.
2. The teacher of mathematics should try to assist the learner in discovering mathematical concepts and ideas.
3. Students learn mathematics by doing mathematics using real world examples and settings.
4. Teachers of mathematics must identify how individual students learn and develop activities or strategies to help them best accomplish objectives placed before them.
5. Teachers of mathematics must be willing to teach to different learning styles and ability levels. Mathematics is for *all* students.
6. Teachers of mathematics need to be able to use more than one instructional strategy for each concept.

7. The teacher of mathematics must help students learn how to learn the concepts of mathematics. Developing an understanding of the process is more helpful than memorizing an algorithm or formula.

The fear of failing must be erased to foster the idea that students can learn from their mistakes. If we are to expect our students to comprehend and deal with complex problems, we need to establish an atmosphere rich with exposures. Each student should become aware of their own ability to invent and explore new ideas and concepts. The effective teacher of mathematics must be willing to capitalize on a student's natural thinking abilities.

Exercises

13. What are the major characteristics you would ascribe to a positive mathematics classroom? Which of these would you control? Which would be dependent on your students? Which of these would depend on administration?

14. Was the mathematics learning environment you experienced in your school years constructivist based? Describe your experiences to amplify your selection.

15. Describe your mathematics classroom of the future.

Change

We live in a rapidly changing society. Technology that was not available to the average person not long ago is now accessible and affordable for the home and school. Our students have access to information that spans the globe. The Internet and e-mail are just two examples of how children can reach across the continents at the touch of a button. One constant is that technology will continue to change. Unfortunately, much of the curriculum seems to have lagged behind. Over the years, many calls for change have been heard. Recently, a variety of works have called for change. They include:

The Underachieving Curriculum: Assessing U.S. School Mathematics From and International Perspective (1987)

Curriculum and Evaluation Standards for School Mathematics (1989)

Everybody Counts: A report to the Nation on the Future of Mathematics Education (1989)

Mathematics Education: Wellspring of U.S. Industrial Strength (1990)

Reshaping School Mathematics: A Philosophy and Framework for Curriculum (1990)

A Call for Change: Recommendations for the Mathematical Preparation of Teachers of Mathematics (1991)

America 2000: An Education Strategy (1991)

Professional Standards for Teaching Mathematics 1991)

The State of Mathematics Achievement: NAPE's 1990 Assessment of the Nation and the Trial Assessment of the States (1991)

Handbook of Research on Mathematics Teaching and Learning (1992)

Assessment Standards for Teaching Mathematics (1995)

Principles and Standards for School Mathematics: Standards 2000 (2000)

These publications discuss the status of school mathematics programs. They describe what has happened in mathematics classrooms of the past, what is happening now, and what should happen in the future. The motivation for these changes comes from a variety of sources outside education. Business and industry want people who:

are capable of setting problems up, not just following formulas;

know how to interpret the numbers or answers they get;

are aware of a variety of approaches for solving problems;

understand the mathematical features of a problem;

can work in groups to reach solutions;

recognize commonalities of mathematics in different problems;

can deal with problems that are not in the format often presented in the learning environment; and

value mathematics as a useful learning and work tool.

Our society has shown a desire for mathematics education to change. Is it time for schools, teachers, and the curriculum to change?

The definitions of a mathematics curriculum vary. Students often describe it in terms of some of the computations they learn in a given class. The students feel that the teacher is the ultimate controller of curricular power. A teacher would define curriculum as what they teach to the students. Administrators view curriculum as a body of course offerings and all other planned school events. Members of the community view the school curriculum as a group of courses designed to produce what they want. A philosopher says the curriculum is the group of courses designed to expose the student to the necessary items that will develop an individual. Perhaps the best definition comes from the idea that curriculum is what happens in your classroom with your students. Many forces impact the mathematics curriculum. Your task becomes one of determining which forces get emphasis and how much.

Test-Driven Curriculum

Many school districts administer standardized tests to determine the mastery of particular concepts for their students. With this in mind, a teacher may be forced to teach exactly the concepts and objectives that appear on the test. What happens if your class scores low on that test? Does this mean that your students have a low aptitude in mathematics? Will you be fired for your classes' low performance on a test? Will your pay get cut because your students do not perform well on a test? You will have to wrestle with questions such as these in the future. Assessment of a student's mathematical abilities should be an ongoing process using a multitude of tools throughout the year. If this scenario occurs, the standardized test will not be the sole definer of the curriculum.

Exercise

16. Is it reasonable to have a test of major proportions at some point during the school year? Why or why not? Describe the impact on the curriculum.

Text-Driven Curriculum

What drives the mathematics curriculum? Who determines the sequence in which you teach your students mathematics? NCTM has published sets of standards as a framework of mathematics that students need to learn. Many states have established objectives for the content that students need to master at each grade level. These lists of state objectives are given to publishers who, in turn, try to produce texts that cover the specified material. A publisher's decision is based on potential sales. A publisher is more apt to accommodate the state offering the largest sales potential. Publishers cannot produce a book for each set of objectives for every state. Instead, one or two texts are produced. The expectation is that the material in the text will meet or exceed the objectives of the states and districts. Generally, this is a safe assumption. If material is in the book that is not on the district or state list of objectives, the teacher can opt to omit it. Basically, the text tries to cover most, if not all, of the topics required. Because each publisher works from the same list of objectives, many texts are similar.

Some texts are clearly different. Saxon, for example, approaches topics in an order and emphasis different from that of most other publishers. Saxon's approach has caused a variety of discussions and opinions to be generated within the mathematics education community. Such developments can be healthy for overall community growth.

Exercises

17. Should you teach in the sequence that the material is presented in the text? Why or why not?

18. Why do new teachers tend to teach mathematics in the sequence presented in the text?

19. Examine several textbooks for a given mathematics concept. Describe their similarities. Are there any significant differences? Is there a text that is notably different from the rest? If there is a different text, rationalize why it should or should not be available for adoption. If there is no different text, discuss why they are all similar.

Teacher-Driven Curriculum

A class consists of students, a teacher, boards, overhead, books, manipulatives, technology, and a collection of stuff. That is the same almost everywhere you go. The boards are different colors; the books vary depending on the publisher. The availability of technology ranges from some students having calculators (the use of which may or may not be permitted) to having computers equipped with the latest and greatest in software offerings. The available technology is one thing that could be quite different. There is one more thing that is the same. In almost every classroom, the expertise and knowledge resides with the teacher. Curricular decisions are influenced by what the teacher knows about mathematical content, how learners think about mathematical concepts, and instructional materials used to teach mathematics (Shulman, 1986).

Ironically, many students like an atmosphere where knowledge and expertise reside with the teacher. The rules are known. Students are basically told what to do and how to do it, which is easier than having to think. Either the student gets the idea as presented or not, right or wrong, no shades of gray. No need for the teacher or students to reflect on responses that vary from the norm. Everyone is on the same wavelength. Expertise and knowledge focused in a teacher contradicts a constructivist environment where students are allowed to investigate, discover, and learn how to become better critical thinkers. Remember, student development is fostered by encouraging the development of self-learning. The student is not in the classroom for the sole purpose of learning how to be a sponge. We want to develop critical thinking skills, not robotic responses. If learners have latitudes in how they can approach a problem, the generated responses stimulate additional thought and insight on the part of everyone.

Imagine what it would be like if all classrooms provided and encouraged flexible thinking, creative approaches, a variety of ideas, an atmosphere of curiosity, and a compilation of prior knowledge to be applied to some new challenging situation. What a wonderful world that would be! Students must be taught and encouraged to think! Teachers can no longer be the center of attention. Rather, they are motivators, stimulators, instigators, co-investigators, participants, and cheerleaders who work very hard. Because teaching is already a demanding, time-consuming profession, perhaps it is unreasonable to ask for such changes in the classroom. Eventually the good students will learn that the world of mathematics can be exciting and invigorating. After all, you did, didn't you?

External Pressures on the Curriculum

Standardized tests, textbooks, and tradition all influence what is covered in the classroom, but there are other forces as well. Societal needs play a role in what is taught. The current value placed on education, coupled with the belief that an educated populace needs adequate mathematical background, sways society's judgment about what is to be covered in the mathematics curriculum.

Effective teaching and learning of mathematics demands a variety of instructional methods to meet the needs of individual students in the curriculum. Educators cannot permit pressures from parents, administrators, specific segments of society, or influential individuals to dictate how mathematics is taught. As a professional educator, it is your responsibility to call on all possible resources: your learning experiences, college mathematics education classes, college education classes, college mathematics classes, internship experiences, mathematical applications from your life, information gathered from reading professional journals, conference attendance, and so on. Compiling your experiences with conscious thought about what you are asking your students to learn will help you define the curriculum in your classroom. So many things available to you are merely guides. You are the qualified professional. You know the students in your class. You would be the most likely person to decide what their mathematical exposures under your tutelage should be. Outside pressures may influence your thoughts, but they should not exclusively dictate what happens with your classes.

Exercise

20. Should you, the teacher, as the local authority on your class solely determine the material to be covered? If yes, why? If no, how much outside influence should be acceptable and why?

The Standards

Some members of the mathematics community realized in the mid-1980s that "business as usual" would not be effective for future mathematics teaching and learning. NCTM took the lead and published *Curriculum and Evaluation Standards for School Mathematics* (referred to in this text as the Standards) in 1989. The guidelines presented in the Standards are formative ideas indicating mathematics learning that is desirable in school settings. The Standards focus on five general goals, which adopt the position that ALL students should:

learn to value mathematics;

develop confidence in their ability to use mathematics;

become problem solvers, not answer finders;

learn to communicate mathematically; and

know how to reason mathematically.

Problem solving, reasoning, communication, and mathematical connections are common strands through all levels, but there are other standards for various grade ranges. The additional standards for Grades K–4 are:

Estimation;
Number sense and numeration;
Concepts of whole number operations;
Whole number computation;
Geometry and spatial sense;
Measurement;
Statistics and Probability;
Fractions and decimals; and
Patterns and relationships.

For Grades 5–8:

Number and number relationships;
Number systems and number theory;
Computation and estimation;
Patterns and functions;
Algebra;
Statistics;
Probability;
Geometry; and
Measurement.

NCTM was one of the first disciplines to develop and publish national standards. It has been shown that when it came to familiarity with the NCTM Standards, mathematics teachers were not adequately educated, trained, or supported (Weiss, 1995). Of the teachers from Grade 8 or lower, fewer than 30% were *well aware* of the contents of the Standards. Fewer than 20% of the same group were *well aware* of the Professional Standards (*Professional Standards for Teaching School Mathematics*; National Council of Teachers of Mathematics, 1991). About 25% of the teachers in Grades 8 and lower were not aware of the Standards.

Exercises

21. Do you think the teaching of mathematics in the elementary school should be different as compared with when you were in elementary school? Why or why not?

22. Have you read the Standards? Will you? Do you need to read them before you begin your teaching career? Why or why not?

Professional Standards

The Professional Standards for Teaching Mathematics (National Council of Teachers of Mathematics, 1991; referred to in this text as the Professional Standards) also deal with how we should change the way we teach mathematics. This document's focus is on teacher knowledge, beliefs, and strategies that assist in delivering the Standards into the classroom. It is important to note that the Professional Standards, like the Standards, are broad frameworks designed to guide school mathematics reform.

Change does not come easy. Offering a document that provides improvements for teaching mathematics does not automatically make this change occur. Barriers include student and teacher beliefs regarding how mathematics is taught that are often developed by prior experiences in mathematics. Student and teacher impressions are not the only obstacles to changing mathematics education. Administrators, parents, and society have strong ideas about how to educate our children as well. The Professional Standards were built on two basic assumptions:

> Teachers are key figures in changing the ways in which mathematics is taught and learned in schools.
> Such changes require that teachers have long-term support and adequate resources. (National Council of Teachers of Mathematics, 1991, p. 2)

The kind of instruction needed to implement the NCTM Standards requires a high degree of individual responsibility and professionalism on the part of each teacher. To give guidance to the development of such professionalism in mathematics teaching, the Professional Standards for Teaching Mathematics consists of five components:

1. Standards for teaching mathematics
2. Standards for the evaluation of the teaching of mathematics
3. Standards for the professional development of teachers of mathematics
4. Standards for the support and development of mathematics teachers and teaching
5. Next steps. (National Council of Teachers of Mathematics, 1991, pp. 4–5)

Exercise

23. Select a vignette from the Professional Standards that you believe to be a description of a good classroom situation. Highlight the strong points of the vignette and describe your impression of the strengths.

Assessment Standards

Assessment is defined as

> . . . the process of gathering evidence about a student's knowledge of, ability to use, and disposition toward, mathematics and of making inferences from that evidence for a variety of purposes. . . . Furthermore, by evaluation we mean the process of determining the worth of, or assigning a value to, something on the basis of careful examination and judgement. (National Council of Teachers of Mathematics, 1995, p. 3)

The Assessment Standards for School Mathematics (National Council of Teachers of Mathematics, 1995b; referred to as the Assessment Standards in this text) are based on research, experiences of the writing team, and ". . . developments related to national efforts to reform the teaching and learning of mathematics. In particular, a recent report from MSEB (Mathematical Sciences Education Board), *Measuring What Counts* (1993), provided an initial scholarly base for the development of these Assessment Standards" (National Council of Teachers of Mathematics, 1995b, p. ix.).

> At present, a new approach to assessment is evolving in many schools and classrooms. Instead of assuming that the purpose of assessment is to rank students on a particular trait, the new approach assumes that high public expectations can be set that every student can strive for and achieve, that different performances can and will meet agreed-on expectations, and that teachers can be fair and consistent judges of diverse student performances. Setting high expectations and striving to achieve them are quite different from comparing students with one another and indicating where each student ranks. A constant theme of this document is that decisions regarding students' achievement should be made on the basis of a convergence of information from a variety of balanced and equitable sources. Further-

more, much of the information needs to be derived by teachers during the process of instruction. (National Council of Teachers of Mathematics, 1995b, p. 1)

The six standards state that assessment should:

1. Reflect the mathematics that all students need to know and be able to do. This refers to providing examples from the real world of students as viewed by students, not adults.
2. Enhance mathematics learning.
3. Promote equity.
4. Be an open process.
5. Promote valid inferences about mathematics learning.
6. Be a coherent process.

We need to value the mathematical development of ALL students. Assessment should not be a tool used to deny access to mathematical learning. Assessment should be used to stimulate growth toward higher mathematical expectations. Demanding less than the best from each student is akin to wasting the potential of the respective individual.

Standards 2000

Standards 2000 (*Principles and Standards for School Mathematics*; National Council of Teachers of Mathematics, 2000) reorganizes the ideas presented in the Standards, Professional Standards, and Assessment Standards. The message is the same, however. Effective teachers of mathematics need to be adept at teaching based on the 10 standards that are listed for all grade levels:

Number and Operation
Algebra
Geometry

Measurement

Data Analysis and Probability

Problem Solving

Reasoning and Proof

Communication

Connections

Representations

These are different ways of categorizing the ideas presented in earlier works. Still the basics are the same and provide direction for the effective teacher of mathematics who is a self-motivated life-long learner.

The Standards, Professional Standards, Assessment Standards, and Standards 2000 all ask for a significant difference in how mathematics is taught and learned. They also implicitly expect ongoing professional development by each teacher of mathematics. Teachers need to see classes taught that model the desired new behavior and continued exposure to new strategies and methods of instruction. Only then can you be expected to consistently deliver effective mathematics classes to their students.

Professional Organizations

The Mathematical Association of America (MAA), NCTM, MSEB, as well as many state and local groups deal specifically with the teaching and learning of mathematics. None of these organizations mandates how to operate your classroom; all of them provide a plethora of suggestions for you. The formats of the information include publications, workshops, conferences, summer institutes, and evaluations of textbooks, software, manipulatives, classroom aids, and so on. You are studying to become a professional educator, and the information is available to

you. As such, you should accept certain responsibilities. One of those is to be a member of your professional organizations. This means NOW, not when you start teaching. NCTM's phone number is 703-620-9840, and www.nctm.org is the Internet address. Student memberships are often half-price. Don't just join, become involved. Learn! Interact with colleagues. Seek out new and better ways to help yourself and your students use mathematical power.

Professional conferences dealing with the teaching of mathematics provide a multitude of opportunities. These meetings give you the chance to hear and meet textbook authors, college faculty, colleagues, and suppliers of support products. Publishers maintain exhibits that show the latest texts, teaching aids, games, software, computers, and calculators. Not only can you look at these items, but you can also talk with a professional about how to use them in a classroom. As a professional, you are obligated to maintain awareness in your chosen area of specialization. Otherwise you continue in the same old rut as the sage on the stage, wondering why students are not absorbing what you tell them.

NCTM publishes newsletters, journals (one is included as a part of the student membership), research journals, and yearbooks on a regular basis. Journals contain articles by classroom teachers, textbook authors, professors, students, and professional authors. Often the presentation is a description of some successful lesson from the classroom. Other national, state, and local organizations provide a variety of alternative publications.

Professionalism carries responsibilities with it. It is your obligation to keep the community and parents aware of recent developments in the field. They need to be educated and reminded about how things are different from when they learned mathematics in school. Otherwise, pressures to continue teaching mathematics as it has always been done will be so great that change will be difficult to accomplish. The broader and stronger your mathematics background and the more you know about how to teach it, the easier it will be for you to establish community trust. It is imperative that you become a self-motivated, lifelong professional who is involved in the field of teaching and learning mathematics. As a professional, you need to evaluate the needs of your students as they embark on the rest of their life-long mathematical journey as consumers and learners.

PLANNING

Teaching mathematics is not simply standing in front of a group of children and telling them how to add and subtract. It is more than grading homework, papers, and tests. There is more to teaching mathematics than telling which page to read and what problems to do for homework. We hope you are aware that becoming an effective teacher of mathematics involves much more. One important aspect of becoming an effective teacher of mathematics is taking the necessary time to plan the lesson that conveys the mathematical ideas and information your students need to learn. Good classes do not just happen, they are carefully planned and orchestrated. Certainly there are deviations from the plan depending on happenings during the class, but the framework is laid out well ahead of time.

Prior to teaching, it is imperative that the topics covered be carefully contemplated and organized to allow time for the ideas to germinate and blend. The advanced planning also provides the opportunity to connect topics from different lessons and subject areas throughout the course.

What Should Be Planned?

This is not a simple question. Your broad course objectives are dictated at the federal, state, district, school, and maybe even department levels. Some schools and districts mandate that all classes are given the same objective to be completed within a given time frame. Even with constraints such as these, there is opportunity for individualization by the teacher. Variation of presentation styles, relating the subject matter to background material, calling on student strengths established earlier in the curriculum, and use of technology can all provide extra time that permits some flexibility for teaching. Curriculum can be altered in a manner that best meets the needs of all students as long as the school or state objectives at the grade level are met. This mandates a look at the full year and establishing an outline that covers the topics, builds needed strengths that will enhance later learning, determines a sequence in which the concepts will covered, and establishes an assessment plan.

As a new teacher, it may happen that you will be given little guidance with planning your yearly objectives. Many times new teachers use the sequence in the mathematics text because of lack of experience. The text may be the only concrete sequence you are given. By your second or third year of teaching at a grade level, you will be more knowledgeable as to which concepts are more difficult for your students. You will be more confident regarding the sequence of the material. Initially you will need to rely on the resources and material you have learned in your mathematics education courses to help you navigate through the curriculum your students need.

Once the long-range plan has been established, consideration should be given to smaller, but still sizeable chunks of information, perhaps determined by chapters or headings in a textbook. You need to reserve the right to delay sections of a chapter, or a whole chapter, until it is more suitable for your class. You may need to alter and perhaps supplement the information in the text with material from the other sources.

Each daily lesson must be carefully prepared and set forth. Pressures or time constraints often hinder the development of well-planned lessons. Consider the person who is about to discuss addition of fractions with a class. Suppose the specific objective is to cover how to add two fractions with unlike denominators. Consider a teacher who did not plan, but skimmed the text for a few seconds prior to class thinking, "OK, I know how to do that." Class begins and the teacher says something like, "Today we are going to add fractions; you know, something like $\frac{1}{4} + \frac{3}{8}$," writing the two fractions on the board while talking. Then there is a short pause and the teacher asks a series of questions such as following, with the class providing appropriate responses before going on to do the next question:

"What is a fraction?"

"Define numerator."

"The denominator of a fraction tells . . . ?"

"In $\frac{1}{4}$, the numerator is . . . ?"

"And the denominator is . . . ?"

"When we add things, basically what do we do?"

What is the teacher doing? These answers are all things the class should know. If they do not, how can the teacher justify dealing with the topic at hand? Ask a class of students what the teacher is doing and they will tell you the teacher is stalling. The teacher, for whatever reason, momentarily forgot how to add fractions with unlike denominators. While each of those mundane questions was being asked, the teacher was probing memory banks, trying to recall how to do the problem; how to organize thoughts; and attempting to devise a coherent explanation. Most of us are quick to say that would never happen to us. Many of us would say that we would not draw a blank on something as simple as that. Maybe or maybe not. The real issue is not whether it *will* happen. The question is *when*? The solution to the dilemma is so simple. *PLAN!*

Lesson Plans

A good rule of thumb for planning is to formulate ideas weeks before they are to be delivered, look the plan over a few times between development and delivery, and take time to review it the day before it happens. This procedure enhances the connections between different plans, stimulates thoughts, and amplifies needed changes. We understand that this takes time, but it is part of being a professional. There will still be many times when changes will be made right before or during the class. Over the years, you will probably need less time to effectively plan your lessons because of your experience and your knowledge of student development.

Once a lesson plan is done, you should look at it periodically between the time it is prepared and when it is to be delivered. This process helps cement the overall lesson into your mind at a level that allows you to deliver a natural presentation. The lesson has become a part of you. Because of your intimate understanding of the material to be covered, you should be able to adjust things quickly and naturally. However, this will not happen unless you organize your teaching so that you consistently prepare daily lesson plans long before they are to be taught.

Planning and Textbooks

Many teachers tend to rely heavily on textbooks in their day-to-day teaching. Typically this is even more common with mathematics classes. Most decisions about what to teach, how to teach it, when to teach it, and the associated exercises are based largely on what is in the textbook. Some people are concerned about the quality of textbooks, the way they are written, and the tremendous influence they have. Prior to the year, carefully read through your teacher's edition of the mathematics text. Many times, it provides helpful ideas for planning. Also, there may be suggestions about common student errors and areas that typically need reinforcement when teaching that particular concept. Remember the teacher's edition can be a wonderful resource and guide, but it is not your only resource.

Textbooks are written to meet the needs of a wide variety of students. Your class may or may not be representative of the sample the authors had in mind. It may be the case that you will need to alter the sequence in which topics are listed in the text to best meet the needs of your students. There is nothing wrong with that as long as appropriate readiness and background are considered. Blindly following the text without consideration for the development and needs of student

can lead to excessive repetition. This constant repetition can lead to bored students who become disenchanted with mathematics.

Exercises

24. Should your lessons follow the structure of the text? Why or why not?

25. Should two teachers in the same grade, with students of the same ability, in the same school, follow the same lesson plans? Why or why not?

26. If you cannot finish the curriculum, how do you decide what to sacrifice? What are the ramifications of eliminating some topics? Is there a way this dilemma can be resolved?

What Constitutes a Daily Lesson Plan?

There must be a reason you are requiring your class to learn this material. What is it? The focus should be on the students learning to perform tasks they could not do prior to the lesson. For example, suppose you are going to teach someone to bake banana nut muffins. This will be the first time the person will have done such a thing.

You say:

"Get the mix."
"Get a big bowl."
"Get a spoon."
"Get one egg."
"Get the milk."
"Get the measuring cup."
"Get the muffin pan."
"Put a paper baking cup in each hole in the pan."

At this point, *you* proceed to do the following:

Turn the oven on to preheat to 400.
Empty the mix into the bowl.
Measure a third of a cup of milk.
Pour the milk into the bowl with the mix.
Break the egg and put it into the bowl.
Blend the ingredients.
Fill each muffin cup until it is half full.
Bake 13 to 15 minutes or until golden brown.
Remove the muffin pan from the oven.
Let the muffins cool.

Now, you say to the person:

"We baked muffins."

You did not let the person measure the milk because of potential spills or perhaps an inability to deal with a third of a cup. You did not let the learner break the egg because of the possibility of shells getting into the mix. Similar excuses can be made for other events that would occur during the making of the muffins.

The muffin example shows that "we" did not make muffins. You did. You used the individual as a "gofer" by saying "Go for this" or "Go for that." The objective in this case was to make muffins. Clearly, the objective was not that the learner would make the muffins. As lessons are considered in the context of this text and the mathematics classrooms described, it is assumed that they will be behaviorally oriented even if they are not so stated. If that assumption is not correct, you run the risk of having a learning environment where the students are not active participants in activities that will assist them in learning the mathematics they will need to become functional citizens.

Questions, lesson notes, and examples are major ingredients for any lesson plan. Each of these is equally significant to the overall development and delivery of the plan. Questions and questioning techniques are crucial. Remember you are trying to stimulate thought in your students because they are active learners in class. Consider the level of questions you are asking. If all your questions are on the knowledge level, there is little or no thought involved because the student is merely repeating information previously encountered. Your lesson plans should include upper level questions. Upper level questions usually cannot be generated quickly, although it does become easier and more reflexive as you mature within your career. Higher order questions require careful thought in advance of the class. Listing upper level questions in your plans shows that you have given them appropriate consideration. Do not worry about including exact wording. You can phrase the question within the context of the class as long as you have the idea in the plans. Another reason for listing your upper level question in your lesson plan or outline is simply so you do not forget to ask it. As you teach your lessons, distractions occur. Without having your upper level questions listed, it is likely you will simply forget to ask them.

Higher level questions strengthen students' reasoning ability and communication skills. Usually questions requiring thought are not easy for students to answer. "How?" and "Why?" can be upper level questions when connected to a response given by a student. Research shows that up to 80% of all questions asked in a classroom are lower level (Fennema & Peterson, 1986; Hart, 1989; Koehler, 1986; Suydam, 1985). Probably the most likely reason for the preponderance of lower level questions is that higher order questions are difficult to create extemporaneously in front of a class. Additionally, upper level questions require an understanding of mathematics that may exceed the teacher's knowledge base.

Most students are curious about things and have questions. Students need to learn to be willing to ask. The following situation was used to stimulate questions. The students entered the classroom to find the teacher sitting on a chair that had been placed on the teacher's desk. The students asked each other what was going on. Some inquired of others whether they should call the principal or another teacher. The level of uncertainty and inquisitiveness was quite high. After a few minutes of this, the teacher hopped off the chair and removed it from the desktop, saying to the class, "Isn't it interesting that you had several questions, but no one asked me. Since I was the one sitting in the chair, wouldn't it be reasonable to ask me why?" The moral of the story— know what to ask and know whom to ask.

Examples are equally as important as questions. Specific examples must be carefully thought out as each lesson is planned. It is logical to assume that many students learn by observing specific examples. Although it is ideal to have students develop and discover mathematics, many times you explain things to them. When you are in a situation where you are explaining something that requires an example, each new problem type should have one written example in your plans, solved in complete detail, just as you expect your students to do it. This should not be an example worked in the text. You will probably use more than one example in your lesson for each type problem, but one worked out in complete detail should be sufficient for your planning.

Your lesson outline notes should reflect the things you will say as the student progresses from a point of not knowing something to a point of knowing it. You should initially assume that your students do not know the material. If they know the topic of the day, why are you teaching it?

The notes should contain the major points that comprise your discussion or development of the topic. There is no need to write out a word by word description of what will be said, just the major points. Some form of an outline (not necessarily formal) is generally deemed most beneficial. You should be able to quickly skim the outline and determine if all the salient points have been covered. Otherwise there is a risk that the discussion will become a random talk session with no apparent point or central theme.

There are many forms of *student assessment* that can be incorporated into your lesson plans to determine student progress. You can give a homework assignment and then check it to see if the subject has been mastered. Quizzes, tests, portfolios, group work, reports, individual projects, and software programs can all be used to provide insight into the progress of students. Each of these methods has strengths and weaknesses you need to be aware of. We discuss these items a little later when we cover assessment.

A Variety of Approaches

Not all students learn the same way. That is why learning modalities are discussed in education classes. You are responsible for knowing your students well enough to determine which is the best method of introducing a topic. Given all the pedagogical options that are available today, a majority of instruction is still exclusively the lecture method, although it is known to be a very ineffective method for student learning. The teacher tells the students how to do a problem type and the class mimics the model established by the teacher (cookie cutter mathematics). Little student thought is required in this format. Thinking and flexibility are not highly valued. It basically becomes the teacher saying, "Here is how you do this. Trust me, I would not lie to you. Don't think about it, just do it." That is a sad commentary, but it is a lot closer to the truth than many of us would like to admit.

Please do not think that the lecture method should never be used in your classroom. Look back to the fourth sentence in the last paragraph and you see *exclusively*. Students get shortchanged in the elementary school learning environment if lecture is the only mode of instruction, and they are deprived of using nonlecture learning styles to help them formulate ideas about mathematics.

You can be a catalyst for change in the elementary classroom. Use technology and manipulatives. Find real-world applications that relate to the students. Create and use models. Insert activities. Establish expectations. You can take a student from an entrance or beginning level to higher ground. You need to try to reach each student. That is why a variety of approaches is so important. The preceding statements are easy to make. The reality is that they might be difficult for you to implement, and the reason is tragically simple. Almost all of your mathematical education has been via the lecture model. The prior statements are asking you to break that pattern. The trouble is, you have few examples to refer to. You lack experience in two facets: teaching and creating lessons. Teaching experience comes with time. Your lesson-creating skills can be practiced and developed starting right now. The basics have been discussed as far as establishing a lesson plan. There is another consideration. You should know more than what you will be teaching. But your mathematical content is compartmentalized into classes and topics. You need to take the time to reflect on the breadth of mathematical knowledge you have and begin to devise ways to cross between the different compartments. That creates new and stimulating ideas for you and your students. As you do this, you should consider taking additional mathematics courses to strengthen your knowledge base. You do not want to be caught in the situation where you are teaching at the precipice of your own knowledge.

We have given you ideas to think about when constructing lesson plans. Many schools and states have prescribed forms and procedures for lesson plans. If you examine those predefined forms, you will notice many of the same ideas. Incorporating these ideas into your lessons can only help you as you begin to teach mathematics.

Classroom Climate

New and stimulating ideas are important to your development. When you teach, you are selling something. If you are not excited about what you are doing, how can you expect your students to be? The Attention, Interest, Desire, and Action (AIDA) method is worth considering as you plan. It is taken from techniques used by many successful salespeople for years. Whatever the product, you need to:

attract *Attention*;
create *Interest*;
establish *Desire*; and
motivate *Action*.

Teaching is no different. As you plan, think of ways to apply AIDA.

Think of a coach in any sport. Players are doing repetitious tasks day after day. How is it that the coach can get players to perform these basic tasks that are not a lot of fun? Part of the reason must be the players' internal drive. You need to achieve that same level of desire and cooperation in the mathematics classroom; enthusiasm on your part is one way to begin.

No matter your level of enthusiasm, discipline problems occur. There is no royal road to student discipline. There is no magic answer. Some of the classroom control you exercise will be planned because of established regulations within your class. However, you will frequently *shoot from the hip* and then hope you were right. Coaches are frequently second-guessed by the *Monday morning quarterbacks* (people who discuss what should have been done after the game or play is over). It is easy to criticize and analyze after the play or game is over. However, in the heat of the game, decisions have to be made on the spur of the moment. That is difficult. Many discipline decisions are made on the spot. You make them and then hope you were right.

No one can tell you what your discipline plan should be. It has to be created by you within the parameters you are given. You and only you know what you are willing to tolerate. Establish guidelines and make your students aware of them. Be firm and, most of all, fair. It is much easier to establish strict rules and back off than it is to be congenial and then try to clamp down. Aside from advice such as that, you are on your own. You need a plan for discipline. Know what is and is not acceptable in your school. Be aware of latitudes provided in your school.

ASSESSMENT

Assessment comes in many shapes and sizes. It is used for many different purposes. Assessment is more than just homework assignments, quizzes, and tests. You look at the work or your students and determine their strengths and weaknesses. You examine your planning, presentation, and discussion methods to decide how they impact the learning styles of your students. You evaluate texts to determine which is most advantageous for your students, school objectives, and school curriculum. Assessment should be ongoing.

The assessment process consists of four phases: planning the assessment, gathering evidence, interpreting the evidence, and using the results. Each part can be characterized through the following questions.

Planning the assessment

What purpose does it serve?

What framework is used to give focus and balance to the activities?

What methods are used for gathering and interpreting evidence?

What criteria are used for judging performance on activities?

What formats are used for summarizing judgments and reporting results?

Gathering evidence

How are activities and tasks created or selected?

How are procedures selected for engaging students in the activities?

How are methods for creating and preserving evidence of the performances to be judged?

Interpreting the evidence

How is the quality of the evidence determined?

How is an understanding of the performances to be inferred from the evidence?

What specific criteria are applied to judge the performances?

Have the criteria been applied appropriately?

How will the judgments be summarized as results?

Using the results

How will the results be reported?

How should inferences from the results be made?

What action will be taken based on the inferences?

How can it be ensured that these results will be incorporated in subsequent instruction and assessment?

Assessing Prior Knowledge

It is difficult to teach your students 2-digit addition with regrouping if your students have not mastered their basic addition facts. You will probably get quite a few blank looks when you use *addend* and *sum* if your students are not familiar with the terms. Having a good grasp of your students' prior knowledge makes teaching and learning of any concept or skill easier.

Students send messages to teachers that give clues about their levels of understanding in any class. Is the teacher receiving these messages? If a teacher asks a class to perform a skill and few of the students can do it, the message should be clear—some background or review work is necessary before proceeding. You need to receive the signal.

In the number trick "1,089" a student selects a 3-digit number without repeating any digits. The selected value is reversed and the smaller of the two 3-digit numbers is subtracted from the larger. In the answer, the tens digit will always be 9. For example, a student selects 351. The reverse is 153. Subtract 153 from 351 and you get 198. Asking for individuals who have a 9 in the tens digit of the answer provides some fast diagnostic information. If only a few hands in the class are raised, you need to examine your instructions.

Typically, most of the students will raise their hands. You can safely assume one of two things of the students who did not raise their hands: The students did not understand/follow your instructions or they have difficulty subtracting when regrouping is involved. There are other possible reasons for the error, but these are the dominant ones. You are now aware of the need to spend some extra time with selected individuals. You have diagnosed a difficulty and can now prescribe a remedy.

Knowing the extent to which prior knowledge and skills are mastered involves diagnosing strengths and weaknesses for each student. This is necessary to:

accurately place students in the curriculum continuum;

assign grades;

evaluate student progress;

help you learn how to teach more effectively;

gather specific rather than global information on individuals; and

structure your teaching style.

Using diagnostic methods to assess prior knowledge is a lot like being a medical doctor. Individuals go to a doctor with symptoms of some illness. The doctor examines the person and compiles all symptoms. Based on the available information, education, and prior experiences, a diagnosis is made, corrective measures are prescribed, and the patient is told to call back in a given amount of time if the situation does not improve. The patient wants to get better and has volunteered information and asked for help. Teachers do not have that luxury. Students frequently try to conceal symptoms and rarely volunteer information. Still, teachers are expected to make these individuals better students of mathematics. Ultimately, the teacher is expected to diagnose and prescribe for each student as needed.

Diagnostic teaching is not a simple task. Like the doctor, you must pull on a wide variety of training, experience, and understanding of the individual involved. You are expected to be aware of the basic psychological construct of all students. It is assumed you know the current social pressures they deal with. As you examine a mathematical illness, you must have a continuum of skills and conceptual developments that precede the problem area. If one, some, or all of those items are missing from the student's background, you are expected to be able to prescribe a series of remedies for the student that will correct all the deficiencies. Ineffective diagnosis and prescription in education can be tragic because it can lead to the mathematical demise of a student. Diagnostic teaching is a serious endeavor and should be approached as such.

Assessing Student Learning

How many questions should be asked to ensure adequate assessment on a particular concept? If one question is asked and the student misses it, are you sure the student does not understand the concept? Maybe it was just a careless mistake. Asking two questions dealing with the concept is better, but how sure can you be? If a student gets one of the two correct, what does this tell you? Maybe asking three questions would do it. If a student gets all three right or all three wrong, you would be fairly certain about the ability level pertaining to this concept. Perhaps five is a better number of questions to ask on a given concept. Your confidence level would be much greater if

a student got all five correct. The problem is, the test becomes extremely long very quickly with five questions per concept. Try to follow these guidelines when constructing your tests:

1. Be sure to have at least three questions for each specific concept.
2. Think about the attention span of your students. A 45-minute test is not realistic for a 9-year-old.
3. Use a variety of types of questions such as multiple choice, short answer, and essay.
4. Don't try to cover too many concepts in one test.

Observation can be a valuable assessment tool. You can watch as you move around the room. As students respond to your questions, notice facial expressions and body language. Be aware of the emotional climate in the room. Observations sometimes lead to the need for additional information. Some students can talk through a problem when they cannot write it. Be careful that they do not look to you for visual clues. This approach is in line with suggestions that students be able to communicate mathematically.

Interviewing requires time and rapport with the student. You are attempting to determine what the student knows. Some students will tell you what they think you want to hear. You need to be able to discern the difference. Time is a major factor in this approach, but the idea should not be discarded as an option.

A checklist can help reduce the pressure of time. As you observe a student, you can check specific items that the student has accomplished. When you reflect on what a student has done, you should be able to quickly establish a picture of what to do to strengthen that student's understanding.

Another method of gathering information is the portfolio. A portfolio should contain examples of the best works of a student as determined by the student. You can provide guidelines that suggest inclusion of an exemplary test paper, a proof, some homework problems, and so on. The portfolio should go beyond that type of information, however. Perhaps journal segments that indicate attitudes and feelings about the study of mathematics are appropriate. Demonstrations of bar graphs and charts constructed from activities done in class would be an example. Reactions to things that have been read could be a possibility. Reflections of various learning activities could be included as well. Remember, however, the items that are inserted into the portfolio should be determined by the student as a means of demonstrating their best work. Portfolios provide excellent examples of student work for parents and administrators to see.

As a teacher, you need to realize that not all assessment ideas are successful or accepted. This compounds the issue immensely. What methods should be adopted? What are trends that will vanish? Will some of the new ideas have a lasting impact on the school mathematics curriculum?

Error Patterns

Sometimes students use an incorrect method or algorithm for solving a problem. Analyzing student errors can be an effective means of student assessment. Here the emphasis is on diagnosing what error has been made and how to correct it. Some errors are easy to determine.

If the subtraction problem 823 − 169 yields a response of 746, you are fairly safe in assuming the student subtracted the smaller digit from the larger in each place, which is a common error pattern. The motivation for such a move is often attributed to the student being told at some time that a "big number cannot be subtracted from a little one." This comes from the desire to have students realize the need for regrouping in the subtraction process. Rather than saying a big number can't be taken from a little one, it would be better to say something like, "You can't take a big number from a little number *yet*" since it can be done in the integers.

Other error patterns are not as easy to determine. Observe the next set of problems, each of which was solved using the same error pattern. You see everything the student showed. What is the error pattern?

831	943	752	830
−276	−178	−249	−428
465	675	413	312

Here we are concerned with how to determine the error and a possible reason so corrective measures to prevent the same situation can be taken. This is not always easy because the root of the problem might begin several years earlier. *Before reading on, you should attempt to determine the common error being made in the four subtraction problems given.* It appears as if subtraction facts are under control. The flaw must lie within the application of the algorithm. Regrouping is performed when necessary so that is not the problem. Where is the regrouping performed? The student is going to the leftmost digit to regroup. In the first problem, the necessary "11" is created for the ones column, "13" in the tens column, and the "8" in the hundreds column is decreased to "6." That error is not easy to determine.

Development of the skills necessary to perform such diagnosis and prescription is rooted in your understanding of the mathematics involved, time, and experience. Divining error patterns is not an easy task, but it can reap large benefits for your students. Regretfully, many teachers look only at the answers and not the work done to get them.

Observe the following problems. What is happening in each problem?

348	613	425	237
+236	+178	+319	+626
684	891	844	963

If you have not assessed the errors in each problem, do so now. Notice that the student performed the needed regrouping into the ones column by adding an additional ten in the tens column for each problem. At the same time, the student also added an additional hundred in the hundreds column.

As your error pattern diagnostic skills increase, the problem areas are easier to detect. It does take conscious thought and practice. Each of the two error pattern types described in the text had four examples. Multiple examples are necessary to enable you to define patterns. You can easily convince yourself of the validity of that statement by attempting the exercises, looking only at the first example in each problem set.

Exercises

27. Determine the error pattern the student made in each of the following problems:

$$42 + 71 = 491$$
$$34 + 28 = 368$$
$$29 + 37 = 2127$$
$$76 + 54 = 7114$$

Describe the error the student is making. List the steps you would employ to assist the student in learning how to do the problem correctly and avoid repeating the same error. Could this error have been caused because the students are not accustomed to seeing addition problems written horizontally?

28. Determine the error pattern the student made in each of the following problems:

4567	389	2468	3421
+7968	+964	+3517	+2476
14635	1453	7085	5897

29. Define an error pattern you think a student would make. State the grade level. Provide sufficient examples. Give your error pattern to a peer to solve. Describe your discussions with your peer about the error pattern and how to correct it.

Assessing You

You need to determine how successfully you created an environment in which the students could learn the material. You also need to determine whether the class understood what was covered. Deciding how well *you* did is not always easy. Some of us tend to be too critical of ourselves. Others are quite lenient when it comes to self-examination and decide that it had to be good because "I" did it. Somewhere between those two extremes is probably where most of us will lie. A few moments for reflection can be very revealing:

Were the examples clear and pertinent?

Did the students ask similar questions repeatedly?

How were the questions I asked answered?

Did the students show reflection and thought?

Were the students able to relate the topic to prior work?

Were the applications clear to the students?

Could the students see the relevance of the topic?

Did I act excited and interested as the lesson was taking place?

Where could the presentation be improved?

Would this lesson be effective with another class?

This is not an exhaustive list of questions to ask as you go over your self-evaluation, but it is a start. Video or audiotaping a class can prove quite revealing. You may also want to create a lesson checklist for yourself. At the end of the day (when you have time), go through the checklist and make notes regarding the effectiveness of the lesson. Be sure to use checklist items that are important to you. Remember this list is a self-assessment of your lesson. You will probably be the only one to see it.

Another form of lesson assessment can be from student feedback. Have students keep a small notebook that can be used as a math journal. Periodically, ask your students to answer questions such as: (a) What was the most fun in mathematics during the past week? (b) What gave you the most trouble? (c) What would you like to learn more about? Collect the students' journals every week or two. This can be extremely valuable for assessing lesson effectiveness as well as student progress throughout the year.

Journals might not be as revealing as we would like because you know who is making the comment. An alternative to that is to have the students write one or two words about the day's lesson in a slip of paper and place it in a box. Here there is no identification available to you, it is quick and easy for the student to do, and you can gain valuable insight into what the students as a whole thought of your lesson.

USING TECHNOLOGY TO TEACH MATHEMATICS

Technology is changing faster than we can adapt to it. New products and upgrades are marketed at a rapid pace, most being bigger, better, and faster than the last. The need for technology in our mathematics classrooms has never been greater.

In the relatively near future, if not now, mathematics and science study will be mandatory of all students because of the demands of our technological times. People in all walks of life will need a higher level of proficiency in mathematics and science. Mathematics is a key to the door of opportunity as students decide about careers, learn to make informed decisions, and function as self-motivated, life-long learners. "Working smarter" is replacing "working harder" mathematically, particularly where more menial tasks (arithmetic would be included here) are concerned. In working smarter, individuals must be mentally fit to absorb new ideas, adapt to change, cope with ambiguity, perceive patterns, and solve unconventional problems (Mathematical Sciences Education Board, 1989). The technology available today through calculators and computers provides an avenue for computation that is faster and more accurate than anything done by hand. If the emphasis on basic computational skills is decreased in the K–12 mathematics curriculum, it will have a dramatic impact not only on what is taught and how it is taught, but also on the role of the classroom teacher. We are not advocating that the teaching of basic computational skills be abandoned. We are encouraging an inclusion of technology as a way of making some computation easier and perhaps more understandable to the student.

Technology can enhance mathematical thinking skills. Young children can now visualize and conceptualize mathematics with the assistance of technology. The earlier technology is used in elementary education, the greater the potential for students achieving a higher level of mathematical understanding. Implementation of technology into our mathematics curriculum is essential.

Learning to Use Technology

Most of the time, some form of technology could be used to enhance student learning of a concept. The important thing is that some form of technology is selected. Regardless of the form of technology, the teacher needs some level of familiarity if it is to be an effective tool. Time and energy need to be invested to learn at least the basics of the technology. This can be done in a variety of ways. Classes can be taken that may or may not offer college credit. Workshops in conjunction with private enterprises or professional meetings are available. There are videotapes that explain the use of technology in various environments. When purchasing technology, assistance and examples can help get you started. Generally speaking, after the introduction, students adapt to it and soon become knowledgeable about the associated technicalities.

Some people resist using technology, no matter the format, until they possess a high degree of comfort and confidence. Yet people seem willing to trust technology almost too much. The mentality seems to be one of, "If the calculator (or computer) says this is the answer, it must be correct." Teachers need to promote and encourage students to use logic, common sense, or estimation when using technology.

Support for Technology

Some responses of mathematics and business leaders regarding technology are:

All mathematics classrooms should have a computer and screen projector available for teacher demonstrations

Students must have computer labs available to them

Schools need to implement effective computer technology into their mathematics education programs. (Mathematical Sciences Education Board, 1990)

Using computers in the classroom generates strong feelings for many mathematics educators. Some do not want technology to become a crutch or shortcut method of learning. Others believe technology can be used as an instruction and teaching tool in the classroom, replacing much of the standard board or overhead tools. Still others indicate that computers can be used as a means of student self-discovery, learning, and development of understanding of mathematical concepts. Technology, whether it is seen as a crutch or tool in the classroom, is a component of today's world.

Studies done by Sigurdson and Olson (1983), Kitabchi (1987), Beyer and Dusewicz (1991), Ferrell (1985), Frick (1989), Salem (1989), and Seaver (1992) all show a significant improvement in achievement when integrating computers and calculators into the mathematics classroom. The information that has been provided by these studies is only a small portion of what is available. The research shows that computers, calculators, and technology accomplish the following in mathematics education:

1. Increased motivation and interest in mathematics.
2. Increased achievement on conceptual mathematical knowledge.
3. Increased achievement on problem-solving skills.
4. Increased enjoyment of mathematics.
5. Increased desire to do well in mathematics.
6. Increased desire to work hard in mathematics.
7. Increase in the number of students who wanted to take more mathematics.
8. Increase in number of females wanting to work in jobs using mathematics.
9. Increased achievement in algebra and geometry.

If the potential is there for increase in mathematical interest and achievement, we must do all we can to give our students the best available education in mathematics.

Change?

Why is it difficult to implement technology in the mathematics curriculum? Are we in the midst of a technological revolution that is being written about and yet little of the revolution seems to be making it into the K–12 setting? The pocket-sized calculator has been available for several years. Research shows use of the calculator does not adversely affect students' learning of mathematics. Yet how many teachers permit calculator use?

Part of the reason for a slow transition toward the use of technology is that we, as human beings, resist change. Some people hold the attitude that, "If it was good enough for me, it is good enough for my children." As technological innovations become available for the mathematics classroom, they can be used to advance learning or hindered by resistance to adopt different approaches. Which way would you have it?

A choice looms. Should technology be integrated into the mathematics education curriculum or not? Two parallel stories are told about a man and a woman. The man learned his arithmetic by doing hand calculations. As advances were made either in the ways in which the calculations were done or the materials available to do them with, the man clung to his way of doing things—by hand using paper and pencil only, no matter the size of the numbers. He persisted through the advent of the calculator, computer, and all other sorts of technological advancements that would have reduced the demand on his manual efforts. After all, he knew how to do it that way—why learn something new? At the same time, the woman, who was a master cook, learned on a wood stove, but progressed through the innovative developments. Each new technological advancement was found in her kitchen during its time: gas stove, electric oven, convection oven, and a microwave oven. Certainly she could have continued with the wood stove as her major cooking tool, but she opted to change with the times. Using the most efficient tools for the task, she can achieve the desired result in the least amount of expended effort.

There is no need to discuss *IF* technology will be inserted into the curriculum.

The question is *WHEN* and *HOW*? Technology is an integral part of our daily lives. Research shows that almost every household owns at least one calculator and over two thirds of the students have access to a computer.

Should calculators be used in the elementary classroom? Recommendations call for the use of calculators as experimental and discovery tools, instructional and reinforcement aids, and a means of curriculum development. Still use in the classrooms continues to focus on the calculator as a way to check work, help with computation, and explore patterns.

Exercises

30. Summarize and react to one article dealing with the use of calculators in a mathematics classroom. Include all bibliographic information.

31. Should calculators be used in the elementary setting? Why or why not?

After seeing the supporting evidence that calculators can enhance mathematical achievement, maybe the question should be: When and how should calculators be used in the classroom? This question is continually debated. How can this be? Calculators have been a hot discussion topic since their introduction into the curriculum. One of the major criticisms has been that it will become an *unremovable* crutch:

> I understand the principle—get them motivated. But I have yet to be convinced that handing them a machine and teaching them how to push the button is the right approach. What do they do when the battery runs out? I see a lot of low-level math among college students who still don't understand multiplication and division. You take away their calculators and give them an exam in which they have to add 20 and 50, and they get it

wrong. And I'm talking about business majors, the people who will soon be running my world. (James R. McKinney, Professor of Mathematics, California Polytechnic State University of Pomona, 1975)

Professor McKinney's comments were typical of those heard when the calculator was introduced into the curriculum. Research has shown results to the contrary of Professor McKinney's fears. The word *crutch* carries negative connotations with it. Why is it that paper and pencils are not classified as crutches? Typically paper and pencil are used to assist with the computations and to record at least the major steps in the solution. Algorithms used for addition, subtraction, multiplication, and division are crutches that we tell students to memorize. What makes the long division algorithm any worse of a crutch than using a calculator to divide large numbers? Should we become purists about crutches and require students to do all computations mentally? After all, how can we say this *crutch* is acceptable but that one is not? Undoubtedly, there was a time when individuals resisted the use of paper and pencil as aids to doing computations. Eventually paper/pencil computations became acceptable. Ultimately you are going to have to decide if your students should be permitted to use calculators as they learn mathematics. It is imperative that you make an informed decision.

When to Use a Calculator

Opponents of calculator usage argue that students need to possess basic arithmetic skills. Almost all authorities agree that a student should be able to do some mental computation. Students do need to learn their basic addition, subtraction, multiplication, and division facts prior to using the calculator. Even after students memorize their basic facts, they still make mistakes. For example, it is rather common for individuals to be confused about whether 7×8 is 54 or 56. A mnemonic like $56 = 7 \times 8$ (5, 6, 7, 8) or the realization that $9 \times 6 = 54$ can be used to resolve the situation. Sometimes calculator use helps avoid the dilemma because the correct product is shown each time. Eventually, some efforts might be required to convince a student it is more convenient to remember the product as opposed to using a calculator each time. It might be that the calculator will provide enough reinforcement for the correct product that the student will remember it, thereby removing the need to use the calculator to find the product of 7×8. In essence, flashcards are used to provide the same reinforcement through repeated visualization. If flashcards are accepted, why aren't calculators?

Like the product of 7×8, a problem involving division by an integral power of 10, a sum of several addends, or the difference between 4,000 and 357 may seem inappropriate for calculator use. If the alternative to an incorrect response to the problem is calculator use, then why not permit it? The calculator is a tool. Is it bad to let the student use the calculator to check their work? Each individual possesses a variety of mathematical talents. The calculator can enhance one's mathematical performance.

When working with word problems, the students are to sift through the words. In the process, the expectation is to set up the arithmetic to be solved. When the words are sifted and the arithmetic is set up, the purpose of the word problem has been accomplished. Students should be permitted to use calculators to perform the operations they deem necessary by their analysis of the problem. If the intent of the

assignment is to have the students practice their arithmetic skills, then it would be wise to choose arithmetic problems. Appropriate word problems would be solved when the required arithmetic has been mastered. Replacing the drudgery of arithmetic in word problems with the emphasis on the conceptual set up of the problem removes some of the anxiety about word problems in general. Students become anxious when faced with word problems. These problems require setup and solution. Give students the tool (the calculator) to assist with the arithmetic so their focus is on setting up the problem.

Calculators can be used to review and reinforce concepts and skills. For example, pair up students, giving each pair one calculator. Have the first student enter 50 into the calculator. Have the next student press the subtraction key and 1, 2, 3, 4, or 5, followed by the = key. The second student then presses the subtraction key followed by 1, 2, 3, 4, or 5 and the = key. The students continue to take turns. The winner is the student who gets 0 after pressing the = key. Does it matter who goes first? Is there any strategy that a student can use to win this game? What problem-solving skills will the students get from playing this game? Do you think they will enjoy playing a subtraction game like this one? This game can be varied using other operations and numbers.

Ultimately, you must decide when to use the calculator. Prompting for the decision will come from the text series, curriculum, parental attitudes, colleagues, and, most of all, your background. You are the local authority in your classroom. You need to become a force that will lead your students into their futures and have them prepared to perform the mathematical skills required of them for the betterment of society.

Exercises

32. Name a mathematical concept that would be hindered by the use of calculators and one that would benefit from the use of calculators. Rationalize your position in both instances.

33. How would you convince a student that memorization of basic fact tables is a necessity?

There are different types of calculators that you will need to consider for your students. Some have large viewing windows that allow more than one line of text. Some allow for fractions to be displayed in true fractional form. Others follow order of operations, whereas some do not. You need to make an informed decision when selecting the most suitable calculator for your students.

Students can begin to learn order of operation rules with a calculator. If they have not been told the rules, a selected series of problems can be given that will lead them to appropriate conclusions. A sequence of problem pairs like $2 \times 3 + 4 = \blacklozenge$ and $2 + 3 \times 4 = \heartsuit$ can be used to guide students to the idea that multiplication is done before addition (assuming the calculator follows order of operations). The number of pairs necessary for students to arrive at the desired conclusion will vary with student ability and the amount of exposure they have had gleaning information from patterns.

Exercises

34. Devise a set of problems that could be used as a basis to teach the order of operations for addition, subtraction, multiplication, and division on the set of counting numbers.

35. Is there any value to using larger numbers for the entries in the problem sets given to students as they are discovering the aspects of order of operations with their calculators? Why or why not?

Typically, when students are first introduced to division, the problems involve a number being divided by one of its factors. As they progress, the division is shifted so a number is divided by a nonfactor. Once this happens, three stages occur: The excess is expressed first as a remainder, then as a fraction, and finally as a decimal. The concept of remainder is best shown by using sets of objects and discussing the number of elements left after the maximum number of sets has been set aside. That is, in $17 \div 3$, five groups of three would be set aside or removed from the 17 objects. Two objects would remain because there are not enough elements to form another set. Casio's FX-55 permits division to be done using remainders. Using the $\div R$ key for $17 \div 3$ displays an answer of $5^{R\,2}$. Most calculators only show the missing factor as a decimal.

Exercise

36. Discuss the advantages or disadvantages of selecting a sequence of exposures that lead students from excess in division being expressed as remainders, then fractions, and finally decimals.

Using the Computer in the Elementary Classroom

Computers are found throughout the elementary setting. They have proliferated at all levels with staggering magnitude.

Schools that had at least one computer in 1983 had at least three in 1985. By 1985, almost every secondary school and over 80% of the elementary schools had computers available for instructional use (Becker, 1986). If the rate of increase kept that pace for the next 10 years, growing threefold every 2 years, today there would be more than 800 computers in each school. That translates to a machine for almost every student in nearly all elementary schools. On the surface this sounds great, but consider the following:

1. Subtract the machines used solely for administrative purposes.
2. Discount the machines set aside for specialized laboratories available only to a select group.
3. Factor in that some machines are older machines and cannot handle the latest software.

How many computers in a school are student accessible? Are they in laboratory settings or equally distributed between all classrooms? How many teachers want to use them? What software is available? When should computers be used? It is a tool that can stimulate thought, individuality, problem-solving skills, and thinking. It is your responsibility to build those desirable traits into each of your lesson plans, and if computers can help, then go for it!

Learning to Use the Computer

Research supports the use of computers in the mathematics classroom. Technology is making a slower entrance into the mathematics curriculum than in the working world. "With approximately 50 percent of school teachers leaving every seven years, it is feasible to make significant changes in the way school mathematics is taught simply by transforming undergrad-

uate mathematics to reflect the new expectations for mathematics" (Mathematical Sciences Education Board, 1989, p. 41). This indicates that an important part of the current teaching population should have been educated during the computer era. Why then is there such limited use of computers as a teaching and learning tool in the mathematics environment?

If we are going to convince our students to use technology as a teaching and learning tool, we should use it ourselves. One source says, "Mathematics faculty will model the use of appropriate technology in the teaching of mathematics so that students can benefit from the opportunities it presents as a medium of instruction" (American Mathematical Association of Two-Year Colleges, 1995). That means you as college students should be seeing technology used in your classes, and you should be using technology as a part of your studies.

Some school systems place a new computer for teacher and classroom use if the teacher will go to two Saturday workshops. The weekend classes show the teachers how to use the computer and software in the classroom. Buying the computers is not enough. Training must also accompany the technology.

Exercises

37. The two major microcomputer platforms are PC and MAC. Which one will you use in your classroom and why?
38. If your school's computer platform is different from the one you prefer, what will you do?

Additional Technology

Video as an instructional tool has been available through slides, film strips, movies, and videotapes. Videodiscs in some areas, like science, are a tremendous asset to learning. These videodiscs can be used in some mathematics classes as a means of demonstrating applications. Unfortunately, videodiscs specifically designed for mathematics are extremely limited.

The digital camera is a recent technological device that has entered the educational setting. Teachers are beginning to realize the potential of capturing real-life images. Digital cameras have the ability to take images that can be used in computer presentations, incorporated in desktop publishing, and shown on Internet Web pages. The Casio QV digital cameras also have the capability to show an image directly on a TV, creating a digital image slide show from the camera. With this option, you can then videotape your slide show for viewing at a later time. For example, you can use a digital camera to take images of your class working on an activity where students are counting and sorting M&Ms® by color. The students then make a table to categorize their candy. After that, the students use the M&Ms® to make a bar graph on small poster board. Since you have taken images of the class doing this activity, you can make a slide show displaying students in action for parents' night. This allows the parents to see the children doing mathematics.

How do we conclude a chapter dealing with technology? There is no end. Some technology mentioned in this text is currently on the cutting edge and exciting, NOW. By the time this is in your hands, it may be out of date. You are fortunate to be entering an age and profession where you will have the opportunity and responsibility to maintain an awareness of the latest developments. As a professional, you are obligated to make the learning of mathematics exciting and progressive for your students. Encourage the use of tech-nology with your students and fellow teachers.

MANIPULATIVES

We have mentioned manipulatives a few times so far and we mention them many more times throughout the rest of this text. They are critical tools in helping children learn mathematics. We discussed Piaget's steps, the first of which is concrete. That is where the manipulatives show up—at the beginning. They continue to show up throughout the curriculum though. New concept beginnings mandate a concrete approach. Refreshing memories and passing through the learning continuum, even if at a very rapid pace, must include the manipulatives at the foundational level. Working with a student who is behind says there is probably a need for some manipulative. Correction of error patterns often can be aided by the use of manipulatives. Uses and needs for manipulatives can be found throughout the curriculum.

We focus on Base 10 blocks, Cuisenaire rods, and number lines as our basic manipulatives. You should have your own set of each manipulative so you can *do* the activities we discuss throughout the remainder of this text. Without the proper tools, you will fail to fully comprehend the full impact of the message we are delivering. More significant, you will fail your future students. We do not list sites regularly in this text, but an example of a site that provides manipulatives on the Internet is http://www.arcytech.org/java/integers.

Conclusion

Decisions, decisions, decisions! As you teach, you are faced with a myriad of situations that require you to decide what to do. You may have the luxury of determining, in advance, what will happen. You may need to state a position within seconds of when a situation arises. The general ideas discussed in this chapter are a resource as you face judgment time. Reflect on the thoughts presented. Expand your knowledge and understanding. As you do, you will be growing as a professional. As you progress through your career, graduate-level courses, in-service opportunities, and professional conferences are wonderful opportunities to update and enhance your teaching skills.

There are so many things that could be considered in thoughts about teaching. Who knows how many other things could be added to the topics we discussed? You need to pay attention to your curriculum and your students. You need to be aware of the various dynamics within your classroom. You need to know the mathematics. You need to be adept at using manipulatives as a teaching or learning tool. You need to know technology and when to use it. It sure looks like what happens in your classroom is up to you.

The only feasible way you can create your own view of teaching mathematics is to be familiar with all of its facets. It takes time and energy to learn about teaching, but the benefits you and your students reap will be worth the effort. It is time to get started with the particulars.

REFERENCES

American Mathematical Association of Two-Year Colleges. (1995). *Crossroads in mathematics: Standards for introductory college mathematics before calculus*. Memphis TN: Author.

Anderson, R. D., et al. (1994). *Issues of curriculum reform in science, mathematics and higher order thinking across the disciplines*. Washington, DC: Department of Education, Office of Research (OR 94-3408).

Becker, H. J. (1986). Instructional use of computers. *Reports from the 1985 National Survey, 1*, 1–9. Baltimore, MD: The Johns Hopkins University, Center for Social Organization of Schools.

Begle, E. G. (1973). Some lessons learned by SMSG. *Mathematics Teacher, 66*, 207–214.

Beyer, F. S., & Dusewicz, R. A. (1991, March). *Impact of computer-managed instruction on small rural schools*. Paper presented at the annual meeting of the American Educational Research Association, Chicago, IL.

Brown, J. S., Collins, A., & Duguid, P. (1989, January/February). Situated cognition and the culture of learning. *Educational Researcher, 18*, 32–42.

Brumbaugh, D. K., Ashe, D. E., Ashe, J. L., & Rock, D. (1997). *Teaching secondary mathematics*. Mahwah, NJ: Lawrence Erlbaum Associates.

Cobb, P., & Steffe, L. P. (1983). The constructivist researcher as teacher and model builder. *Journal for Research in Mathematics Education, 14*(2), 82–94.

Crosswhite, J. F. (1986). Better teaching, better mathematics: Are they enough? *Arithmetic Teacher, 34*(2), 54.

Cummings, F. (1995). Equity in reforming mathematics and science education. *The Common Denominator, 1*(3), 1–2.

Fennema, E., & Peterson, P. L. (1986). Teacher-student interaction and sex-related differences in learning mathematics. *Teaching and Teacher Education, 2*(1), 19–42.

Ferrell, B. G. (1985, March). *Computer ImmersionProject: Evaluating the impact of computers on learning*. Paper presented at the annual meeting of the American Educational Research Association, Chicago, IL.

Fey, J. (1980). Mathematics education research on curriculum and instruction. In R. J. Shumway (Ed.), *Research in mathematics education* (pp. 388–432). Reston, VA: National Council of Teachers of Mathematics.

Hart, L. E. (1989). Classroom processes, sex of student, and confidence in learning mathematics. *Journal for Research in Mathematics Education, 20*(3), 242–260.

Kitabchi, G. (1987, November). *Evaluation of the Apple classroom of tomorrow*. Paper presented at the annual meeting of the Mid-South Educational Research Association, Mobile, AL.

Koehler, M. S. (1986). Effective mathematics teaching and sex-related differences in Algebra I classes (Doctoral dissertation, University of Wisconsin, 1985). *Dissertation Abstracts International, 46,* 2953A.

Kronholz, J. (1998, June 16). Low X-pectations: Students fear algebra, and then comes the ninth-grade crunch. *The Wall Street Journal.* (*http:// www.middleweb.com/Backstories1-HTML*)

Mathematical Sciences Education Board. (1989). *Everybody counts.* Washington, DC: National Academy Press.

Mathematical Sciences Education Board. (1990). *Reshaping school mathematics: A philosophy and framework for curriculum.* Washington, DC: National Academy Press.

National Advisory Committee on Mathematical Education. (1975). *Overview and analysis of school mathematics in grades K–12.* Washington, DC: Conference Board of Mathematical Sciences.

National Council of Teachers of Mathematics. (1989). *Curriculum and evaluation standards for school mathematics.* Reston, VA: Author.

National Council of Teachers of Mathematics. (1991). *Professional standards for teaching mathematics.* Reston, VA: Author.

National Council of Teachers of Mathematics (NCTM). (1995a). *Addenda series:* Reston, VA: Author.

National Council of Teachers of Mathematics (NCTM). (1995b). *Assessment standards for teaching mathematics.* Reston, VA: Author.

National Council of Teachers of Mathematics. (2000). *Principles and standards for school mathematics.* Reston, VA: Author.

Oberlin, Lynn. (1985). *How to teach children to hate mathematics.* Gainesville, FL: University of Florida Press.

Porter, A. C., Floden, R. F., Freeman, D. J., Schmidt, W. H., & Schwille, J. R. (1986). *Content determinants (with research instrumentation appendices).* Research Series No 179. East Lansing, MI: Institute for Research on Teaching, Michigan State University.

Salem, J. R. (1989). Using Logo and Basic to teach mathematics to fifth and sixth-graders. *Dissertation Abstracts International, 50*(05), 1242A (University Microfilm No. 8914935).

Scieszka, J. (1995). *The math curse.* New York: Viking.

Seever, M. (1992). *Achievement and enrollment evaluation of the Central Computers Unlimited Magnet Middle School 1990–1991.* Kansas City, MO: Kansas City School District.

Shulman, L. S. (1986). Those who understand: Knowledge growth in teaching. *Education Researcher, 15*(2), 4–14.

Sigurdson, S. E., & Olson, A. T. (1983). *Utilization of microcomputers in elementary mathematics* (Final Report). Edmonton, Alberta: Alberta Department of Education.

Steffe, L. P., & Killion, K. (1986, July). Mathematics teaching: A specification in a constrionist frame of reference. In L. Burton & C. Hoyles (Eds.), *Proceedings of the Tenth International Conference, Psychology of Mathematics Education* (pp. 207–216). London: University of London Institute of Education.

Suydam, M. (1985). Questions? *Arithmetic Teacher, 32*(6), 18.

Weiss, I. R. (1995, April). *Mathematics teachers' response to the reform agenda.* Paper presented at the American Educational Research Association Meeting. San Francisco, CA. (ERIC Document Reproduction Services No. ED 387 346)

2
Number and Operations

Get ready. Get set! Go!! That sums up this section. Here is where most of what you will be teaching throughout your professional career will be covered. Notice the word *most* in the last sentence. That is spelled **m o s t**, not **a l l**. Please do not fall into the trap of neglecting to cover algebra, geometry, measurement, data analysis, probability, problem solving, reasoning, and proof. Even after elementary students know the foundations of all these topics, they still need to be able to communicate their knowledge in understandable mathematical language, connect the different topics together because they are all intertwined, and, finally, see representations of the material in the real world. Ironically, we place the majority of what you will be covering in your career as a teacher of elementary mathematics in this one section and then put each of the other topics mentioned earlier in a section all their own. Closer examination of that approach makes sense, however, because we do not want you to miss things you may not have covered (or maybe you for-

got you did) in your career as an elementary student. So, let the adventure begin!

EARLY CHILDHOOD

Children enter elementary school with high expectations about learning mathematics because they have seen a lot of it in their lives already:

Are we there yet? (distance)

Am I taller than you? (length)

Who has more? (number)

Wanna bet? (probability)

Will you help me with this puzzle? (shapes)

Why? (proof)

How do I . . . ? (problem solving)

It is imperative that we capitalize on these exposures and many like them. This process starts formalizing the foundations that help these children appreciate the many and varied facets of mathematics. We may know very little about a child's background, skills, level of exposure to mathematics, anticipations, or expectations, but we do know children learn at different paces and in different ways. Different children learn distinct things by the end of their school experience, therefore it is up to us to gently guide each child along a path of learning. Mathematical experiences were not isolated incidents in the child's life before school, and we must take care to prevent isolating mathematics as a subject in school by infusing it with other subjects. A child learns in complex patterns with multiple links to other subjects, contexts, and ideas. Have you heard the expression "every class is an English class"? Well, this powerful message can be extended to include mathematics in every class! If this powerful message speaks to you, the future teacher of elementary school mathematics, you will seek ways to provide connections among subjects.

Seriously now, how much mathematics can a little child possible know? For example, ask a student to draw a family picture. More than likely, the adults will be larger than the rest of the family members, particularly if the artist and all siblings are relatively young. If there is an infant in the family, that individual will probably be the smallest person in the picture. This portrays that the artist is aware of an important mathematics concept—relative size. The scale might not be accurate, but the idea is there. In art class, you have an opportunity to reinforce mathematics in the context of large, small, and relative sizes. Similar opportunities for the integration of mathematics are available in almost all subject areas. There is a problem with that last statement, however. It could be difficult for you to integrate mathematics into other subject areas because of your own experiences, which probably did not involve that. Furthermore, your strength (or lack of it) in mathematics will help (or hinder) integrating mathematics into other subjects. Students are accustomed to dealing with multiple ideas at one time, and we should stand ready to capitalize on these natural links.

Readiness

Hughes (1993) discusses the idea that young children enter school with more mathematical than had previously been believed. They are aware of concepts like size, shape, time, money, numbers, logic, geometry, and so on. They even have an intuitive awareness of ideas involving concepts far beyond their formalized knowledge base. For example, most children realize that if they walk faster, or even run, they can get from one place to another in a shorter amount of time. In this natural way, the idea that running gets you where you want to go quicker than walking is developing. As adults, we apply that concept regularly. We know that if we drive faster we can get where we want to go sooner as long as we do not stop to have a conversation with some law enforcement official.

Our task as teachers of mathematics is to realize and capitalize on this knowledge base. The simple fact that our children are not all on the same page of the playbook at the same time creates huge barriers for some children. It also means that you face a formidable task because your classes will include children with a unique collection of background information, expectations, and drives. You must consider this wide variety of exposures particularly in the early childhood grades. Where will you begin and how fast will you move when the children in your class have wide background differences or when some of them do not have readiness skills?

The simple answer is to ensure that background skills are provided for all children. That is so easy to say and so difficult to accomplish. Some students will recognize numerals and perhaps even have memorized some addition facts. Some may be aware of procedures such as putting two toys together with three more toys to get five toys and then getting the same result as starting with three toys and putting two more with them. That is, some students are informally aware of the idea that

2 + 3 = 3 + 2. More formally, we would say the student is beginning to become aware of the commutative property of addition on the set of whole numbers. Certainly we would not expect the student to be able to spout all that terminology, nor should we burden little children with these terms, but recognition that the formative idea is there is critical. How can a teacher possibly provide an appropriate background and valid enrichment activities for students when a child with rich readiness skills is in the same class with a child who is unable to even recognize numerals?

Deciding Where the Kids Are

Maybe we could give all little children a test to determine their backgrounds and look for commonalities. How in the world could we do that? When children initially enter school, many cannot read or write, and their verbal/language skills may vary greatly. Some little children are very shy. What medium could be used to determine readiness skills accurately? Certainly you could conduct some Piaget-type conservation tasks to determine whether they possess basic conservation skills relating to number, length, or space. But how could you complete such time-intensive individual investigations in a classroom situation?

On that first day of school, you will have little or no knowledge of who your young charges are, what they know, or what they are able to do. There are things you can observe, which may provide direction. How well do they function with manipulatives? Are they able to do a task in more than one way? Suppose you give a child some triangles, circles, and squares. Each shape has some red ones and some blue ones. You ask the child to sort the shapes into two groups. Perhaps the child will put all the red ones in one group and the rest in another. You could compliment the child and then put all the blocks back into one group. Using the same words to ask the same child to perform the same task might provide surprising results. Some children will group the pieces by color again. Others might group them by shape. Those who do a different grouping the second time are probably more flexible in their thinking skills. This is significant information to consider as you begin to teach young children. Those who can look at a concept from more than one vantage point are developmentally farther along than those who cannot.

What kind of conceptual background has been developed at home? Is a child accustomed to doing things alone? Consider a parent and child going to a bank to deposit money into the child's savings account. Does the adult complete the transaction and then say, "Well, we made a deposit to your account," or is the child allowed to be a part of the operation. The child may not be able to fill out the deposit slip, but could place the money on the teller's counter, explain that it is a deposit, and thank the teller. Allowing the child to take such an important role could be first steps toward real self-reliance, even though the parent was closely supervising the transaction.

Present a child with a new and different task and then quietly watch the reactions. Some children will wait to be guided. Some will begin to explore the situation and look for possible resolutions. Others will ask for help. Those are not all the possible reactions, but you should understand the point. Different children are going to behave differently in various situations. You must find a way to accommodate these disparities in your classroom while keeping the children headed in a common direction.

Most students will have learned some facts by rote before starting school. They will have heard all sorts of facts and ideas and perhaps may even be able to consistently perform some tasks. You may have heard about a little child counting while waiting for the bus on the first day of kindergarten. Arriving at 100, the question was whether that would be enough if the teacher asked someone to count in class. The child was very proud of the ability to count and it showed. A closer look revealed that words were merely being uttered, and there was only a limited idea of the background that would provide meaning for the carefully memorized words. Rote work is a part of the learning environment. Prior to school, children will have experienced repetitive reciting. They learn language from hearing a word over and over. As they attempt to say the word, they will be corrected and encouraged. The same is true for number experiences.

Children may receive mixed signals if your classroom learning activities include more than rote work. If learning at home was almost all rote and you present an environment that does not place a premium on rote learning, a dilemma may be created for the child. You may find that some children and parents resist your efforts to encourage thinking, analyzing, and seeing an idea in different ways.

Your expectations for a child may be quite different from their parents' expectations. Parents are likely to use a single, familiar format or algorithm while helping their child. These caring parents will try to help the child learn exactly what they learned in the same way they learned it. Consider adding two 2-digit addends with regrouping. If a parent consistently helps the child write problems with one addend carefully aligned above a second addend, the child might assume mastery before they are able to handle the problem in any format. If you then present the same problems written horizontally, the child might become quite discouraged. The algorithm may have been learned without leaning anything about place value. Recall the error pattern discussed earlier when the student was doing problems like 42 + 36 and getting sums of 456.

Finally, and perhaps most significant, you must always be aware of any attitudes the student brings from home. In many homes, mathematics has not been viewed in a favorable light. That attitude might be telegraphed within the classroom. When you begin to teach mathematics, do not be surprised if you encounter low levels of enthusiasm or excitement.

Exercises

39. Select a child who is at the beginning school age and conduct a conservation of number activity. Describe the results of your experiment.

40. Observe a kindergarten or first-grade student who is placed in an unusual environment. Describe how the child reacts.

41. Describe a plan you could implement to help the parents of your students view mathematics in a more positive light.

Classroom Activities

Mathematics education research clearly shows the value of using manipulatives to introduce topics (Hatfield, 1994). This is the concrete stage, providing a firm foundation for growth through the semi-concrete and semi-abstract stages, with the ultimate goal of reaching the abstract level. This process cannot be rushed and will not be the same for each student. You must guide a child's mathematical development by beginning each concept at the concrete stage and supporting progress through all levels. That means you need to ensure the proper mathematical development of each child by beginning at the concrete stage of learning and helping them progress through the various developmental stages to the abstract level of knowledge. As you decide what to do in your curriculum, your decisions must be guided by the characteristics of the learners and the topics to be learned. Young children rely on sensory information, amplifying the need for concrete beginnings. A child who has not physically moved two sets of objects together to form a single set will likely struggle. As the child manipulates the sets of objects, a mental image of what is going on begins to form. Over time, the child will be able to use this image to form mental pictures instead of handling physical objects (concrete). Growth continues as the child begins to create sketches (semi-concrete) and then uses tally marks or some other shorthand way to represent the sets (semi-abstract). Finally, the child will learn to use numerals to represent the cardinality of the initial sets and the combined set (abstract). It is unlikely that abstract thinkers remember much about how they functioned before they could think abstractly. This is a skill needed by teachers, who must ensure that students receive the most important classroom gift—time. Hurrying ensures a weak foundation. Are *you* able to use concrete thinking skills?

Because your students will not be able to think as you do, you must develop a conceptualization of thinking the way they do. On that first day of school, some of your students will have fairly sophisticated number skills, some will have no number skills, and most will be some-

where between these extremes. You cannot just stand there, smiling and wondering. Start with pre-number activities using manipulatives. Questions such as, "Does this set have more, fewer, or the same number as that set?" becomes the emphasis. As students become competent in comparing, begin to introduce ordering. The need for a short way to show the ordering process leads the children to numbers.

You will probably find your students able to classify things before they have developed the language skills needed to explain what they have done. You can help them develop classification skills along with language skills by keeping a box of assorted *stuff* available. Initially ask them to sort the objects any way they want. Later specify how things should be sorted, perhaps by stating some desired characteristic that will determine what does or does not belong in the set. Begin to name the objects as a set of whatever they are. Later present the children with a set of familiar objects like spoons. Ask the children what they see. Some children will respond that they see spoons. That is fine. Eventually someone will say that they see a set of spoons. That subtle difference is significant. The recognition of set indicates an advancement in both mathematics and language skills. As always, this developmental sequence takes time and generally is not the same for any two children.

At an early point along the developmental line, you could consider using loops of yarn to enclose two sets of objects. Then enclose the two sets with another (longer) piece of yarn to enclose both sets. Place additional objects inside the larger set, but not in either of the subsets. Ask the child to move one additional object into one of the smaller sets, and then ask the child to clarify why the object was placed in the selected subset. Notice that this yarn activity is open ended and no two children need supply the same answer. You might want to let students look through that old box of assorted *stuff* and supply their own set objects.

Children need to have fun with numbers. That can be accomplished through counting games that involve counting forward, skip counting, counting on, counting backward, or guessing how many objects are in a set. Those activities should be followed by situations that lead to combining, separating sets, getting two groups to have the same number of elements in them, adding elements to a set, or removing some elements from sets. Events such as these provide a natural lead-in to operations on numbers.

Children do not always need a teacher to explain the concepts of measurement. The plain and simple fact is that children need to measure some real items. Then they need to measure some more real items. Then . . . well, you get the idea! One popular approach to teaching children how to measure involves using units that are now called non-standard. There are wonderful activities available that address old-fashioned measures. If you explain to children that the distance from a person's fingertips to their elbow is the non-standard measure called a *cubit*, you should also explain that it was once used in construction. As a point of interest, you might look up the difference between the Roman cubit and the Egyptian cubit. For little children, "long, long, ago" is enough because they are not able to grasp the concept of ancient. After you talk with them about the foot, which is now a standard measure, you might have them walk about the room and compare their feet to see just how non-standard this measure was long, long, ago.

Following your discussion of standard and non-standard measures, you might allow them to devise their own standard measure such as a brand-new pencil, a large paper clip, or a segment of string that is as long as a selected class member is tall. Using their own selection to measure a few objects in or out of the classroom can be fun. Because the measure is standard, they can check one another for accuracy. Be sure to allow plenty of time for measuring and move to metric and inch–foot–pound measures only when the students have mastered the concept. There is one huge underlying assumption that is made with measurement, and ignoring this assumption leads to difficulties for many students.

In Piaget's conservation-of-length task, a child is asked to determine whether two objects (typically a pair of clay hotdog-style shapes) are the same length. Once the child decides the two are the same length, one of the two is moved. Figure 2.1 shows the initial setup where the child would say the objects are the same length in Scene 1, whereas Scene 2 depicts what the child would see after one of the objects would be moved. A child who is not conserving length will indicate that one of the two shapes in Scene 2 of Fig. 2.1 is longer than the other, although seconds earlier the same child had agreed that the two shapes were the same length. This can be translated to saying that, for this nonlength-conserving child, the length of the object is not constant. If a nonlength-conserving child is asked to determine how long something is, no matter what unit is used, the unit is often moved along the object. In other words, for a nonlength-conserving child, we are

Scene 1   Scene 2

FIG. 2.1.

asking that a measurement be made with what is essentially a ruler that expands and contracts. You should proceed with great caution, being a constant advocate for a child who does not yet conserve length. Otherwise the unexpected responses you see may lead to incorrect assumptions about the abilities of perfectly normal nonconserving children.

With appropriate consideration given to conservation tasks, children should be doing things with measurement as a part of their early number experiences. You can begin asking them questions that carry number responses related to things such as: How many? How big? How far? How long? Each of these questions may be answered with a number or word, but you should encourage more. For example, if asked how far it is from Orlando, Florida, to Atlanta, Georgia, you might get answers like 8, 500, far, or a long time. More information is needed to get a complete picture (8 hours, 500 miles, a long time to ride). You should encourage your students to develop a preference for more information. That is, rather than just saying that one item is longer than another, it would be advisable to get them interested in how much longer one is than the other.

Another connection between fun and learning in mathematics is found in patterns, often a focus area in early childhood settings. You can start out with simple things like showing a child a sequence of colored chips (R B R B R B R B) and asking what chip would come next. You can build on this with a transition into "counting on." In this game, you or a student provide the first few numbers of a simple sequence and then ask for the next number. Of course, you will begin with 1, 2, 3, 4, . . . or 2, 4, 6, 8. Eventually the patterns will become quite complex and challenging. Your students will love to try to stump you!

Shapes and patterns go hand in hand. Your students will be talking about shapes long before they are ready to begin work with geometric shapes. Because shapes are part of the world that children experience before entering school, most will have experience with points, lines, planes, and spaces. In school, even in the early years, they need to build on that background to develop a spatial sense and realize that geometry surrounds them in their world. They start out recognizing different common shapes and go on to using classifications of shapes. For example, initially they might count the number of sides on polygons to classify them. Quadrilaterals come as squares, rectangles, rhombi, parallelograms, trapezoids, and, of course, weird quadrilaterals without special names or features. They are all polygons. They are also all quadrilaterals (another classification). Some of them are parallelograms and some are not. Recognition of these classification schemes will help students analyze relations that exist between different shapes—another important aspect of mathematics and life skills.

Data may represent the name of an android to many children, but data surround them. Without anyone noticing, children take advantage of many opportunities to analyze data even at an early age. For example, children often compare their number of toys with those of other children. This inclination can be extended to activities such as creating a bar graph to indicate how many students in a class were born during the same month of the year. During early school experiences, this can be accomplished by placing small sticky notes on a chart with the longest bar indicating the month with the most birthdays. This provides a gentle introduction to formal data collection and interpretation.

Thinking, problem solving, reasoning skills, and the methods we use to introduce, reinforce, and assess these skills will have a large impact on other subject areas as well. Students must learn to how discern good logic from poor before they can determine whether an argument is sound. Careful nurturing of reasoning skills provides a background for proof, which is an essential part of mathematics. An important aspect of proof is the knowledge that even a whole group of confirming examples offered as evidence of why something is true rarely proves an issue, whereas a single counterexample clearly disproves the issue. Let us assume that all children in a given class were born in May. One could offer that as proof that everyone is born in May. We know that is not correct, but it does show how an example does not prove something. It is important that children learn how to use logic to make convincing arguments in favor of their point. With the birthday example, one could cite an individual with a June birthday as a counterexample of the premise. You begin building the proof idea by asking questions like: How do you know?

NUMBER SENSE

At an early age, children begin the fascination of dumping bags or boxes of objects on the floor. Next, children become amused at returning the objects to the box or bag just so they can dump the blocks on the floor again. Eventually, children begin to separate the dumped objects into groups with similar characteristics. Soon the separate piles are placed into different boxes. The children have begun to classify objects by arranging them into individual sets. When children begin making these sets, do you think they know how many objects are in each of their sets? Do they care? Eventually they will want to know how many of one

thing they have as compared with another. They will probably want to know how many pennies they have compared with the number of dimes. Eventually, we want our children to have a good feel or number sense of the quantity they have collected.

Try the following activity with a group of people. You will need an overhead projector and 15 pennies. Tell them you are going to display a number of pennies on the overhead. Their job is to decide how many pennies are shown and write the quantity. They are not to shout out their answer. Begin the activity by placing one penny on the overhead. Quickly turn the overhead on, then off. The class will see a brief display on the screen. The people should immediately write the number of pennies they see. A right or wrong answer is not the focus of this activity. Have those who saw only one penny raise their hand. Next, ask for a show of hands by those who saw two pennies. Ask those who saw three pennies to raise their hands. Repeat the activity again using three pennies, then four, then eight, then seven, and finally nine pennies on the overhead, each time asking for a show of hands to indicate how many pennies were observed. Vary the quantity of pennies and spread them out on the overhead as shown in Fig. 2.2. Do not always increase the num-

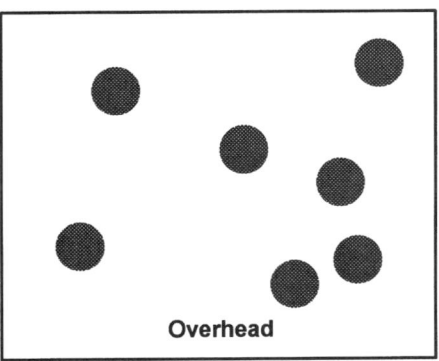

FIG. 2.2.

ber of pennies from the previous amount, and do not arrange the pennies in the same pattern.

At what point did you notice a significant difference between the correct number and the groups' responses? Did this surprise you? Quite often there is a significant disparity between five and seven. The age level of the student probably will impact the results. Younger students may only have a grasp on twoness and threeness, whereas some older students may even be able to see eight or nine pennies at one time.

When you put two pennies on the overhead, did all the students see exactly two pennies? Do you think they counted two pennies or did they actually see two? If a student saw two, then they probably have a grasp of the concept of twoness. They actually know abstractly what the numeral 2 represents.

Repeat the activity again with six pennies. This time arrange the pennies as shown in Fig. 2.3. Did most of the students get the correct answer? Do you think these students have a grasp of the concept of sixness? More than likely, most of the students subliminally and rapidly grouped the pennies into two groups of three or three groups of two and then counted the groups to get six. If the students tried to mentally group the pennies,

they are using the basis of multiplication at least at an informal level. Try the activity again by scattering 10 pennies on the screen in no particular pattern. Ask how many students saw 6, 7, 8, 9, 10, 11, 12, 13, and 14. Next, take all the pennies off and then place 10 back on the overhead. You are doing this so the students do not know that you are still using the same number of coins. Arrange the 10 pennies in a similar pattern to Fig. 2.3 and repeat the activity. Again ask how many students saw 6, 7, 8, 9, 10, 11, 12, 13, and 14. Did more students see 10 on the second try?

This activity is a wonderful introduction to number sense, sets, and also potentially for multiplication. The students can see the power of arranging objects into groups for the purpose of determining the number of things in a set. Remember, it is important to give the students a useful application of the mathematics that they learn.

Exercises

42. What do you think would happen if you used pennies, dimes, and quarters (or other different size objects) at the same time?

43. How could the penny flashing activity be used for another operation?

Counting to 100 and having a true number sense for 100 are not the same. Even as adults, 100 is a difficult quantity to see. If you took 100 dollar bills and stacked them on a table, do you think the average adult would see 100 dollar bills? Would they even come close? How about if you took the stack of bills and tossed them up in the air? When they come to rest on the ground, scattered all over the place, will you see 100?

When teaching mathematics, we use counting and grouping skills to identify numbers. For example, if you divided that

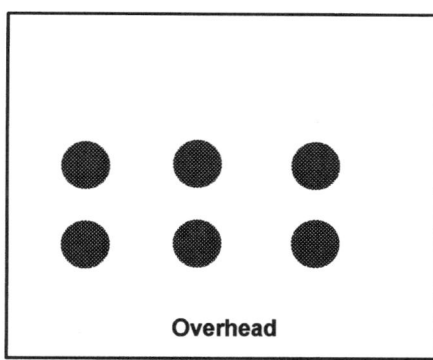

Overhead

FIG. 2.3.

stack of 100 dollar bills into separate stacks with five bills in each stack, you could count the number of stacks to determine the total number of bills. You might have a better understanding of 20 stacks of five or even five stacks of 20. Consider a student who sees a movie where a kidnapper asks for $2 million in unmarked twenties. The criminal wants the money delivered in a duffel bag by one person to a trash can in a back alley. Later the movie shows a person carrying a gym bag with the money. If the kidnapper wanted unmarked 20-dollar bills, the duffel bag would have 100,000 twenty-dollar bills. Because each bill weighs approximately one gram, the weight of the money inside the gym bag would be about 100,000 grams or approximately 223 pounds. Could the kidnapper carry the bag? Would the duffel bag be large enough to hold the money?

Exercises

44. Give a similar example to the money and the briefcase where children see inappropriate uses of numbers in real life.

45. Would it be appropriate to bring a stack of 100-dollar bills into class to show students how ridiculous the ransom requests are in movies? Why or why not?

Manipulatives and Number Sense

When children enter school, they come from an environment where much of the learning was based on experiences with physical objects. One of the tragedies is that many times children are asked to skip directly from the concrete experiences to abstract concepts, bypassing the semiconcrete and semiabstract stages of learning. As children progress through school, we need to take the students on a journey that will allow them to develop from the concrete to abstract level.

Pattern blocks are manipulatives that can help students increase their ability to sort and classify. A typical set of pattern blocks includes:

Green	Triangles
Orange	Squares
Blue	Rhombi
Red	Trapezoids
Yellow	Hexagons

Other pattern block sets may include other shapes, and the color of the shapes may be different than the colors given before. For example, a set produced by another company contains triangles that are three different colors, thick or thin, and large or small.

When introducing a new manipulative, it is important to give the children ample opportunity to play and explore with the new items. You might first have the students separate their blocks into piles by colors. Next, have them group their blocks into piles of like shapes. Ask the students to compare their results to previous ones. If students are asked to group blocks so the shapes in each pile have the same number sides, how many piles will they have?

As children grow mathematically, they will need to know that the piles they have been creating are called sets. A set is a collection or group of things that is well defined. A set may be a group of like objects (usually the case) or a group of unlike ones (uncommon but correct). The only requirement is that it be clear whether or not a given thing (element) belongs in the set. Cardinal number (cardinality) of a set shifts the focus to the number of elements in a set.

Children begin at the concrete level by physically placing things into sets. As they

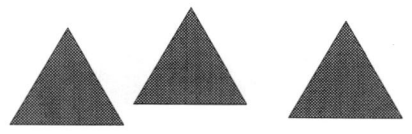

FIG. 2.4.

mature, students should be introduced to semi-concrete concepts by drawing pictures of the sets they constructed with their hands. For example, if students arranged their pattern blocks into sets by color and one of the sets contains three green triangles, then they would draw a picture similar to Fig. 2.4. Instead of working with the actual blocks, they use the drawings to represent the concrete objects. This lends itself to a gradual movement toward the abstract level that the students will encounter later in mathematics. As students successfully sort, classify, and perform operations on objects at the semi-concrete level, they begin to move to the semi-abstract level by using figures or marks to represents the cardinality of a set as shown in Fig. 2.5.

Now students use symbols to represent drawings or pictures of real objects. As you look at the tally marks, you might think that it would be easier to simply write 7 rather than 7HH //. Try to think on your students' level. To determine the cardinality of a set, many of your students are counting each object in the group. The tally marks represent a symbolic form of the set that students can still count. The numeral 7 is an abstract sense of the

quantity 7. When looking at the numeral 7, do you in any way, shape, or form see the quantity 7 represented? Of course not, you just know 7 means the quantity 7. This is a completely abstract concept because you are allowing a symbol or character to represent the tally marks that represent the picture that represented the objects in the set.

Exercises

46. Describe three other ways students could group pattern blocks?

47. Name two other manipulatives that younger students could use to sort and classify. Explain how the manipulatives could be used.

Comparison

As students continue to sort and classify different sets, it is natural for them to begin to compare different sets. When children look at two bags of candy, they think about which one is larger, which one has more, which items are bigger, and which ones taste better. The children are using comparison to decide which bag to choose. One method a child can use to answer the question is one-to-one correspondence. Figure 2.6 shows two bags with several types of candy. By matching a piece in one bag to a single piece in the

Can be represented by 7HH //

FIG. 2.5.

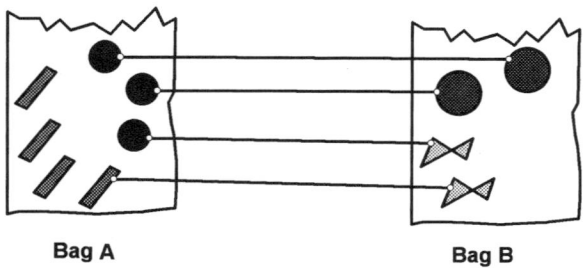

Bag A   Bag B

FIG. 2.6.

other, one can see that Bag A has more candy. A student might also realize that Bag A has more types of candy. The child can also see that the candy in Bag B is larger than the corresponding pieces in Bag A. As the awareness level increases, the student is better equipped to make a more informed decision as to which bag should be selected and why.

Number Properties

Ask for number properties (also called field axioms or field properties); if you get an answer, you will probably hear something like, "The commutative property and that kind of stuff." That is right and wrong. Properly said, you are going to talk about the commutative property of addition (or multiplication) on the set of whole (or some other appropriate set) numbers. When talking properties, two essential ingredients are the operation and a set of elements. The smallest set where all the number properties are present is the rational numbers. In that set, you have:

Closure	+ or × two rationals and get a rational
Commutative	$a + b = b + a$ and $a \times b = b \times a$
Associative	$a + (b + c) = (a + b) + c$ and $a \times (b \times c) = (a \times b) \times c$
Identity	$a + 0 = 0 + a = a$ and $a \times 1 = 1 \times a = a$

Inverse	$a + (-a) = (-a) + a = 0$ and $a \times \dfrac{1}{a} = \dfrac{1}{a} \times a = 1$
Distributive	$a \times (b + c) = (a \times b) + (a \times c)$

These properties are encountered throughout the elementary program and should be taught when appropriate. The idea of problem pairing as discussed in Part 1 is one way to introduce the properties.

You could also lay useful foundations at the concrete stage. When a child is combining two sets, it does matter if the sets are interchanged. Children could be encouraged to combine two objects on the left with three objects on the right. After doing that, they could place the same three objects on the left and the same two on the right. Then end result is a set with the same five objects in it.

Closure can be communicated with a set of pattern blocks. How many different shapes can you make using some or all of the triangles? No additional triangles may be introduced to the discussion. The variety of results may be considerable, but there is a limit to how many can be created *unless* new triangles are permitted.

Similar approaches can be used to establish the meaning of any of the properties. Understanding can be enhanced by investigating the property ideas in various sets and using different operations. For example, is the set of digits {0, 1, 2, 3, 4, 5, 6, 7, 8, 9} closed for (under) addition? Some students might say yes because 2 + 3 = 5, 4 + 5 = 9, and 0 + 6 = 6. However, 6 + 7 = 13, and 13 is not an element of the original set (digits). Thus the statement that the digits are closed under addition is false since closure demands that any two elements from the set are operated on, giving a result that is an element of the set. Will subtraction commute in the integers? In general, the answer is no. Examples such as $5 - 2 \neq 2 - 5$ will usually convince students, particularly if you ask whether $5 minus $2 is the same as $2 minus $5. An interesting extension question is whether subtraction will ever commute in the integers. The answer is yes; $5 - 5$ will commute as will any situation where a number is subtracted from itself.

Exercises

48. Describe how you would help a student learn that the whole numbers are not closed for division.

49. Is there ever a time when there would be a distributive property of multiplication over subtraction on the set of counting numbers?

50. Select one number property that has not had some idea for presentation given in this text, and describe how you would present it to a class having the appropriate readiness skills.

Place Value

Understanding place value is critical to much of a student's arithmetic development. We all know that. Yet place value gets far less developmental attention than it should. You have seen texts with presentations similar to that of Fig. 2.7. All too frequently that is about the extent of exposure students get to place value before they are expected to competently use the idea in their work.

When adding whole numbers, they are instructed to regroup (carry) from the ones to the tens column and show it by placing a 1 above the top value in the tens column. That 1 represents one ten, but frequently that idea is not stressed enough so the student makes a useful connection. Perhaps a similar explanation is given for regrouping from tens to hundreds. Before long it is assumed that the student can apply similar logic to subsequent places, and the presumption is that place value is understood and can be applied easily. The reality of the situation is that often the student can mechanically do what is asked but has no idea why the moves are being made. Far more tragically, that same student is not aware enough to be concerned about why it works.

Place value is so easy to teach. Start with a set of Base 10 blocks similar to those shown in Fig. 2.8. At the concrete level, the students learn to trade 10 units for one ten and vice versa. Similarly, they learn to trade 10 tens for one hundred. They also should learn that one hundred can be traded for nine tens and 10 ones (the most convenient and common way) or eight tens and 20 ones, and so on. As they make these trades, discussion should fo-

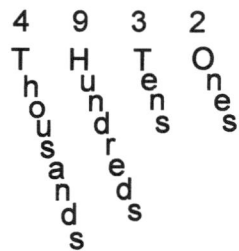

FIG. 2.7.

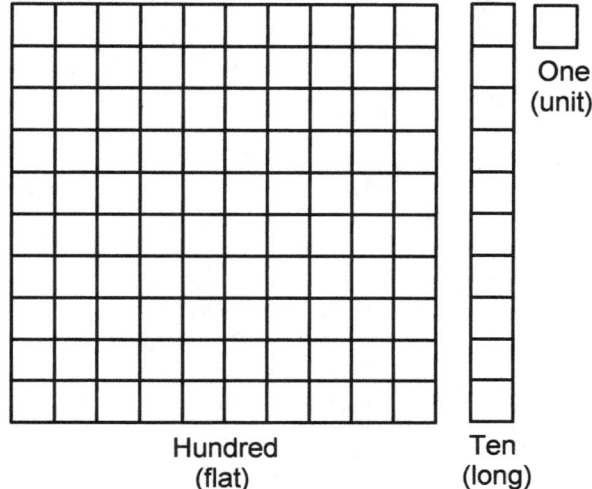

FIG. 2.8.

cus on the idea of one 10 being equivalent to 10 ones. Certainly appropriate U.S. coins could be inserted here to amplify the relationships. Regroupings using Base 10 blocks will be revisited later during the discussions about addition and subtraction where place value will be amplified.

WHOLE NUMBER OPERATIONS

Addition

Throughout this chapter, all the other chapters in this book, and your career as a teacher of elementary mathematics, you should ask if the child is ready for the concept being covered. If a child does not know the addition facts, how can we expect that child to do multidigit addition involving regrouping? Where does addition begin? A logical answer is that we start with sets. The student plays with small collections of objects, which leads to exploring the cardinality of sets. The answer

to "How many?" is the cardinal number, and that starts the groundwork for addition. Two sets are joined together (union), and the total number of elements is to be determined. As long as the two sets are disjoint (no common elements), the cardinality of the union of the two sets will equal the sum of the cardinalities of the two original sets. This is a critical formative stage to help the child be ready to encounter addition.

Sequence for Teaching Addition of Whole Numbers

The following list of steps is not exhaustive. It is the beginning of the sequence used to generate students' ability to do all whole number addition problems. At some stage in the sequence, each student should realize that the same procedure (regrouping or not) is being repeated in each place value. At that point, the generalization of the addition algorithm is estab-

Facts

Sums <10 (Need place value of 2 digits before going on)	
$10 \leq sum \leq 18$	
Multiples of 10 + multiples of 10 (sums < 100)	Example: 20 + 30
2 digits + 1 digit with no regrouping	Example: 23 + 4
2 digits + 2 digits with no regrouping	Example: 23 + 45
2 digits + 1 digit with regrouping of the ones	Example: 27 + 8
2 digits + 2 digits with regrouping of ones only	Example: 27 + 38
(Need place value of 3 digits before going on)	
2 digits + 2 digits with regrouping of tens only	Example: 85 + 91
2 digits + 2 digits with regrouping of both places	Example: 87 + 45
NOTE: Some 3-digit problems could be done before all 2 digit types are completed.	
3 digits + 1 digit with no regrouping	Example: 246 + 0
3 digits + 2 digits with no regrouping	Example: 246 + 30
3 digits + 3 digits with no regrouping	Example: 246 + 301
3 digits + 1 digit with regrouping of the ones	Example: 246 + 7
3 digits + 2 digits with regrouping of ones only	Example: 426 + 57
3 digits + 2 digits with regrouping of tens only	Example: 482 + 91
3 digits + 2 digits with regrouping of tens and ones	Example: 417 + 96
3 digits + 3 digits with regrouping of ones only	Example: 317 + 608

lished, and such fine detailing as shown here is no longer necessary.

Exercises

51. When will 4-digit place value need to be discussed in the addition sequence and why?
52. Complete the prior addition sequence until all three-digit + three-digit examples are done. Do an example with each entry.
53. Some elements of the 2D + 2D and 3D + 3D sequences given earlier could be switched around. Which ones and why?

Some might argue that the addition sequence shown is overkill. Most textbooks do not break the sequence into such fine detail. The small incremental steps are most helpful for a student who tends to struggle. At the same time, the carefully sequenced steps do no harm to a better student. In fact, the likelihood is that the small steps will help all students understand the addition concept better.

You should notice that the examples given in the sample sequence avoid duplicating digits. This assists students as they look at examples and track numbers. Duplication of digits can add unnecessary confusion for some students. This is not to be construed as saying that digits should not be duplicated in examples. All that is being said is that in the initial examples avoid duplication of digits for the benefit of your students. Eventually duplication of digits must occur.

Although all the examples are listed horizontally in our addition sequence, you should list problems both horizontally and vertically as you present the various steps in the addition sequence to your students. They need to be comfortable dealing with both formats. Also, you should some-

times place the smaller addend first, especially in 4 + 23 and $\begin{array}{r}4\\+23\end{array}$. Some might say that if the student understands the concept, this variable listing idea is not necessary. However, it can also be said that the variable listing of the problems will enhance students' understanding. This form of an addition problem is not overly common in many texts, but students should deal with a large variety of forms as they learn about adding whole numbers.

The order listed in the sequence is not absolute. The facts should come first for obvious reasons. The advantage of splitting them into sums less than 10 followed by sums of 10 through 18 is that if the children are not ready for place value, they can still deal with addition. For example, they could work with sums of three addends, where the sum is less than 10. They can work with number families (e.g., all the pairs that give a sum of five). They can begin to learn the basics of the commutative property of addition on the set of whole numbers, the associative property of addition on the wholes, and the additive identity on the wholes. These property concepts should continue throughout the development of addition with whole numbers. Early on in the discussion about addition, you need to identify the terms "addend" (the numbers being added) and "sum" (the answer in addition). This assists the students in identifying the things they are working with and also lays essential groundwork for subsequent work in subtraction.

The following examples are addition facts: 3 + 4 = 7; 0 + 5 = 5; 9 + 8 = 17; 6 + 6 = 12. The following examples are not addition facts: 10 + 3 = 13; 5 + 12 = 17; 10 + 12 = 22; 18 + 0 = 18. Given that, the class would be asked to define an addition fact. Here the child is an active participant in the learning environment as opposed to be a passive learner. Rather than being told the definition and asked to memorize it, the student is to determine the definition based on examples of what are and are not addition facts. The expectation is that each child (and you) will conclude that an addition fact involves three whole numbers, at least two of which must be a single digit. The number facts for all operations (addition, subtraction, multiplication, and division) have now been defined if this statement is generalized.

As you begin to deal with the complete set of addition facts, you can ask questions like, "What is the largest sum in the addition facts and why?" Because a number fact always involves three whole numbers, at least two of which must be single digits, the largest fact sum is 18. This is an example of the type of upper level question that needs to be asked of your students at every opportunity to stimulate their learning.

After the facts are learned, consider multiples of 10. This can be relatively easy for the students if you have done things like 2 oranges + 3 oranges = 5 oranges. Starting concretely, they would deal with situations involving 2 tens and 3 more tens, concluding the total is 5 tens. They should be thinking that this is similar to the problem with the oranges. The 2 tens would be written as 20, and so on, and they have 20 + 30 = 50. Before long, they should conclude that adding multiples of 10 is just like doing the addition facts, but with a zero on the end.

After this, either 2 digits plus 1 digit with no regrouping or 2 digits plus 2 digits with no regrouping could be done. After one of those two types is done, the other generally follows. If your students are not ready for regrouping, you could do 3 digit plus 1 digit with no regrouping. Of course, the 3-digit addend must be preceded by a discussion of place value. This sequencing

decision is also influenced by the idea of not necessarily wanting to present your students with too many hard or easy concepts in a row. You do not want to discourage them, and you also do not want them to become too arrogant about their ability. You are the local authority in your classroom, and you need to make those decisions based on your students.

Sets and the Addition of Whole Numbers

Sets of objects provide the background necessary for addition. The students begin by dealing with a situation similar to Fig. 2.9. They would decide the cardinality of set A (expressed as N(A) or n(A)) and the cardinality of set B and finally the cardinality of the union of sets A and B. Notice there is no duplication of shapes in Fig. 2.9. At the concrete stage, this is not a problem because the elements of one set are counted, the elements of the second set are counted, and finally the elements in the union of the two sets are counted. However, it does become a problem if the sets are: R = {2, 3, 4, 5, 6} and S = {4, 6, 8}. The union of R and S is {2, 3, 4, 5, 6, 8} and N(R) + N(S) ≠ N(R ∪ S).

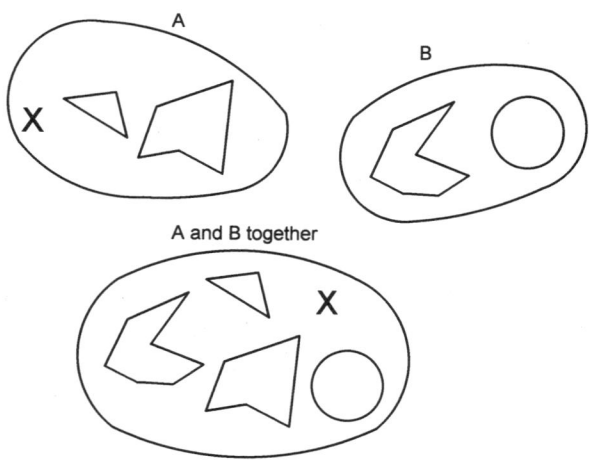

FIG. 2.9.

Thus, the sets being used need to be disjoint to avoid complications.

Exercise

54. If set A is your copy of the text for this class and set B is another copy of the same text (same edition), are sets A and B disjoint?

Base 10 Blocks and the Addition of Whole Numbers

The examples dealing with sets could just as easily be done with Base 10 blocks or bean sticks. The advantage is that the exposure comes early in the students' experiences. Do not forget, students need time to play with any manipulative. One of the first formal activities with Base 10 blocks after that free play period is the art of trading. Students need to realize that 10 ones (unit blocks or units) can be traded for one 10 (long) and vice versa. Of course, along with the 10 block being introduced comes a place value discussion. With this background, addition facts become fairly simple.

If the fact being learned is 7 + 8, the units are placed together and then 10 of them are traded for a long. The final result would be one long and five units as shown in Fig. 2.10. In Fig. 2.10, the straight and curved line segments show one way the individual cubes could be combined to create the long and remaining units. It is conceivable that a student would just count 1, 2, 3, . . . , 14, 15 to determine the sum. This student is probably not as developmentally advanced in mathematics as a student who would *count on* (counting on is the process of beginning in the middle of a counting sequence and going on) from seven or eight to the total of 15. Even if a student counts on, the one who starts with eight might be more mathematically ad-

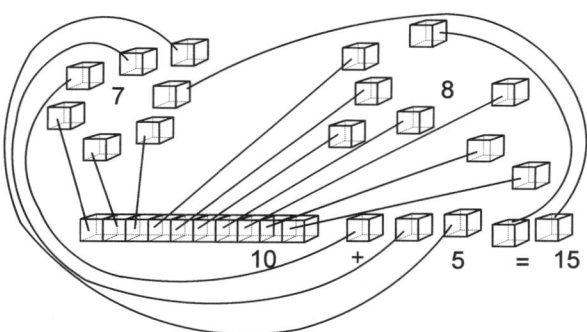

FIG. 2.10.

vanced than the one who starts from seven. Counting on is difficult for some students as they begin to learn about adding whole numbers. It should be noted, however, that the question was to determine the sum of 7 + 8 and no stipulation was given on what method should be used. Thus, any student getting the sum (legally) has succeeded.

Once the concrete stages of 7 + 8 = 15 are developed, the student should make the transition to working with pictures of the blocks. For us as adults, this might seem like a trivially small difference, but it is significant as the students grow mathematically. If necessary, they can refer back to the actual blocks and build parallel lines of thought. The pictures would be followed by a listing of "Us," which would represent the pictures of the individual units that stand for the individual blocks. Notice here again that the connection can be made with the concrete if necessary. Figure 2.11 shows one way the "Us" could be arranged to show 7 + 8 = 15.

There are all sorts of grouping procedures that can be used to get the sum of 15 for 7 + 8. You could "take two out of the seven," leaving five there. Then put those two with the eight to make 10. Then 10 + 5 = 15. You could "take three out of eight," leaving five there. Then put those three with the seven to make 10 and 10 + 5 = 15. These are abstract processes that grow out of grouping as shown

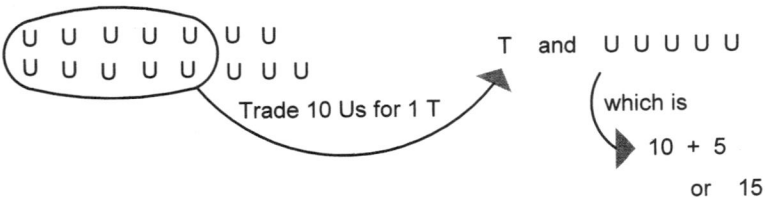

FIG. 2.11.

in Fig. 2.11. They are good things for your students to conclude and should be encouraged. At some stage, now that the students know 7 + 8 = 15, the fact needs to be memorized.

The process used to do 7 + 8 = 15 is applied in essentially any addition problem when the Base 10 blocks are used. The only difference is the numbers involved. Consider 289 + 427. If necessary, the problem could be done with the blocks. Figure 2.12 shows the stages that would occur using pictures of the blocks to show the sum of 716. The trading 10 ones for one ten and 10 tens for one hundred lend themselves well to using the standard algorithm for adding 289 + 427 abstractly, which would look like

$$
\begin{array}{r}
11 \\
289 \\
+427 \\
\hline
716
\end{array}
$$

These same processes could be used with more than two addends.

An intermediate step in the form of technology can be useful. One such ex-

ample is IBM's "Exploring Math Concepts" (IBM, 1995) series. Within that software is the capability to build problems like 158 + 296 and then represent each addend with pictures of the appropriate Base 10 blocks. Once that is done, the student has the option of asking the software to take the 14 units and make a 10. Similarly, 10 of the 15 tens could be traded for one 100. In each case, the action on the screen closely duplicates the student's actions as the blocks are manipulated. This close parallel between the concrete manipulation and figures moving on the screen helps the student transfer away from the concrete stage.

Exercises

55. Describe how you would use the Base 10 blocks to teach an addition fact. Explain each stage, beginning with the concrete and going through the abstract level where the fact is memorized. Your explanation could be a series of pictures like in Fig. 2.11, a verbal description of what you would do, or a combination of words and pictures.

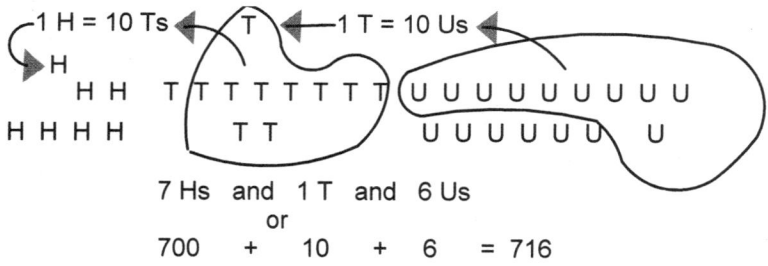

FIG. 2.12.

56. Describe how you would use the Base 10 blocks to teach finding the sum of two addends where there is regrouping out of all three place values. Explain each stage, beginning with the concrete and going through the abstract level where the algorithm is used. Your explanation could be a series of pictures such as Fig. 2.12, a verbal description of what you would do, or a combination of words and pictures.

57. A *doubles* addition fact has both addends being the same. How many *doubles* addition facts are there?

58. How many addition facts are known once the student is aware that zero is the additive identity in addition of whole numbers?

59. How many addition facts are known once the student realizes that adding one to a number will give the next consecutive counting number?

60. Assuming the student is aware that zero is the additive identity in addition of whole numbers and that adding one to a number gives the next consecutive counting number, how many addition facts are known?

Cuisenaire Rods and the Addition of Whole Numbers

As initial exploration takes place, some student will create something like Fig. 2.13. That is a wonderful opportunity for

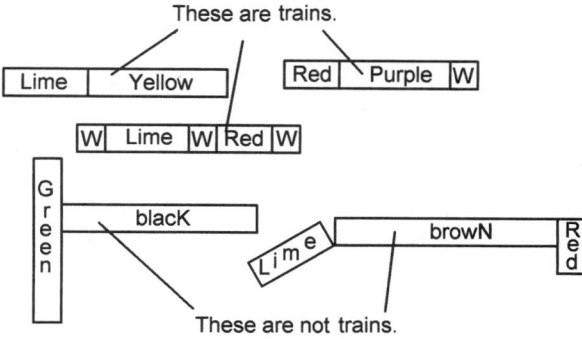

FIG. 2.13.

you to explain the concept of a train when discussing the Cuisenaire Rods.

When White is the unit within the Cuisenaire Rods, it can be shown that Red is equivalent to two Whites or units. That would be done in a manner similar to that shown in Fig. 2.14 except it would be

FIG. 2.14.

established by the students manipulating the actual rods. Figure 2.14 also shows the confirmation that Green is equivalent to a train made up of six White rods or, when White is the unit, Green is six. A similar procedure would be used to confirm the numerical values for all 10 Cuisenaire Rods. When White is the unit: Red = 2, Lime = 3, Purple = 4, Yellow = 5, Green = 6, blacK = 7, browN = 8, bluE = 9, and Orange = 10.

Suppose the fact you are dealing with is 9 + 4. You would need a bluE–Purple train and then that would need to be interpreted as shown in Fig. 2.15. Certainly you could place White rods beneath the bluE–Purple

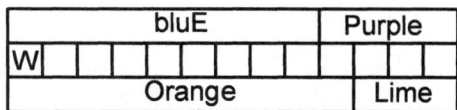

FIG. 2.15.

train to show that 9 + 4 = 13. However, a unique way might be to place an Orange–Lime train beneath the bluE–Purple train to show a sum of 13. The advantage to the Orange–Lime train is the emphasis on place value because Orange = 10 and Lime = 3, so the Orange–Lime train is equivalent to 10 + 3. The student is seeing a representation of expanded notation.

Once the addition problems go beyond facts, the Cuisenaire Rods can become cumbersome because of the length of the trains. That is not to be construed as a statement that the Cuisenaire Rods should not be used with sums greater than 18. Something like 158 + 296 would be possible to show but quite unrealistic. The hope would be that the students would be functioning at the abstract level before the Cuisenaire Rods would be needed to show 158 + 296.

The Cuisenaire Rods have a distinct advantage for providing subliminal background pertaining to the commutative and associative properties of addition on the set of whole numbers. Figure 2.16 shows how the Cuisenaire Rods can be used to show 3 + 5 = 5 + 3, whereas Fig. 2.17 shows how they can be used to show 2 + (5 + 4) = (2 + 5) + 4. There are other configurations that would show the associative property of addition on whole numbers. Some would argue that the one shown in Fig. 2.17 is too complex and confusing. If you start with the center line in Fig. 2.17 and work up or down, much of the confusion is eliminated.

The encounters your students have with the commutative property for addition on the set of whole numbers using the Cuisenaire Rods can be amplified through the use of problem pairs. As they establish 3 + 4 and 4 + 3 with the rods and they begin to practice the sums abstractly, a part of a written assignment could look something like:

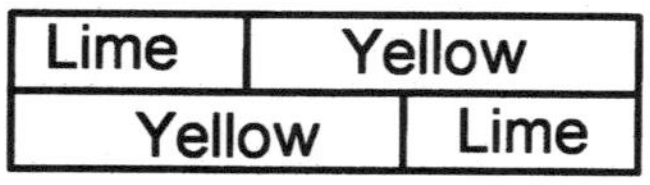

Lime	Yellow
Yellow	Lime

FIG. 2.16.

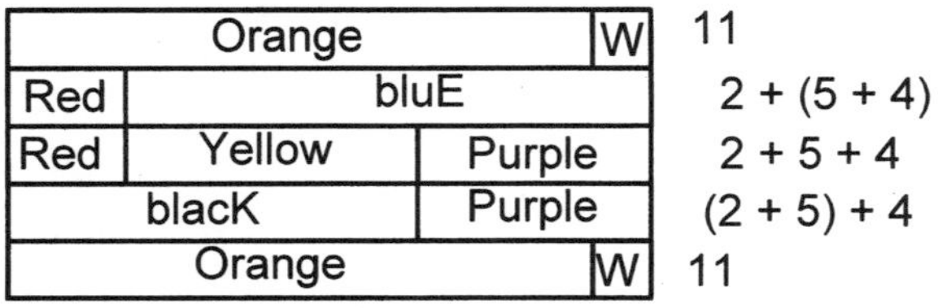

Orange		W	11
Red	bluE		2 + (5 + 4)
Red	Yellow	Purple	2 + 5 + 4
blacK		Purple	(2 + 5) + 4
Orange		W	11

FIG. 2.17.

1) 3 + 4 = ___
2) 4 + 3 = ___
3) 7 + 6 = ___
4) 6 + 7 = ___

The intent would be for them to realize that the answer to problem number 2 is the same as the answer for problem number 1, and so on. Once the student does a few pairs, the hope would be that, once 7 + 6 is done, the student automatically enters 13 for the sum of 6 + 7. Discussion at this point should have the student saying something like, "The numbers are reversed but the answers are the same." That response is a crude expression of the commutative property of addition on the set of whole numbers.

Exercises

61. Based on the pictures in Fig. 2.13, define a train as used with Cuisenaire Rods.

62. Describe what you would accept from a student using the Cuisenaire Rods to confirm that blacK = 7 when White is the unit.

63. Describe how you would use the Cuisenaire Rods to teach an addition fact. Explain each stage, beginning with the concrete and going through the abstract level where the fact is memorized. Your explanation could be a series of pictures similar to those in Fig. 2.15, a verbal description of what you would do, or a combination of words and pictures.

64. Do 25 + 9 using the Cuisenaire Rods, and show the result with pictures.

The Number Line and the Addition of Whole Numbers

Addition on the number line is similar to the pictures generated when using Cuisenaire Rods. Figure 2.18 shows 7 + 6 done

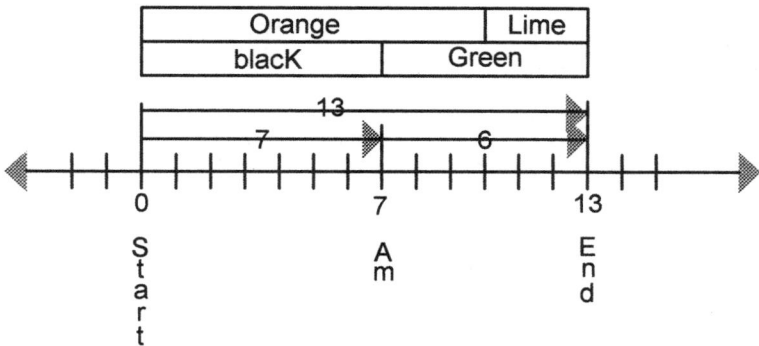

FIG. 2.18.

with the Cuisenaire Rods and below that the same problem on the number line. This problem could also be modeled for younger children by using a number line on the floor that they would walk on. The words *Start* (always zero), *Am* (intermediate location or position as the problem is worked), and *End* (sum) are significant to all number line addition problems. You always start at zero and, for now, move in a positive direction. Arrows are used here, but hops or curves could be used to show the span from 0 to 7 and from 7 to 13 as well as the total change from 0 to 13. It is not necessary to use a dashed segment

to show the total change or sum, but it is helpful for students who struggle to see which number is the answer.

As with the Cuisenaire Rods, larger sums can become cumbersome on the number line, but they can be done. Sums such as 20 + 30 are easy to show on the number line. Parallel descriptions between 2 + 3 on the number line and 20 + 30 should be developed. Figure 2.19 shows both sums on different number lines, which can help students see the similarities. The different scales have to be brought out as part of the discussion.

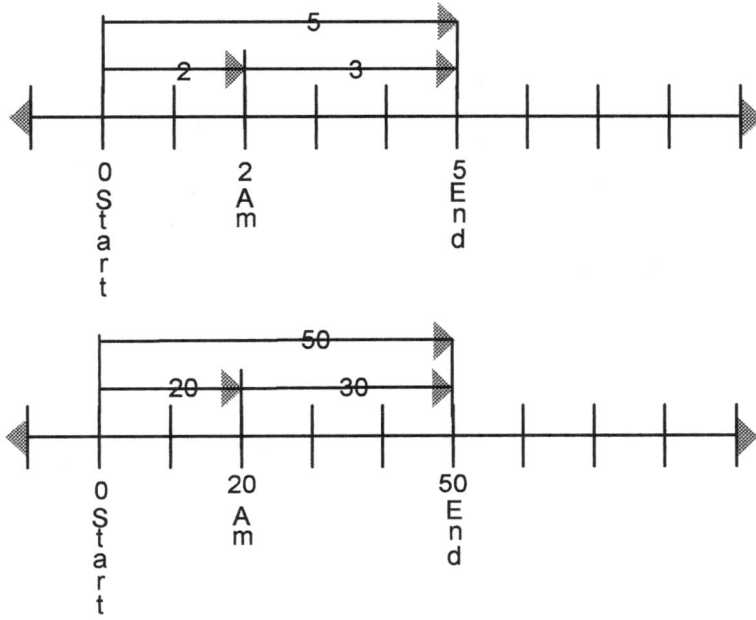

FIG. 2.19.

Exercises

65. Do 9 + 7 on the number line using the procedure described in this text.

66. Show that 8 + 4 = 4 + 8 on the number line using the procedure described in this text.

67. Discuss how you would use the number line to introduce 20 + 30, assuming that the students have used the number line to learn their addition facts. What should the students conclude when doing 20 + 30?

Alternate Methods for Adding Whole Numbers

There is a logical transition toward the addition algorithm. First, the student uses Base 10 blocks to learn the addition facts and then progresses to various addition problems pertinent to the readiness stages. The objective is to move away from the concrete and toward the abstract algorithm as rapidly as is realistic for each student. The beauty of the blocks is that they can be used to reinforce any addition problem if a student wavers and needs additional support in the concept development. Doing a problem like 896 + 784 with the Base 10 blocks is possible, although some might prefer to not have so many pieces to deal with. The stage that follows the actual blocks would be pictures of them, and here again the sum could be demonstrated as in Fig. 2.10. Rather than using pictures, you could use "H" for hundred, "T" for ten, and "U" for units or ones as shown in Fig. 2.12. That would be followed by expanded notation addition (800 + 90 + 6) + (700 + 80 + 4). Once expanded notation addition is mastered, it can be collapsed into what we call our

standard algorithm by showing the regroupings in the next column.

That last paragraph contains the total developmental sequence from concrete to abstract. The amount of time it takes students to progress through the stages varies with each individual. One thing is certain: Rushing to a stage before a student is ready will hamper that individual's development. Adjusting the way things are done at the concrete level and then passing that idea through the various stages between that and the abstract level can provide the basis for alternate algorithms.

The algorithm normally used for addition is the most popular because it is the one most people have been taught to use. It is the one that is used in most textbooks, but it is by no means the only one that exists. There will be times when you will have a student who is not able to grasp that method. You will have students who have already mastered the standard addition algorithm. Asking them to do more than maintenance practice is not as appealing as perhaps asking them to investigate alternate methods for adding whole numbers. You might consider paring a student that has not mastered the algorithm with one who has.

The partial sum approach to addition is dependent on prior exposure to doing problems like 500 + 700 and the students realizing that this problem is much like 5 + 7, only the 5 and 7 are not in the ones column. They would also need to be aware of the basics of zero being the identity element for addition on the set of whole numbers. With that background, a problem like 896 + 784 would be done:

```
  896
 +784
   10
  170    (90 + 80, not 9 + 8 as is commonly said)
+1500    (800 + 700, not 8 + 7 as is commonly said)
 1680
```

You should notice that the 1 in both the tens and hundreds columns of the partial sums actually are the regroups or trades (carries would be the common word) normally found at the top of the respective columns from the preceding place value column sums which are. This is a powerful way to show expanded notation addition and eases the transition to our standard addition algorithm. After all, that is what we want students to be able to use *and understand* isn't it?

Reading involves motions going from left to right. The standard addition algorithm has students starting at the right and moving to the left. If you look at Fig. 2.12, you should be able to see how the trades can be made in any sequence. That is, the first one could involve trading ten tens for one 100 followed by swapping 10 ones for one ten. The end result would still be the same. That is the basis for the scratch method for adding whole numbers. The procedure is shown with 896 + 784:

$$
\begin{array}{r}
896 \\
+784 \\
\hline
15\overset{6}{\cancel{7}}0 \\
68
\end{array}
$$

Notice that the 5 is scratched out and a 6 is placed below it. Starting from the left, the first sum is 800 + 700, which is 1500. The 15 is written as a part of the sum in the appropriate place values and the zeros are not shown. Then the addition in the tens column is completed, giving a sum of 17 (really 170). The zero presents no problem because it is the additive identity. The 7 is written in the tens place of the sum. However, the 1 that is regrouped (really 100) has to be accounted for. The 100 is shown by scratching out the 5 and inserting a 6. If they were shown, the problem would be:

$$
\begin{array}{r}
896 \\
+784 \\
\hline
1500 \quad (800 + 700) \\
170 \quad (90 + 80) \\
+10 \\
\hline
1680
\end{array}
$$

Here the regrouping 1s are at the bottom of the hundreds and tens columns, which could prompt the scratch method.

If you do a problem like 896 + 784 with Base 10 blocks, more than likely you will do the flats first (unless someone instructs you to start elsewhere). Students frequently do the same thing. The rationale is that the big ones are easier to deal with first. Eventually each block type is dealt with and the sum is determined. Sometimes if the biggest block is done first, an additional step might need to be inserted into the process because of a new regrouping. This is very much like what happens with the scratch method.

The partial sum method should show you that addition of whole numbers can be started in any column and taken in any order as long as the place value of each column is used. The reason we use our standard algorithm is because it is essentially the only one that has been taught. There is another method, developed by Barton Hutchings, that can be intriguing and useful for students. Suppose the task is to find the sum of 9, 8, 9, 7, 9 in column addition. Before showing Dr. Hutchings' Low Stress Addition, consider what is going on in your head as you find this sum. The first part, 9 + 8, is easy because it is a fact, yielding a sum of 17. The next step is to find the sum of 17 and 9, which is not a fact. Students will have worked this problem, but in the formative stages of their development it probably was shown as:

$$
\begin{array}{r}
1 \quad \text{(regroup 10 ones as 1 ten)} \\
17 \\
+9 \\
\hline
26
\end{array}
$$

The difficulty is that many students are unable to do a problem such as this in a mental format. As 17 is added to 9, what really happens in your head is the 17 is expressed as 10 + 7. The 10 is remembered and the sum of 7 and 9, which is a fact, is determined to be 16. That 16 is actually 10 + 6, so now the aggregate is 10 + (10 + 6) = (10 + 10) + 6 = 20 + 6 = 26. Granted, you do the problem much more reflexively than that, but if you think about it, that is what is going on in your head.

The Low Stress algorithm eliminates the need to remember all those multiples of 10 and keeps the problem as a collection of addition facts. The following demonstration shows the addition of 9 + 8 + 9 + 7 + 9:

```
    9
    8
1   7   (9 + 8 = 17—first two addends)
    9
1   6   (7 (from the 17) + 9 = 16)
    7
1   3   (6 (from the 16) + 7 = 13)
+   9
 1      (10 from 3 (from the 13) + 9)
    2   (2 from 3 + 9)
+4 0    (sum the 10s at the left)
 4 2    (partial sum not normally used here).
```

This method can be used with more than single-digit addends. You just need a little more space between columns and any regroup from a value is placed at the top of the respective next column. Students sometimes are confused by a sum like 3 + 4 + 9 when using Low Stress addition, but it reacts like the others.

```
    3
    4
      7   (3 + 4 = 7)
+   9
 1        (10 from 7 + 9)
      6   (6 from 7 + 9)
+ 1 0
    1 6   (partial sum not normally used here)
```

These are not the only alternate methods for adding whole numbers. The basis for you to provide them with different ways of finding sums is here, however. The rest is up to you.

Exercises

68. Do 967 + 579 + 418 using the partial sum method.

69. Do 967 + 579 + 408 using the scratch method.

70. Do 687 + 579 + 498 using the Low Stress method.

71. Explain the scratch method to someone who does not know how to add that way.

72. Explain the Low Stress method to someone who does not know how to add that way.

Error Patterns

Whenever computations are done, errors occur. At times, the incorrect responses are a result of carelessness or not thinking. At other times, the errors occur because of a lack of understanding of the algorithm being used. Some errors are rather typical, whereas others are unique to individuals. As you look at a student's paper, your responsibility is to determine the source of incorrect thinking. In a sense, you are playing doctor. You see the symptoms. You call on your knowledge and experience. You diagnose the problem. You prescribe a solution. Sometimes you cure the problem. Sometimes you have to work with the individual again. As you work to correct error patterns, the continuum of the curriculum has to impact your decisions. You know where you want the student to be in the curriculum. You have to look at the continuum and plug the erring individual in at the right spot. If you go back too far, the student becomes bored because that is known information. Do not go back far enough and the student is frustrated because of a lack of background. When doctors prescribe, they face the same dilemma. The medical profession is different because the prescription can have life-and-death consequences. Your decisions will not have physical ramifications, but they could have an impact on the mathematical life (or death) of your student. This is a serious business.

A typical error in adding whole numbers involves ignoring any regrouping. A student would say that $684 + 979 + 763 = 2216$. Assume that no matter how many problems the student does, this process is repeated each time. Notice that it appears as if the student knows the addition facts and is able to do column addition. Sometimes a comment or a note on the paper is all it takes to correct the situation. Sometimes you have to follow the developmental continuum all the way back to the concrete stage. Generally, if you have to go back to the beginning stages, once the student realizes the error, the progress back to the place you are with the other students could be quite rapid.

Rather than provide additional examples of typical error patterns, the rest of this section consists of error pattern exercises. In each exercise, multiple examples of the error are provided. Your task is to describe the error pattern and discuss how you would correct a student who is making that error. The desire is for the student to learn to use the addition algorithm properly. Merely saying the algorithm to the student is not adequate. There is a flaw in the thought process being used. You need to determine the flaw and get it corrected.

Exercises

73.

4689	538	9681
5794	721	4032
+ 157	+ 746	+ 6195
9420	1995	19708

74.

4689	538	9681
5794	721	4032
+ 157	+ 746	+ 6195
14420	2095	21708

75.

4689	538	9681
5794	721	4032
+ 157	+ 746	+ 6195
14840	2105	21908

Subtraction of Whole Numbers

There are many things in life that are done and then undone, such as putting on shoes and then taking them off. Subtraction is the undoing of addition. That is one of the reasons the two topics are introduced as close together as they are in the curriculum. Some people argue they should be taught together because they are so closely related.

Readiness

As a child approaches addition of whole numbers, readiness includes numberness (sense of how many are in a set), conservation of number, place value, and background with the manipulatives. For children to begin subtraction of whole numbers, the basics of addition should be in hand. That does not mean the child should have all addition problem types under control. However, the child should know the addition facts and have at least some exposure to a few of the initial steps in the addition sequence presented in the section on adding whole numbers.

Many children are not developmentally ready to deal with subtraction when they first see it, particularly if the coverage is abstract. We know that developmentally children are ready to deal with basic multiplication at about the same time they are ready to deal with addition. Some authorities adopt the position that multiplication should be started with, or shortly after, addition, delaying subtraction until the students are developmentally ready. Yet we continue to teach subtraction after addition. Why? Tradition. That is the way we have always done it, so why change. That might not be a good reason by the way.

Subtraction requires a certain reversibility of thought or the ability to work a problem backward. In addition, each addend is considered until the sum is determined. In subtraction, the student is given the sum and one addend and is looking for the other addend or the missing addend. Conceptually, that is difficult for many students to do.

Concrete exposure is important in subtraction. If you start with sets, the take-away model for subtraction can seem natural. A set of objects is presented and then some of them are taken away. The initial set is the sum. The objects removed are the known part of the sum or the addend. The elements of the set that are left after the removal represent the missing addend. Did you notice the terminology connection with addition? Figure 2.20

models take-away subtraction. This missing addend is often called the difference. We use missing addend because the terminology is a link to addition.

The comparison model is another concrete model for subtraction using sets. In this procedure, two sets are given, one representing the sum and the other indicating the known addend. A one-to-one correspondence is established between the two sets, making as many pairs as possible. The cardinality of the elements of the set representing the sum that do not have partners gives the missing addend. An example of comparison subtraction is given in Fig. 2.21.

Looking at Fig. 2.21, you might ask why the segment between the pentagon and rectangle crosses the segment between the star and the triangle. You might also ask why the circle in the larger set was skipped. These are good questions and they show you are thinking. Generally, the segments would not cross and the circle would not be skipped. Rather, the third segment from the left would join the pentagon and star, and the fourth one would join the circle and rectangle as shown in Fig. 2.22. At the same time, sometimes it is advisable to present students will different examples to raise questions similar to those at the beginning of this paragraph. Then the students realize that the emphasis is on making that one-to-one correspondence between elements and

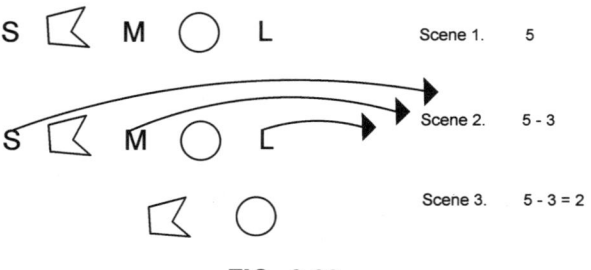

FIG. 2.20.

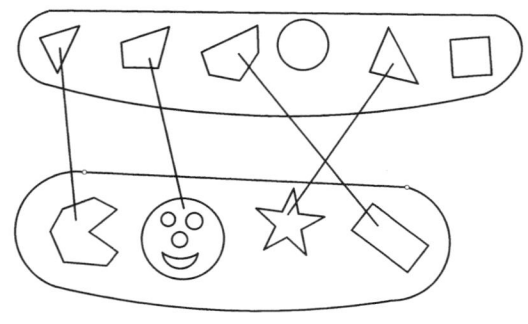

FIG. 2.21.

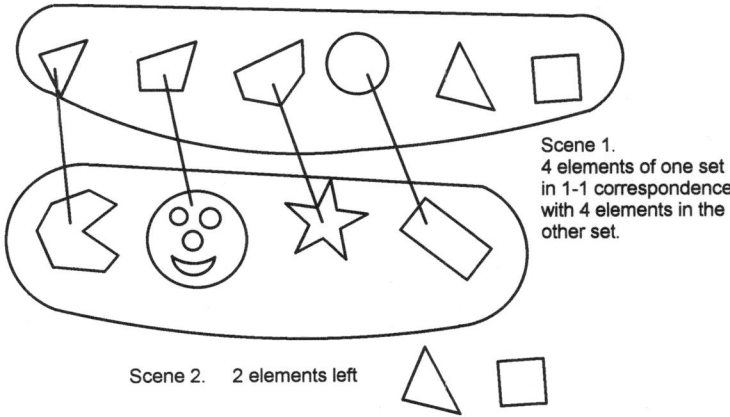

Scene 1.
4 elements of one set
in 1-1 correspondence
with 4 elements in the
other set.

Scene 2.   2 elements left

FIG. 2.22.

seeing what is left. One big advantage to doing the pairing in an orderly manner is that it is easier to see what is happening.

The missing addend is the third model for subtraction. It is the most abstract of the three and is more dependent on addition facts. It also provides a clear link to addition. In the missing addend model of subtraction, a problem like 9 – 3 = ? would be reworded. The 9 is the sum and the 3 is the known addend. The question becomes: "What number is added to 3 to get 9?" As you soon see, this model works wonderfully well with the Cuisenaire Rods and number line. Furthermore, this model works well with subtraction of signed numbers, which is discussed later.

Sets and the Subtraction of Whole Numbers

Regrouping in subtraction creates a monumental hurdle for some students. That is why the initial concrete exposure is so critical. Sets work well with the take-away and comparison subtraction models. Figure 2.20 shows elements of a set used to do take-away subtraction. The assumption is that the student is able to deal with cardinality of sets. Scene 1 shows the initial set. Scene 2 shows some elements being taken away. Scene 3 shows the elements

that are left and thus, 5 – 3 = 2. Taking away the last three elements might help some students. Eventually they should realize that it does not matter which elements are removed. The significant issue is the number of elements at the beginning (sum), the number taken away (addend), and the number left (missing addend).

Comparison subtraction is shown in Figs. 2.21 and 2.22. Notice that each element in the set representing the addend is paired with an element in the sum set. After the pairing, there are still two elements left in the set representing the sum that cannot be paired because there are no more elements in the addend set. Those two elements represent the missing addend. You should also have perceived that the elements were paired in a more typical fashion in Fig. 2.22 as contrasted with Fig. 2.21. If you did, give yourself a pat on the back. You are starting to think about how material is presented.

Exercises

76. Explain to an individual just beginning subtraction how to do take-away subtraction using a set of objects. Describe the reaction and advantages or disadvantages of the approach you used.

77. Explain to an individual just beginning subtraction how to do comparison

subtraction using a set of objects. Describe the reaction and advantages or disadvantages of the approach you used.

Cuisenaire Rods and the Subtraction of Whole Numbers

The Cuisenaire Rods could be used to do either comparison or take-away subtraction *if* the rods were used as individual pieces and carried none of the rod definitions with them. Another way would be to use only the White rods for either of those models. The strength of the Cuisenaire Rods in subtraction of whole numbers lies in dealing with the missing addend model. The assumption is that the students have the appropriate readiness skills with the manipulative.

Earlier we said the problem 9 – 3 = ? would be reworded. The 9 is the sum and the 3 is the known addend. The question becomes: "What number is added to 3 to get 9?" Figure 2.23 shows that situation in terms of the Rods. The bluE rod represents the 9 and what is known. The Lime rod shows how much of that bluE rod is known. The task is to find a rod that will, when joined with the Lime rod, make a train as long as the bluE rod. You can see in Fig. 2.23 that the Green rod is needed. Because the students are familiar with the Rods, they know this is equivalent to six White rods so it is 6 to them.

One interesting developmental issue involves selecting the Green rod. If you are familiar with the Rods, and because you already know how to subtract, you might *cheat* and think something like: "bluE is 9 and Lime is 3; 9 – 3 = 6; 6 is Green." Children learning to do subtraction will

not be able to do that. Some will select rods and see if they fit. Suppose a student selects Purple. Placement shows it to be too short. Assume that student picks blacK next and determines it is too long. At this point, you, in your big kid wisdom, would say the needed rod is longer than Purple and shorter than blacK. The temptation would be to tell the student that. *Don't do it! Don't say anything.* The student may next pick the browN rod and learn it is too long. That is fine. In the process, the student discovers a basic idea related to limits.

The Cuisenaire Rods can be used in this manner to do any whole number subtraction problem. As the numbers in the problem get larger, the rods become cumbersome because of the many pieces. However, the important thing is that they can still be used if they are needed. Actually, the Base 10 blocks are much more efficient to use for problems involving larger numbers.

Exercises

78. Do 13 – 6 with the Cuisenaire Rods. Try not to *cheat* by doing it mentally. Rather, *pretend* you do not know how to subtract and randomly place the rods as if you had no idea what to do until you find the right one. Describe your thoughts after you complete that process.

79. Do 57 – 26 with the Cuisenaire Rods. Describe your thoughts after you complete the problem.

The Number Line and the Subtraction of Whole Numbers

As with the Cuisenaire Rods, the number line works well with the missing addend model. Figure 2.24 shows Fig. 2.23 as the

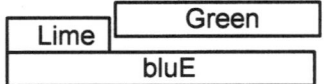

FIG. 2.23.

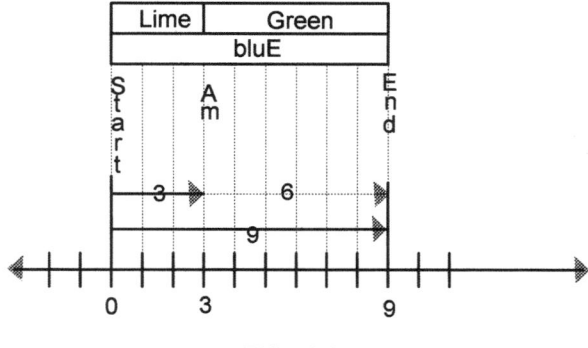

FIG. 2.24.

top part and then the number line as the bottom part. In the process, you can see how easily the Cuisenaire Rods transfer to the number line. You should also see that the number line solution only involves a counting process to determine the missing addend.

The number line could be used to do larger subtraction problems, but it rapidly becomes cumbersome. The optimal choice for doing most subtraction problems beyond facts is the Base 10 blocks.

Exercises

80. Do 13 – 6 on the number line. Describe your thoughts after you complete that process.

81. Do 57 – 26 on the number line. Describe your thoughts after you complete the problem.

82. Discuss the similarities and differences between the Cuisenaire Rods and the number line for doing subtraction facts. Which would you prefer to use with children and why?

Base 10 Blocks and the Subtraction of Whole Numbers

The Base 10 blocks could be used to show subtraction facts if the units were used in either the take-away or compari-

son models. The longs or ten rods could perhaps be used with some of the larger facts, but even then trades would need to be done.

The subtraction sequence is significant and needs careful attention. The process shown for the subtraction example in this section would be similar for any problem in the sequence. Figure 2.25 shows $\begin{array}{r} 426 \\ -189 \end{array}$ using the letter names for the Base 10 blocks with the comparison model. The different scenes are important to show the regrouping process. Eventually those regroupings become the values typically placed above digits in the sum.

Figure 2.26 shows $\begin{array}{r} 426 \\ -189 \end{array}$ using the letter names for the Base 10 blocks with the take-away model. This procedure works well with the blocks, but it may not transfer to the standard algorithm as well as the comparison model, where both the sum and addend are shown at once. You should be able to do subtraction of whole number problems using the Base 10 blocks with either model.

Prior to what is shown in Fig. 2.25, the students should physically manipulate the blocks to solve each type of subtraction problem leading up to and beyond $\begin{array}{r} 426 \\ -189 \end{array}$.

Then they should do the problems using pictures of the Base 10 blocks. The students should not be rushed from the blocks to the pictures of the blocks. You have to wait until they are ready to move out of the concrete stage, which may or may hot happen all at once.

Similarly, the students should not be rushed from the pictures of the blocks to the letter names for the blocks. Granted, we want them to use an algorithm for subtraction as rapidly as possible, but not at the expense of a lack of understanding of

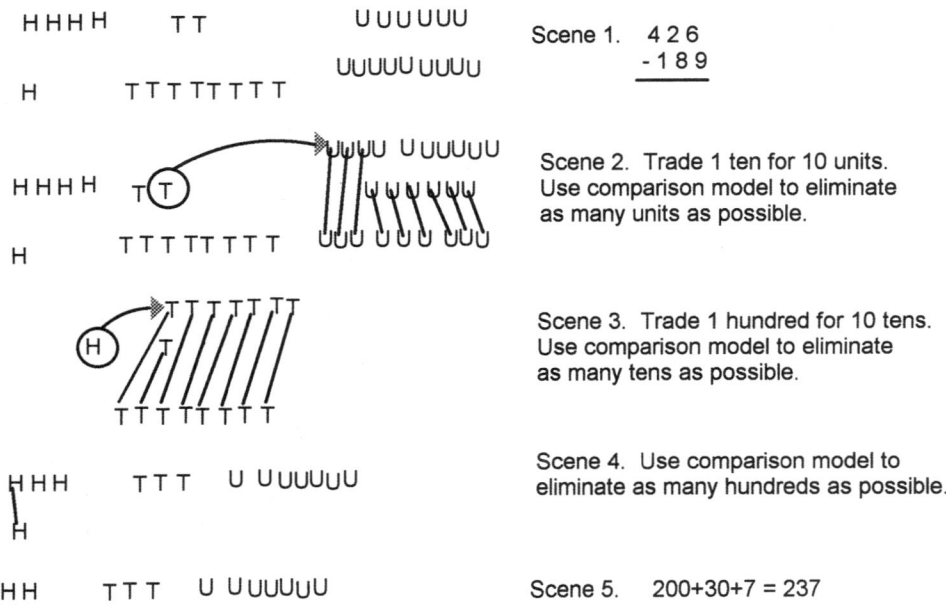

Scene 1.   4 2 6
            -1 8 9

Scene 2. Trade 1 ten for 10 units. Use comparison model to eliminate as many units as possible.

Scene 3. Trade 1 hundred for 10 tens. Use comparison model to eliminate as many tens as possible.

Scene 4. Use comparison model to eliminate as many hundreds as possible.

Scene 5.   200+30+7 = 237

FIG. 2.25.

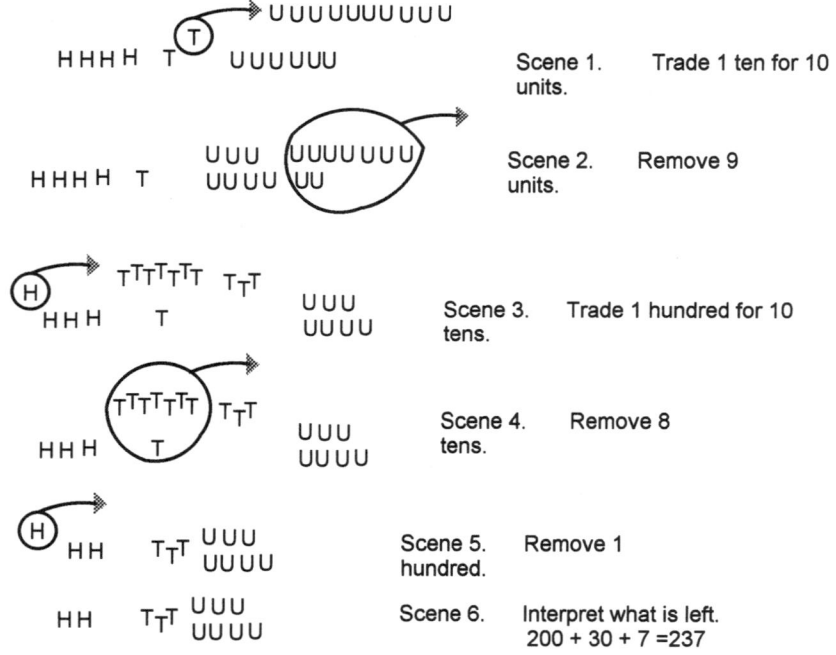

Scene 1.   Trade 1 ten for 10 units.

Scene 2.   Remove 9 units.

Scene 3.   Trade 1 hundred for 10 tens.

Scene 4.   Remove 8 tens.

Scene 5.   Remove 1 hundred.

Scene 6.   Interpret what is left.
                200 + 30 + 7 =237

FIG. 2.26.

the algorithm on their part. It takes time. Once they have worked with the letter names of the Base 10 blocks, the transition to expanded notation subtraction is relatively easy. After that, they can move to

the standard notation and an algorithm. It is advantageous to add an intermediate step involving denominate numbers (numerals with words after them—4 hundreds) between the letter names for the blocks and the expanded notation subtraction. Some authorities argue that the students should be permitted to discover their own algorithms and use them. The counterargument to this point is that discovery takes a long time; if students use different algorithms, they might confuse one algorithm with another. We all can make excuses to fit the position we adopt on such matters. You need to decide what position you will take and then develop a rationale you will use to defend it. Merely saying "because I said so," "because the book does it that way," or "because that is how I was taught" is not sufficient.

Exercises

83. Use the Base 10 blocks to do 357 − 198. Describe with pictures and scenes, words, or a combination of the two how a student would transition through the concrete, semi-concrete, and semi-abstract stages to the standard algorithm.

84. Use letter names for Base 10 blocks to do 3001 − 1469. Discuss the advantages of a concrete approach to this particular problem.

85. Outline how you would convince a colleague to use Base 10 blocks to teach subtraction of whole numbers.

Sequence Considerations for Teaching Subtraction of Whole Numbers

Certainly the subtraction facts must be mastered before expecting students to do any subtraction problem beyond the facts. Otherwise the students do not have the appropriate tools or readiness. After the facts are learned and assuming concrete exposure continues, it seems

reasonable to deal with multiples of ten minus multiples of ten, perhaps limiting the sum to less than 100 at first. This limit of 90 would be influenced by the students' abilities to deal with place value. The concept of multiples of ten is particularly useful when regrouping problems are encountered, especially in the developmental steps between the concrete stage and the standard subtraction algorithm.

As each new subtraction problem type is encountered, place value and regrouping skills are critical. If your curriculum or textbook does not treat something like 325 − 74 different from 325 − 78, then you need to supplement it with the appropriate intermediate steps. In the case of these two examples, the assumption would be that the students have already done problems involving 3 digits minus 2 digits with no regrouping and problems dealing with 3 digits minus 2 digits with regrouping out of the tens into the ones. Problems such as 325 − 74 should be done before 325 − 78 because the skill of regrouping out of the hundreds into the tens is included in 325 − 78 as is the skill of regrouping out of the tens into the ones. Student experience with both of these types individually is desirable prior to putting them together in a problem like 325 − 78. At some point in time, the students proclaim that regrouping in subtraction is the same no matter what place values are involved.

Alternate Methods for Subtracting Whole Numbers

The algorithm for subtracting whole numbers typically found in textbooks is not the only one. Some people prefer using the borrow-payback method of subtraction. The problem 426 − 189 would be done as follows:

```
      1       10 ones added to sum (notice no regrouping)
   4  2  6
 - 1  8  9
```

```
      1
   4  2  6
         9     Additional 10 subtracted. Ten has been
 - 1  8  9     added to the sum (10 ones) and to the missing
               addend (1 ten) so the problem is not changed.
```

```
      1
   4  2  6
         9
 - 1  8  9
         7     16 - 9 = 7
```

```
   1  1        10 tens added to sum
   4  2  6
         9
 - 1  8  9
         7
```

```
   1  1
   4  2  6
      2  9     Additional 100 subtracted. 100 has been added
 - ᵻ  8  9     to the sum (10 tens) and to the missing ad-
         7     dend (1 hundred) so the problem is not changed.
```

```
   1  1
   4  2  6
      2  9
 - ᵻ  8  9
      3  7     120 - 90 = 30 (Note zeros not written on
               problem)
```

```
   1  1
   4  2  6
      2  9
 - ᵻ  8  9
   2  3  7     400 - 200 = 200.
```

Borrow-payback subtraction may seem confusing, but it could be because it is new to you. Do a few subtraction problems that way and you may grow to like it. It is your obligation to teach your students how to subtract. Notice that the last sentence did not say it is your obligation to teach your students to subtract the way you do.

A common error involves students subtracting the little number from the big one in each place value column. Thus, the problem 5123 − 1684 would be 4561. Integer subtraction uses the idea of taking the little number from the big one in each column. The problem 5123 − 1684 would be:

```
   5  1  2  3
 - 1  6  8  4
         -1      (3 - 4 = -1)
      -6  0      (20 - 80 = -60)
   -5  0  0      (100 - 600 = -500)
 + 4  0  0  0    (5000 - 1000 = 4000)
   3  4  3  9    (4000 - 500 - 60 - 1 = 3439)
```

This is an unusual method and would not be appropriate for most students learning to subtract whole numbers particularly because of the use of integers. However, children who are accustomed to playing card games where the score can go in the hole have been known to do quite well with this method.

Another error is prompted by problems like 3001 − 487, which can generate the answer 624 when students are unclear about regrouping. In your sequence, subtraction involving zeros should get special consideration at the concrete level for each new place value to avoid this dilemma. There is an easy way to do this problem that your students will enjoy. Rewrite 3001 as 2999 + 2. The problem is then done (2999 − 487) + 2, and the real beauty is that all regrouping in the subtraction has been eliminated. This procedure can be extended to something like 5023 − 1496, which would become (4999 − 1469) + 24. Try it; you'll like it.

Students often get the perception that subtraction cannot be done moving from left to right. That is not the case. Consider 523 − 176. Starting from the left, 500 − 100 = 400. There is a need to have more than 2 tens in the center column because the task is to subtract 7 tens from 2 tens. The regrouping is accomplished by scratching the 4 out in the subtraction answer and making it a 3, writing the 3 below the 4. Now the answer is 300 + 50 (remember the zeros are typically not written, but they help clarify this discussion). Moving to the ones shows a need to regroup again to get 13 − 6. That is accomplished by scratching out the 5 in the tens column of the answer and writing a 4 below it. Now the 7 ones are placed in the answer and the problem is done, giving 347. The entire process would look like:

```
      12  13
   5   2   3
 − 1   7   6
 ───────────
   4   5   7
   3   4
```

Exercises

86. Do 67953 − 18076 using the borrow–payback method. Describe your thought process as you do it.

87. Do 67953 − 18076 using integer subtraction. Describe your thought process as you do it.

88. Do 5007 − 2345 by renaming 5007 as 4999 + 8. Do you think this is a good method to show students? Why or why not?

89. Do 5007 − 2345 using the scratch method for subtraction. Do you think this is a good method to show students? Why or why not?

Error Patterns

We provided a brief discussion of two error patterns and how to correct them in the last section. Rather than provide discussion of typical error patterns, this section consists of error pattern exercises. In each exercise, multiple examples of the error are provided. Your task is to describe the error and discuss how you would correct a student who is making that error. The desire is for the student to learn to use the subtraction algorithm

properly. Merely saying the algorithm to the student is not adequate. There is a flaw in the thought process being used, and your task is to determine what it is and get it corrected. This activity requires that you are aware of the continuum for learning subtraction of whole numbers.

Exercises

90.	4361	5231	63421	653
	−1879	−1879	−21879	−128
	3518	4648	42458	535
91.	4361	5231	63421	653
	−1879	−1879	−21879	−128
	532	1462	12652	435
92.	4361	5231	63421	653
	−1879	−1879	−21879	−128
	3592	4462	42652	525
93.	4361	5231	63421	653
	−1879	−1879	−21879	−128
	382	1252	9442	325

Multiplication of Whole Numbers

Multiplication, like addition and subtraction, should be based on concrete experiences. Assuming a traditional sequence and manipulative background, the development of multiplication facts can be relatively easy until the shift is made to multidigit factors. Then the pace will slow considerably until the basic concept of applying the facts with regrouping is mastered, after which students may move along quickly again. Although we often refer to the *standard algorithm* in this chapter and throughout the text, you should not "write too much into that statement." Our standard algorithm is probably how you do multiplication and how it is shown in most textbooks. There are several methods that could be used to do multiplication problems and any one of them could become the standard algorithm for your class.

Readiness

Rather than rushing into subtraction, consider pairing multiplication with addition. Repeated addition is one model for multiplication, which means that multiplication is a natural extension of addition. Any sort of manipulative can be used to combine groups of items to find a total. One natural use of repeated addition flows from the fact that, during group work, there may be five groups with four students in each group. Students may decide that there are 20 students in the classroom without counting. Figure 2.27 shows $3 + 3 + 3 + 3$ on the number line. Certainly the problem could be stated as "Three plus three plus three plus three equals twelve." It could also be presented as "Four groups of three equal twelve." Stating it both ways provides a natural transition that students may be able to construct on their own.

Multiplication can also be shown a different way starting with the number line. Actually this procedure leads to the array model for multiplication as shown in Fig. 2.28. Initially the idea of placing the side of a square on each unit of the number line is discussed. Rather than continuing on across the number line, as was done in Fig. 2.27, the next set of three is placed below the first. The process is duplicated for each repetition of the addend. The end result is a rectangle that is the addend wide and the number of addends high. In this case, it is three units wide and there are four groups or sets of

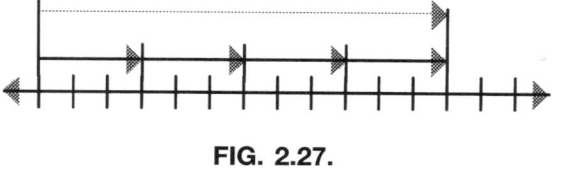

FIG. 2.27.

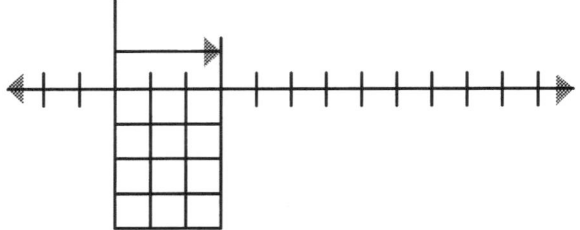

FIG. 2.28.

them. Initially, this could be introduced using small plastic unit squares, quickly moving to the pictorial representation. The verbal transition is that these four sets of three give 12, or 4 threes are 12, and finally $4 \times 3 = 12$. This provides a natural, concrete shift from repeated addition to formal multiplication. The teacher or a student could model the shift on an overhead graph while the students at their desks first mimic the actions and then suggest exercises to challenge one another.

If your students are accustomed to working with sets, the set model for multiplication may be appropriate. The union of several sets is a natural lead-in to addition. Another set operation that is often overlooked is cross-products or set multiplication. If your wardrobe consisted of three shirts and two pairs of pants, how many different outfits could you make? Assume that the shirts go only on top and the pants go only on bottom. Your only concern would be to answer the question regarding the different possible outfits. Figure 2.29 shows one way the answer could be determined. Because there are three shirts and two pairs of pants, you would have six possible different outfits. A shorthand way of writing that is $3 \times 2 = 6$.

With the repeated addition model, the array model, or the cross-product model for multiplication, a smooth transition is possible if the concrete background has been established. It bears repeating that all of the models are dependent on concrete beginnings and that multiplication

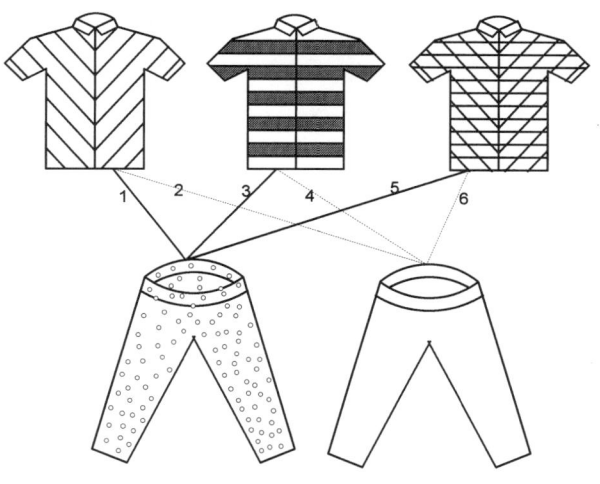

FIG. 2.29.

seems to be a natural outgrowth from the initial exposure.

Exercises

94. Reflect on the idea of introducing multiplication before subtraction. Summarize your thoughts in writing.

95. Of the three multiplication models mentioned in the text, which appeals the most to you and why?

96. Investigate an elementary mathematics textbook that introduces multiplication. Which model is used? Is the appropriate concrete background established before the students are moved to the pictorial and abstract level of dealing with multiplication?

Sequence for Teaching Multiplication of Whole Numbers

We use factor for each number being multiplied and product for the answer when multiplication is completed. A sequence for teaching multiplication facts follows.

Typically the multiplication sequence is not divided this finely. However, you need to be aware of how it is developed in case you encounter a student who needs to take smaller steps along the continuum. Once students master the concept of the multiplication algorithm, these small incremental changes will not be as necessary. We discuss the process in more detail later.

As with addition and subtraction of whole numbers, the multiplication facts must be mastered before moving on. Multiplication offers a few new hurdles to students. As a part of multiplying, they have to be able to add. More significant, they need to recognize multiplication problems in a different format. Suppose for the sake of this discussion that we consider only problems written vertically. The students will have seen multiplication facts written $\begin{array}{r} 6 \\ \times 7 \\ \hline 42 \end{array}$. However, when they start dealing with the multiplication algorithm, they will encounter situations where one factor is not directly over the other. For

Facts	
Products <10 (Review place value of 2 digits before going on)	
10 ≤ product ≤ 81	
Single digit × multiple of 10 (product <100)	Example: 20 × 3
2 digit × 1 digit with no regrouping	Example: 34 × 2
2 digit × 2 digit with no regrouping	Example: 34 × 21
2 digit × 1 digit with regrouping out of the ones	Example: 17 × 8
2 digit × 2 digit with regrouping out of ones only	Example: 17 × 16
(Need place value of 3 digits before going on)	
2 digit × 2 digit with regrouping out of tens only	Example: 42 × 34
2 digit × 2 digit with regrouping out of both places	Example: 87 × 45

example, in $\begin{array}{r}57\\ \times\ 8\end{array}$ the 8 × 7 appears natural, but the 8 × 50 is different because of the alignment. This slight misalignment is not a big thing for adults, but for a student who is struggling with the basics of multiplication it can be catastrophic. Rarely will you see $\begin{array}{r}8\\ \times 57\end{array}$, but you should consider discussing the situation with your students. It is all a part of building an understanding of multiplication.

As you know, multiplication should start concretely and progress through the various stages until the ability to find all products abstractly is developed. After learning basic multiplication facts, time should be spent on multiplication of multiples of 10 by single-digit numbers. This not only assists in the conceptual development of multiplication, but also reinforces the idea of place value as shown with 2 × 6 = 12, 20 × 6 = 120, and 200 × 6 = 1200. After a strong framework has been built with basic facts and multiples of 10 by single-digit numbers, problems like 23 × 4 can be addressed. Traditionally, the students were told to do 4 × 23 by putting the 2 of the 12 below the 4 and the 1 of the 12 above the 2 of 23. Then they were told to multiply the 4 by 2 (really 20) and, after getting that product, add the 1, which was carried, placing the sum to the left of the 2 from the 12. This should make sense to you because that is probably how you do the problem. However, it sure could seem confusing to a beginner.

The partial product method for multiplication can alleviate part of the dilemma. Assuming the appropriate background, the problem 23 × 4 can be treated as (20 + 3) × 4, which becomes (20 × 4) + (3 × 4). You have already laid the groundwork for this problem because 20 × 4 and 3 × 4 have already been done. Both of these are old problems, and you are actually employing a good teaching technique—taking a new problem and breaking it into parts that the students have already mastered. You also have an application of the distributive property of multiplication over addition on the set of whole numbers. As they do a few, they generalize and contrive a form of the algorithm. Then you can help them clarify and formalize the developments. In this way, they are much better off than students who are simply given an algorithm before they have a firm understanding of the concept. This partial product problem shown in a vertical format would be:

```
  23
×  4
  12   (from 4 × 3)
  80   (from 4 × 20—implies an understanding of
  92      place value)
```

From here, it is relatively easy to convert to the standard algorithm.

A more complex problem that can be done via partial product would be

```
   568
×   97
    56   (7 × 8)
   420   (7 × 60)
  3500   (7 × 500—first three lines become
            standard algorithm first line)
   720   (90 × 8—the old fashioned algorithm's first
            line!)
  5400   (90 × 60)
 45000   (90 × 500—last three lines become
            standard algorithm second line)
 55096
```

The partial product amplifies students' understanding of place value. It is also a simple matter to convert to the standard algorithm. At some point along the continuum, the partial product process can be abandoned in favor of the standard algorithm, but only when the students understand the notation and connect it with what is actually happening.

One of the beauties of the partial product approach to multiplication is the ability to establish background for future work in multiplication. The process can be applied to multiplication of decimals and fractions and could be extended to algebra. Fast forward your students to an algebra class and assume they possess the appropriate background skills to do $(2n + 3) \times 4$. The problem should be written in the vertical format first and related to whole number multiplication using the partial product format:

$$
\begin{array}{r}
2n + 3 \\
\times 4 \\
\hline
12 \quad (4 \times 3) \\
8n \quad (4 \times 2n) \\
\hline
8n + 12
\end{array}
$$

We have not given a complete sequence for multiplication. By now you should be aware of the need to pay attention to even the smallest changes in problem types. Use that information, along with the beginning of the sequence that has been provided, to build a reasonable multiplication continuum for your students. Do not forget to start with the concrete and move through the stages to the abstract algorithm.

Number Line and Multiplication of Whole Numbers

Figure 2.27 shows how multiplication is done on the number line. The commutative property of multiplication on whole numbers could be shown or amplified with the number line as shown in Fig. 2.30. Placement of the sets of arrows either both above, both below, or one

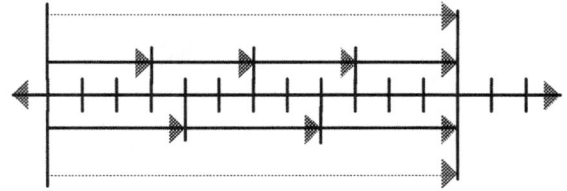

FIG. 2.30.

above and one below is not overly significant. What is important is that both sets of arrows are shown to bring out the idea that $4 \times 3 = 3 \times 4$. Figure 2.28 could be used to show the commutative property of multiplication on whole numbers as well. The argument would be that the number line was used to establish each original array as shown in Fig. 2.31. The examples you use need to be carefully selected. For example, children will understand 4 hops of 0, but they will struggle with 0 hops of 4. Certainly the facts involving zero as a factor must be considered, but not at first and only when you feel the children are ready to encounter the difficulties associated with zero as a factor.

Before long, the number line and its derivatives are deemed too cumbersome for the sake of convenience. As the factors increase in magnitude, the number line becomes so long that it is difficult to grasp its size. As you consider the different learning modalities of your students, remember that the number line is an alter-

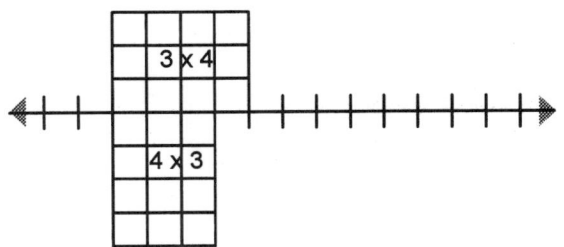

FIG. 2.31.

native. It may be awkward with big factors and products, but it does work.

Exercises

97. Would you use the number line to show that $4 \times 1 = 4$? Why or why not?

98. Use the number line to show $(2 \times 3) \times 4 = 2 \times (3 \times 4)$.

99. Use the array model to show $(2 \times 3) \times 4 = 2 \times (3 \times 4)$.

Cuisenaire Rods and Multiplication of Whole Numbers

The array method for multiplication works well with the Cuisenaire Rods. Form a *cross* with the two factor rods as shown in Fig. 2.32, where the Purple (4 rod) is on top of the Lime (3 rod). The task becomes one of completing the rectangle (you always get a rectangle when multiplying). In this case, your rectangle is comprised of Lime rods laid side by side until the total width is Purple long. Figure 2.33 shows the Purple on top of the four Limes. One advantage of this configuration is that the weaker students could count the little squares (equivalent to the unit, White) to confirm that four groups or sets (should we say *groups*) of three, or four threes, is

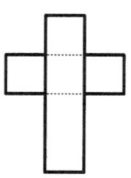

FIG. 2.32.

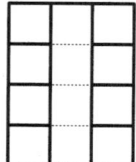

FIG. 2.33.

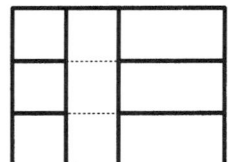

FIG. 2.34.

12. Did you notice that this looks a lot like the array model too? Figure 2.34 shows placing the Lime on top of the Purple, but it is not as easy to see the 12 smaller squares. The Cuisenaire Rods can be used to show the commutative property of multiplication on the set of whole numbers, as shown in Fig. 2.35. Notice that the left picture in Fig. 2.35 amplifies the connection with the array model.

There is another way to show multiplication with Cuisenaire Rods; it is beneficial when considering multiplication of fractions. Rather than making a cross, visualize a rectangle with a border around it. Next, place the two factor rods along the border as demonstrated in Fig. 2.36. Figure 2.37 shows how the product could be shown by building a rectangle that is Lime long and Purple wide. As discussed

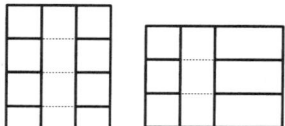

FIG. 2.35.

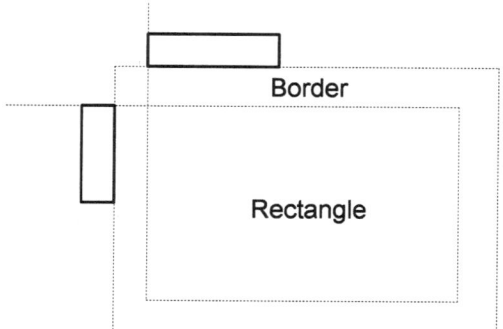

FIG. 2.36.

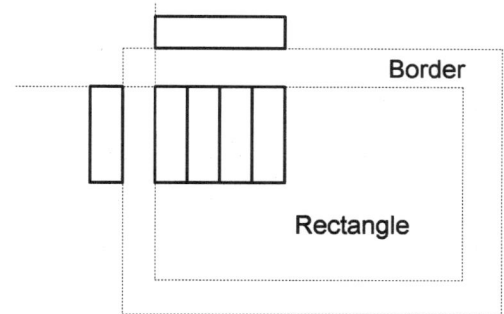

FIG. 2.37.

earlier, the product could be shown as Purple long and Lime wide and configured so the number of White units could be counted if necessary.

Either process is useful in helping students learn their multiplication facts. When larger factors are used, sets of rods may be combined or substitutions might be made for some of the rods. For example, a Lime–Purple train could be substituted for a blacK rod. This is good because it reinforces that 3 + 4 = 7. It also has a shortcoming because the student must remember that the Lime–Purple train represents the blacK and the picture of the rectangle for the product might be confusing. Another shortcoming of the rods, as with most concrete or semiconcrete models, is that as the factors get

larger it becomes cumbersome to show what is happening. However, it is important to remember that they can be used to *show* the product if necessary.

Exercises

100. Use the cross method to show 7 × 8 with the Cuisenaire Rods.

101. Use the bordered rectangle method to show 7 × 8 with the Cuisenaire Rods.

102. Show that 5 × 4 = 4 × 5 with the Cuisenaire Rods. Is one configuration more advantageous than the other? Why or why not?

Base 10 Blocks and Multiplication of Whole Numbers

The Base 10 blocks do not work well for multiplication facts. You could use the necessary number of unit rods, but that would be tedious. However, once the facts are established, Base 10 blocks rapidly become the manipulative of choice for many people because of the smaller number of pieces used and the connection to the partial product method for multiplying two factors. Figure 2.38 shows the product 14 × 12. This is a modification

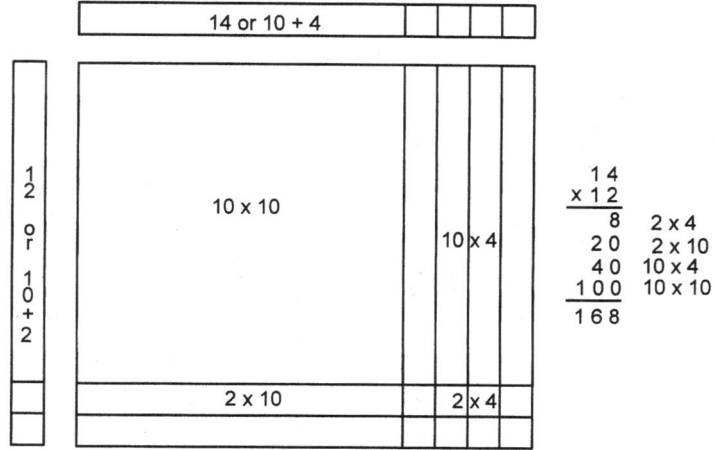

FIG. 2.38.

of the border rectangle method discussed earlier with the Cuisenaire Rods. It also amplifies earlier work with expanded notation. One beauty of this approach is its connection to algebra, which is discussed shortly.

Although the Base 10 blocks can be used with larger problems, they too become unwieldy rather quickly. That only amplifies the necessity for doing the smaller multiplication problems concretely to help the students understand the intricacies of place value and the steps involved in multiplication. As with all manipulatives, the objective is to abandon them as quickly as possible in favor of abstractions that lead to the algorithms. However, they cannot be discarded before the students have mastered the concepts—development takes time.

Figure 2.39 shows the algebra connection to the Base 10 blocks. The problem being done is $(x + 4)(x + 2)$ rather than $(10 + 4)(10 + 2)$, and all that happens is the 10 rod is renamed as x. Everything else remains the same. Although you probably will not discuss this algebra connection in your elementary class, when your students reach the point in their mathemati-

cal careers where the product of two binomials is discussed, they will have the feeling that the process seems familiar.

The semi-concrete approach to reaching a product using expanded notation is an excellent precursor for the F.O.I.L. (Firsts, Outers, Inners, Lasts) technique you probably learned in algebra. You started by multiplying the first terms of each binomial. In our example $(x + 4)(x + 2)$, the first term in each binomial is x. Their product is x^2. So x^2 would be product of the Firsts. When looking at the two binomials together, $(x + 4)(x + 2)$, the left x and the 2 are on the outsides. Their product is 2x. So 2x would be product of the Outers. The inner terms of $(x + 4)(x + 2)$ are 4 and the right x. 4x is their product. The last term for each binomial is 4 and 2, yielding a product of 8 for the Lasts. You need to be careful to distinguish between learning things like F.O.I.L. without understanding what is happening for your students. If you learn without understanding, you are using a rule mechanically, which is not a good thing. Take a look at the partial product part of Fig. 2.38 and you should be able to identify the four parts of F.O.I.L. You could do the same thing with Fig. 2.39.

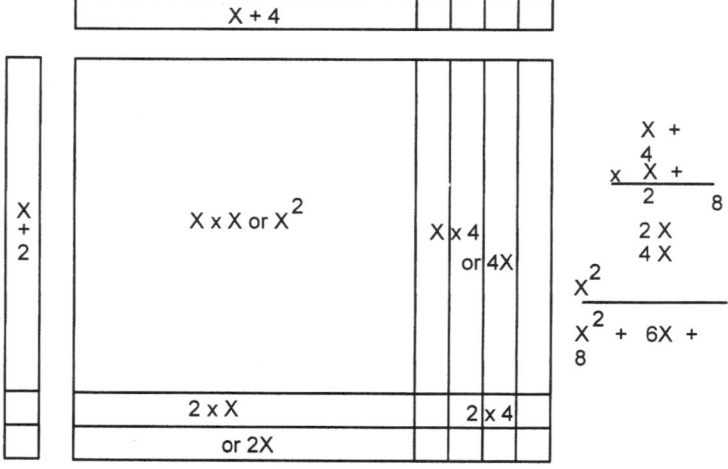

FIG. 2.39.

Alternate Methods for Multiplication of Whole Numbers

The concrete approach may become unwieldy. The partial product method has already been discussed and can be a viable option for those who are not ready for the standard algorithm. Even with larger factors, the partial product works well.

```
        3 4 6 9
      × 5 8 7
            6 3      (7 × 9)
          4 2 0      (7 × 60)
        2 8 0 0      (7 × 400)
      2 1 0 0 0      (7 × 3000)
          7 2 0      (80 × 9)
        4 8 0 0      (80 × 60)
      3 2 0 0 0      (80 × 400)
    2 4 0 0 0 0      (80 × 3000)
        4 5 0 0      (500 × 9)
      3 0 0 0 0      (500 × 60)
    2 0 0 0 0 0      (500 × 400)
    1 5 0 0 0 0 0    (500 × 3000)
    2 0 3 6 3 0 3
```

That problem looks long compared with the standard algorithm, but it is a process that works and condenses to it when the student is ready. (Teacher, can't I just use a calculator?)

Look at 14 × 12 from the beginning. If your students do not know their multiplication facts, asking them to do this problem is not reasonable. Given that they know the facts, there is a developmental sequence that would help them all arrive at the ability to use and understand the algorithm. Figure 2.36 shows what would be done concretely. The next stage in the sequence would involve students drawing something like Fig. 2.38. Then the parts of the figure would be named by their partial product names, followed by an organized written summary similar to

the one to the right of the block representations in Fig. 2.38. Finally, that expanded abstraction would be condensed to the algorithm normally used.

There are other ways of doing multiplication problems, and they can be used in two contexts. Certainly, any algorithm is as good as any other, and it is conceivable that a student would opt to use an algorithm different from the one you or other students use. That is an acceptable thing. However, it does require some responsibility on the part of you and the student. Both of you need to understand how the selected procedure works so you are able to assist the student when difficulties occur. That is why most teachers insist that students all use the same algorithm. At first you might say that idea makes good sense. However, why should the student be forced to do things the way you (or the book) do them as long as the student understands what is being done? Part of your responsibility of being the teacher involves understanding different algorithms so you are able to work with students in their mental environment. Again, how do you justify forcing a student to do things your way? Answer that question very carefully and give it some serious reflection before you adopt a position. Some students may not grasp the approach you use and need an alternative. Others may comprehend the approach quickly, and these optional methods could be used to provide them with mental stimulation. One of those methods is lattice multiplication. Figure 2.40 shows the product 3469 × 587. The tens digit of the product of individual digits is placed above and to the left of the diagonal in the appropriate cell, and the ones digit is below and to the right of that same diagonal. Some segments are darker to show which addends in any given diagonal column are used. This method can be introduced

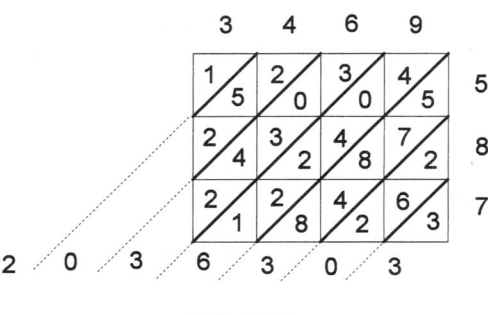

3   4   6   9

1/5 2/0 3/0 4/5   5

2/4 3/2 4/8 7/2   8

2/1 2/8 4/2 6/3   7

2   0   3   6   3   0   3

FIG. 2.40.

by saying: "If you know your multiplication facts and how to add, you can do any whole number multiplication problem in the world." For some students, such a challenge is too tempting and they learn in spite of themselves.

Another appealing challenge could be: "If you know how to double numbers, divide by two, and add, you can do any whole number multiplication problem in the world." The method is called Russian peasant multiplication or the simple halving doubling method. It involves selecting one factor and successively dividing it by two until you arrive at one. The other factor is doubled each time there is a halving. In the process, if a halving yields a half, that half is ignored. You need to insist, for example, that the students respond that $11\frac{1}{2}$ is half of 23. Note that 11.5 could be used, but the typical response is $11\frac{1}{2}$. Once the students say that $11\frac{1}{2}$ is half of 23, tell them to ignore the half as they proceed. It is important that students not form the habit of saying 11 is half of 23. Once one is the value in the halving column, each row of the halving column that has an even value in it is eliminated along with its corresponding partner in the doubling column. Finally, the remaining elements of the doubling column, including the initial factor if it remains, are added, giving the desired product. For example,

23	254	Halving the left column, what is half of 23?
11	508	Half of 23 is 11.5 but forget the 0.5.
5	1016	Half of 11 is 5.5 but forget the 0.5.
2	2032	Half of 5 is 2.5 but forget the 0.5.
1	4064	Half of 2 is one.

The row "2———2032" is eliminated because in the halving column, 2 is even. 254 + 508 + 1016 + 4064 = 5842. Notice that in this example, because 23 is odd, the initial factor of 254 is included in the sum. If, for example, the problem had been 24 × 254, the factor of 254 would have been excluded from the sum (assuming you opt to halve 24). In this example, the temptation is to make 254 the head of the halving column because it is even, but it too will lead to an odd value eventually ($\frac{254}{2} = 127$). Because the idea is to get the halving column to one, starting with the smaller factor accomplishes that objective faster.

There are other ways to do multiplication, but the ones given here provide you with alternatives. You should not present these alternative methods to members of the class unless you need to have something to challenge some students or another way to multiply for students who labor with the standard algorithm. Eventually struggling students conclude that, although these ways work, there has to be a simpler way. When they ask, you can show them the world's slickest, quickest way to multiply (short of technology), which is the standard algorithm. Yes, you tried to show them earlier and they resisted. Now they are asking for it. Big difference!

Exercises

103. Compare the Russian peasant method with lattice multiplication approach. Which do you prefer and why?

104. Compare lattice multiplication with the partial product method. Which do you prefer and why?

105. The partial product method for multiplication is a modification of "Napier's Bones." Describe Napier's Bones and how they would be used to do 45 × 73.

106. Using Russian peasant multiplication to do 106 × 37, which factor would you select as the one to be halved and why?

107. Create a three-digit times two-digit problem and do it using partial product, lattice, and Russian peasant multiplication.

Error Patterns

Rather than provide additional examples of typical error patterns, the rest of this section consists of error pattern exercises. In each exercise, several examples of the error are provided. Your task is to describe the error pattern and discuss how you would correct a student who is making that error. The desire is for the student to learn to use the multiplication algorithm properly. Merely saying the algorithm to the student is not adequate. There is a flaw in the thought process being used, and you need to determine the error and get it corrected.

Exercises

108.

45	69	387
× 28	× 74	× 59
320	246	2723
90	423	1505
1220	4476	17773

109.

45	69	387
× 28	× 74	× 59
360	246	3483
90	483	1935
450	759	5418

110.

45	69	387
× 28	× 74	× 59
360	276	3483
130	513	2695
1660	5406	30433

111.

45	69	387
× 28	× 74	× 59
640	366	13563
100	843	4055
1640	8796	54113

112.

45	69	387
× 28	× 74	× 59
360	276	3483
90	483	1935
1260	4006	12733

Division of Whole Numbers

Often children have a basic idea of how to add and subtract even before they get to school. This stems from various play activities they participate in as they are growing up, but those foundations are independent of the formalized school presentations they get.

Division is a different story, however. Division was probably difficult for you to do. More than likely, it is still not overly easy for you to do long-hand division. Typically people avoid doing long division if at all possible. Is it any wonder students have trouble doing and liking division?

Readiness

Why is division so difficult and why do we avoid it? Division is complex and that certainly is a part of the reason. All of a sudden the word "division" appears in the child's mathematical curriculum development and the hard work begins. Success is dependent on good skills in rounding, estimation, place value, mental arithmetic, multiplication, subtraction, and unusual formats for doing the whole number algorithms.

Before proceeding with this chapter, you need to do $78\overline{)541554}$ so we can talk about it. No calculators on this one—do it by hand. As you work, make a list of all the potential sources of errors a student could make.

You should have done the division problem before reading this. Without knowledge of the division facts, a student is doomed before beginning. Typically we round the 78 to 80 to make things a little easier. Of course that makes the estimation easier, but rounding is difficult for some children. Do we always round up in division?

Once the factor is rounded and part of the missing factor (maybe you call it the quotient) is estimated, placement of the number comes into play. Where does it go? This part of the missing factor (6 in this case) is then to be multiplied by the factor and the product placed below the 541554. Before the placement is encountered, finding the product of 6 and 78 could be a challenge. First, the format is different. Although the 6 is improperly

placed in $78\overline{)541554}^{\,6}$, it does show the

unusual format. Actually that is 6000, (which would put the 6 in the proper location), but we typically do not write the zeros. The students generally are told where to put the 6 without benefit of the explanation that it is really 6000. Anyhow, the student now has to find 6 × 78. Its setup is strange, however. Before multiplication was almost always set up like $\begin{array}{r}78\\\times6\end{array}$. Rarely

would the student even see $\begin{array}{r}6\\\times78\end{array}$, let alone

something like $\begin{array}{r}\times78\quad ^{6}\\\hline 468\end{array}$. Weird! This new

format is confusing for many children.

Assuming the student gets to the point of

$$78\overline{)541554}^{\,\,6000}$$
$$-\quad 468$$

(with the zeros there to show

proper placement), a new set of difficulties arise. Remember all of the problems associated with subtraction involving regrouping? Here they are again!

Suppose the student gets beyond the subtraction troubles and now sees

$$78\overline{)\,541554}^{\,\,6000}$$

. Essentially that is $78\overline{)73554}$,

$$-468000$$
$$\overline{73554}$$

but it sure looks different. Another set of potential problems, and so it goes. Like we said, division is not easy. No wonder students struggle with it.

The other part is that little is done to develop any informal feel for division. The idea discussed earlier about multiplication of whole numbers always giving a rectangle will help with division. Given that idea, the number being divided (product) is the rectangle. The number you divide by (factor) is a known dimension of the rectangle. Your task is to determine the other dimension (missing factor) of the rectangle. This little bit of background certainly lowers the degree of difficulty for students as they initially encounter division.

You may have thought that *product*, *factor*, and *missing factor* are strange words to be using with division. More than likely, you were thinking *divisor* (number you are dividing by), *dividend* (number being divided), and *quotient* (answer) were the words that should be used with division. We use *product*, *factor*, and *missing factor*. We have our reasons. It helps connect multiplication with division. Avoiding *divisor*, *dividend*, and *quotient* eliminates three vocabulary words for the students to learn. You could counter that it is only three words, but those three, plus three more if you use *minuend, subtrahend,* and *difference* in subtraction (instead of *sum, addend,* and *missing addend*), give six words. The list can grow. Doesn't our responsibility involve making the learning environment as reasonable as possible? If so, doesn't a reduction in the number of new words that have to be learned help? Another retort could be that the textbook uses *divisor, dividend,* and *quotient.* You could use *factor, product,* and *missing factor* and, in the process, expand your students' horizons, making them mathematically bilingual for this stage of their development. Of course, that does increase the number of words they have to learn.

Background information for division is important. However, it is not wise to start division too early. As with subtraction, division involves reversibility of thought at this stage. Unlike subtraction, where there is generally some intuition about what will happen in the operation, students have little or no feel for division initially other than perhaps an idea of distributing things by saying "One for you, one for me. . . ." The complexities in division are so great that it is wise to delay the exposure until students are in the more advanced developmental stages that generally appear in the intermediate grades, and definitely not until they have a sound command of multiplication (and subtraction).

Exercises

113. List the advantages and disadvantages of using *divisor, dividend,* and *quotient* as opposed to *factor, product,* and *missing factor.* Which set of words do you prefer and why?

114. Do you think the idea of a division problem being a rectangle where one dimension is known and you are looking for the other one is a reasonable approach to introducing division? Why or why not?

115. Is it reasonable to think of having your students attempt division of whole numbers before they are well founded in the skills related to multiplication? Why or why not?

116. Did you notice there is no comma in $78\overline{)541554}$, whereas in place value we teach students the comma should be there? Is this a potential distraction for students? Why or why not?

117. Finish the discussion started in the text that deals with potential sources of errors when doing $78\overline{)541554}$. Explain in general terms why long division is difficult for students.

Sequence for Teaching Division of Whole Numbers

As with each whole number operation, division facts are essential before taking your students to any type of division problem. Division facts are much easier to learn if the students know their multiplication facts and understand the rectangle or array concept for developing them. Figure 2.41 shows $8\overline{)56}$, where the factor (browN) is known and the task is to build a rectan-

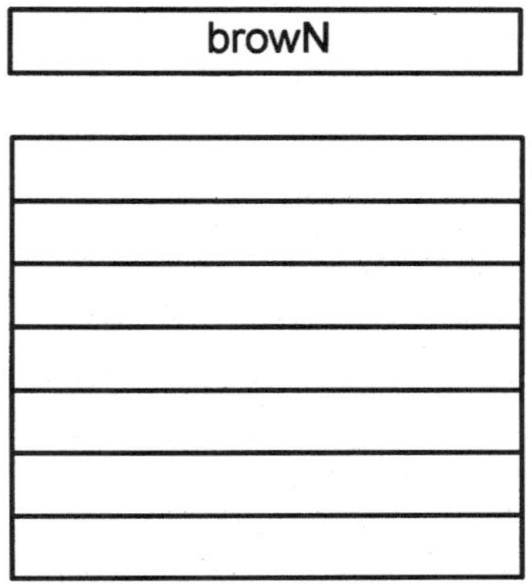

FIG. 2.41.

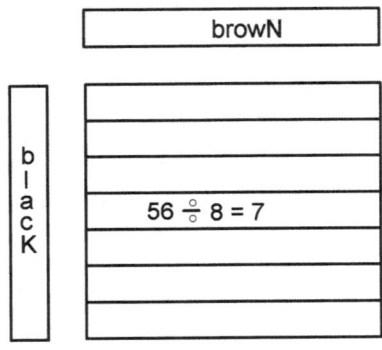

FIG. 2.42.

gle browN wide until 56 units are represented. The missing dimension is as long as the blacK rod, which is seven, when White is the unit (see Fig. 2.42).

Once the division facts have been mastered, deal with multiples of 10 divided by a digit (60 ÷ 2). The students should quickly recognize the connection to 6 ÷ 2 with a zero on the end. The discussion could focus on the idea of dividing 60 things equally between two people. Review multiplication problems like 30 × 2 and things should go relatively quickly. The students should conclude that the answer is 3 with a zero on the end. Similar problem types (600 ÷ 2, 6000 ÷ 2, etc.) should be somewhat easy once the first conclusion is achieved, assuming related concepts have been developed with multiplication.

Next, the students should see problems like 24 ÷ 2. The 24 could be renamed as 20 + 4, which decomposes the new problem into two problems that have been seen before. There is an abundance of 2s in this problem and it could be argued that, at this stage of development, those 2s should not present any difficulty for students. Still, a better example might be 68 ÷ 2 just in case. The discussion for solving 24 ÷ 2 could also be developed by dividing 20 things equally between two people and also dividing four things equally between the same two people. Each person then has 10 + 2 items, which is the expanded

notation for 12. At this point, the students should begin making connections.

Next, the problem could be written
$$2\overline{)20+4}^{\,10+2}$$, which eventually condenses to
$$2\overline{)24}^{\,12}$$. If desired, the typical division work could also be shown as $2\overline{)20+4}^{\,10+2}$ or $2\overline{)24}^{\,12}$.

$$\begin{array}{r} 10+2 \\ 2\overline{)20+4} \\ \underline{20+4} \\ 4 \\ \underline{4} \\ 0 \end{array} \qquad \begin{array}{r} 12 \\ 2\overline{)24} \\ \underline{20} \\ 4 \\ \underline{4} \\ 0 \end{array}$$

Similar developments could be created for any long division scenario.

The next problem type should be 36 ÷ 2. This problem is different because the tendency might be to rename the problem as 30 + 6, but that does not give familiar work. Rather the problem should be expressed as 20 + 16, which does give two familiar problems and closely resembles the development discussed in the last paragraph.

After these problem types, you need to develop ideas related to 60 ÷ 20 before moving to problems where the factor consists of two digits. That is because of the typical encouragement to round the factor to some multiple of 10, 100, and so on. The students should associate 60 ÷ 20 with 6 ÷ 2 and realize the zero is absent in the missing factor. It is easier for students to do this if they have a strong command of the related multiplication situations. This development, coupled with the lead-in to the standard algorithm presented with 24 ÷ 2, should provide adequate background to move to multidigit factors and products as long as it is done in small increments. Interspersed with all these developments is the idea of repeated subtraction division, which is discussed in the alternate approaches to division section of this chapter.

We have opted to deal only with division problems that involve whole numbers here. We discuss division problems that result in remainders when division involving decimals is discussed. It is critical to consider remainders in division, however, because not all division problems result in no remainder.

Exercises

118. Complete the problem $2\overline{)68}$, but do it in the format $2\overline{)60+8}$. Describe your impressions as you complete the problem.

119. Do $68\overline{)8000+300+60+4}$ by rounding 68 to 70. Describe your impressions as you complete the problem.

120. Is it necessary to differentiate between problem types like $68 \div 2$ and $36 \div 2$? Why or why not?

Manipulatives for Division of Whole Numbers

Manipulatives are difficult for division mainly because of the sheer magnitude of the number of pieces that are needed. Figure 2.42 shows how the division facts could be developed concretely with the Cuisenaire Rods. As either the factor goes above 9 or the product exceeds 81, the process becomes cumbersome. Some argue that even problems like $72 \div 9$ are difficult to do with the rods because of the need to substitute rods for the bluE one unless sets are combined. The contention is that whatever train is used for the bluE rod will distract some students.

Figure 2.43 shows how $168 \div 12$ could be done with the Base 10 blocks or Cuisenaire Rods. As you see, it works, but there are a lot of pieces. Neither this discussion nor the one with the Cuisenaire

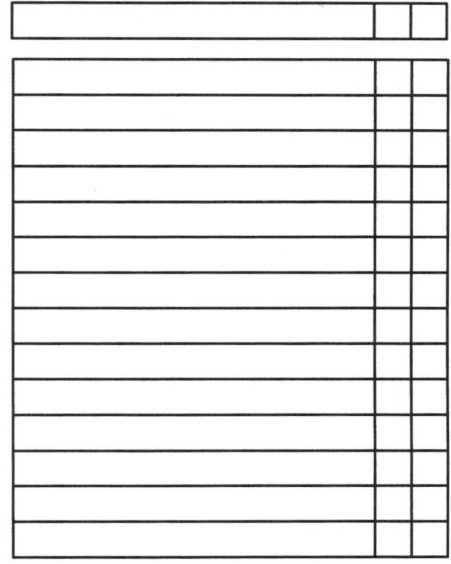

FIG. 2.43.

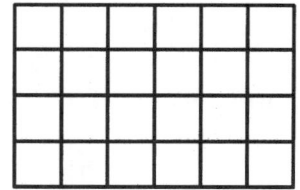

FIG. 2.44.

Rods will make much sense to students unless they have developed multiplication using these manipulatives and the idea of the product being a rectangle.

The array method could be used instead of the Cuisenaire Rods or Base 10 blocks. Figure 2.44 shows how an array could be used to show $24 \div 6$. You should notice the similarities between the array and both the Cuisenaire Rods and the Base 10 blocks.

Exercises

121. Show how $35 \div 7$ could be developed using the Cuisenaire Rods.

122. Show how $35 \div 7$ could be developed using an array.

123. Show how 169 ÷ 13 could be developed using an array.

124. Is there value in using manipulatives with division of whole numbers? Why or why not?

Alternate Methods for Dividing Whole Numbers

Background for division needs to be established concretely. One component of that development involves the physical partitioning of items with a one-for-you, one-for-me approach. As this is done, emphasis should be given to associating the problem and answers with the resultant numbers.

A crucial element in the development of the division algorithm is repeated subtraction division. If this is done first, students encounter fewer difficulties as they try to master the standard algorithm. When doing the standard division algorithm, estimations must be precise. In the repeated subtraction approach to division, it is acceptable for estimations to be low or precise. Considering how weak the estimation and rounding skills of most students are, this is a significant asset. Students need to be familiar with multiplying digits by multiples of 10 when doing repeated subtraction division, but this should have been developed earlier and therefore is not a hurdle.

The easiest way to visualize how repeated subtraction division works is to think of a large pile of stir sticks that represent the product. Consider 28567 ÷ 49 and you have a pile of 28,567 sticks. The question for all division problems is, How many factors are contained in the product? In this case, the question becomes, How many 49s are in 28,567? Certainly we could remove one group of 49 from the 28,567 sticks, leaving 28,518 sticks.

Another batch of 49 could be removed, leaving 28,469 sticks. This process could continue 581 more times and we would learn that a total of 583 sets of 49 are contained in 28,567 sticks. Even the most patient of individuals would tire of that process before too long.

If the idea of multiples of 10 is employed in repeated subtraction, short cuts begin to appear. Suppose after the second group of 49 is removed, leaving 28,469 sticks, it dawns on the person to remove 10 bunches of 49 or 490 sticks. This speeds things up and two more sets of 10 bunches of 49 sticks could be removed as well. Thus, at this stage, 32 bunches of 49 sticks have been removed, leaving 26,999. We still have a long way to go.

Hopefully someone will capitalize on the idea of multiplying 49 by 10 and extend it to multiplying by 100 or 1000. Alas, 1000 is too big and is eliminated. Things should start to accelerate now. Someone usually realizes that bunches could be removed 200 or 300 at a time as well. Now old skills come into play because quick mental multiplication of 300 by 49 with 14,700 sticks removed leaves 12,299. We cannot take out 300 more because 14,700 is greater than 12,296, but we could take out 200 bunches of 49, leaving 2499 sticks. We have already done 49 × 300, so 49 × 30 should come quickly; then we could take out 20 more bundles of 49, leaving 49 sticks. Someone might want to try 50 × 49, which is fine. Either way, there is one bunch of 49 sticks left. The only question remaining is how many bunches of 49 have been removed altogether? The answer is
1 + 1 + 10 + 10 + 10 + 300 + 200 + 50 + 1 or 583, which is the missing factor. The significant part of this discussion is that estimates on or below the actual value are acceptable. As estimation skills increase, the repeated subtraction division method collapses to the standard algorithm.

```
    49)28567
    -    49      1
       28518
    -    49      1
       28469
    -   490     10
       27979
    -   490     10
       27489
    -   490     10
       26999
    - 14700    300
       12299
    -  9800    200
        2499
    -  2450     50
          49
    -    49      1
           0    583
```

FIG. 2.45.

In Fig. 2.45, the number of bundles of 49 removed is recorded to the right of each removal. The recording could also be above the division symbol, which looks more like the standard algorithm. As the student's estimation skills increase, the repeated subtraction approach gets closer and closer to the standard algorithm.

One could justifiably ask why we used the example 28567 ÷ 49 as opposed to one with smaller values. It is a good question. We feel that this problem will help you see how repeated subtraction works. Using the process with smaller numbers is easily accomplished. Finally, you might say that a calculator should be used with a problem like this. We agree. Having said that, we are also aware that many curricula and tests require students to be able to do problems such as 28567 ÷ 49 by hand.

Exercises

125. Multiply a two-digit number by a one-digit number. Use the product and the one-digit factor to create a division problem, making the two-digit factor become the missing factor. Now do the division problem using the repeated subtraction approach. *You may not estimate accurately!* Give a low estimate for both the ones value and the tens value (see Fig. 2.45 for a model of how to estimate low) so you get a feel for how repeated subtraction division works.

126. Multiply a two-digit number by a three-digit number. Use the product and the two-digit factor to create a division problem, making the three-digit factor become the missing factor. Now do the division problem using the repeated subtraction approach. *You may not estimate accurately!* Give a low estimate in the ones, tens, and hundreds values so you get a feel for how repeated subtraction division works.

127. Write a summary of your impressions on the advantages and disadvantages of repeated subtraction division.

Error Patterns

Error patterns exist in division. They include rounding, estimation, place value, mental arithmetic, multiplication, subtraction, as well as unusual formats for doing the whole number algorithms. These errors are varied and require close examination of student work to identify them. It is important to define and correct division errors as quickly as possible.

Exercises

128. Describe or write a short story that uses division of whole numbers as an integral part of its development.

129. Describe a number trick that involves division.

FRACTION OPERATIONS

Equivalent Fractions and Multiplication of Fractions

Students encounter fractions early in their lives when they hear things like:

"The TV program lasts a half hour."
"Share half of the cookie with your friend."
"See the quarter moon."

These exposures can be advantageous as children begin to formalize their learning, but they can also lead to misconceptions.

Ask a youngster to tear a piece of paper in half and you will probably see something like Fig. 2.46. They hear the words.

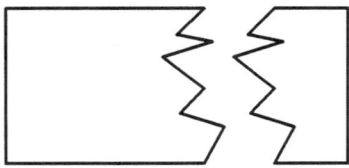

FIG. 2.46.

Yet because of unspecific daily language use, children may not have an accurate interpretation of what is being conveyed. For example, exactly what is "half of a cookie"? That phrase or something similar is frequently encountered in the early experiences of a child. But what is half a cookie? Literally, a *half* means one of two equal sized pieces. As adults, we know the intent and accept that "pretty close" is usually good enough.

When teaching children about fractions, is "pretty close" good enough? *NO.* It is important that a child be aware that a *half* means one of two equal sized pieces. Later, the approximations and inaccuracies accepted in our common language will suffice, but not at the beginning learn-

ing stages of mathematics. At the same time, it is unrealistic to expect a preschool child to be able to say that one half is one of two equal sized pieces. So what do we as educators do? We develop the concept carefully and accurately, but do not press the children to verbalize the desired precision until later in their development.

The idea of a half can be conveyed at an informal level by using a candy bar as a manipulative. The assignment would be to have the child share the candy with another. The child breaks the candy in half and the friend picks first. It is amazing how well the concept of half is now understood.

Paper Folding to Show Fractions

Capitalize on that idea by having the students fold a piece of paper in half. Then ask them how they know it is a half. Ultimately they will say something similar to the edges match for the two sides. Depending on the age, that may or may not be as far as you go with the discussion. If you have older or more capable students, you might want to fold a piece as shown in Fig. 2.47. Ask,

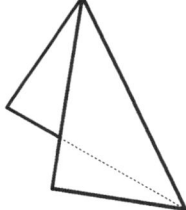

FIG. 2.47.

"Would this be acceptable?" This should prompt some discussion and alteration of their definition, which should lead to halves being equal sized pieces.

Egg Cartons to Show Fractions

Another manipulative for demonstrating halves is egg cartons. For a more extensive discussion of egg cartons as a manipulative to teach fractions, please see http://pegasus.cc.ucf.edu/~mathed/egg. html. As with any manipulative, it is best if each child has a set to do the activities. Start with the bottom tray from a dozen eggs to serve as the unit (suppose the carton is pink). Later you will see how other parts or combinations of egg cartons could also serve as the unit. It is best if the lid and any flap are removed. The unit should look like Fig. 2.48. Once the students have investigated the egg carton and determined the various features such as 12 holes, 2 wide and 6 long, and that

FIG. 2.48.

each hole is the same size (we assume), the investigation of fractions a la egg cartons can begin. The examples will deal with two equivalent fractions, but more than two can readily be handled.

A second carton, preferably a different color (assume blue), should be cut into two equal pieces, each of which is 1 by 6 holes. Both of the two pieces should be placed into the pink carton and then one of them removed, resulting in an arrangement shown in Fig. 2.49. Each child

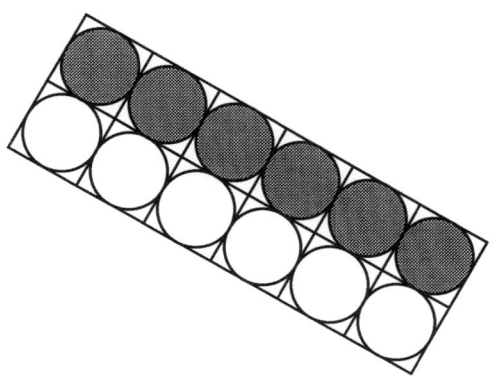

FIG. 2.49.

should now determine what part of the pink carton is represented by the blue piece. They should realize it is one of two equal pieces because they put two blue pieces that were the same size in and took one out. This idea of a half is rather easy for adults to conceptualize, but it could present quite a challenge for a young child in the formative stages of developing the idea of a fraction. The potential degree of difficulty for children only amplifies the need to have manipulatives to assist with the learning of fractions.

Figure 2.50 shows a different configuration for a half using egg cartons. It is im-

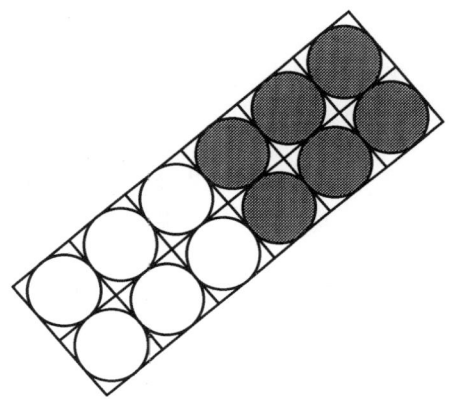

FIG. 2.50.

portant for the children to have different arrangements to represent various fractions. This helps them realize the true definition of half—one of two equal sized pieces. As this idea develops, they will more readily accept different sized units, which will lead to equivalent fractions and ultimately common denominators as fractions are added, subtracted, and divided.

Figure 2.48 shows the egg carton in what is commonly called *standard position*. If students consistently see figures in standard position, they sometimes form the incorrect idea that shapes cannot be presented in a different orientation. Nothing could be farther from the truth. In fact, the standard position idea can lead to problems. This is why it is important to

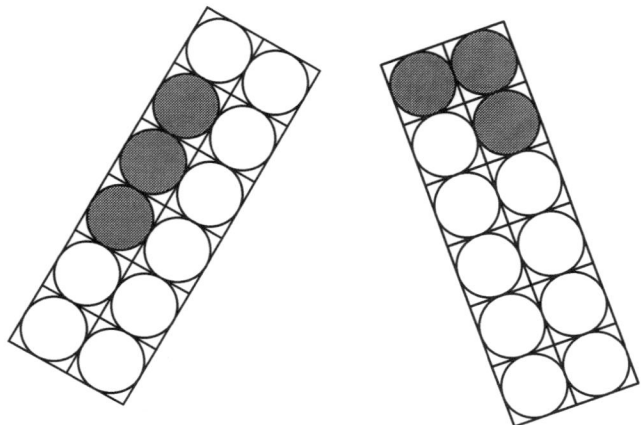

FIG. 2.51.

show Figs. 2.49 and 2.50 along with Fig. 2.48.

It is now known that there are different ways to represent $\frac{1}{2}$. Similar discussions should take place for other fractions. Consider $\frac{1}{4}$, which can be configured in more than one way as shown in Fig. 2.51. Figure 2.52 shows one way to arrange the parts to help students conclude that a "3-holer" (yellow) would represent $\frac{1}{4}$ when a 12-holer (pink) is the unit. Remove the yel-

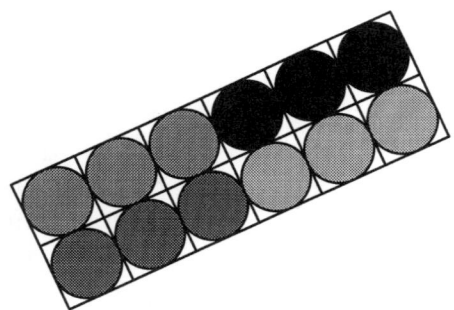

FIG. 2.52.

low $\frac{1}{4}$ and place a blue piece in the unit (pink). Put 2 yellow pieces inside the blue one. Discuss that these two yellow pieces represent $\frac{2}{4}$ of the unit. After that is clear and understood, remove the two yellow

pieces and reveal the blue piece. Ask what the blue represents with respect to pink and lead to the conclusion that $\frac{2}{4}$ represents the same thing as $\frac{1}{2}$. The fundamentals of equivalent fractions have now been concretely established.

Similar examples using other basic equivalent fractions need to be established using the egg cartons. Once several other examples have been worked concretely by the students, it is time to begin seeking a generalization. The possibility exists that the time lapse between the physical creation of equivalent fractions with the egg cartons could be greater than a year.

Exercises

130. Use egg cartons to show $\frac{2}{3} = \frac{4}{6}$.

131. Use egg cartons to show $1\frac{5}{12} = \frac{17}{12}$.

Cuisenaire Rod Background for Fractions

Cuisenaire Rods are a powerful manipulative that can assist children as they learn to operate with fractions. Students need to do a multitude of developmental activities like the ones discussed in this section before attempting to operate on fractions. It is assumed that students possess the appropriate background experiences with Cuisenaire Rods (or a suitable substitute) before utilizing the following instructional activities. For a more extensive discussion of using the Cuisenaire Rods, please see http://pegasus.cc.ucf.edu/~mathed/crods.html.

Can you use three same-colored rods to make a train that is the same length as the Green rod? You might try using three White rods, but that is too short. A train made out of three Lime rods would be too long. Ultimately, you should determine that three Red rods are just right. Some children will not realize that if White is too short and Lime is to long, the logical conclusion is that the resultant rod must be longer than a White and shorter than a Lime. This is a critical skill in the basics of limits. You are encouraged to resist the temptation to tell the children this conclusion. Let them play with the rods and discover this for themselves. This activity and ones like it establish the background for the idea that a unit may be divided into a number of equal sized pieces.

At this stage of development, students need to deal with other rods that can be equated to a number of shorter rods all the same length. For example, can they make a train of four rods, all the same color, as long as a 2-Orange train, or the Purple rod, or the browN rod, and so on? After encountering several problems with solutions, impossible ones can be introduced. For example, can a train consisting of three rods all the same color be formed to match the length of the blacK rod? Several of these problems need to be done before proceeding.

Once several problems have been completed, a different type should be presented. If Yellow represents one, what is two? If Red represents one, what is two? These activities are critical for getting the students to realize that the size of the unit can change. In measurement, we often change units, so this becomes a valuable skill. It also provides background for the idea of Least Common Denominator in operations with fractions. At this point in the development, fractions would not be considered. As before, several of these problems need to be done before proceeding to the next concept.

Cuisenaire Rods and Fractions

Finally, it is time to shift to building the idea of fractions. It is essential to remember that the preceding examples must be well established. If Red is the unit, what is White? We know it is not a whole unit, so we have to find out what part of the unit White is. It takes two Whites to make a train as long as the Red rod (sound familiar?). So, one White represents one out of two equal sized pieces (two Whites), or one out of two equal parts, or one out of two, or one half (notice the transition from the rods to our typical verbiage). This transition is important because it helps the children connect the concrete exposure with our common language, and therefore they have a mental image of what is described by one-half.

If Red is the unit, what is Lime? Lime is the same as a train consisting of a Red and White. The Red is the unit, so you have one unit and a little more. How much more do you have? This was answered in the previous paragraph, so we know that the solution is one and one-half. However, the Lime is the same as three Whites too. If White is a half, then *three of those Whites* would be the *same as three of those halves*. Notice you now have two different answers for the same problem: three halves and one and one-half. We have just discussed converting mixed numbers to improper fractions. Several of these problems need to be done before proceeding.

Cuisenaire Rods and Equivalent Fractions

Cuisenaire Rods make it easy to show equivalent fractions. For example, if browN is the unit, two Purples make a train that is the same length as the browN. Therefore, one Purple must represent one-half. Similarly, four Reds are the same length as a browN so Red is one-fourth. Eight White rods are also the same length as a browN. However, four Whites represent $\frac{4}{8}$, which is equivalent to one Purple or $\frac{1}{2}$ and two Reds represent $\frac{2}{4}$, which is equivalent to one Purple or $\frac{1}{2}$ as shown in Fig. 2.53.

Exercises

132. Use the Cuisenaire Rods (or a suitable substitute) to show that if Green is the unit, $\frac{2}{3} = \frac{4}{6}$.

133. Use the Cuisenaire Rods (or a suitable substitute) to show that if the Orange–Red train is the unit, $\frac{1}{2} = \frac{2}{4} = \frac{3}{6} = \frac{6}{12}$.

Number Line and Equivalent Fractions

We assume the student is familiar with using the number line. Initially it is advantageous to have the number line on a strip

of paper (adding machine tape works well). Mark only zero and one, having them several inches apart. One-half is easy to locate by folding the strip so the zero mark is on top of the one mark. The fold identifies the location of one-half. Then fold the strip in half again to determine the one-fourth. Opening the strip would reveal the location of one-fourth, two-fourths (notice it is on top of one-half), three-fourths, and four-fourths (on top of one) points. Refold to one-fourth of a unit and fold that part in half to locate each of the eighths. Figure 2.54 shows what has been described. It should look similar to Fig. 2.53 as far as where the marks are and how they are determined. The connection between the Cuisenaire Rods and the number line is natural and strong.

A piece of paper is also a handy tool for determining thirds. Most adults have attempted to fold an 8.5 × 11-inch piece of paper into thirds so it fits into a business envelope. As long as the folds are close to being at the third marks, things work out

White

W	W	W	W	W	W	W	W
Red		Red		Red		Red	
Purple				Purple			
browN							

FIG. 2.53.

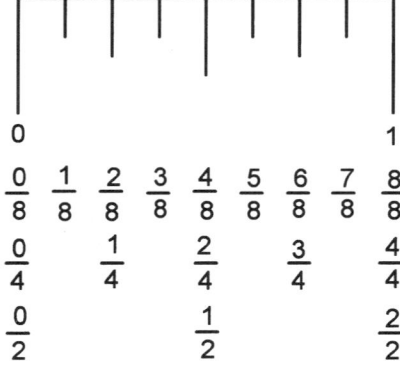

FIG. 2.54.

fine. In fact, the proper way to fold a business letter is to make it so the last fold leaves the top edge about a half-inch above the initial fold as shown in Fig. 2.55.

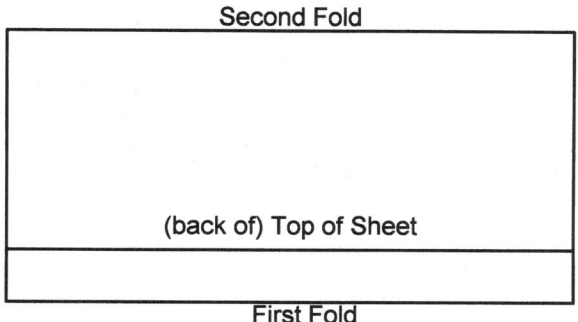

Second Fold

(back of) Top of Sheet

First Fold

FIG. 2.55.

As practical as this might seem for letters, it is not sufficient when introducing children to fractions. One third has to be one of three *equal sized pieces* initially for children. The paper number line is an easy way to get exact thirds, particularly if activities similar to those described earlier with the Cuisenaire Rods have been done.

Establish a unit length on a strip of paper (adding machine tape is still a good choice). Fold the paper in half and in half again. The strip has just been divided into four equal sized pieces. Tear the strip at either the one-fourth or three-fourth mark and discard the smaller piece. The remaining piece is now divided into thirds

and becomes the new unit. Figure 2.56 shows this.

Exercises

134. Use the strip of paper routine to establish a unit divided into sevenths.

135. Use the strip of paper routine to establish a unit divided into fifths.

Equivalent Fractions and Multiplication

Frequently, children discuss equivalent fractions prior to being exposed to the idea of multiplication of fractions. For example, to show that $\frac{1}{3} = \frac{2}{6}$, we show the children $\frac{1 \times 2}{3 \times 2} = \frac{2}{6}$, which is a modification of $\frac{1}{3} \times \frac{2}{2} = \frac{2}{6}$. The children memorize the routine, but often have no idea what is really happening. Manipulatives remove the mystery. Elaborate on the equivalent fraction activities already discussed and the idea that equivalent fractions stem from multiplying or dividing the numerator and denominator of a fraction by the same value is established.

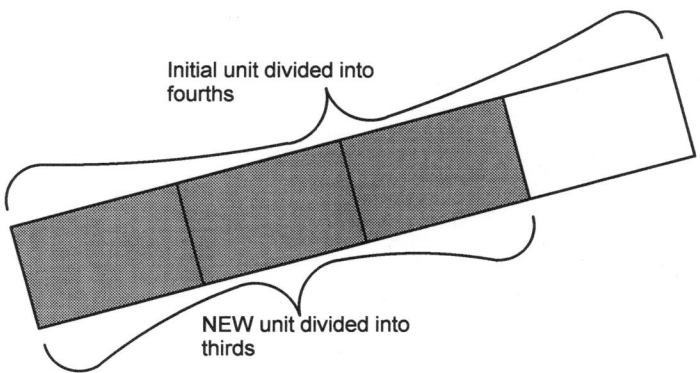

Initial unit divided into fourths

NEW unit divided into thirds

FIG. 2.56.

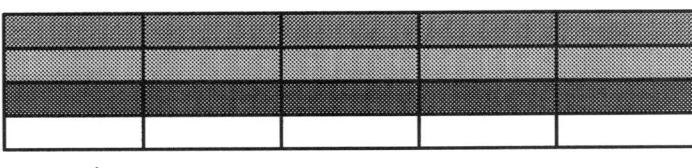

$\frac{1}{4}$ of five is shown by each shaded row

FIG. 2.57.

Array Multiplication of Fractions

When sequencing multiplication using fractional numbers, the first problem type would involve a whole number times a fractional number. Figure 2.57 shows five unit squares side by side (a 1 × 5 rectangle in standard position). Each of the units is also divided horizontally into fourths so each row of Fig. 2.57 represents $\frac{1}{4}$ of 5. At the same time, within any one of the unit squares, each row represents $\frac{1}{4}$, and there are five $\frac{1}{4}$s on each row representing $\frac{5}{4}$. Counting the total number of little shaded $\frac{1}{4}$s gives $\frac{15}{4}$. This shows the product for the problem $5 \times \frac{3}{4}$. If addition of fractions has been developed, then this product could also be shown in the repeated addition format.

The array method for showing multiplication of fractions is probably the easiest to produce. The discussion here focuses on the product of two fractions. If there is a need to physically show the product of more than two fractions, one way is to find the product of the first two and then use that product with the third fraction, repeating the process until all fraction factors are considered. Any product will result in a rectangle. Figure 2.58 shows the array method for $\frac{2}{3} \times \frac{5}{7}$. Notice there

are no common factors. Certainly problems like $\frac{2}{3} \times \frac{3}{4}$ must be discussed with your students. At first, however, it is best to avoid making matters any more complicated than necessary. Figure 2.58 depicts one way the array can be shown. Looking at the figure, you see 21 unit rectangles (who said they had to be squares?). Of the 21 unit rectangles, 14 (or $\frac{2}{3}$) of the total are shaded one way and 15 or $\frac{5}{7}$ are shaded another. The overlap region covered by both shadings represents $\frac{2}{3}$ of $\frac{5}{7}$ or $\frac{5}{7}$ of $\frac{2}{3}$ of the total number of unit rectangles. So, $\frac{2}{3}$ of $\frac{5}{7}$ or $\frac{5}{7}$ of $\frac{2}{3}$ is $\frac{10}{21}$ and the product is shown.

Traditionally students are asked to express answers to problems like $\frac{2}{3} \times \frac{6}{7}$ in lowest terms (reduce, simplify, or divide out common factors). Suppose a student

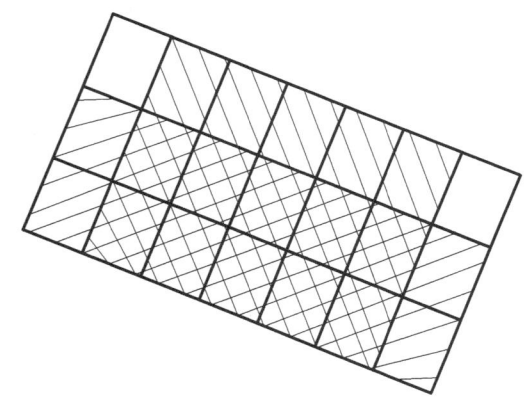

FIG. 2.58.

is asked to reduce $\frac{12}{84}$ and gives $\frac{12}{84}$, something smaller, which is what reduced means. We know that is not the intention of the statement, but in the strictest sense of the word, the fraction has been reduced. A similar discussion could be made about "simplify" from the standpoint of asking why one fraction is simpler than one of its equivalent forms. Again, we know what we mean by simplify, but the word is not overly descriptive. It appears as if "divide out common factors" is the best way to say what is going on as fractions are reduced or simplified. Mathematically that is a true statement.

Exercises

136. Is it reasonable to expect young children to be able to say divide out common factors and understand what they mean?

137. Show someone who is not in your class how to reduce a fraction and describe their reaction.

138. Should students be expected to express fractions where the greatest common factor between the numerator and denominator is one? Why or why not?

139. Describe another way Fig. 2.58 could be shown. Is there an advantage to the way you show it as opposed to the one shown in the text? Why or why not?

Because they have already dealt with equivalent fractions, the students should be able to handle the intricacies involved in multiplication of fractions. They can work the problem by saying $\frac{2}{3} \times \frac{6}{7} = \frac{2 \times 6}{3 \times 7}$, which gives $\frac{12}{21}$. The traditional task now is to find a fraction that is equivalent to $\frac{12}{21}$,

where the numerator and denominator are relatively prime (Greatest Common Factor of the numerator and denominator is 1). The prior work with equivalent fractions should make this a relatively easy task. Is there a better way to get the numerator and denominator to be relatively prime? In this particular example, $\frac{2}{3} \times \frac{6}{7}$ becomes $\frac{4}{7}$. After students do several problems concretely, they should be encouraged to look for patterns. As they create equivalent fractions, students should eventually notice that the numerator and denominator are both divided by three (in this case). That should lead them to conclude that the division can be done before multiplying (thus the phrase dividing out common factors).

$$\frac{2}{\overset{}{\underset{1}{\cancel{3}}}} \times \frac{\overset{2}{\cancel{6}}}{7} = \frac{4}{7}$$

Students tend to resist doing the division first. It is not incorrect to multiply the numerators and denominators first and then divide out common factors. Often it is more difficult because larger numbers are involved. Eventually students encounter problems like $\frac{2}{3} \times \frac{3}{4} \times \frac{4}{5} \times \frac{6}{7} \times \frac{7}{8}$, which are much easier to do if the common factors are divided out initially.

Exercises

140. What could be a major difficulty for students who do $\frac{2}{3} \times \frac{3}{4} \times \frac{4}{5} \times \frac{6}{7} \times \frac{7}{8}$ by first finding $2 \times 3 \times 4 \times 6 \times 7$ and $3 \times 4 \times 5 \times 7 \times 8$?

141. Describe how you would help a student see the advantage of dividing out

common factors first in problems like $\frac{2}{3} \times \frac{3}{4} \times \frac{4}{5} \times \frac{6}{7} \times \frac{7}{8}$.

Multiplication With the Cuisenaire Rods

Remembering that all students do not use the same learning modality, you need to have alternate plans for showing multiplication. Multiplication of fractions has a different procedure than addition, subtraction, and division. It is the easiest to master, which is why we deal with it first. Consider $\frac{1}{2} \times \frac{1}{4}$. You are looking for a unit that can be expressed in terms of halves as well as in terms of a fourth of one of those halves. Suppose the student starts with a Red rod. Half of Red would be a White, but there is no way within the set of rods to represent a fourth of a White. Continuing, Red is half of Purple, but there is no rod that represents a fourth of a Red (remember, we need to be able to take a fourth of the half). The next "halfable" candidate is Green, but its half, Lime, is not "fourthable." The browN rod is "halfable" with Purple, which is also "fourthable" by using a White. So the answer to the question "What rod can you take a half of and, at the same time, take a fourth of a half?" is browN. One-fourth of one-half is represented by White. The only thing left is to interpret what this represents. When browN is the unit, White is $\frac{1}{8}$. So, $\frac{1}{4}$ of $\frac{1}{2}$ is $\frac{1}{8}$ as shown in Fig. 2.59.

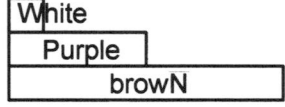

FIG. 2.59.

The same solution exists for $\frac{1}{2}$ of $\frac{1}{4}$, which indicates that the commutative property of multiplication is operational on the rational numbers.

Multiplication with the Cuisenaire Rods was discussed in the whole number section of this text. Those skills can be used to show multiplication of fractions, and the results are similar to those established with arrays. The denominators of the two factors are placed as shown in Fig. 2.60 and the rectangle showing that product is built. Then the numerators for the respective denominators are placed on top and that rectangle is built on top of the rectangle established by the two denominators. The answer is the number of White rods in the top product over the number of White rods in the bottom product. This is a good process because it shows the product of the numerators over the product of the denominators, which is what the students will eventually do. The one shortcoming of this process is that it encourages multiplication before dividing out common factors.

The same problem as done in Fig. 2.58, $\frac{2}{3} \times \frac{5}{7}$, is shown in Fig. 2.60. Notice the nu-

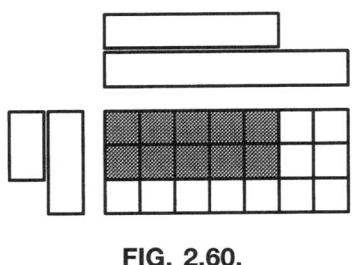

FIG. 2.60.

merator location is different. It is best to physically place the numerator rod on top of the denominator rod, but they were placed above or to the side to help you better see both numerators and both denominators. The shaded section shows the product of the numerators. It is easy to determine that the numerator of the product is equivalent to 10 White rods while the denominator is equivalent to 21 White rods.

Exercises

142. Explain the similarities between Figs. 2.58 and 2.60.

143. Explain the differences between Figs. 2.58 and 2.60.

144. Discuss the advantages or disadvantages of doing multiplication with either the array method or Cuisenaire Rods (remember there are two different ways with the Rods).

Multiplying Mixed Numbers

Once the procedures for multiplying fractions have been established concretely, the students should be led to the generalized abstract methods as quickly as possible. When the students are functioning at the abstract level for multiplication, mixed numbers are easy to deal with because they can be converted to improper fractions.

The product of mixed numbers can be shown concretely with an array in a manner similar to that used for finding the product of whole numbers. Figure 2.61 shows the product of $1\frac{2}{3} \times 1\frac{3}{4}$. Each of the shaded strips to the right of $\frac{1}{4}$ of a unit square and below the right side of the unit square represents $\frac{1}{4}$ of a unit. Considering the entire length of the shaded region to the right of $\frac{1}{4}$ of a unit square would mean you are considering $\frac{1}{4}$ of the entire two units shown at the top of the figure. A similar discussion would hold for the $\frac{1}{3}$ vertical strips. Notice the region where the $\frac{1}{4}$ strips and $\frac{1}{3}$ columns intersect. Each of those small rectangular regions represents $\frac{1}{3}$ of $\frac{1}{4}$ or $\frac{1}{12}$ and there are six of them or $\frac{6}{12}$. This pictorial explanation appears complex, but if the stu-

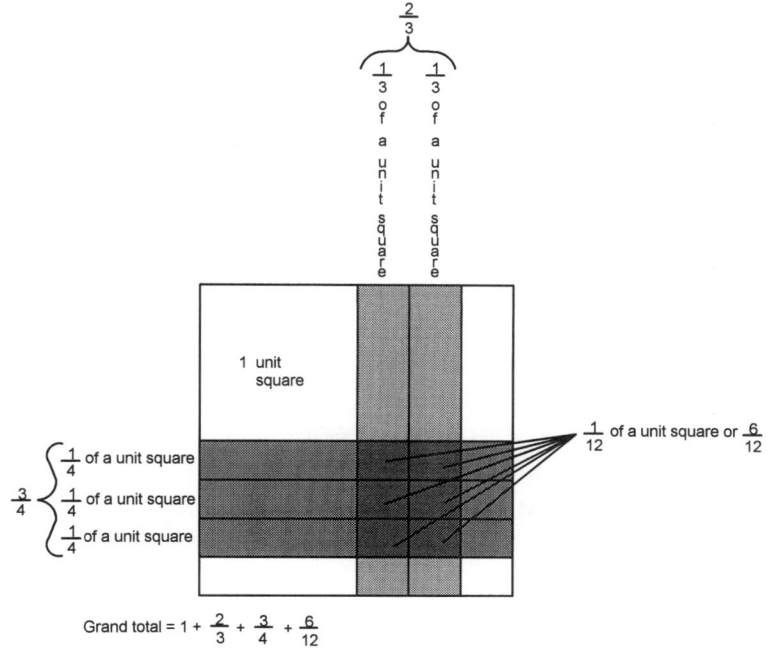

FIG. 2.61.

dents are familiar with showing partial products, they should be able to understand this presentation.

Figure 2.62 shows $2\frac{1}{4} \times 3\frac{1}{3}$, but without

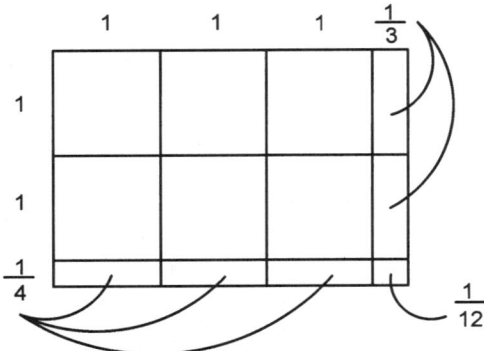

FIG. 2.62.

any of the regions that would not be a part of the product (notice this is a partial product interpretation mentioned in the section dealing with multiplication of whole numbers). Interpretation of the figure is based on the realization of what the partial regions represent in terms of a unit. The six units are easy to see, and the remaining partial units depict the indicated values. Final interpretation of the product is determined by finding $\frac{1}{3} + \frac{1}{3} + \frac{1}{4} + \frac{1}{4} + \frac{1}{4} + \frac{1}{12}$, which is $\frac{18}{12}$ or $1\frac{1}{2}$. Adding that to the six units shown gives a grand total of $7\frac{1}{2}$, which is $2\frac{1}{4} \times 3\frac{1}{3}$. It should be noted that the interpretation of $2\frac{1}{4} \times 3\frac{1}{3}$ is dependent on the ability to add fractional numbers with different denominators. Addition of fractional numbers has not been discussed in the sequencing used in this text so readiness would become a consideration. However, if the traditional sequencing is followed, this would not be a problem. Another alternative would be to follow this text's sequencing of doing equivalence and

multiplication first. Next, deal with addition of fractional numbers and simply delay discussion of multiplying mixed fractional numbers. After addition involving different denominators has been developed, return to multiplication of mixed numbers. Logically, when considering the spiral curriculum, it would probably be the case that addition would be developed before multiplication was entirely completed.

Addition of Fractions: Suggested Sequence for Student Development

Addition of fractions is a broad concept. There are several different problem types under that heading, ranging from a relatively simple idea of adding two unit fractions with the same denominator to adding mixed numbers with denominators that share a common factor. Between those two problem types are several different situations involving addition of fractions. Table 2.1 represents all the basic fraction addition problems. Although only two addends are shown in Table 2.1, consideration should be given to problems that involve more than two addends as the concept of fraction addition is developed. Not all the possible fraction addition problems are presented in Table 2.1. For example, an intermediate problem like $\frac{1}{7} + \frac{2}{7}$ could be inserted between the first two entries of the top row. This might be an essential step for some students in enhancing their understanding because it contains one unit fraction

The examples in Table 2.1 avoid the duplication of digits. Frequently students learn processes for doing problems by tracking numbers in the examples. If the sample problems do not contain redundancy of digits (except for the same de-

TABLE 2.1
Addition of Fractions Sequence

Variable	Unit	Non-Unit	Mixed
Same Denominators	$\frac{1}{7} + \frac{1}{7}$	$\frac{2}{7} + \frac{3}{7}$	$1\frac{2}{7} + 8\frac{3}{7}$
Related Denominators	$\frac{1}{7} + \frac{1}{14}$	$\frac{3}{7} + \frac{5}{14}$	$1\frac{3}{7} + 8\frac{5}{14}$
Unrelated Denominators	$\frac{1}{5} + \frac{1}{7}$	$\frac{2}{5} + \frac{3}{7}$	$4\frac{2}{5} + 6\frac{3}{7}$
Quasi-Related Denominators	$\frac{1}{4} + \frac{1}{6}$	$\frac{3}{4} + \frac{5}{6}$	$2\frac{3}{4} + 11\frac{5}{6}$

nominators), they are easier for the students to study. Eventually digits will be used more than once within a problem type.

By the time students investigate addition of fractions with unlike denominators, they should have some experience with equivalent fractions. Typically the requirement is to express a fraction sum (and all other final results) in its simplest, lowest terms. Although there is a need for students to practice the skill of dividing out all common factors to get that simplest answer, it is not advisable to present them with that requirement during their early encounters with addition of fractions. As with repeating digits in a problem, eventually sums that are not in lowest terms could be generated, but avoiding them at first can help some students master addition of fractions.

The sums of the first sample problems are all less than one. Ultimately, conversion of a sum from an improper fraction to a mixed number is encountered. However, in the spirit of helping students master the task at hand, avoid expecting them to perform this extra maneuver when beginning fraction addition. Later when the students are more experienced and conversion between improper fractions and mixed numbers is reflexive, this is not an issue.

There are many ways to progress through the problem types presented in Table 2.1. Certainly one could do all of the types where the denominator is the same with possible additions like $\frac{1}{7} + \frac{2}{7}$ between the first two entries of the top row. Doing this would mandate digression from the sequence to introduce mixed numbers in the first row, but that assuredly could be done. After all the problem types involving the same denominator are completed, the skills necessary for students to do the second row of problem types could be addressed, followed by the third and fourth rows. Rather than doing all problem types with the same denominator first, $\frac{1}{7} + \frac{1}{7}$ could be followed by $\frac{1}{7} + \frac{1}{14}$. You might consider doing problems like $\frac{1}{7} + \frac{2}{7}$ between $\frac{1}{7} + \frac{1}{7}$ and $\frac{1}{7} + \frac{1}{14}$ to make smaller steps between concepts. More than likely, you would not do all of the problem types in Table 2.1 in one year. Guiding students through a sequence of the Table 2.1 concepts is influenced by their ability. Other considerations include ideas like whether the students have found the past few concepts presented to be easy. If the students mastered the previous concepts with ease, it might be appropriate to offer them a more challenging topic. That would indicate which problem type would be next. By the same token, if the students have found the last concepts difficult, it might be time to discuss something relatively easy for them.

Typically textbooks do not provide such precise considerations of topic sequencing. They can't! The text authors do not know your students, their backgrounds, or their ability levels. You are the local authority for your students. As such, you are the one who should make decisions. Blindly following the sequence presented by the text or standards in the order listed may not be the best route for you students. That is why careful consideration of the topics presented in Table 2.1 is so critical.

Why Use Manipulatives to Add Fractions?

Logically manipulatives would be used with each fraction addition problem type. The procedures explained here are similar for any of the problems. Our examples focus on $\frac{1}{3} + \frac{1}{4}$ under the assumption that you could do a comparable development with any fraction addition problem type.

Manipulatives are convenient tools for helping children understand why operation rules work as they do. Frequently children are given a procedure for adding fractions and told to follow the algorithm when presented with a problem such as $\frac{1}{3} + \frac{1}{4}$. Here is a set of rules to follow that is typically given to an elementary student during the discussion on adding fractions:

"Find the Least Common Denominator (LCD)."

"Divide the denominator of the first fraction into the LCD."

"Multiply the numerator of the first fraction by the answer you got when you divided the first denominator into the LCD."

"Divide the denominator of the second fraction into the LCD."

"Multiply the numerator of the second fraction by the answer you got when you divided the second denominator into the LCD."

"Add the two new products."

"Put the sum over the LCD."

You are probably familiar with that set of instructions because you were told that procedure earlier in your education. Perhaps you have done enough practice problems that the instructions have become engrained in your head.

Make an audio recording of yourself reading that section of statements in quotes pertaining to adding two fractions. As you record, read it as fast as you can. Play the tape back and you might get some feel for how it sounds to a student who does not comprehend the procedure. Granted, you would probably speak much more slowly with children, but the intent is to note how it could sound to a student who does not understand the process.

Adding Fractions Using Egg Cartons

Egg cartons are one tool that can be used to find $\frac{1}{3} + \frac{1}{4}$. The students must be familiar with expressing fractional parts of a unit with egg cartons (see http://pegasus.cc.ucf.edu/~mathed/egg.html for a detailed discussion). The initial task is to determine a unit that can be expressed in terms of thirds and fourths at the same time. One procedure is to have the children consider different cartons as the unit and see if they work (guess and check). Another method lends some organization to the search by starting with a 1-holer (egg carton with one hole) and increasing the size of the unit one hole at a time until a suitable unit is located. If they know that the unit has to be a 12-holer, there is no need to be working with the concrete because they are already functioning abstractly.

N-holer	Accept	Reason
1-holer	No	Can't find $\frac{1}{3}$ or $\frac{1}{4}$
2-holer	No	Can't find $\frac{1}{3}$ or $\frac{1}{4}$
3-holer	No	Can find $\frac{1}{3}$ but not $\frac{1}{4}$
4-holer	No	Can find $\frac{1}{4}$ but not $\frac{1}{3}$
5-holer	No	Can't find $\frac{1}{3}$ or $\frac{1}{4}$
6-holer	No	Can find $\frac{1}{3}$ but not $\frac{1}{4}$
7-holer	No	Can't find $\frac{1}{3}$ or $\frac{1}{4}$
8-holer	No	Can find $\frac{1}{4}$ but not $\frac{1}{3}$
9-holer	No	Can find $\frac{1}{3}$ but not $\frac{1}{4}$
10-holer	No	Can't find $\frac{1}{3}$ or $\frac{1}{4}$
11-holer	No	Can't find $\frac{1}{3}$ or $\frac{1}{4}$
12-holer	YES	Can find $\frac{1}{4}$ and $\frac{1}{3}$

The process might appear tedious, but it does provide a concrete way to establish a unit. Figure 2.63 shows how egg cartons can be used to determine the sum of $\frac{1}{4}$ and $\frac{1}{3}$. Counting the number of filled

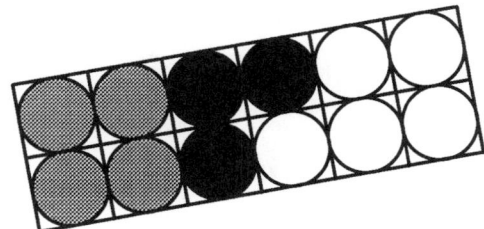

FIG. 2.63.

holes (7) and comparing that with the number of holes in the unit (12) gives $\frac{7}{12}$,

which is the sum of $\frac{1}{4}$ and $\frac{1}{3}$. Writing this result along with other examples, which would be done in a similar manner using egg cartons, could yield

$$\frac{1}{3} + \frac{1}{4} = \frac{7}{12}$$
$$\frac{1}{2} + \frac{1}{3} = \frac{5}{6}$$
$$\frac{1}{2} + \frac{1}{7} = \frac{9}{14}$$

It is hard to tell how many examples like this need to be done, but eventually some enterprising student is going to develop a generalization something like: "All you need to do is multiply the denominators to get the denominator (notice LCD in this case?) of the answer and add the denominators to get the numerator of the answer." AHA! Celebrate because that student is well along the way of discovering the rule used to add fractions. Granted these are unit fractions and additional work would be necessary to complete the concept, but a powerful foundation has been established.

A problem like $\frac{2}{3} + \frac{1}{4}$ can be used as a next step in developing the complete algorithm for adding fractions. The problem would be solved using egg cartons as described earlier (or any other manipulative). After several problems of this type are done and listed, a discussion similar to the one used when finding the sum of two unit fractions can be created to lead the students to the desired generalization.

$$\frac{2}{3} + \frac{1}{4} = \frac{11}{12}$$
$$\frac{2}{5} + \frac{1}{3} = \frac{11}{15}$$
$$\frac{3}{7} + \frac{1}{5} = \frac{22}{35}$$

The conversation here would be similar in that the product of the denominators of the two fractions being added is the denominator of the sum. Before, the numerator of the sum was determined by adding the denominators of the addends in problems like $\frac{1}{3} + \frac{1}{5} = \frac{8}{15}$, but that will not work now. In the example $\frac{2}{5} + \frac{1}{3} = \frac{11}{15}$ and using the idea of adding denominators to get the numerator, you need to ask how to get 11 from 5 and 3. The sum of 5 and 3 is not enough. Using different combinations leads to the conclusion that the only way to get 11 using 5s and 3s is to have two 3s and one 5 or 3 + 3 + 5 = 11. But 3 + 3 can be written as (2)(3), and a major piece of the complete algorithm for adding fractions is supplied. Some extension of this discussion finalizes the desired algorithm.

Did you notice that in the last set of three examples all of the numerators are multiples of 11? If you did, give yourself a pat on the back. You are beginning to be sensitive to issues that can give students wrong impressions and perhaps even generate an error pattern. In this case, a student could conclude sums of a unit and nonunit fraction will always have a numerator that is a multiple of 11. Stranger things have happened.

Exercises

145. Use egg cartons to show the sum $\frac{1}{2} + \frac{1}{3}$. Describe the process necessary to determine the LCD. Remember, if the LCD can be determined abstractly, there is no need to use the egg cartons. Assume you do not know how to find the LCD abstractly and role-play using egg cartons to gain insight into what your students will experience.

146. Use egg cartons to show the sum $\frac{2}{3} + \frac{1}{4}$.

147. Use egg cartons to show the sum $\frac{4}{5} + \frac{2}{3}$. Explain your answer.

Adding Fractions Using Cuisenaire Rods

Procedures for finding $\frac{1}{3} + \frac{1}{4}$ with the Cuisenaire Rods (see http://pegasus.cc.ucf.edu/~mathed/crods.html for detailed instructions) are similar to those for egg cartons. The first task is to establish the unit needed. Rather than asking about an N-holer, the rod color is asked. Can the White rod serve as a unit? No, because you can't find a third or fourth of it.

Rod	Accept	Reason
White	No	Can't find $\frac{1}{3}$ or $\frac{1}{4}$
Red	No	Can't find $\frac{1}{3}$ or $\frac{1}{4}$
Lime	No	Can find $\frac{1}{3}$ but not $\frac{1}{4}$
Purple	No	Can find $\frac{1}{4}$ but not $\frac{1}{3}$
Yellow	No	Can't find $\frac{1}{3}$ or $\frac{1}{4}$
Green	No	Can find $\frac{1}{3}$ but not $\frac{1}{4}$
blacK	No	Can't find $\frac{1}{3}$ or $\frac{1}{4}$
browN	No	Can find $\frac{1}{4}$ but not $\frac{1}{3}$
bluE	No	Can find $\frac{1}{3}$ but not $\frac{1}{4}$
Orange	No	Can't find $\frac{1}{3}$ or $\frac{1}{4}$
Orange–White train	No	Can't find $\frac{1}{3}$ or $\frac{1}{4}$
Orange–Red train	YES	Can find $\frac{1}{3}$ and $\frac{1}{4}$

Figure 2.64 shows how the Cuisenaire Rods would be used to obtain the answer to $\frac{1}{3} + \frac{1}{4}$.

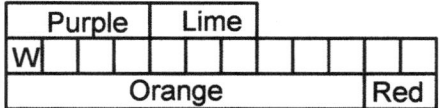

FIG. 2.64.

Although a variety of combinations could be used to represent the unit rod, the Orange–Red train is used to amplify place value (10 + 2 or one ten [Orange] and two ones [Red]).

If the students are not comprehending the abstractions, they can be referred to a manipulative, but it will take a significant effort on your part to sell them on the idea. Once abstractions are started with a concept, a concrete approach is often visualized as being too childish.

In the egg carton discussion, a generalization for multiplying the denominators and adding the numerators was discussed. It would be duplicated here if the Cuisenaire Rods were the manipulative of choice. Remember the ultimate goal is to have the students use and understand the algorithm commonly applied when adding fractions. (Listen to that tape you made earlier.)

Exercises

148. Use Cuisenaire Rods to show the sum $\frac{1}{2} + \frac{1}{3}$. Describe the process necessary to determine the LCD. Remember, if the LCD can be determined abstractly, there is no need to use the Cuisenaire Rods. Assume you do not know how to find the LCD abstractly and role-play using Cuisenaire Rods to gain insight into what your students will experience.

149. Use Cuisenaire Rods to show the sum $\frac{2}{3} + \frac{1}{4}$.

150. Use Cuisenaire Rods to show the sum $\frac{4}{5} + \frac{2}{3}$. Explain your answer.

Adding Fractions and Error Patterns

One common error pattern when adding fractions has the numerators being added and placed over the sum of the denominators. Manipulatives can help prevent that error before it happens. Suppose the problem is $\frac{2}{7} + \frac{3}{7}$, which frequently generates the incorrect response of $\frac{5}{14}$. Often this error is corrected by telling a student that the denominators are not added. Once again, the teacher is stating a fact that the student must simply believe. For some students, such an explanation is sufficient. For others, however, you might need to proceed from the concrete beginning up through the levels to the abstract application of the algorithm. Your knowledge of the student, content, and pedagogy will help you place the student properly in the sequence. Figure 2.65 shows how egg cartons could be used to pro-

FIG. 2.65.

vide the correct answer. The assumption is that the student is familiar with using egg cartons to add fractions. Otherwise, the background discussed in the beginning of this chapter would need to be established. Certainly, more complex addition problems that students use to employ this error pattern will be encountered. The sequence for explaining the error concretely could be established.

Exercises

151. Suppose a student says $\frac{2}{3} + \frac{1}{8} = \frac{3}{11}$. Describe how you would use egg cartons to establish the actual sum of $\frac{19}{24}$.

152. Suppose a student says $\frac{2}{3} + \frac{1}{2} = \frac{3}{5}$. Describe how you would use Cuisenaire Rods to establish the actual sum of $\frac{7}{6}$ (or $1\frac{1}{6}$).

153. Define an error pattern for adding fractions that is different from placing the sum of the numerators over the sum of the denominators of the addends. Describe how you would help a student correct such an error.

Subtraction of Fractions: Suggested Sequence for Student Development

The development of a subtraction sequence development will be left to you in the first exercise in this section. There are some unique situations that occur with subtraction that do not happen with addition. For example, what is the answer when one unit fraction is subtracted from another unit fraction when the denominators are the same? Similarly, if a unit fraction is subtracted from another unit fraction where one denominator is a multiple of the other, is there a pattern? Questions such as these can be investigated as part of the outgrowth of developing a sequence for subtracting fractions.

When students operate on fractions, they will have seen subtraction of whole numbers. It is likely that the beginning topics for subtraction of fractions will oc-cur along with or soon after the beginning topics for addition of fractions. This is not too illogical as long as manipulatives are used in the formative stages.

Exercises

154. Create a sequence for subtracting fractions starting with two unit fractions with the same denominator and ending with mixed numbers with quasirelated denominators.

155. As the addition sequence for fractions was developed, some discussion focused on providing steps that were not listed in the table. For example, $\frac{1}{7} + \frac{2}{7}$ was listed as a potential entry between $\frac{1}{7} + \frac{1}{7}$ and $\frac{2}{7} + \frac{3}{7}$. Does the subtraction sequence you created allow for such detail or would it need to be added?

Manipulatives and Subtracting Fractions

Manipulatives are just as critical when dealing with the subtraction of fractions as they are when introducing any other operation. The students should have used manipulatives to establish how to add fractions and conceivably moved to abstractions for parts of addition. It is not prudent to assume these same students are capable of dealing with the abstractions related to subtraction of fractions without concrete exposure. The slow, careful development discussed in addition would be appropriate for the initial stages of subtraction of fractions. It is possible that the students would be able to move through those concrete stages quickly because of the exposure in the formative stages of adding fractions. This would also be true as far as using the manipulatives to establish generalizations and algorithms for subtracting fractions. The weaker the background established with other operations, the more difficult it will be for students to call on those experiences as they encounter new concepts to be learned.

Subtracting Fractions Using Egg Cartons

Assuming that the students know how to determine the unit (see http://pegasus.cc. ucf.edu/~mathed/egg.html for a detailed explanation), subtraction of fractions is not difficult. If the problem is $\frac{1}{3} - \frac{1}{4}$, the unit would be a 12-holer. The sum, $\frac{1}{3}$, would be represented by a 4-holer, and the addend, $\frac{1}{4}$, by a 3-holer. The task is to determine the missing addend, which in this case would be $\frac{1}{12}$. This is shown in Fig. 2.66, where the unit is established as

FIG. 2.66.

a 12-holer and a 3-holer ($\frac{1}{4}$) is placed inside a 4-holer ($\frac{1}{3}$). The one hole that is not filled represents the missing addend and is interpreted as one of 12 equal sized pieces or $\frac{1}{12}$.

An example that would appear at the beginning of the subtraction of fractions learning sequence would be $\frac{5}{7} - \frac{2}{7}$. As-

suming the student knows that a 7-holer would serve as the unit, Fig. 2.67 shows the egg carton solution. Two of the five

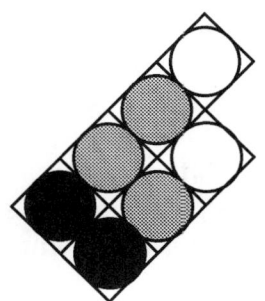

FIG. 2.67.

filled holes are double filled, leaving 3 of the 7 in the unit filled once, showing $\frac{5}{7} - \frac{2}{7}$. A few problems like those shown in Table 2.2 should be done.

TABLE 2.2
Egg Carton Subtraction

Examples for egg cartons
$\frac{5}{7} - \frac{2}{7} = \frac{3}{7}$
$\frac{7}{9} - \frac{5}{9} = \frac{2}{9}$
$\frac{11}{13} - \frac{6}{13} = \frac{5}{13}$

Because the students have encountered problems similar to these when adding fractions was developed, it should be rather easy for them to generalize the algorithm for subtracting fractions when the denominators are the same. It is assumed the students would realize that when the denominators are the same, the smaller numerator is subtracted from the larger and the denominator of the missing addend would be the same as the other denominators in the problem.

There is one new item to be considered at this point. Notice the last sentence in the previous paragraph says the smaller numerator is subtracted from the larger.

At this stage of development, that is an adequate representation of the situation. However, eventually the students will need to realize that the larger numerator could be subtracted from the smaller, resulting in a negative missing addend. Do not let the students generalize that you cannot subtract the larger numerator from the smaller. Although that outgrowth would not likely occur in the elementary school environment, it is important not to confuse the students for their mathematical future.

Exercises

156. Create a subtraction problem with related denominators and describe how to solve it concretely with egg cartons. Include an account of how to determine the LCD in your discussion.

157. List at least three subtraction problems with unrelated denominators and specify the conclusion they could generate.

Subtracting Fractions Using Cuisenaire Rods

As with the egg cartons, the assumption is that the students are appropriately familiar with using the Cuisenaire Rods. A major part of the familiarity is the idea of finding the unit. Furthermore, it is assumed that the student is familiar with using the missing addend approach to subtraction. If the students have done whole number subtraction and addition of fractions with the Cuisenaire Rods, subtraction of fractions should seem relatively easy for them. Sequencing of the problem types is an important aspect of the presentation.

A problem like $\frac{4}{7} - \frac{1}{7}$ is a good place to start. Certainly there are other problems

that could be used. Consideration should still be given to items like avoiding the need to divide out common factors in the missing addend in a problem like $\frac{7}{9} - \frac{4}{9} = \frac{3}{9}$. By the same token, a problem such as $\frac{4}{5} - \frac{2}{5} = \frac{2}{5}$ is a poor choice because the addend and missing addend are the same. This may seem trivial to you, but remember you have had a lot more experience than your students. When the addend and missing addend are the same, some students might conclude that this will always be the case and do some incorrect "creative mathematics."

Solving $\frac{4}{7} - \frac{1}{7}$ with the Cuisenaire Rods involves determining the unit rod first. In this case, the blacK rod is the first one that can be divided into sevenths (i.e., it is *seventhable*). If the students have been using the Cuisenaire Rods for a while, they might be at the level where they would conclude that the blacK rod is the first candidate for the unit because it is the first one that can be made equal to seven White rods. Either way, the unit is determined. You should note that a student, who automatically begins with the blacK rod *because* it is the first one that can be made equal to seven White rods, is probably closer to functioning at the abstract level than the student who uses the "Can White be the unit?; Can Red be the unit? . . ." process described earlier.

With blacK as the unit in $\frac{4}{7} - \frac{1}{7}$, the sum is represented by Purple. The known addend is White and the task is to find the missing addend, which in this case is Lime. Lime here is interpreted as $\frac{3}{7}$ because blacK is the unit and Lime represents three out of seven White rods. This is shown in Fig. 2.68.

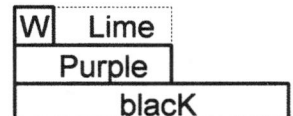

FIG. 2.68.

Figure 2.69 shows what could be the next problem type to be considered when doing fraction subtraction, $\frac{1}{7} - \frac{1}{14}$. Determining the unit is still the key. The students could be aware that the blacK rod is the first one that is seventhable. That realization alone is not enough to get the unit rod. Yet coupled with the idea that 14 is twice seven, some students will conclude the next possible candidate for the unit rod must be two blacK rods. Certainly two blacK rods can be expressed in terms of seven equal sized pieces (Red). The only question remaining is whether a two blacK rod train can be expressed in terms of 14 equal sized pieces. Happily, White will work and the unit is determined.

You should watch your students as they work through determining the unit for problems like this. If they are aware that two blacK rods are needed, they might conclude that one White expresses a seventh of each of the blacK rods. At the same time, they could conclude that one White would be one of 14 equal sized pieces if two blacK rods are considered. A student who is functioning at this level is much closer to the idea of LCD than one who has to build the picture physically with the rods. The student who is closer to the abstraction does not necessarily possess more native intelligence than the one who works it concretely. The only thing that can be concluded here is that one student is farther along the abstraction trail on this problem type than the other. At the same time, the student who is able to deal with the situation at a more abstract level is providing you some indicators that could imply a higher level of development and perhaps more mathematical awareness.

Now that the unit is determined, $\frac{1}{7} - \frac{1}{14}$ can be done on the rods with relative ease as shown in Fig. 2.69. The different configurations are shown in Fig. 2.69 mainly for your convenience. It would not be necessary to show all of these or to have your students do them all. It is helpful for some and confusing for others, so decide carefully. The top of Fig. 2.69 shows the solution to the problem $\frac{1}{7} - \frac{1}{14}$, where Red represents $\frac{1}{7}$ and White represents $\frac{1}{14}$. The White with the dashed sides is the missing addend of $\frac{1}{14}$.

The problem $\frac{1}{7} - \frac{1}{14}$ might not be the best choice because the addend and missing addend are the same. However, if you want to stimulate your students to think about generalizations, perhaps you would want to do several problems such as:

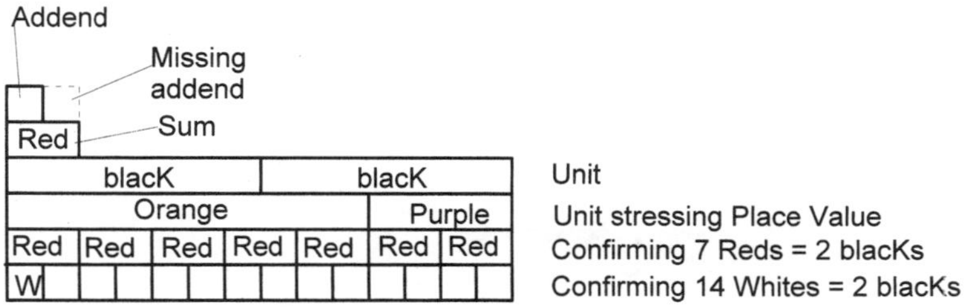

Addend

Missing addend

Sum

Red						

blacK				blacK		

Orange					Purple	

Red	Red	Red	Red	Red	Red	Red

W						

Unit

Unit stressing Place Value
Confirming 7 Reds = 2 blacKs
Confirming 14 Whites = 2 blacKs

FIG. 2.69.

$$\frac{1}{7} - \frac{1}{14}$$

$$\frac{1}{3} - \frac{1}{6}$$

$$\frac{1}{11} - \frac{1}{22}$$

$$\frac{1}{5} - \frac{1}{10}$$

because there are some things students should be able to conclude. First, the second denominator is twice the first in each problem. Second, the addend and missing addend are the same in each case. These may not be monumental conclusions or generalizations, but they are a means to help students learn to look for unusual happenings as they do problems. This ability to notice different things can be an asset as they progress toward their mathematical future.

Exercises

158. Suppose you asked your students to do a series of problems like $\frac{1}{4} - \frac{1}{12}$, $\frac{1}{5} - \frac{1}{15}$, $\frac{1}{6} - \frac{1}{18}$, and so on. What generalization could they be expected to develop?

159. If the problems from the last exercise were followed by sets of problems like $\frac{1}{4} - \frac{1}{16}$, which would be followed by problems like $\frac{1}{4} - \frac{1}{20}$, which would be followed by problems like $\frac{1}{4} - \frac{1}{24}$, and so on for as

long as necessary, what generalization could students be expected to develop?

160. Create a subtraction problem with related denominators, and describe how to solve it concretely with Cuisenaire Rods. Include an account of how to determine the LCD in your discussion.

Subtracting Fractions Using the Number Line

As with other operations involving fractions, the number line could be used, although it may not be as easy to comprehend for some students. The student needs to know how to find the LCD to use the number line. If that knowledge is available, the abstract level is present. Therefore, dealing with the situation at the concrete level has to be questioned.

A paper number line can be created to do the problem $\frac{1}{3} - \frac{1}{4}$ concretely. Use a strip of adding machine tape for the number line, making it about a foot and a half long to begin. Fold the tape into fourths and tear one of the end fourths off, establishing thirds. Use this strip of paper (somewhere around 13 or 14 inches long now) as the unit. Starting from the left, mark the first fold crease as $\frac{1}{3}$ and the second fold crease as $\frac{2}{3}$. Now fold the entire strip into fourths and, starting from the left, mark the *new* fold creases as $\frac{1}{4}$, $\frac{2}{4}$, and $\frac{3}{4}$, respectively, as shown in Fig. 2.70. The paper unit is divided into three

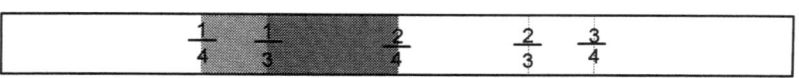

FIG. 2.70.

sized sections as shown by the lighter shading between $\frac{1}{4}$ and $\frac{1}{3}$, the darker shading between $\frac{1}{3}$ and $\frac{2}{4}$, and the white section between zero and $\frac{1}{4}$. Examination shows there are other sections congruent to the ones already mentioned.

Figure 2.71 shows the unit folded at the $\frac{1}{4}$ and $\frac{1}{3}$ points. Continue the folding process by laying this small section along the part from zero to $\frac{1}{4}$. Then fold back and forth like you are making a fan as shown in Fig. 2.72. The small section will fit twice between $\frac{1}{3}$ and $\frac{2}{4}$. That small section will fit three times between zero and $\frac{1}{4}$. When the fan is completed and the small sections are counted, you will have a unit divided into 12 equal sized segments. Those segments can be used to establish that $\frac{1}{3}$ equals $\frac{4}{12}$ and $\frac{1}{4}$ equals $\frac{3}{12}$. Using the missing addend process for subtraction on a number line, it can be shown that $\frac{1}{3} - \frac{1}{4}$ is $\frac{1}{12}$. Granted, this paper-folding procedure is not simple, but it does work. As you work thorough it, you should increase your understanding of subtracting fractions.

Subtracting Fractions and Error Patterns

Subtraction has its own set of problems and error patterns that could appear in subtraction with fractions. Other opportunities for errors exist that are unique to subtraction of fractions. For example, when doing $\frac{1}{5} - \frac{1}{7}$, the students could conclude that the denominator should be the product of 5 and 7 as they did in addition of unit fractions with unrelated denominators. They could subtract five from seven and get two for the numerator. We know the order of the denominators in the problem will influence the sign of the missing addend, and they may or may not. The point is that they could do an absolute value thing and, not realizing it, get the correct signed answer. Unless you are paying close attention, an error pattern could be generated.

Exercises

161. Do $\frac{3}{4} - \frac{2}{3}$ on a paper number line.

162. Describe your reaction to doing fraction subtraction problems on a paper number line.

163. Define an error pattern for subtraction of fractions. Create three sub-

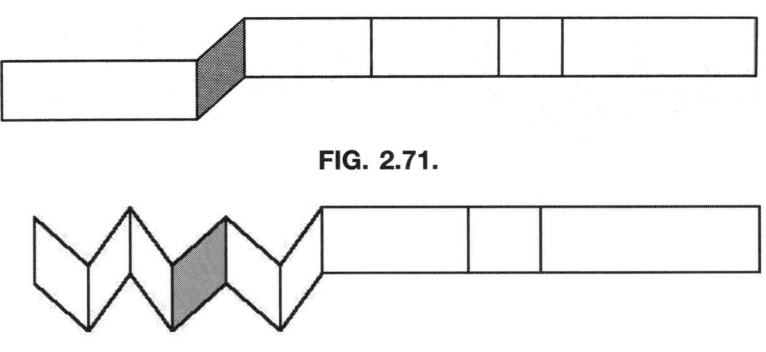

FIG. 2.71.

FIG. 2.72.

traction fraction problems using the error pattern. Give those three problems to another person in your class and ask them to describe the error pattern. Assess the description. Note that if you create multiple-choice tests and include error patterns such as this, you can gather additional information about your students. It takes time to create the questions, but the gains are significant.

164. Describe how you would correct the error you just created.

Division of Fractions: Suggested Sequence for Student Development

The question in $4\overline{)24}$ (or $24 \div 4$) is *how many sets of fours are in 24?* If the problem is $\frac{1}{2} \div \frac{1}{8}$, the question is *how many eighths are in a half?* There are some intermediate steps between $24 \div 4$ and $\frac{1}{2} \div \frac{1}{8}$. It has to be assumed that students are familiar with a concrete definition of a fraction as established with the Cuisenaire Rods. A whole number divided by a fraction should be done prior to a fraction divided by a fraction. For example, *how many halves are in three* could be done as shown in Fig. 2.73.

As the division sequence for fractions is constructed, consideration should be

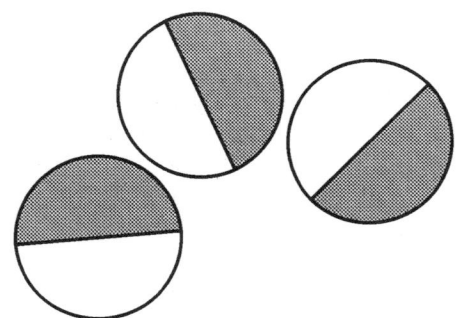

FIG. 2.73.

given to the specific problem types that result in answers that are whole numbers first. Only after several division problems of this type are done should the students encounter problems such as $\frac{2}{3} \div \frac{3}{4}$.

Exercise

165. List at least one other problem type that should be done with students before they encounter $\frac{1}{2} \div \frac{1}{8}$.

Manipulatives and Dividing Fractions

Division of fractions is certainly one area where concrete applications are extremely important. Although several manipulatives can be used to develop the concepts related to fraction division, the Cuisenaire Rods are one of the easiest assuming the students have had prior exposure. The one item that is most frequently overlooked is the question that asks *how many factors are in the product* for a given problem.

Dividing Fractions Using Cuisenaire Rods

Division of fractions using the Cuisenaire Rods is simple if two things are in place: experience in finding the LCD and knowledge of the question that is being asked in a division problem. If the problem is $\frac{1}{2} \div \frac{1}{8}$, the unit rod is the browN rod and the question is *how many eighths are in a half?* Selection of the browN rod is natural at this point of the students' development because it is the first one that can be divided into eight equal sized pieces by using White. Similarly, Purple represents a half of a browN. Figure 2.74 shows the

W	Eighth
Purple	Half
browN	Unit

FIG. 2.74.

problem using browN as the unit. Because White represents an eighth and Purple stands for a half, the question of *how many eighths are in a half* can be stated as "How many Whites are in a Purple?" This is easy for students to see and answer. "How many Whites are in a Purple?" can then be restated as "How many eighths are in a half?"

So, $\frac{1}{2} \div \frac{1}{8} = 4$, and one problem of this type has been done. Several more problems of this same type need to be done. For example, when the students see several problems of the type shown in Table 2.3, they will begin to arrive at some con-

TABLE 2.3
Division With Cuisenaire Rods

$$\frac{1}{3} \div \frac{1}{6} = 2$$
$$\frac{1}{4} \div \frac{1}{20} = 5$$
$$\frac{1}{5} \div \frac{1}{15} = 3$$

clusions about what is happening. For those who do not see, you can ask some questions to stimulate their thinking. For the problem $\frac{1}{2} \div \frac{1}{8} = 4$, you could ask for a connection between the denominators and the answer. If that does not work, perhaps you could ask how a two and eight could be used to give a four. The response eventually should be $8 \div 2 = 4$.

Now you begin asking how the problem $\frac{1}{2} \div \frac{1}{8} = 4$ could be changed to give the answer in terms of dividing the eight by the

two. Because the students have experience with multiplication of fractions, they should recognize that $\frac{1}{2} \times 8 = 4$ and, more specifically, that $\frac{1}{2} \times \frac{8}{1} = 4$. Your next question focuses on how this last problem of $\frac{1}{2} \times \frac{8}{1} = 4$ is related to $\frac{1}{2} \div \frac{1}{8} = 4$. It should not take long for the idea of inverting the second fraction and changing from division to multiplication to begin to develop.

Once the foundation is laid, different fraction division problems need to be done. If the problem is $\frac{2}{3} \div \frac{3}{4}$, you want to know *how many $\frac{3}{4}$s are in $\frac{2}{3}$*. Figure 2.75 shows how the missing factor is determined. The question is, "How many three

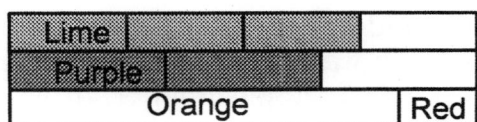

Lime			
Purple			
Orange			Red

FIG. 2.75.

Lime trains fit in a two Purple train?" It can be seen that one three Lime train will not fit in one two Purple train. The question now becomes how much of the three Lime train is a two Purple train. Notice that the three Lime train is now the basis for discussion, and this becomes much like some of the formative activities for fractions. Figure 2.76 shows only the three Lime train and the two Purple train. From that, it can be determined that it takes nine Whites to make a train equivalent in length to the three Lime train and that the two Purple train takes up eight of

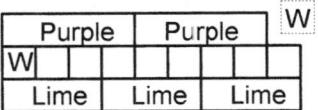

Purple	Purple	W
W		
Lime	Lime	Lime

FIG. 2.76.

those nine White rods. Eight out of nine Whites are used, or $\frac{8}{9}$s. Thus, $\frac{2}{3} \div \frac{3}{4} = \frac{8}{9}$.

What if the problem is $\frac{3}{4} \div \frac{2}{3}$? The situation would look like Fig. 2.75 again, but the interpretation would be different. Now the question is, "How many $\frac{2}{3}$s are in $\frac{3}{4}$?" Here the two Purple train is the basis for comparison, and the question can be translated to "How many two Purple trains fit in a three Lime train?" Figure 2.77 shows that it takes eight White rods to make a train the same length as the

Lime	Lime	Lime
W									W
Purple	Purple

FIG. 2.77.

two Purple train. It also shows that the three Lime train is one White rod longer than the two Purple train. The question now becomes one of determining the value of a White rod. Because it takes eight White rods to make a train as long as the two Purple train, a White is one of eight equal sized pieces, or $\frac{1}{8}$. Thus, the three Lime train represents one whole two Purple train and $\frac{1}{8}$ more, so $\frac{3}{4} \div \frac{2}{3} = 1\frac{1}{8}$.

Exercises

166. Do $\frac{7}{8} \div \frac{3}{4}$ with the Cuisenaire Rods and explain why the answer is $1\frac{1}{6}$.

167. Do $\frac{3}{4} \div \frac{7}{8}$ with the Cuisenaire Rods and explain why the answer is $\frac{6}{7}$.

168. Do $\frac{3}{4} \div \frac{4}{5}$ with the Cuisenaire Rods and explain why the answer is $\frac{15}{16}$.

169. Do $\frac{4}{5} \div \frac{3}{4}$ with the Cuisenaire Rods and explain why the answer is $\frac{16}{15}$.

Dividing Fractions Using Pattern Blocks

Pattern Blocks can be used to show division of fractions. If the hexagon is defined as a unit, then the trapezoid could be shown to be $\frac{1}{2}$, the rhombus would be $\frac{1}{3}$, and the triangle would designate $\frac{1}{6}$. If you wanted to do $\frac{1}{2} \div \frac{1}{6}$, the question would be how many $\frac{1}{6}$s fit in $\frac{1}{2}$ or how many triangles fit in a trapezoid as shown in Fig. 2.78. You should take the time now to learn more about Pattern Blocks and how they can be used to show fraction operations.

Equivalent Fraction Division

Whole number division is difficult for students. Division of fractions is even more difficult because many students do not understand what division is all about, which is compounded by unclear impressions of fractions. Fraction division is also

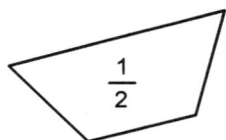
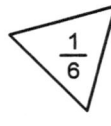
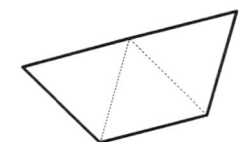

FIG. 2.78.

confusing for students because it does not look like division. They have learned to work division by using a format that looks like $6\overline{)42}$. Fractions can also be placed in that format for division. Introduce fraction division as *being easy to do* by taking a new, complex problem and expressing it in terms of familiar skills. Those old skills are finding the LCD, equivalent fractions, and using the familiar division format. Suppose the problem is $\frac{1}{2} \div \frac{1}{8}$. The LCD is 8, $\frac{1}{2} = \frac{4}{8}$, and the format would be $\frac{1}{8}\overline{)\frac{4}{8}}$. Now the question is *how many $\frac{1}{8}$s are in $\frac{4}{8}$* or, because the denominators are the same, *how many ones are in four?* The completed fraction division would be

$$\frac{1}{8}\overline{)\begin{array}{c}4\\ \frac{4}{8}\\ \frac{4}{8}\\ \hline 0\end{array}}$$

Assuming that students are familiar with division that results in remainders expressed as a fraction, the equivalent fraction process can be used for any fraction problem. A problem like $\frac{3}{4} \div \frac{2}{3}$ becomes $\frac{9}{12} \div \frac{8}{12}$ or $\frac{8}{12}\overline{)\frac{9}{12}}$. It does not take many problems in this format before students realize they could just do $8\overline{)9}$ and the new, seemingly difficult problem type is just like something that has been done many times before. Think about the idea of finding the LCD first and then dividing the numerators as just described. Does it make you wonder why division of fractions is not taught this way?

A problem like $\frac{3}{4} \div \frac{2}{3}$ becomes $\frac{9}{12} \div \frac{8}{12}$, but at this point the development could

vary. Rather than expressing it as $\frac{8}{12}\overline{)\frac{9}{12}}$, the students could express it as $\frac{9 \div 8}{12 \div 12} = \frac{9 \div 8}{1}$, which becomes $\frac{9}{8}$ or $1\frac{1}{8}$. You should notice (as should your students) that this acts a lot like multiplication of fractions.

Exercises

170. Do $\frac{4}{5} \div \frac{7}{8}$ using the equivalent fraction process. Make up at least two more fraction division problems where the denominators are unrelated and do them using the equivalent fraction process. After you have done at least those three problems, describe your feelings of the equivalent fraction division process.

171. Find a student (or adult not in your class) with the appropriate background to be dividing fractions and demonstrate equivalent fraction division. Describe their reaction to what you show them.

Error Patterns in Division of Fractions

Error patterns that occur in division fall into two basic types: inverting the first fraction rather than the second or arithmetic ones. Although the arithmetic ones are varied, they should be relatively easy to control and correct. Students sometimes lack adequate skills in dividing out common factors either after the fraction division problem has been converted to multiplication or in expressing the missing factor in terms of its equivalent, where the numerator and denominator are relatively prime.

The other error of inverting the first fraction rather than the second and then multiplying is also rather easy to control. First, it is important to do the problems concretely. That should lead the students to the conclusion of inverting the second fraction and multiplying. The second thing, and this is critical, is that when the rule for division is stated, the students should be encouraged to say "Invert the second fraction and multiply" as opposed to "Invert and multiply."

One objective of a modern mathematics education is to provide students with real-life examples. When asked to provide a real-life example of a fraction divided by a fraction (for now, exclude situations like $\frac{2}{1}$, where the denominator is 1), a common response involves "halving a recipe," which actually means to divide by two. In the desired context, a fraction divided by a fraction would be something like $\frac{3}{4} \div \frac{1}{2}$ or even $3 \div \frac{1}{2}$, where the factor is a fraction. Examples such as this are not easy to find, and yet the world is full of them.

Exercises

172. Discuss an error pattern different from those described in the text. Explain how you would help a student learn to avoid the error.

173. Find an example of a fraction divided by a fraction—something like $3 \div \frac{1}{2}$. For this assignment, dividing something in half would be like dividing by $\frac{2}{1}$, which is not acceptable.

DECIMAL OPERATIONS

Addition of Decimals

Students encounter decimals when dealing with money or using calculators. If a student has experimented at all with a calculator, the likelihood is great that decimals have appeared in some form. It could have been as division was explored, unless they were using a calculator that had been set to report the answer in terms of a remainder or a fraction (e.g., Casio *fx-65*). Perhaps the student was merely trying out the decimal point on the calculator.

As far as money is concerned, it is fairly certain that the student will have seen prices involving cent signs as a part of class work in the lower grades. It is equally likely that prices involving the dollar sign and decimal points have been encountered in different shopping environments. Given these exposures and other potential ones, the students generally come to decimals and decimal addition with some informal background and understanding.

Readiness

As a part of readiness for adding decimals, students should have a solid understanding of place value and the concept of regrouping. The students have probably already dealt with fractions. They need to be aware that decimals are another way of writing special fractions, in which the denominator is some power of 10. Fractions mean division. In the case of $\frac{7}{10}$, they should realize that $\frac{7}{10}$ means $7 \div 10$ or $7\overline{)10}$, which can also be expressed as 0.7. Calculators that have a "F<->D" key can be a great asset at this point. Enter a fraction like $\frac{3}{10}$ and then touch the "F<->D" key. The result will probably be 0.3 (some calculators might not put the zero in front of the decimal point).

In introducing decimals, there is a temptation to provide some oral drill to emphasize knowledge of place value. You would read something like, "Five thousand seven hundred ninety-eight and one hundred twenty-three thousandths." We suggest avoiding that practice. There is no question the students need to recognize that five thousand seven hundred ninety-eight and one hundred twenty-three thousandths is a word expression of 5,798.123. However, oral drill involving such statements sets students up for failure in some instances. First, consider your enunciation skills. Do you say things clearly enough that students are able to distinguish between thousands and thousandths? Certainly if you concentrate the difference is obvious. However, if you are in normal speech patterns, is it still so obvious? The students' listening skills are even more critical. After you have taught for a few days, you will become acutely aware of how students do not listen as well as we would like. Thus, when you start with thousands and thousandths, the opportunity for difficulty arises.

By the time students encounter a formalized approach to addition of decimals, they should have command of addition facts as well as some abstract process for doing addition. If the students are in control of these factors as well as the necessary basic exposure to decimals, addition with decimals should be relatively easy. Without an adequate background in addition, place value, and regrouping, the student could be destined to suffer some difficult times.

One additional factor that must be considered is related to place value. Traditionally, students have done ragged addition problems (3698 + 2 + 10 + 547) by being told to line up the ones. Besides relying heavily on an understanding of place value and the ones digit, which would align the ones as

3698
2
10
+ 547, the student still needs to under-

stand that there are unwritten zeros holding places in the problem. That is, some students struggle with what belongs in what column and thus are instructed to insert zeros so that the problem becomes

3698
0002
0010
+0547. At this point, alignment difficulties may be solved and what digits are involved in each column clarified. Some students are instructed to turn their paper sideways and use each space between segments as a column, as shown in Fig.

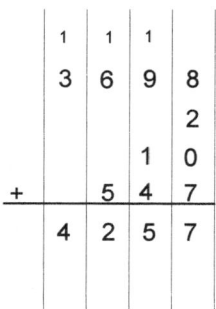

FIG. 2.79.

2.79. You could refer the students to a digital clock where 5 o'clock is shown as 05:00. Somewhere along the line, we stop writing all the extra zeros. Student understanding can be helped by asking how they write their own age. If a student is 9 years old, do they write 09? Their age could be written as 09, but we typically do not do this. Why not?

Before being ready to deal with addition of decimals, the students also must realize that 0.4 = 0.40. They should have encountered the idea that $\frac{4}{10}, \frac{40}{100}, \frac{400}{1000}$, and so on are equivalent fractions. If they have done that, and if the concept that $\frac{4}{10} = 0.4$ has been covered, the notion that

$$0.4 = \frac{4}{10} = \frac{40}{100} = \frac{400}{1000} = 0.4 = 0.40 = 0.400$$

should be relatively easy for the students.

In their whole number experiences, they have learned that putting zeros at the end of a number changes the number. Now they are hearing that it is permissible to put zeros at the end of a decimal value as long as they are on the right side of the decimal point. We understand that the decimal point makes a huge difference in the discussion, but students may not. Thus, this takes careful development, and the result will be much less confusing when adding ragged decimals, particularly when the instruction starts with manipulatives.

Exercises

174. Create a lesson plan using the calculator in a manner that will help students discover that fractions like $\frac{3}{10} = 0.3$.

175. What happens when you enter 0.700 in your calculator and touch =, enter, or EXE? Do this activity with a friend and explain the result.

176. Create a lesson plan to help students realize that $0.32 = 0.320 = 0.3200 = \dots$.

Sequence for Teaching Addition of Decimals

Before a sequence for addition of decimals can be created, the students must be in control of addition facts, regrouping, place value, addition of multidigit addends, addition involving addends with a varying number of digits, and the idea that $0.8 = 0.80 = 0.800 \dots$. With that background, addition of decimals is fairly easy.

Traditionally, students have been told that they merely needed to line up the decimal point and then proceed as if adding whole numbers. If they write a zero in front of the decimal point, there is no need for that rule. They learned to line up the ones in whole number addition. For a value like 0.6, the ones digit is zero. When lining up the ones, the decimal points are automatically lined up. This might not seem like a big deal to you, but if you use that with your students, you just eliminated one thing that has to be memorized. That helps your students.

Given the discussion about lining up the ones digits, the sequence for adding decimals is pretty much under control. It is assumed that the students have mastered whole number addition. If they have not, you should question why you are asking them to add decimals.

There is one new hurdle in addition of decimals assuming the students are ready. Ragged decimal values like $0.35 + 6.941 + 295.7$ can be a source of difficulty because of the missing zeros at the end of the addends. The students are accustomed to seeing the last digits aligned in vertical form. Look what can happen with the ending zeros missing and not lining up the ones digits.

$$\begin{array}{r} 0.35 \\ 6.941 \\ +295.7 \\ \hline \end{array}$$

Because they have dealt with the idea that $0.35 = 0.350$ and they elect to have an alignment for the right-most digit, it can be accomplished by inserting the appropriate zeros. The earlier example of $0.35 + 6.941 + 295.7$ would become

$$\begin{array}{r} 0.350 \\ 6.941 \\ +295.700 \\ \hline \end{array}.$$

This *should* look familiar to the students, except for the decimal point, but that too is an old issue.

Exercises

177. Suppose you have several students who struggle with addition of whole

numbers. How do you rationalize asking them to add decimals?

178. Do you think writing a decimal at the end of a sentence would cause problems for students? For example, find the sum of 43.6 and 9.2. Defend your position in writing.

Adding Decimals Using Calculators

The calculator has already been discussed as a means of introducing decimals to students. In fact, if students have the opportunity to use calculators, the likelihood is quite high that they will be asking about decimals before they work with them in the school curriculum. The reason for that is simple. They see decimal answers on their calculator when they experiment. Calculators: Don't leave home without them.

Adding Decimals Using Base 10 Blocks

Base 10 blocks work extremely well as you introduce students to addition of decimals. Rather than the small square being the unit, other blocks represent the unit. If you are adding 2.3 + 4.5, the long (we cannot call it the ten now because it is the one) could serve as the unit. Because the little square is one of 10 equal parts, or $\frac{1}{10}$, we have a means to express a part of

the whole. We would not use $\frac{1}{10}$, however, but rather we would use 0.1 because we are in decimals. Figure 2.80 shows how the Base 10 blocks would be used to show 2.3 + 4.5, with the long serving as the unit.

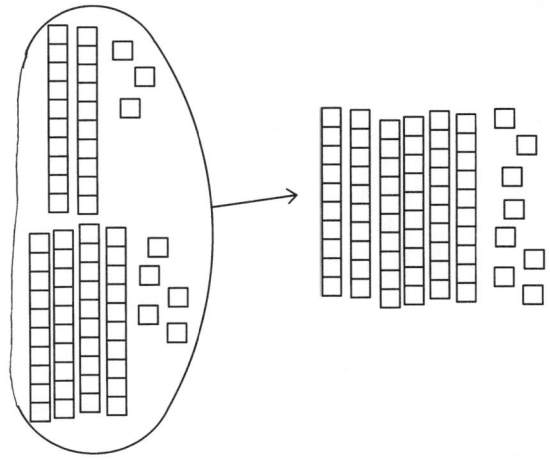

FIG. 2.80.

If the flat had been selected to serve as the unit, then one long would represent 0.1. Figure 2.80 would still look similar, but flats would replace the longs and longs would be where the small squares are. If we opted to use the flat as the unit, then 2.3 + 4.5 could be expressed as shown in Fig. 2.81. You should notice that "H," "T," and "U" are replaced with "F" (Flat), "L" (Long), and "C" (Cube), respectively. This is done because of the potential confusion that could stem from the idea that "H" represents 100, which is significant because the Flat now represents the unit.

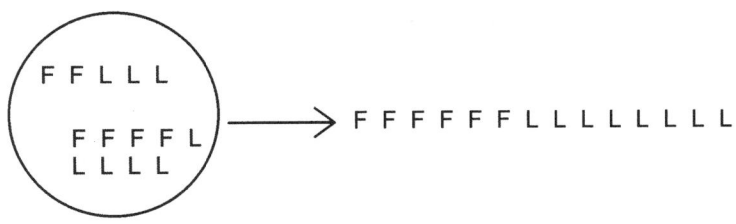

FIG. 2.81.

Using the Number Line to Add Decimals

The number line works for adding decimals, but it can become cumbersome in a hurry. Figure 2.82 shows 0.7 + 0.6, which is relatively easy to show on the number line. Look at Fig. 2.18 and you can see that the number line part of that figure is similar to Fig. 2.82. This comparison should convince you that the procedures for adding whole numbers and decimals on a number line are the same.

Although the students are older when they encounter addition of decimals, they still need the concrete exposure. Which manipulative you use is not nearly as important as the decision to use a manipulative. The students should progress rather quickly to the abstract stage of adding decimals because of prior exposure and readiness skills they bring to the process. However, the transition has to be at a natural pace for them. Forcing the issue too quickly could result in students having difficulty remembering how to add decimals.

Exercises

179. Do you agree that the statement "Calculators: Don't leave home without them" applies to you?

180. Do you agree that the statement "Calculators: Don't leave home without them" applies to your students?

181. Explain why your answers to the last two questions were the same or different.

182. Describe how you would use the Base 10 blocks to show 1.69 + 0.7 + 4.5.

183. Would you use the number line to demonstrate that the sum of 1.69, 0.7, and 4.5 is 6.89? Why or why not?

Alternate Methods for Adding Decimals

Assuming that the prerequisite skills discussed earlier in this chapter are within the capabilities of the students, there should not be a great need for alternate methods for learning to add decimals at this level. However, alternate methods could provide options for enrichment for some students who master the concept of adding decimals faster than their colleagues.

Exercises

184. Show how to do 6.86 + 0.94 + 7.35 using the scratch method for addition.

185. Describe how you would relate the Base 10 blocks to the partial sum method for adding 6.86 + 0.94 + 7.35

Error Patterns

The error patterns that appeared while adding whole numbers should be corrected by now. If that is not the case, then

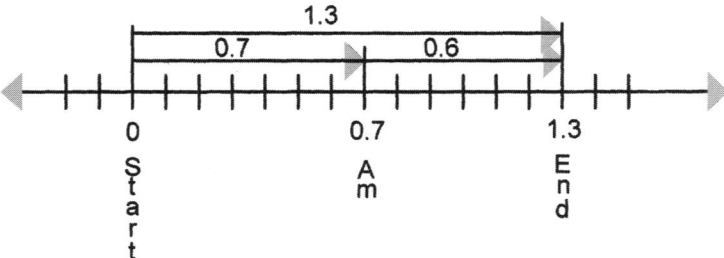

FIG. 2.82.

any of those behaviors could reappear. One additional error occurs when students encounter ragged decimal addition. They are accustomed to lining up the last digit when dealing with addends having varying numbers of digits (43 + 2,869 + 5). If the problem is 43 + 2.869 + 0.5, the students are given a new rule about lining up the decimal points. If they have been taught to line up the ones digits and to write 0.5 rather than the way it is frequently seen, there is no need for the rule about lining up decimal points. Thus, the risk of errors in addition of decimals is minimized by the assurance that the students have the appropriate readiness skills before embarking into the study of decimal addition.

Exercises

186. Suppose a student consistently gives the sum of problems like:

3.2 + 0.98 + 4.657 as 47.87
2.178 + 4.6 + 0.35 as 22.59
0.46 + 1.3 + 5.278 as 53.37

Describe the error being made, including how the decimal is being placed in the answer.

187. Outline how you would correct the error the student is making in the problems given in Exercise 186.

188. Describe how you would suggest introducing the addition of decimals to help avoid errors such as the one described in Exercise 186.

189. Suppose a student consistently gives the sum of problems like:

3.2 + 0.98 + 4.657 as 883.7
2.178 + 4.6 + 0.35 as 712.8
0.46 + 1.3 + 5.278 as 703.8

Describe the error being made, including how the decimal is being placed in the answer.

Subtraction of Decimals

As with the addition of decimals, subtraction undoubtedly will have been encountered prior to the formalized study of the operation. Good bets for exposure would still be in the realms of money and calculators. It is assumed that the concept about 0.7 = 0.70, = 0.700 . . . has been developed. Of course, typical subtraction error patterns will appear unless they have been resolved earlier in your students' school careers. Ragged decimal problems hold the potential to create specific problems.

Readiness

You should expect students to have command of subtraction facts, subtraction involving regrouping, place value, and the manipulative that will be used as a part of the instruction. Given this background, things should move rather smoothly. Without this background, how do you justify asking them to add decimals?

Sequence for Teaching Subtraction of Decimals

The sequence for subtraction of decimals should parallel that of whole numbers. It is assumed that the manipulative of choice will be available, although the students should move from the concrete to the abstract stage rather quickly. Initially problems like 0.8 − 0.5 should be done and generalized that the subtraction is essentially an application of known facts except for the presence of the decimal points. A concrete introduction similar to those used for whole number subtraction and decimal addition will facilitate the learning, too. For example, if, in a three-dimensional set of Base 10 blocks, Long is defined as the unit, then the little Cube represents 0.1. So, 0.8 – 0.5 becomes 8 Cubes – 5 Cubes, leaving 3 Cubes, just like with whole number subtraction. Figure 2.83 shows the take-away modeling of this problem.

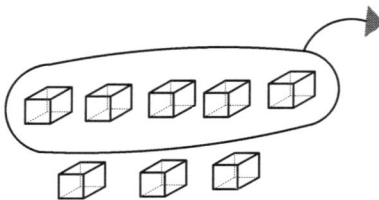

FIG. 2.83.

One potential source of difficulty is ragged decimals, especially in problems like 1.8 – 0.93. The idea of inserting the zero showing 1.8 = 1.80 and then regrouping the one and eight-tenths as one and seven-tenths plus ten hundredths is critical. That is, 1.8 = 1.7 + 0.10. So the problem becomes:

$$
\begin{array}{r}
1.8 = 1.7 + 0.10 \\
-0.93 = \underline{0.9 + 0.03} \\
0.8 + 0.07 = 0.87
\end{array}
$$

Again, the Base 10 blocks become an invaluable asset. If the students have the appropriate background with them, this should not be difficult. Without that concrete exposure first, however, you are asking for trouble.

Exercise

190. Develop a sequence for subtraction of decimals that incorporates all concepts from the basics through complete mastery.

Manipulatives for Subtraction of Decimals

As students experiment, a calculator provides them the opportunity to see what the answer is supposed to be. In many cases, students will correctly conclude that decimal subtraction is a lot like whole number subtraction. If the emphasis has been placed on lining up the ones place for the operation, there is not a need to discuss lining up decimal points. Furthermore, problems like 1.8 – 0.93 can be done, and many students will surmise it is a lot like 180 – 93, with the alignment taken care of automatically. Ironically this approach can amplify the idea that 1.8 = 1.80.

The number line could be used to show subtraction of decimals as is shown in Fig. 2.84, which is actually Fig. 2.24 with-

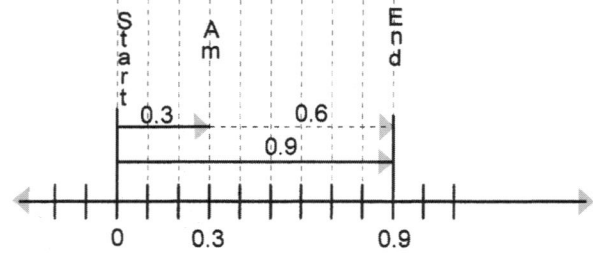

FIG. 2.84.

out the Cuisenaire Rods, and changes from 3 to 0.3 and 9 to 0.9. The number line could be used to show other problems, even ones like 1.8 – 0.93, but it would be a cumbersome task. The point is, it could be done.

The Base 10 blocks are most useful when dealing with decimal subtraction. If the students are familiar with using either egg cartons or Cuisenaire rods with fractions, they know that different pieces can be used to represent the unit. That knowledge is invaluable with Base 10 blocks and decimal subtraction. With that information, 4.2 – 0.89, which is shown in Fig.

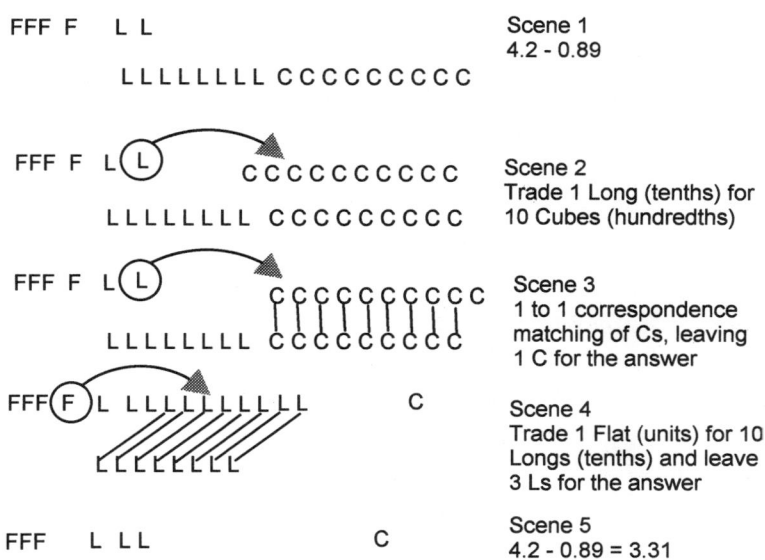

FFF F   L L   Scene 1
                                                4.2 - 0.89
      L L L L L L L L C C C C C C C C C

FFF F L Ⓛ   C C C C C C C C C   Scene 2
                                                Trade 1 Long (tenths) for
      L L L L L L L L C C C C C C C C C   10 Cubes (hundredths)

FFF F L Ⓛ   C C C C C C C C C   Scene 3
                                                1 to 1 correspondence
      L L L L L L L L C C C C C C C C   matching of Cs, leaving
                                                1 C for the answer

FFFⒻ L L L L L L L L L L L   C   Scene 4
                                                Trade 1 Flat (units) for 10
      L L L L L L L   Longs (tenths) and leave
                                                3 Ls for the answer

FFF   L L L   C   Scene 5
                                                4.2 - 0.89 = 3.31

FIG. 2.85.

2.85, becomes relatively simple to do, where the Flat is used to express the unit.

Look back to Fig. 2.25 and you will see a lot of similarities between it and Fig. 2.85. The Base 10 blocks can be used in a similar manner to do many decimal subtraction problems and lead students to the desired abstractions. This probably sounds like a broken record to you by now, but it is imperative that you provide your students with the concrete exposures at the beginning of each new topic.

Exercises

191. Show how to do $0.71 - 0.58$ on the number line.

192. Show how to do $0.71 - 0.58$ with the Base 10 blocks.

193. By now you should have formulated an opinion of which manipulative you prefer to use. Discuss why you have prioritized them as you have. Rationalize why it is necessary to be able to develop a concept using more than one manipulative.

194. Should more than one manipulative be used to develop a concept?

195. Describe whether you feel a calculator is a valuable tool for teaching the subtraction of decimals and why.

196. Describe how you would use a calculator to help students do a problem like $5.2 - 1.679$.

Error Patterns

Any of the error patterns that occur with whole numbers can reappear. That is another reason that it is so important to spot and correct the errors properly in the beginning. Problems like $4.7 - 1.635$ present a whole new opportunity for errors because of the unexpressed zeros in the hundredths and thousandths places of the sum (4.7). Even after those zeros are inserted, the difficulties associated with subtraction problems having sums ending in zeros can occur. In $4.700 - 1.635$, you could still use the idea of converting 4.700 to $4.699 + 0.001$ and reexpressing the problem as $4.699 - 1.635 + 0.001$. This avoids difficulties associated with regrouping in subtraction as was stated in the error pattern section dealing with subtraction of whole numbers. However, the complications associated with decimals might increase the degree of difficulty for some students.

Multiplication of Decimals

Decimal multiplication is not too difficult for many students. They probably will have experimented with calculators and perhaps even begun to formulate some conclusions about what is happening. We discuss methods for capitalizing on this background later. By now students should be aware of the idea that the world of mathematics is an ever-expanding collection of ideas that build on prior experiences. It is important that you help them see that each new topic adds power to their abilities to manage the world around them.

Readiness

Multiplication facts, multiplication algorithms, place value, decimal placement, insertion of zeros in decimals, and probably some exposure to money will likely all be a part of the readiness skills students need for succeeding with multiplication of decimals. Any weakness in those and related topics will only lead to difficulties in the new arena of decimal multiplication. Some old friends will show up too: number line, array method for multiplication, calculators, and the repeated addition definition for multiplication. Reminder exposures to these concepts could prove quite useful. Notice that, once again, this is a pretty direct hint that there is a need to begin with some sort of concrete exposure for multiplying decimals and then proceed toward the abstract as quickly as possible.

The students should be aware that there is a decimal point to the right of any integer. If that is not part of their repertoire, you need to spend some time es-

tablishing it. The idea is necessary for when decimal places will be counted in products involving decimal factors. To some extent, this becomes an extension of the ability to insert zeros after the last significant digit to the right of a decimal point (0.8 = 0.80 = 0.800 . . .), which is essential background information.

Sequence for Teaching Multiplication of Decimals

Assuming appropriate background understanding of multiplication, you should start with a whole number times a decimal—something like 4 × 0.3. This can easily be shown with the number line, an array, Base 10 blocks, or the calculator. The problem and answer should be recorded as each problem is completed. After doing a few like this, the students should conclude that they are multiplying the 4 and 3 like they always do. They should also realize that the product is changed only by the placement of the decimal point. At this juncture, it will not be clear to the students that they locate the decimal point by counting from the right. However, it is a beginning because they become aware of the need to have the decimal point in the answer.

Next the students should do problems like 4 × 0.03. Again, this can easily be shown with a number line, an array, Base 10 blocks, or the calculator. They should now realize that there are two decimal places in the problem and two in the answer. Because of the product being 0.12, they should conclude that the counting comes from the right. This is the first place that prior knowledge about each integer having an unwritten decimal point at the right end comes into play.

At this point, you could proceed to other problems like 6 × 0.27 or even 6 × 0.027. Notice, however, that the product is such that there is no need to insert a zero into it to accommodate the appropriate number of decimal places. That zero insertion problem type should be delayed until the students are more comfortable working with decimals in products. The careful sequencing presented here is essential if you want to provide the easiest, most efficient curriculum path by which your students will learn about multiplication involving decimals.

So far we have only dealt with two factors—where one was a whole number and the other involved a decimal. This process could continue to include problems like 4.2 × 3. This would amplify and strengthen the idea of placement of the decimal point in the product. Eventually you are going to need to consider problems where both factors contain a decimal part.

Problems like 0.3 × 0.4 are a reasonable place to start because they can easily be shown with an array. This concrete demonstration rationalizes why the decimal point is placed as it is in the product. This should not prove to be too much of a hurdle if the appropriate prior exposure to decimal products has been developed in a manner similar to what we have described. As in all the other problem types, the problem should be recorded along with the product as 0.4 × 0.3 = 0.12. Once some similar problems have been done, the students should arrive at the desired conclusion about the location of the decimal point in the product. This is the first exposure to decimals in both factors, so time needs to be taken to develop the idea of counting the number of decimal places in the problem to determine the number of decimal places in the product. You will probably need to do more than this one problem type to solidify the desired generalization. For example, you might want to do something like 0.7 × 0.43. If you establish the appropriate background early,

this generalization should develop rather quickly. Again, avoid any situation where there is a need to insert a zero at this time.

Eventually you are going to need to develop the ideas involved with problems like 0.2 × 0.3. Calculators can be used to generate the desired suspicions in your students. With appropriate background, students will quickly become aware of the need to have more digits to make the answer correct. This background is based on the generalization dealing with counting decimal places from the right-most digit in the product, and that the total number of decimal places in the two factors gives the number of decimal places in the product. The only thing missing is the idea of inserting a zero between the decimal point and the 6. They have seen it on their calculators. It is easily rationalized via the array. However, in all of their mathematical lives, students have been discouraged from adding digits to a number because of the impact on the answer. They have already experienced the ability to insert zeros in certain locations with decimals and whole numbers. This one is different, but you can develop it rather easily with the appropriate background.

With this last piece of information, students should now be able to derive the general rule that will work for multiplying any decimal values. That is, they count the number of decimal places in the factors and establish that many places in the product, counting from the right and inserting zeros to the right of the decimal point as needed to make the count come out correct.

Manipulatives for Multiplication of Decimals

The exposure to decimals on a calculator has been mentioned in both addition and subtraction of decimals. It becomes clear here, too. The students could use the calculator to do problems mentioned in the sequence section of this chapter. Doing this provides a lot of information and should raise suspicions about what the generalization should be for multiplication problems involving decimals. The more work you and your colleagues have done with these students on patterns and generalizations, the easier it will be for them to draw the appropriate conclusions.

If there is a need for a more concrete exposure, either the Base 10 blocks or the number line can be used for some basic problems. If the problem is 4 × 0.3, Fig. 2.86 shows how it would be done

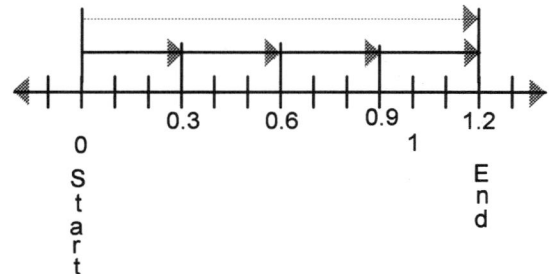

FIG. 2.86.

with the number line. Figure 2.87 shows how it would be done with Base 10

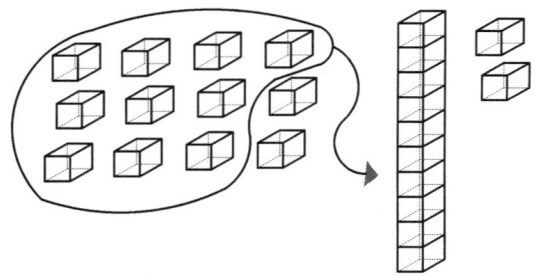

FIG. 2.87.

blocks. Both methods assume prior exposure to the manipulative. The Base 10 blocks would have defined a Long as the unit. Similar problems could be done with either manipulative, although the number line can become cumbersome rather quickly, and the Base 10 blocks may need to have the unit block redefined. At

this stage, most of the problem types can be shown concretely.

Excluding the calculator, the array is the best method for showing something like 0.2 × 0.3. For best results, it probably should be used to do other problems involving decimal factors unless the students are comfortable with using different manipulatives. Figure 2.88 shows the ar-

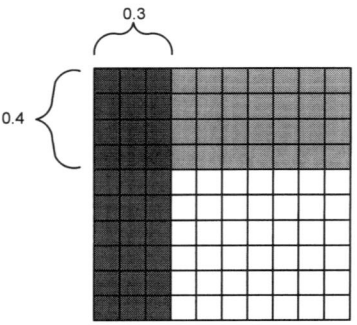

FIG. 2.88.

ray model being used with 0.3 × 0.4, whereas Fig. 2.89 shows how an array would be used to show 0.2 × 0.3. In both cases, each small square represents

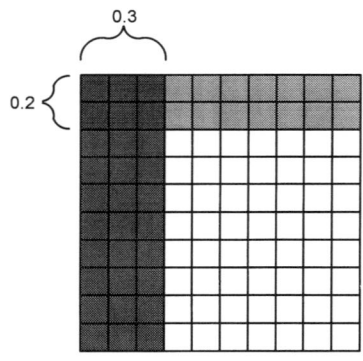

FIG. 2.89.

0.01. In Fig. 2.88, there are enough small squares that it is not necessary to insert a zero into the product. However, Fig. 2.89 shows the product of 0.2 × 0.3 as 6 little squares or 6 hundredths. The students should know that this represents 0.06. Thus, they need to conclude that a zero needs to be inserted appropriately in the product. Now the complete generalization for placement of the decimal point in a product for decimals can be developed. Of course, the students need to do more than these examples, and discussions need to be held about zero insertion, how many are appropriate, and their location. That is, the students need to understand that there is a rhyme and reason to inserting zeros in decimal products.

Exercises

197. Show how to do 4 × 0.6 on the number line.
198. Show how to do 12 × 0.3 with the Base 10 blocks.
199. Show how to do 0.2 × 0.4 on an array.

Alternate Methods for Multiplying Decimals

Given the concept of decimal location in products, any of the alternate methods for multiplication can be used with decimal factors. As was the case in whole number multiplication, these alternate methods could be used to enrich the understanding of students who quickly grasp the concept of decimal multiplication. Use of alternative algorithms would also show they work in environments other than whole numbers. Of course, one of these alternate ways might be the preferred method of multiplication for some student. Partial product can provide some interesting review of place value and zero insertion. Lattice multiplication is done exactly like it was with whole numbers. The only difference is decimal placement. Do not forget about Russian peasant multiplication or the simple halving doubling method. With this one, you would need to treat the factors as whole numbers for the sake of simplicity and then place the decimal at the

end of the work. Notice that this assumes the student already knows how to locate the decimal point in the product.

Exercises

200. Using Russian peasant multiplication to do 1.06 × 3.7, which factor would you select as the one to be halved and why?
201. Create a three-digit (hundredths) times a two-digit problem (tenths) and do it using partial product, lattice, and Russian peasant multiplication.

Error Patterns

Most multiplication errors should have been corrected by this time. However, there might be remnants of any of them, and so there is a need to watch carefully. The corrective procedures would be exactly the same as described when dealing with whole number multiplication. Multiplication of decimals introduces one new error pattern and that involves proper placement of the decimal point in the product. The correction involves elaboration of the generalizations discussed previously about decimal location in the product.

Division of Decimals

More than likely, the students have gotten beyond division with no remainder in their work with fractions. If that is the case, decimal division is easier to master. Is it reasonable to put the words *division* and *easy* in the same sentence? Without exposure to division with remainders, decimal division is still manageable for many students if they have appropriate introductions to it. Remainders in division must be considered because sometimes a problem with a remainder makes sense and sometimes it does not. For example, if you are talking about dividing a dozen cookies between eight children, each child can get a cookie and a half or 1.5 cookies. On the other hand, if you are talking about dividing a dozen ball bats between eight children, a bat and a half does not make much sense.

One idea that needs discussion is the appropriateness of problem expectations. There is no question that students need to do division problems by hand. There is debate over how much is enough, however. Just as with whole number division, the facts are a foregone conclusion. Certainly it would seem reasonable for a student to do something like 3.8 ÷ 2 mentally regardless of the format $\left(2\overline{)3.8} \text{ or } \frac{3.8}{2}\right)$. Similarly, it would seem unreasonable to expect a student to do 43.81025 ÷ 796.38624 by hand. Somewhere between those two problems is a cutoff point at which the calculator becomes acceptable and necessary.

Exercises

202. Provide a written defense of your position on what is an appropriate problem type to permit students to use calculators when doing decimal division problems.

203. Assume that your position for permitting the use of calculators in decimal division differs from that of your department, school, district, or state standards. What do you do and why?

Prior to starting division with decimals, the students need to be well founded in the basics of division, place value, equivalent fractions, rounding, approximation, estimation, multiplication, and subtraction. The assumption is that they are function-

ing well beyond introductory levels with each of these concepts. If the students have encountered equivalent fractions, division of decimals can be broken into four categories: $\frac{whole}{whole}$, $\frac{decimal}{whole}$, $\frac{whole}{decimal}$, and $\frac{decimal}{decimal}$. With fraction background, each of these four problem types can be expressed as $\frac{whole}{whole}$ through equivalent fractions achieved by multiplying both the numerator and denominator of the given fraction by an appropriate power of 10. Actually, the students will soon realize that the only necessity is to have the denominator of the fraction be a whole number. That is equivalent to moving the decimal point the appropriate number of places in both the factor (divisor) and product (dividend), like you probably learned to do sometime earlier in your academic career.

Sequence for Teaching Division of Decimals

The ultimate objective in teaching students how to divide decimals is to have them generalize how to move the decimal points in the factor and product to yield the algorithm you probably use, which is essentially dividing something by a whole number. As long as there is a remainder of zero in division, the situation is not overly difficult. In division of whole numbers, we discussed problems that only have a remainder of zero. Now there is a need to go beyond that. The idea that division problems always have a remainder of zero should be unrealistic to students, particularly if they think at all about their lives in which they encounter situations where items are divided equally between participants and there are some extras. Initially that excess is expressed as a remainder, then as a fraction, and finally as a decimal. The idea of a remainder is fairly easy to grasp. If the students have encountered fractions, they more than likely will have seen excess expressed in terms of a half. Given that, conversion of that half to 0.5 is a relatively simple task, and the stage is set for decimal division involving situations that have nonzero excess.

Look back at the sequencing section on division of whole numbers and any one of those problems could be done with decimals rather easily. Even something like $78\overline{)735.54}$ does not present much of a challenge, *IF* the student knows how to divide and has an inkling of where to place the decimal point in the missing factor (quotient). A problem like $7.8\overline{)73554}$ may present a little bit of a challenge because of the need to reset the decimal point in the factor and in the product. However, if the students have been exposed to equivalent fractions, even this is a relatively simple task. The problem can be restated as:

$$\frac{73554}{7.8} = \left(\frac{73554}{7.8}\right)\left(\frac{10}{10}\right)$$

$$= \frac{735540}{78} \; .$$

At this point, the problem is similar to what was encountered earlier in the curriculum when dividing with whole numbers. The only hurdle is to determine what to multiply the fraction by. Basic knowledge of decimal multiplication by powers of 10 quickly reduces this to an almost trivial level.

Any decimal division problem can be treated in a similar manner. The students do need to be made aware of the impact on the decimal point when both the numerator and denominator (factor and product, respectively) of a fraction are multiplied by a power of 10. More than likely, you were taught the rule that said to move the decimal point to the right end in the factor and then move it the same number of places in the product. Multiplying the numerator and denominator by the same power of 10 explains why that motion is appropriate. The only other clarification that is needed involves amplification of the idea that there is a decimal point at the right end of any whole number. That ending decimal point might need to be inserted in the product to provide proper placement of a decimal point in the missing factor of a division problem involving decimals.

Exercises

204. Make up a problem involving a whole number divided by a decimal. Explain how to convert your problem to one where it is a whole number divided by a whole number.

205. Make up a problem involving a decimal divided by a decimal. Explain how to convert your problem to one where it is a whole number divided by a whole number.

206. Is it necessary to convert all problems involving a decimal divided by a decimal to one involving a whole divided by a whole? Why or why not?

Manipulatives for Division of Decimals

As discussed with whole numbers, manipulatives can be used with division, but they become cumbersome quickly because of the magnitudes involved. The calculator is a wonderful ally at any stage of learning, but that is particularly true with division of decimals. An organized set of decimal division problems done with a calculator, where the problem and results are recorded and analyzed, can lead students to the generalization about moving the decimal point in division problems.

Error Patterns

All the error pattern potentials that existed with whole number division may still show up. The hope is that these errors would have been corrected and thus moot points. Location and movement of decimal points in division provide fertile ground for errors, particularly involving left to right or right to left and from where to commence the counting. Aside from those rather standard errors, you almost need to carefully examine a student's work to determine exactly what is happening.

INTEGER OPERATIONS

Addition of Integers

By the time students consider addition of integers, they should be well versed in the addition of whole numbers. They should have been exposed to the addition of fractions. They probably have even worked some with the addition of decimals. Now with integers, they see signed numbers (positive or negative) as well as the operation sign, plus (+).

For years, the students have done $4 + 3 = 7$. With integers, we make a big deal about rewriting the problem as $^+4 + ^+3 = ^+7$. Teachers typically insist that the students say "*Positive* four plus *positive* three equals *positive* seven." We do that to help them prepare to deal with addition problems involving negative numbers. We know that, but the students do not. Eventually we tell the students that

there is no need to worry about saying "*Positive* four plus *positive* three equals *positive* seven." We allow them to revert to saying four plus three is seven because everyone knows the numbers are positive if there is no sign present. Some students have got to be thinking, "Why don't they make up their minds? First I do it without signs; then they insist I say positive; then they say to not worry about the signs." Students do have a point. It is imperative that we are clear as we present integers to them.

Readiness

Integer addition is difficult to accomplish if the students are not proficient with addition of whole numbers. Ironically, they have to be proficient at subtraction of whole numbers as well because addition of integers with opposite signs involves subtraction.

Addition of integers is a binary operation as was the case with addition of whole numbers. More than two addends can be considered, but no matter how capable the students are, they can only deal with two addends at a time. Once the sum of two addends is determined, that sum becomes one addend and the next addend would be considered. For example, in $^+4 + ^+3 + ^+6$, the student would do $^+4 + ^+3 = ^+7$ first and then $^+7 + ^+6 = ^+13$. Of course, some might prefer to do $^+4 + ^+6 = ^+10$ first, but still only two addends are dealt with at any one time. One source of confusion is that, in $^+4 + ^+3 = ^+7$, the students are dealing with a *positive* three *plus* a *positive* four yielding a *positive* seven. The *positive* sign of the number can be confusing for some students.

Finally, it is helpful if the students have exposure to the number line prior to considering adding integers. Although there are methods for adding integers that involve colored chips (one color for positive and another for negative), we will focus on using the number line, which, we believe, is the most beneficial way to approach addition, subtraction, and part of multiplication of integers. With the chips, the students must remember which chip is positive and which is negative and then develop a set of rules for working with the chips that later must be translated to abstractions. The number line transitions are easier and more natural for students.

Exercises

207. Describe your impression of the concept of addition of integers at this point. Include a discussion of whether you think it is hard or easy to learn and why you hold that position.

208. What do you think about the idea that we have students adding positive numbers in the early grades, then insist that they insert the signs, and later tell them not to worry about the signs?

Sequence for Adding Integers

Initially, the existence of negative numbers has to be established. Traditionally this is done with discussions about temperature (Florida students have trouble thinking in terms of below zero), below sea level (Colorado students have trouble identifying with this), debt (most students will know the word, but might not have an understanding of the concept), or above or below ground level. There are many other means for developing the idea of positive and negative numbers. You need to select one (or more) that your students can identify with.

There are four problem types involved in the addition of integers:

$$^+4 + {}^+6 = {}^+10$$
$$^-4 + {}^-6 = {}^-10$$
$$^+4 + {}^-6 = {}^-2$$
$$^-4 + {}^+6 = {}^+2$$

Problems where the addends have the same sign should be considered first and then generalized. You probably generalized the rule to be "When adding numbers with like signs, add the absolute values (number without the sign) and give the answer the common sign." After that conclusion is drawn, deal with problems involving addends of opposite signs and generalize them. You probably say something like, "When adding numbers with unlike signs, subtract the smaller absolute value from the larger absolute value, and give the answer the sign of the larger absolute value." The generalizations you say are fine, but you do need to figure out a means to help your students arrive at the same conclusions, and you should not just tell them the rules.

Building those two generalizations is not too difficult. Give the students several problems (using the calculator or number line) where the signs of the addends are the same. The addition of positive values should be easy for them. They should notice that when adding two negative values, the answer is the sum of the two addends, but the sign of the sum is negative. With those conclusions, the generalization of adding *like normal* and giving the sum the sign of the addends develop quickly.

After completing the work where the signs of the addends are the same, introduce problems where the addends have opposite signs. Initially the absolute values of the addends should be relatively small so there is little opportunity for students to be distracted. As students do problems like $^+5 + {}^-3 = {}^+2$, focus on the numbers involved and ask how a two can be derived out of a five and a three. They should tell you it comes from $5 - 3 = 2$. At that point, develop the idea that $5 - 3 = 2$ and $^+5 + {}^-3 = {}^+2$ are two different ways of doing the same problem. They should conclude that the sign of the second number is changed, and the operation is changed from addition to subtraction. You have to be careful about letting students say they are subtracting the little number from the big one because that will not always be true.

Finally, approach problems like $^-5 + {}^+3 = {}^-2$. Here again the students will essentially be doing $5 - 3 = 2$, but the operation is changed from addition to subtraction. The answer gets the sign of the larger absolute value, which is what happened before, but it was not immediately as apparent in the earlier example. Again you need to focus the discussion on the two problems and how the two different ways of doing the problem can be interchanged. Ultimately the students should conclude that when adding numbers of opposite signs, they should subtract the smaller absolute value from the larger absolute value and give the answer the sign of the larger absolute value.

You might ask why we discuss integers and absolute value to the extent we do in an elementary education book. It is imperative that your knowledge base exceed that which you are teaching.

Exercises

209. Describe two different ways you would introduce the idea of negative numbers to your students. Include a discussion about why you feel your selections would be good to use with students.

210. Create a set of problems that you would use to teach students that, when adding numbers of like signs, they add and give the sum the common sign. Develop an outline of the lesson that would be used with the problem set.

211. Create a set of problems you would use to teach students that, when adding numbers of unlike signs, they subtract the smaller absolute value from the larger absolute value and give the answer the sign of the larger absolute value. Develop an outline of the lesson that would be used with the problem set.

Tools for Adding Integers

The calculator can be an ally when teaching students about adding integers. Give them problems grouped as described earlier (adding integers with the same signs and then adding integers with opposite signs). Have the students write each problem and the associated answer. As they look for patterns, they should generalize the rule for adding integers with the same signs and integers with different signs. If they are accustomed to looking for patterns and generalizing, this should go rather quickly.

With colored chips, suppose Blue is positive and Green is negative. The problem $^+2 + {}^+3$ is translated to be 2 Bs put together with 3 more Bs, giving 5 Bs or $^+5$. The students should not need to do many problems like this to become comfortable with the idea that adding two (or more) positive integers yields a positive integer for the sum. Using Gs for problems like $^-2 + {}^-3$ should lead to a similar conclusion for negative addends. At this point, the students should combine these two ideas into one generalization, stating that when the signs of the addends are the same the sum is determined by regular addition and holds the common sign of the addends.

Sums of opposite signed addends are relatively easy to show with colored chips

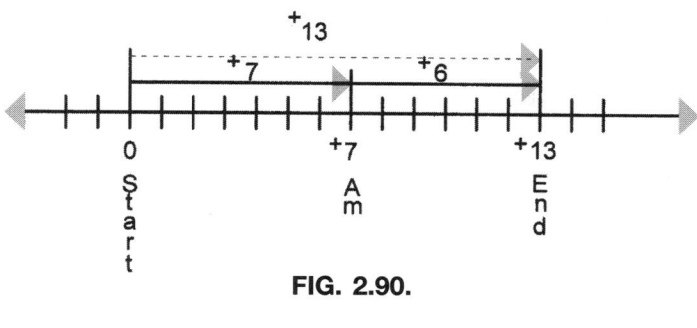

FIG. 2.90.

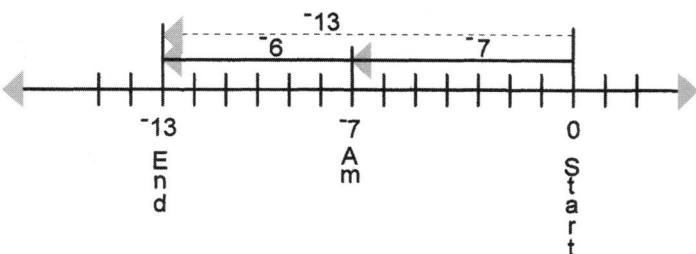

FIG. 2.91.

too. The students must realize that a B and a G together counterbalance each other or yield zero. Given that, $^-2 + {}^+3$ would be expressed by 2 Gs and 3 Bs. However, 2 Gs could be paired with 2 Bs and they would be the same as zero, leaving only one B as the sum. That would then be interpreted as $^+1$, showing that $^-2 + {}^+3 = {}^+1$. Similarly, $^+2 + {}^-3 = {}^-1$ because, after the paring, one G would be left. At this point, you would develop the generalization in the manner described earlier.

The number line is also an effective way to develop the rules for adding integers. Figure 2.90 is a duplication of part of Fig. 2.18 without the Cuisenaire Rods. As you look back at Fig. 2.18 and compare it with Fig. 2.90, you should notice that the only difference is the presence of the signs of the numbers in $^+7 + {}^+6 = {}^+13$. The process for doing the problem on the number line is exactly the same as with whole numbers. Figure 2.91 shows $^-7 + {}^-6 = {}^-13$ on the number line. This too should be easy for the students if they have had prior experience with adding whole numbers on the number line. Of course, the problem $^-7 + {}^-6 = {}^-13$ is dependent on the creation

of the negative part of the number line. It is imperative that they have experience on the number line for addition if it is going to be used with subtraction of integers. Short of patterning, the number line is the only way to show subtraction of integers effectively at a concrete or semiconcrete level.

The sum of addends with opposite signs still needs to be shown on the number line to build the other generalization. Figure 2.92 shows $^+7 + {}^-3 = {}^+4$ on the number line. Notice that the first addend is $^+7$ and the second is $^-3$, resulting in the positioning at $^+4$. The only thing left is to determine how to get from where you start (0) to where you end up ($^+4$). In this case, you travel four units in the positive direction, yielding a sum of $^+4$.

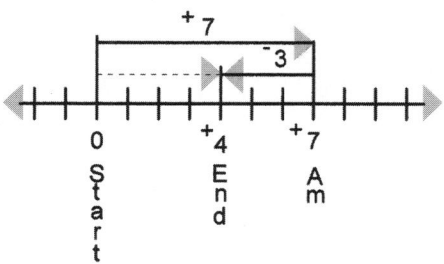

FIG. 2.92.

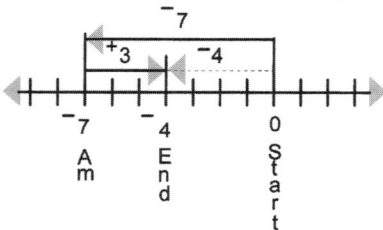

FIG. 2.93.

The companion problem to $^+7 + ^-3 = ^+4$ is $^-7 + ^+3 = ^-4$. Figure 2.93 shows how it would be done on the number line. Here, the first addend is $^-7$ and the second one is $^+3$, resulting in ending up at $^-4$. The student should conclude that, as they start at 0 and go four units to the left or negative direction, they arrive at the sum $^-4$. Doing a variety of these problems should lead to the conclusion that the smaller absolute value is subtracted from the larger and the answer is given the sign of the larger absolute value.

Exercises

212. How could absolute value be explained to your students?
213. Describe how the calculator could be used to help develop generalizations about adding signed numbers.
214. Do $^+7 + ^+3 = ^+10$ on a number line and write a lesson plan to introduce your students to finding the sum of two positive integers.
215. Do $^-7 + ^-3 = ^-10$ on a number line and write a lesson plan to introduce your students to finding the sum of two negative integers.
216. Describe how you would use problems like $^+7 + ^+3 = ^+10$ and $^-7 + ^-3 = ^-10$ along with the number line to help your students generalize that, when adding two integers with the same signs, add the absolute values and give the answer the common sign.

217. Do $^+9 + ^-3 = ^+6$ on a number line and write a lesson plan to introduce your students to finding the sum of a positive and a negative integer.
218. Do $^-9 + ^+3 = ^-6$ on a number line and write a lesson plan to introduce your students to finding the sum of a negative and a positive integer.
219. Describe how you would use problems like $^+9 + ^-3 = ^+6$ and $^-9 + ^+3 = ^-6$ along with the number line to help your students generalize that, when adding two integers with opposite signs, subtract the smaller absolute value from the larger and give the answer the sign of the larger absolute value.

Subtraction of Integers

Subtraction of integers may seem strange to students. One interpretation of the rule says that, to subtract integers, you change the sign of the second number and follow the rules for addition. However, the rule for addition of integers with unlike signs states that you subtract. So, to subtract, you think add, which really involves subtracting some of the time. You probably said those last three sentences are pretty confusing and yet that is what you were taught. IF students develop the ideas for subtraction of integers on the number line, calculator, or with colored chips, the rule about changing the sign of the second number and adding is relatively easy for them to generate and comprehend. There is a message in that last statement. Did you get it? Concrete introduction is critical.

Readiness

At this stage, it is assumed the students understand integers and the meaning of associating a sign with a number. It is further assumed that they have successfully added integers. Of course, they need to be adept at working with whole numbers for all operations, but particularly with addition and subtraction. Given that, they should be ready to encounter subtraction of integers.

Sequence for Subtracting Integers

At this level, sequencing is not much of a factor. The goal is to have them establish the idea that, when subtracting integers, you change the sign of the second number and follow the rules for addition of integers. Within that setting, the four problem types the students will encounter are:

$$^+8 - {}^-3 = {}^+11$$
$$^-8 - {}^+3 = {}^-11$$
$$^+8 - {}^+3 = {}^+5$$
$$^-8 - {}^-3 = {}^-5$$

Students should complete problems like $^+8 - {}^-3 = {}^+11$ and $^-8 - {}^+3 = {}^-11$ first. After rewriting the problems for addition, they ultimately involve adding numbers with like signs. As they are done on the number line, calculator, or colored chips, do several of each type. As the students do them, they should record the problem and answer. After several are listed, ask the students how they can get 11 out of 8 and 3 (or whatever the numbers would be), ignoring the signs of the number for the time being. Once that is established, ask them how they can get $^+11$ out of $^+8$ and $^-3$. They should conclude that they need to add a $^+3$ to a $^+8$ to get $^+11$. What they really said was that they needed to change the sign of the second number and add. You will need to help them formalize the verbalization of this concept, but the basics are there. The discussion and development for problems like

$^-8 - {}^+3 = {}^-11$ would be similar with appropriate sign changes in the discussion.

Next deal with problems such as $^+8 - {}^+3 = {}^+5$ and $^-8 - {}^-3 = {}^-5$. The development should come from work with the number line, calculator, or colored chips. Once several problems of each type are done, the discussions will be similar to those used when doing problems like $^+8 - {}^-3 = {}^+11$ and $^-8 - {}^+3 = {}^-11$. However, the question now focuses on how they can get $^+5$ out of $^+8$ and $^+3$. You may elect to deal with the situation without signs at first, as suggested earlier. Ultimately, the students should conclude that, to make the numbers match what they are seeing from their work with the calculator, number line, or colored chips, the sign of the second number has to be changed and then the rules for addition are to be followed. You need to ensure that the students understand what is happening.

Exercises

220. Create a problem set to help students generalize a rule for dealing with problems like $^+8 - {}^+3 = {}^+5$ and $^-8 - {}^-3 = {}^-5$. State the generalization you expect them to generate from these problems.

221. Create a problem set to help students generalize a rule for dealing with problems like $^+8 - {}^-3 = {}^+11$ and $^-8 - {}^+3 = {}^-11$. State the generalization you expect them to generate from these problems.

222. Explain how the two generalizations developed in Exercises 220 and 221 can be stated as one generalization for the subtraction of one integer from another.

Tools for Subtracting Integers

We focus on the number line, colored chips, and calculator to develop the concept of subtracting integers. You should not assume that these are the only ways to develop the idea. We are merely presenting the position we think are the easiest for the students to understand. Any of the colored chips, calculator, or number line activities involve the student doing several problems similar to either $^+8 - {}^+3 = {}^+5$, $^-8 - {}^-3 = {}^-5$, $^+8 - {}^-3 = {}^+11$, or $^-8 - {}^+3 = {}^-11$, recording the problem and answer, and then drawing conclusions.

The number line is a powerful tool for showing how to determine the missing addend in the subtraction of integers. The problem $^+3 - {}^+8 = ?$ is rewritten as $^+8 + ? = {}^+3$. Figure 2.94 shows what this would look like on the number line. The

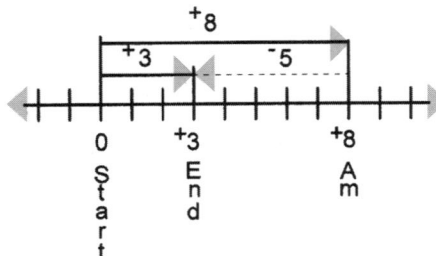

FIG. 2.94.

addend is $^+8$ and locates where you are. The sum of $^+3$ tells you where you want to

finish. Your number line task is to show how to get from where you are to where you want to finish. In this case, you move $^-5$ or 5 spaces in a negative direction, which is the missing addend.

All number line subtraction problems would be done in a similar fashion and would be explained in a similar manner. You have an addend and a sum and are looking for the missing addend. In each case, you locate the addend and that shows where you are. You locate the sum, which shows where you want to finish. Your task is to summarize the movement needed to get from where you are to where you want to end up in terms of how many spaces are used and the direction of the motion. Figure 2.95 shows $^+8 - {}^-3 = {}^+11$, while Fig. 2.96 shows $^-8 - {}^+3 = {}^-11$. As stated earlier, you need to do several problems of each type with your students on the number line and then help them derive the desired algorithm from those examples.

The process would be similar with the calculator. You would give the students several problems of each type (one type at a time) to do on the calculator. Each problem and the result would be re-

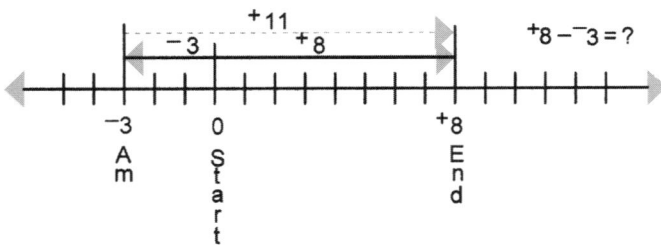

FIG. 2.95.

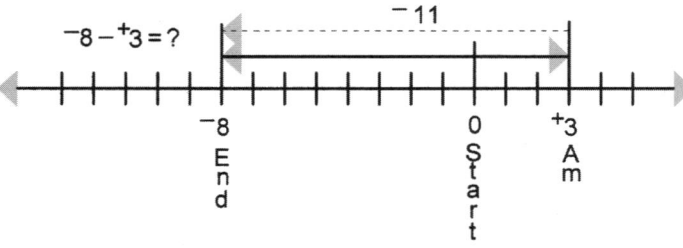

FIG. 2.96.

corded. After several problems of a given type are recorded, discussion would focus on what has happened with the numbers that would yield the indicated result. As a generalization from a problem type is added to the list, attempts could be made to compile generalizations into one bigger generalization. Ultimately the students should conclude that the rule about changing the sign of the second number and adding works for all integer subtraction problems.

The colored chips present an interesting way to look at subtraction of integers. In the process, a concept that is quite valuable in future mathematics work can be formulated. It involves the idea that zero can be expressed in a multitude of convenient ways. With the colored chips, the students need to realize that a positive (Blue) and a negative (Green) counterbalance each other or give a net result of zero. When additional chips of a given color are needed to solve a problem, adequate pairs of chips representing zero can be inserted.

With the chips, subtraction is viewed as a take-away model. Thus, to subtract, chips need to be taken away. Suppose you had to do $^+2 - {^+5}$ with the colored chips. You would start out with 2 Bs to represent the $^+2$. However, the problem indicates that you need to remove 5 Bs and you only have 2. The dilemma is resolved by inserting three zeros in the form of three Bs and three Gs. Now you have a set consisting of 5 Bs and 3 Gs. This allows you to remove 5 Bs. That leaves 3 Gs, which are interpreted as a negative three. Thus, $^+2 - {^+5} = {^-3}$ has been shown with the chips. As discussed earlier, you need to have students do several of each type and then draw conclusions about that particular type of problem.

Consider $^+2 - {^-6}$. The need is to remove six Gs. To generate the 6Bs that need to

be subtracted, 6 Bs and 6 Gs should be placed with the already existing 2 Bs. Now you have 8 Bs and 6 Gs; the negative six that needed to be represented can be removed, leaving 8 Bs, which represents a positive eight.

Exercises

223. Do $^-8 - {^-3} = {^-5}$ on the number line and with chips and explain your answer.

224. Do $^-5 - {^+8} = {^-13}$ on the number line and with chips and explain your answer.

225. Describe how you would lead a class to the generalization for changing the sign of the second number and following the rules for addition when dealing with the subtraction of integers.

226. Create a lesson plan covering each of the four problem types for subtracting integers represented by colored chips or by the number line. Be sure to include detailed examples and questions that would lead to the desired generalizations.

Error Patterns

Error patterns involving the subtraction of integers generally involve incorrect signs, omission of signs, or difficulty with subtraction. A more elaborate discussion of fundamental subtraction error patterns is found in whole number subtraction. Manipulative foundation, along with precise work as the concepts are developed, and an emphasis on paying attention to what is being done generally solve many of the problems.

Multiplication of Integers

There are only two conclusions students need to generate when considering multiplication of integers. If there is an even number of negative factors, the product will be positive; if there is an odd number of negative factors, the product will be negative (assuming none of the factors is zero). These both should develop relatively quickly assuming the students have the appropriate background. Some would argue that we should just tell the children the rules. However, that makes them dependent on an outside source for their knowledge. Certainly students cannot create all mathematics, and they will be told many things. Our goal is to teach them to think through things on their own by providing them with a variety of reasonable exposures. Generalizations such as we discuss here are within the capabilities of elementary school students, and the value is much greater than simply telling them the rules.

Readiness

By the time the students get to multiplication of integers, they *should* have mastered their multiplication facts. They *should* be adept at using a multiplication algorithm. They *should* be familiar with working with signed numbers. The hope is that they *should* have some background with the number line, colored chips, or calculator through addition and subtraction of integers. If all of that holds true, multiplication of integers is not too difficult. With this in mind, it is still prudent to provide a quick review of addition and subtraction of integers before introducing multiplication and the repeated addition model for multiplication because that can be one of the methods used to explain multiplication of integers.

Sequence for Teaching Multiplication of Integers

If the students possess the appropriate readiness skills to deal with the multiplication of integers, the size of the factors is not significant. Thus, it is not unreasonable to deal only with single digits. It generally does make the learning a little easier for the students because the focus can be on the signs of the factors as opposed to multiplication skills.

Because multiplication of integers is a binary operation, we focus on using two factors. If more than two factors are involved, the product of two factors must be found first. Then that product becomes one of two factors that generates a new product, until all factors are considered. For example, when finding the product of $^-2 \times {}^+4 \times {}^+5$, you find the product of $^-2 \times {}^+4$, which is $^-8$. Then you find the product of $^-8$ and $^+5$, which is $^-40$. So if the students know how to deal with two factors, they should be able to work with more than two rather quickly. With that assumption in mind, multiplication of integers requires consideration of four problem types:

positive times positive,
positive times negative,
negative times positive, and
negative times negative, taken in that order.

If the students have ever dealt with multiplication as repeated addition, multiplication of two positive factors has already been done. They should have completed a problem like $4 \times 3 = ?$ The only difference now is that the problem is $^+4 \times {}^+3 = ?$ This does create one interesting dilemma, however, and it is essentially the same thing that was presented earlier. The students have found the product of 4 and 3 to be 12, and now they find the product of $^+4$ and $^+3$ to be $^+12$. They may have also heard statements like, "Any time a number does not have a sign, it is positive" or "If the number does have a positive sign with it, the sign could be left off because it is *understood*." So all along they have known that 4 × 3 = 12, and now they learn that $^+4$ × $^+3$ = $^+12$. Students question the need to include the signs of the numbers because the answer is really 12. We insist that the sign be included because we know they will need the sign when they get to problems involving negative factors. Ironically, as with addition of positive addends, we soon tell the students that the signs can be ignored in multiplication if everything is positive. No wonder they get confused.

Following the positive times a positive problem types with a positive times a negative is significant. The ability to show a positive times a negative on the number line in a manner similar to what could be used to show the product of two positive factors is important. The students should quickly be able to generalize that a positive times a negative yields a negative product because of experiences with repeated addition with negative addends.

Assuming the students have dealt with the commutative property of multiplication on whole numbers, they probably suspect there is a commutative property for multiplication on integers. With that in mind, a negative factor times a positive factor can be *commuted* into a positive factor times a negative factor. Therefore, three of the four problem types are done.

The fourth problem type, which involves two negative factors, presents a little more of a challenge to explain to students. One way to get students to the point of knowing that a negative factor times a negative factor yields a positive product involves using a calculator and problem sets that involve generalizing from several answers *known to be right*. Care must be taken to ensure that the signs of the factors are properly entered and considered as the problems are done. Doing problems like

$$^-4 \times {}^-3 = {}^+12$$
$$^-5 \times {}^-7 = {}^+35$$
$$^-2 \times {}^-3 = {}^+6$$

should quickly lead students to conclude that when two factors are negative the product is positive.

Patterning is another way to develop the idea that a negative factor times a negative factor yields a positive product. The assumption is that the students know how to do the other three integer multiplication problem types when they get to the following problem set. The students need to make the comments beside each problem type as they are completed in front of the class. Each time from the second problem on, there is a comparison between the respective problem and the preceding one as the written words (or some similar statements) are uttered by the group.

$^-6 \times {}^+6 = {}^-36$

$^-6 \times {}^+5 = {}^-30$ Comparing this line with the previous line, the students would say: 1st factor stays the same; 2nd factor decreases by 1, product increases by 6.

$^-6 \times {}^+4 = {}^-24$ 1st factor stays the same; 2nd factor decreases by 1, product increases by 6.

$^-6 \times {}^+3 = {}^-18$ 1st factor stays the same; 2nd factor decreases by 1, product increases by 6.

$^-6 \times {}^+2 = {}^-12$ 1st factor stays the same; 2nd factor decreases by 1, product increases by 6.

$^-6 \times {}^+1 = {}^-6$ 1st factor stays the same; 2nd factor decreases by 1, product increases by 6.

$^-6 \times 0 = 0$ 1st factor stays the same; 2nd factor decreases by 1, product increases by 6.

$^-6 \times {}^-1 = {}^+6$ 1st factor stays the same; 2nd factor decreases by 1, product increases by 6.

The set of problems needs to be long enough so that the students reflexively (and probably sounding quite bored) say, "Stays the same, decreases by one, increases by six" phrases. The reasoning behind the length is that, by the time they get to $^-6 \times {}^-1 = {}^+6$, they will say the words without thinking. BANG! They just got a positive product out of two negative factors. Now the discussion should shift to the idea of patterning and how it has to continue as you rationalize this unusual revelation.

Two final generalizations can be developed after all four integer multiplication problem types are done. One is that if the two factors have the same sign, the product is positive. The other generalization is that if the two factors have different signs, the product will be negative. These can then be extended to the conclusion that if the number of negative factors in a multiplication problem is even, the product is positive, and if the number of negative factors in a multiplication problem is odd, the product is negative (assuming none of the factors is zero).

Exercises

227. Outline a lesson on how to introduce a problem like $[(^-3 \times {}^-4) \times {}^-5] \times {}^+2 = ?$

228. Do the sequence of problems with students that started with $^-6 \times {}^+6 = {}^-36$ and ended with $^-6 \times {}^-1 = {}^+6$ with someone. As you do it, focus on their reaction to the comments that are made as any problem is compared with the preceding one. Write your reflections to their responses and actions.

229. Describe how you would convince students that $^-7 \times {}^+4 = {}^-28$.

230. Describe how you would convince students that the product of two factors with the same sign is positive.

231. Describe how you would convince students that the product of two factors with opposite signs is negative.

Manipulatives for Multiplication of Integers

The idea of using a calculator to do problem sets to stimulate generalizations is one important approach used to assist students to deal with the product of two integers. Another alternative focuses on the number line.

The number line is a good tool for showing many operations. However, it works well for only part of multiplication. Figure 2.97 shows how the number line

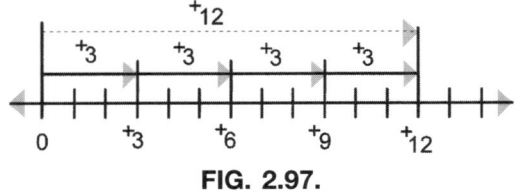

FIG. 2.97.

can be used to deal with problems like $^+4 \times {}^+3 = {}^+12$. Essentially, it shows the same configuration that appeared in Fig. 2.27 except that Fig. 2.97 deals with integers rather than whole numbers. Because the whole numbers are non-negative integers, they should look the same.

Figure 2.98 shows $^+4 \times {}^-3 = {}^-12$, the only other problem type involving the product

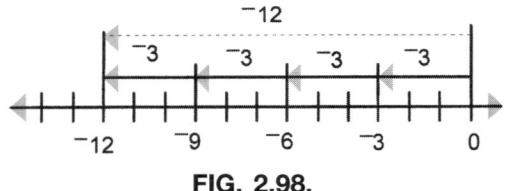

FIG. 2.98.

of two integers that can be shown on the number line. You are looking at four sets of negative three in $^+4 \times {}^-3 = {}^-12$, which is for all practical purposes a mirror image of $^+4 \times {}^+3 = {}^+12$ reflected at zero on the number line. Problems like $^-4 \times {}^+3 = {}^-12$

cannot be shown on the number line because it requires a negative four sets, which does not make sense. The same reasoning would be used for problems like ⁻4 × ⁻3 = ⁺12.

The colored chips could be used to show ⁺4 × ⁺3 = ⁺12. Using the set definition for multiplication, this problem represents putting together four sets of positive three. If Blue represents positive, then the student would have four sets of three Bs. Compiling all of the chips yields 12 Bs or ⁺12, and the problem is completed. Remember, the students need to do several problems of this type before concluding that a positive times a positive is a positive.

The product of a positive and a negative would be done in a similar manner to that of a positive times a positive. If the problem is ⁺3 × ⁻6, the student would need three sets of ⁻6 or three sets of six Gs. Combining all of the chips would yield 18 Gs or a product of ⁻18. Several problems of this type would need to be done to lead the students to the appropriate conclusion.

When it was mentioned earlier, you should have been thinking that the "commutative property of multiplication on the set of integers" approach was rather abstract. The colored chips can be used to approach the problem from a concrete vantage point. The zero idea comes into play again. Suppose the problem is ⁻3 × ⁺2. This indicates that three sets of positive two need to be taken out of the situation. But you do not have any chips to work with yet. As many as necessary can be inserted by using the zero idea. Because there is a need for a ⁺6, insert six zeros. Now the ⁺6 can be removed in the form of six Bs, leaving six Gs. Because the necessary action has been accomplished, the problem is completed, and the six Gs represent the answer, which is also ⁻6.

Finally comes the product of two negative factors. The colored chips could be used here as well. Suppose the problem being considered is ⁻3 × ⁻4. The problem indicates that three sets of negative four must be removed. Using the zero idea, three sets of negative four can be inserted into the situation, but they would be accompanied by three sets of positive four because each negative is generated from a zero that is represented by a positive and a negative pair. Now that the necessary 12 Gs are present, they can be removed and the requirements of the problem are satisfied. The removal of the 12 Gs leaves 12 Bs, which represent the conclusion of the problem or ⁺12.

Exercises

232. Do ⁺3 × ⁺5 = ⁺15 on the number line.
233. Do ⁺3 × ⁻5 = ⁻15 on the number line.
234. Outline a lesson that would use the calculator to help students generalize that if the signs of two factors are the same, the product is positive.
235. Outline a lesson that would use the calculator to help students generalize that if the signs of two factors are different, the product is negative.
236. Create a lesson plan covering each of the four problem types for multiplying integers represented by colored chips. Be sure to include detailed examples and questions that would lead to the desired generalizations.

Error Patterns

Initially we assumed that the students have had adequate experience with multiplication of whole numbers before embarking on multiplication with integers. Given that, the error patterns that develop with integer multiplication revolve around sign errors. Most often, the errors stem from ignoring a sign or two and considering the factors like whole numbers. By taking the time to carefully develop the concepts concretely as described throughout this chapter, many of the potential errors associate with multiplication of integers can be alleviated.

Division of Integers

Division causes frustration for all ages. When signed numbers are involved, the despair is not as bad because generally long-hand division is not involved. The ultimate goal is to arrive at the generalization that, in division, if the signs are the same, the answer (missing factor) will be positive, and if the two signs are opposite, the missing factor will be negative. These are the same generalizations that were developed in multiplication of integers.

Readiness

We must assume the student knows the division facts and has dealt with multiplication of integers before encountering division of integers.

Sequence for Teaching Division of Integers

The division of integers follows the same path as that of multiplication. First you deal with problems in which the signs of the numbers are the same and reach a generalization. That is, you first introduce

problems like, $^+4\overline{)^+20}$ or $\dfrac{^+20}{^+4}$ and $^-4\overline{)^-20}$ or $\dfrac{^-20}{^-4}$, concluding that when the signs are the same the sign of the missing factor will be positive. After that, deal with problems in which the signs of the numbers are different and reach a generalization. Include examples such as, $^-4\overline{)^+20}$ or $\dfrac{^+20}{^-4}$ and $^+4\overline{)^-20}$ or $\dfrac{^-20}{^+4}$, concluding that if the numbers involved in the division are of opposite signs, the missing factor will be negative.

Manipulatives for Division of Integers

The calculator is the most efficient method to use for helping students discover the generalizations involved with division of integers. You should give them four different problem sets. First, introduce, model, or explain problems like $^+4\overline{)^+20}$ or $\dfrac{^+20}{^+4}$ only and have students list the problem and the answer. When enough have been done, they should state their conclusion in writing. Next, introduce problems such as $^-4\overline{)^-20}$ or $\dfrac{^-20}{^-4}$ only and have them list the problem and the answer. Once again, when enough problems have been completed, they should state their conclusion in writing. After they have finished both of these problem sets, they should combine the two conclusions into one that deals with division problems, where the signs of the two numbers involved are the same. This should come quickly because they will have generated a similar conclusion with the multiplication of integers.

After the students have done the problems with the signs of the numbers being the same, they should do the third set of problems like $-4\overline{)^{+}20}$ or $\dfrac{^{+}20}{^{-}4}$. (They could do problems like $^{+}4\overline{)^{-}20}$ or $\dfrac{^{-}20}{^{+}4}$ first.) They should list the problem and the answer. When enough have been done, they should state their conclusion in writing. Finally, they should work on problems like $^{+}4\overline{)^{-}20}$ or $\dfrac{^{-}20}{^{+}4}$ (or $^{-}4\overline{)^{+}20}$ or $\dfrac{^{+}20}{^{-}4}$). Once again, when enough have been done, they should state their written conclusion. After they have completed the third and fourth problem sets, they should combine the two conclusions into one that deals with division problems in which the signs of the two numbers involved are opposite.

When considering division with the colored chips, remember that you are given the product and one factor, and that you are looking for the other factor. Realizing that a product is generated by two factors and being familiar with multiplication of integers makes the situation relatively easy. If you had $^{+}12 \div {}^{+}3$, the problem could be interpreted as $^{+}3 \times ? = {}^{+}12$ and the answer is apparent from the known facts about multiplication of integers. Answer "How many sets of positive three chips are needed to make $^{+}12$?" and you have what you need. If the problem had been $^{+}12 \div {}^{-}3$, the question becomes, "How many sets of what kind of chips need to be taken out to leave a total of $^{+}12$?" In this particular case, you would need to take out three sets of $^{-}4$. Because there are no negative chips to start with, you would need to use 12 zeros to get the necessary chips to be removed. When they are taken out, you are left with 12 Bs, which represent the $^{+}12$.

It is relatively easy to show $^{-}12 \div {}^{+}3$ with the chips. You need to decide how many chips go into each of three sets that will be put into your situation, leaving a total of $^{-}12$, so you would use three sets of $^{-}4$. However, if the problem is $^{-}12 \div {}^{-}3$, the question focuses on how many chips in each of three sets must taken out to leave 12 Bs. There are none to start with, so you need to use enough zeros to get the necessary number of Bs to remove. You will have 12 Bs and 12 Gs, but when you remove the three sets of 4 Bs each, you are left with the desired 12 Gs.

Exercises

237. Create a lesson plan that includes a pair of problem sets for division where the signs of the two numbers involved in the division are the same. Describe in the lesson plan how the problem sets could be used within a class period to lead the students to this conclusion: When the signs of the numbers in a division problem are the same, the missing factor is positive.

238. Create a lesson plan that includes a pair of problem sets for division where the signs of the two numbers involved in the division are opposite. Describe in the lesson plan how the problem sets could be used within a class period to lead the students to this conclusion: When the signs of the numbers in a division problem are opposites, the missing factor is negative.

239. Create a lesson plan covering each of the four problem types for dividing integers represented by colored chips. Be sure to include detailed examples and questions that would lead to the desired generalizations.

Error Patterns

The error patterns for dividing integers are not unique. All errors that occurred in the beginning of division as discussed in whole numbers may still surface. Furthermore, errors related to signed numbers are possible as well.

NUMBER NOTATION

There is more to mathematics than the mastery of addition, subtraction, multiplication, and division. As students progress through the elementary curriculum, they learn a great deal of new mathematics, some of which is dependent on the four operations on some set of numbers. For example, it is extremely significant for children to learn multiplication prior to determining the least common denominator (LCD) of two numbers. As students continue to progress and learn more mathematics, they inevitably encounter larger numbers.

Calculators in the Classroom

As students move through the mathematics curriculum, they begin to solve problems involving larger numbers. Many times the concepts being taught have nothing to do with the operations being performed. For example, finding the area of a rectangle requires the multiplication of two numbers. The goal is for the student to use square units, not to teach how to find the product of two numbers. Suppose a student found the area of the rectangle in Fig. 2.99 to be 182 in² and explained that the area was determined by multiplying the length by the width, which

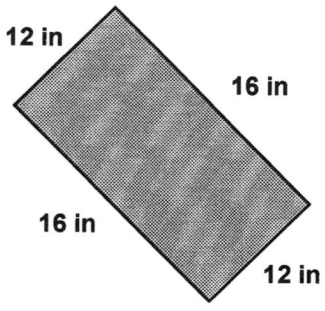

FIG. 2.99.

are 16 and 12 inches, respectively. If the problem is worth five points on a quiz, how many points would you deduct? Determining the area of the rectangle is the focus of the assessment. Does this student understand the process? Because the actual answer is 192 in², should any points be deducted? It appears as if there might just be a computational error. That can happen to anyone. Is the emphasis here on the process of finding the area or getting the arithmetic correct? Do not misunderstand, correct arithmetic is essential, but it is not the only thing in the elementary curriculum that is important.

As the magnitude of the numbers continues to increase, a controversial topic slowly creeps into the mathematics curriculum—the calculator. As mastery of basic facts is completed as well as a comfort level of doing addition, subtraction, and multiplication of two- and three-digit numbers, the use of technology for computations begins to show merit. We use technology to do the arithmetic because we have mastered the basics (barring arithmetic errors from time to time) and are dealing with larger concepts where arithmetic skills are assumed. Can't the same be said of our work with students?

If you used to do arithmetic, how can you justify that your students perform operations on large numbers by hand, *assuming they have mastered the basics*? Are calculators unavailable to them because you were not permitted to use them when you were in school? Many parents feel that if it was good enough for them, then it must be good enough for their child. That is only just beginning. How are you going to justify calculator use to the parents? How do you sell the school administration? What happens if there is a school rule that says no calculators in the classroom?

Once children learn basic computational skills and have an understanding of the algorithm being used, what is gained by repeatedly performing operations on larger numbers? It does take up time in the day! Like it or not, calculators and computers are here to stay. In the real world, businesses are looking for people who can collect data, analyze information, and make informed decisions from this process. They are not looking for people who can do arithmetic. Technology does that! Maybe the issue is not when technology should be used, but when technology should not be used.

Exercises

240. At what grade level should children begin to use calculators?

241. If you are in an interview for your first teaching position and a principal asks you for your position on the use of calculators, what will you say?

242. When should technology not be used in the elementary curriculum?

Expanded Notation

When students learned place value, standard notation and expanded notation were introduced. Standard notation allowed the student to connect place value with our Hindu Arabic numeration system. For example, the number 247 is in standard notation and can be displayed using Base 10 blocks as shown in Fig. 2.100. You can ask a student to divide the Base 10 blocks into individual sets as shown with the dashed line segments in Fig. 2.101. This activity will help the student make a connection between standard and expanded notation.

Ask the students to determine the number represented by the hundred squares in the leftmost set (200) followed by the number represented by the tens (40) in the center set and lastly the number represented by the unit squares (7) in the

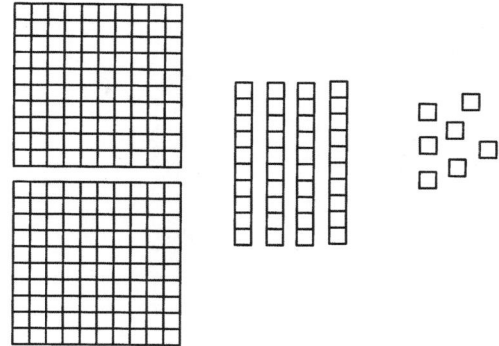

FIG. 2.100.

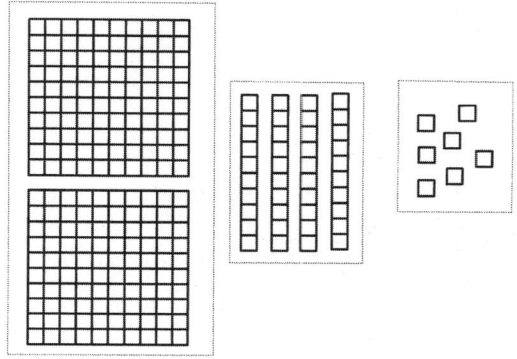

FIG. 2.101.

right set. This total can be written as 200 + 40 + 7 in expanded notation. It is extremely important for students to concretely work with expanded notation to build a strong foundation for place value. This will make the transition to larger numbers much easier. As the concept of place value is absorbed and connected to expanded notation, the Base 10 blocks activity can be taken one step farther.

Have the students take out a piece of paper and a set of Base 10 blocks. Students could work in pairs. Instruct the children to turn their paper in a landscape or hot dog position. Then ask the students to use the manipulatives to represent 265 across their paper and write the expanded notation below each section as shown in Fig. 2.102. Now have the students draw a line segment between the types of Base 10 blocks as shown in Fig.

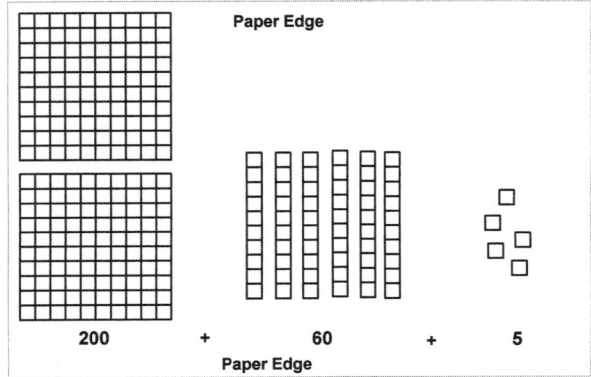

FIG. 2.102.

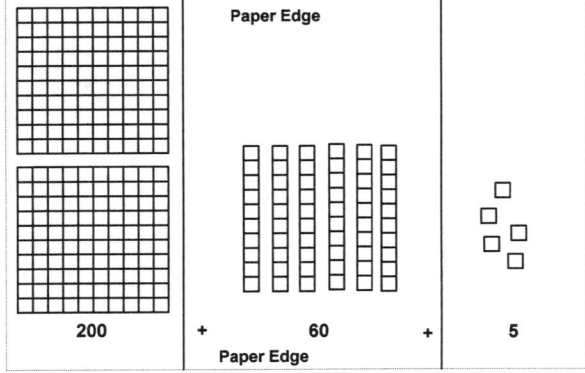

FIG. 2.103.

2.103. These dividing segments allow students to individually work with the hundreds, tens, and ones places.

If multiplication has been developed, children can begin to make the connection that 200 + 40 + 7 can also be represented as 2 × 100 + 4 × 10 + 7 × 1. Ask the student how many blocks are in the hundreds place. Because there are two hundreds blocks, 200 can be rewritten as 2 × 100. This should make sense to the students as long as the proper foundations of multiplication were developed, such that 2 × 3 was introduced as two sets of three. Similarly, 2 × 100 should be two sets of 100. Have the students write 2 × 100 below 200 on their sheet so they can visually make the connection between the Base 10 blocks (concrete representation), 200, and 2 × 100. Have the

students continue the task by determining and writing 6 × 10 below 60 to represent six sets of 10. Finally, instruct the children to complete the process by determining how many units are in the rightmost set by writing 5 × 1 to represent five sets of one each. Figure 2.104 can be used to help students make a connection

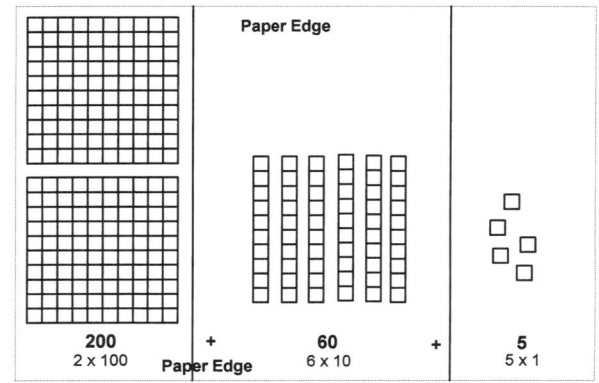

FIG. 2.104.

between the manipulative and the notation representing a given number.

It is important to provide a multitude of examples for the students as well as ample time to allow them to see the relationship. Please provide time for the majority of students to see the connection between the manipulative and expanded notation. Notice that we said the *majority* of students. We are not suggesting that you only need to teach to the majority, but unfortunately you may not be able to spend 5 days teaching a concept when the majority of students have mastered the skill. This is one of the reasons that many students dislike mathematics. They tend to find it boring because they are asked to repeatedly complete the same tasks reviewing the same topics after they have mastered them. You will need to move on for the majority of the students and still provide time for those students struggling to make the proper learning association. This can be difficult to manage and do.

Learning centers throughout the room provide an excellent avenue for reteaching difficult material. Those students who have mastered certain topics could work at centers on cooperative or individual skills involving previously learned material. Several TAG exercises in this text would serve as center material and activities. They also provide enjoyment and growth for students who have mastered a topic while allowing you the opportunity to work with others who are having difficulty with a concept. This time will give you a better chance to make individual observations and diagnosis.

Exercises

243. Outline an idea for a learning center that would promote the concept of standard and expanded notation.

244. Make a list of inexpensive replacements for Base 10 blocks.

Exponents and Exponential Notation

Because place value tends to be a difficult concept for many students to master, it is important that you provide a multitude of strategies and activities allowing students to confidently develop the idea. As students progress through the development of the concept of place value, they eventually need to deal with *exponential notation*, which requires knowledge of *exponents*. After learning the facts, students typically deal with multiplying by tens. To introduce exponents, begin by reviewing multiplication by tens and powers of 10. For example, ask students to complete an exercise like:

3 × 10

8 × 10

4 × 10

15 × 10

12 × 10

26 × 10

Before long, many students will say they simply affixed a zero at the right end of the non-10 factor to obtain the product. In a follow-up question, you would ask what is 10 × 10 and how would they use the "putting a zero on the end" idea with that problem. Because 10 happens to be the other factor here as well, you can attach a zero on the right end of 10 to get 100 for 10 × 10. What is 100 × 10? Because you are multiplying by 10, the product will be 100 with another zero attached to the right side, yielding 1000. It would be good for students to confirm that their quick way does work by using technology or an algorithm to compute the answer. Would you recommend a calculator for this particular problem?

Many students find multiplying by 10 to be a quick mathematical feat. Wouldn't it be great if we could find a way to capitalize on this confidence? In 10 × 10, students should notice two tens are involved and in 100 they should notice two zeros are involved. A parallel discussion could be developed with 100 × 10 as 10 × 10 × 10, or 3 tens and the product 1000 having 3 zeros in it. The process would continue in a similar manner with larger factors and products. The goal is to stimulate a new way to write what these problems are showing (two tens as factors and two zeros in the product, three tens as factors and three zeros in the product). Once again, patterning is present. Now a shortcut way of writing 10 × 10 is equivalent to 10^2, where 10 is called the *base* and 2 is labeled the *power* or *exponent*. If 100 is equivalent to 10 × 10 and 10 × 10 is equivalent to 10^2, then what can be said about 100 and 10^2? Students need to see the connection between 100 and 10^2. Ask about the meaning of the 2 in 10^2. Your students are liable to suggest ideas like 10^2 means 10 × 10 or 10^2 means the number has two zeros, which connects to the idea that 100 has two zeros in it. If your students buy into that, then 10^1 will be easy because the number that yields 10 can only contain one zero. Therefore, 10^1 equals 10. This can also help initially justify that 10^0 equals one because one is 10 with zero zeros.

When introducing exponents, have students complete exercises like: Change the number in standard form to one using only factors of tens and then to a number using exponents. Explain why your use of exponents makes this number equivalent to the original number.

1000
100
10000
10
100000

By having students write an explanation of their process, you can get a better diagnostic idea of their comprehension of exponents. When introducing exponents, be sure to begin with powers of 10 and do not rush to attempt other numbers until the idea with tens as factors is mastered. As you do this development with your students, you are establishing critical background essential for the development of algebra.

Exercises

245. Show why 5^0 is one.
246. Is anything to the zero power one?

As the development of exponents progresses, students are ready to make the connection among standard, expanded, and exponential notation. Have students take out a sheet of paper and Base 10 blocks once again. This activity is similar to the one used to develop Fig. 2.104.

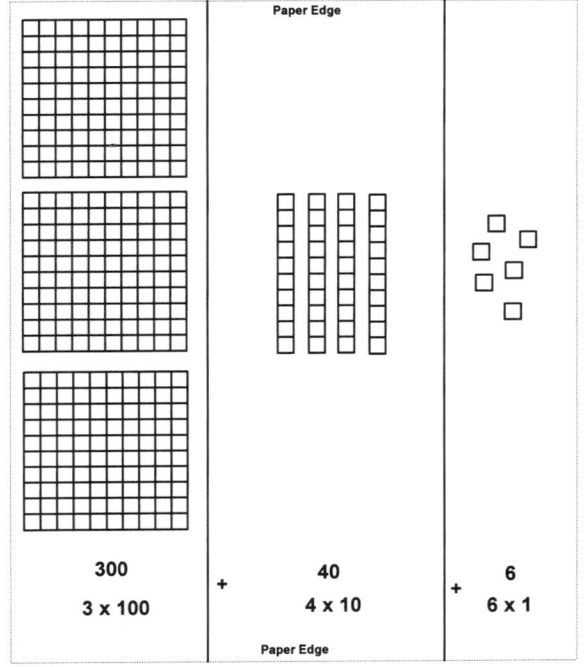

FIG. 2.105.

Have students use Base 10 blocks to represent 346 on a landscaped piece of paper. Also have each student draw a line segment separating each place into its own section. Students need to write the number represented in each section below the Base 10 blocks and its expanded form as shown in Fig. 2.105.

The next task is to have students represent 100 using only exponents and write the new representation of 300 below 3×100 in the hundreds place. Then have each student represent 10 in the tens place using only exponents and write the new representation below 4×10. Last, repeat this process for the units place. The final result should look similar to Fig. 2.106. This activity allows the student to make the connection among the Base 10 blocks, standard notation (346), expanded notation ($3 \times 100 + 4 \times 10 + 6 \times 1$), and exponential notation ($3 \times 10^2 + 4 \times 10^1 + 6 \times 10^0$). We urge you to allow your students multiple concrete opportunities to develop the connections provided by these activities.

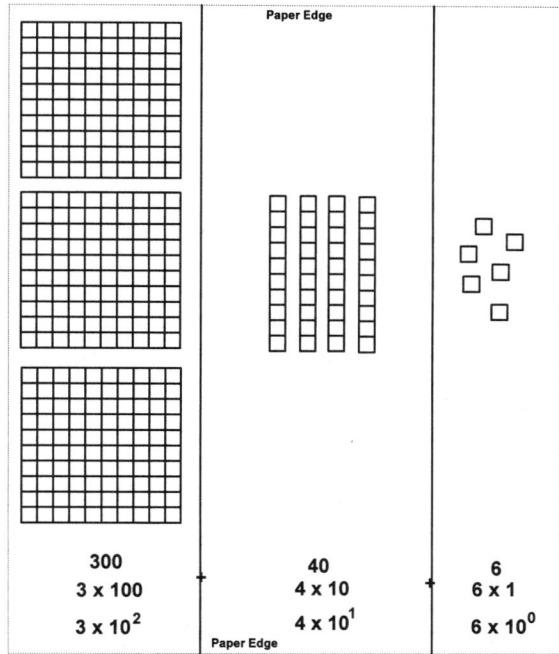

FIG. 2.106.

These connections are extremely important in mathematical development for middle school and beyond.

Conclusion

Although children come to school with a variety of experiences, they are unaccustomed to formal educational settings. It is your responsibility to provide them with solid beginnings and traverse from concrete to abstract thinking as they learn to operate with numbers. Your attitude, excitement, emphasis of concrete beginnings, encouragement, and guidance will combine into a powerful influencing force for the rest of your students' lives.

Operating with numbers is not easy. The examples discussed here are only a part of the picture. Similarly, a clear sequence that pays attention to small details as influenced by the readiness and ability levels of your students needs to be established. You should work *concretely* with problem types different from those described to ensure that you can create the necessary learning environment that is most productive for your students. Practice these skills now. You will be extremely busy when you start teaching as a full-time profession.

REFERENCES

Brumbaugh, L. S. (1994). *Scratch your brain where it itches*, Book A-1. Pacific Grove, CA: Critical Thinking Press & Software.

Bureau of Engraving and Printing. (1998). Facts and trivia. [http://www.bep.treas.gov/forum.cfm 6/1/98]

Exploring math concepts. (1995). Atlanta, GA: International Business Machines Corporation.

Hatfield, M. M. (1994, October). Use of manipulative devices: Elementary school cooperating teachers self-report. *School Science and Mathematics, 94*(6), 303–309.

Hughes, M. (1993). *Children and number*. Cambridge, MA: Blackwell.

Hutchings, B. (1976). Low-stress algorithms. *Measurement in school mathematics, 1976 yearbook*. Reston, VA: National Council of Teachers of Mathematics.

Teaching Children Mathematics. Reston, VA: National Council of Teachers of Mathematics.

3
Algebra in the Elementary Classroom

FOCAL POINTS

- The Beginnings of Algebra
- Laying the Foundation for Algebra
- Integrating Algebra in the Elementary Classroom
- Formulas
- Formulas for Elementary Mathematics

Consider the following problem, which is rich in algebraic opportunities (as well as many others). Pete and Repeat are traveling the 96 miles from Pahokee to Holopow on their bikes. Pete can average 8 miles per hour (mph) and Repeat can average 12 mph. Show on the following chart how far they each would be after 1, 2, and 3 hours, respectively.

Pahokee  Holopaw

Algebra is often thought to be a specific subject area studied in the middle school and beyond. Realistically, components of algebra begin to appear early in the curriculum, if only in a problem like $2 + 3 = ?$ Algebraically, this might be expressed as $2 + 3 = x$, but that difference is not major. Similarly, the study of subtraction facts written in the form $? + 4 = 7$ gives strong direction toward an algebra-based solution involving subtracting 4 from both sides of the equation to determine the missing addend. The moral of the story, then, is that algebra and related opportunities to provide critical groundwork for your students abound in the elementary school curriculum. We ask that you regularly scan the material you are working through with your students to determine algebraic connections and use that information to enhance your students' learning opportunities.

Place the information about the travels of Pete and Repeat into the table.

Hours	1	2	3	4	5	6		
Pete								
Repeat								

Questions such as the following should be asked about the information in the table or graph to stimulate the foundations of algebraic thinking.

Describe a pattern for each row of the table.

How far from Pahokee is each rider after 3 hours?

How long will it take each rider to travel 24 miles?

After Repeat gets to Holopaw, how long will it take Pete to get there?

Write an explanation of how you got your answer.

If H is the number of hours traveled and M is the distance covered in miles, write a rule that shows the relation between M and H for each rider.

Use the rule you just devised to show how far each rider can go in an hour.

How far would each rider go between Hour 4 and Hour 5?

If it is 96 miles from Pahokee to Holopaw, how long will it take each rider to make the trip?

If you join Pete and Repeat on the bike trip between Pahokee and Holopaw and you know M = 11H shows your rate of travel, what does the 11 tell you about how you travel?

What question would 96 = 12H answer?

What question would D = (8)(14) answer?

Exercises

247. What mathematical content could be covered in the Pete–Repeat example?

248. What pedagogy could be covered with the Pete–Repeat example?

249. What NCTM Standards 2000 are covered in the Pete–Repeat example?

Believe it or not, algebra did not simply appear within the last 60 years. Some students probably wonder what really smart person discovered this mathematics that required us to use letters instead of numbers. Many might question why we always have to find the missing x rather than d, Q, or M? What was so special about x? The Babylonians were using algebra basics in 2000 B.C. It has been discovered that they were solving second- and third-degree equations of the form $x^3 + x^2 = b$ (Eves, 1990). Of course, the Babylonians did not use the letters x or b, nor did they use our current numeral or place value system and exponents as we know them.

The first records dealing with adding or subtracting the same magnitude on both sides of an equation are found in the Arabic writings of Al-Khowarizmi (Mohammed ben Musa, which means Mahomet, the son of Moses) about 830 A.D. Leonardo da Pisa (Fibonacci) introduced some basics of algebra to Italy about 1200 A.D. while Robert Recorde introduced it to England in a 1557 A.D. publication. Those introductions were not the algebra as we know it today, but the ideas were present. Algebraic methods and notations have been improved and revised through the centuries. Unlike arithmetic, where 3 + 4 = 7, algebraic notations like x + y = z take on different meanings in different contexts. Thus, the subject of algebra provides challenges for some individuals because of their difficulty in dealing with the abstractions associated with unknowns.

Descartes (about 1637 A.D.) contributed to the development of algebraic symbolization. He used symbolic notation to express algebraic calculations. He also used letters at the beginning of the alphabet (a, b, c) to denote known quantities and letters from the end of the alphabet (x, y, z), particularly x, to indicate unknown quantities. (Does this sound familiar from your high school days?)

When should we introduce algebra in our mathematics curriculum? When is it introduced into the curriculum right now? Organizations such as NCTM suggest that *all* students can learn mathematics. That means all students can learn algebra at the appropriate time in their development. This philosophy is not totally acceptable to everyone in our society.

Traditionalists say, and many parents agree, that "The mathematics I learned and the way I learned it was good enough for me, so it is good enough for my child." Unfortunately, that statement is far from true. Individuals with skills limited to computation offer little to society mathematically, and that lack of mathematical skill limits their career opportunities. Technology can do the arithmetic. Society needs thinkers. Still discussion continues relating to what should be learned in mathematics and how it should be taught. The resistance to curricular and conceptual change is formidable. Today's world is much more mathematical than yesterday's, in that productivity in today's world requires greater mathematical abilities and more complex problem-solving skills than did yesterday's. Even most common percents, ratios, and discounts are done with calculators instead of by hand. Tomorrow's world will be even more mathematical than today's. Should we continue to introduce algebra into the curriculum in the ninth grade as we did 20 years ago? That is already changing, and many middle schools offer Algebra I as part of their regular curriculum. Is it possible that our students have the developmental capability to begin learning algebraic concepts in elementary school? Does this mean we can introduce algebraic concepts in first grade or fifth?

WHEN DOES ALGEBRA BEGIN?

When do children start to learn algebra? When should we begin to teach students algebra? Children learn the basics of algebra at an early age. When children first learn addition, they begin to learn algebra. You may not recognize it because an x or y is not present. When learning their addition facts, children solve problems such as $3 + 4 = \square$. The box represents the sum the students are trying to find. The box represents a variable. In reality, there is no difference between $3 + 4 = \square$ and $3 + 4 = x$. Either way, the student is being asked to find an unknown. Many times students see blanks such as $3 + 4 = \underline{\quad}$ rather than boxes. When students are asked to fill in the blank with the correct response, they are solving an algebraic equation.

The use of algebra at an early age can significantly help teach many different mathematical concepts. Such a prominent example exists when teaching subtraction. While students are mastering addition, the idea of subtraction can be subtly introduced. Recall that when teaching addition we use the terms *addend + addend equals sum*, and when teaching subtraction we use *sum − addend = missing addend*. There is a significant difference among $3 + 4 = \square$, $3 + \square = 7$, and $\square + 4 = 7$. Although all three mathematical sentences require knowledge of basic facts, the last two provide excellent leads toward subtraction because both have a sum and an addend and are looking for a missing addend. These problems also require some problem-solving skills. As students attempt to solve $3 + \square = 7$, they need to revise the problem to find, "what's missing?" They are looking for the missing addend. Three added to what number will give you seven? As you introduce this problem-solving approach (which should begin at some concrete level initially), recall your introductory algebra class in high school. As you learned how to solve an equation for x, the first type probably was something like $3 + x = 7$. Amazing how it looks so similar to $3 + \square = 7$. The only difference is the shape of the variable. Of course, you were instructed to solve the equation by subtracting three from both sides, yielding $x = 4$. An elementary student is simply asked to fill in the box with the missing number. You now have elementary students using algebra to learn addition and subtraction.

Exercises

250. Have some early elementary students solve 15 problems: Five in the form of 3 + 4 = □ with a box as a missing addend, 5 in the form of 3 + □ = 7 with the box as the second addend, and 5 in the form of □ + 4 = 7 with the box as the first addend. Which problem type was easiest for the students? Which did the students find the hardest? Why do you suppose this occurred?

251. Look at the table of contents of an Algebra 1 textbook. What concepts could possibly be introduced in the elementary classroom using manipulatives?

LAYING THE FOUNDATION FOR ALGEBRA

The use of manipulatives should be an ongoing occurrence in the classroom. It is important that students begin by learning mathematics on the concrete level and slowly progress when they are ready for other levels of development. Although algebra is an abstract way to view mathematical concepts, the use of manipulatives can help integrate it into the elementary curriculum. Suppose one student has three blocks and another student has seven as shown in Fig. 3.1.

First Student   **Second Student**

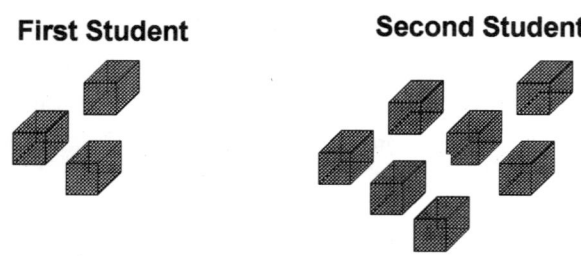

FIG. 3.1.

The question that the first student must answer is how many blocks do I need to have as many as the other student? In reality, you are asking the first student to solve a problem of the form 3 + □ = 7. The exception is that the student is doing this problem on a more concrete level by using manipulatives. Here are the beginnings of the foundation for algebra. The student is looking for the missing addend. One strategy the student might take is to line up both sets of blocks as shown in Fig. 3.2.

First Student

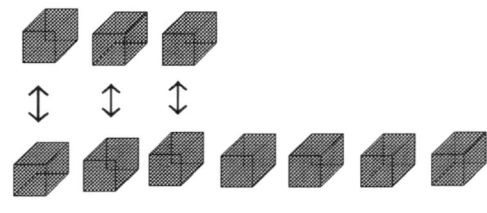

Second Student

FIG. 3.2.

This would allow the student to concretely look for a one-to-one correspondence and find the number of missing blocks needed to obtain seven. The student can begin adding blocks until the number of blocks in both sets is the same. This could also be solved via the take-away model. That is, the second student's set would have three blocks removed (to match those of the first student) and then the residue could be counted.

Another method would involve the use of technology in the form of a calculator. Suppose the student is given a set of problems like 3 + □ = 7. Is there any way this problem can be done with a calculator? The answer is yes, but first the situation must be interpreted. What does this problem actually mean? Seven is the known sum and 3 is the known addend. The box represents the missing addend. Thus, the problem presents a sum and an addend. The other addend can be determined by subtracting the known addend from the sum. Thus, the calculator is used to solve 7 − 3 = □. In the process, the student is exposed to a subtraction fact. Once this exposure occurs, the intent would be for that student to memorize that fact.

The preceding processes may seem trivial, but in reality using an x or y is much the same. If you were asked to find the missing addend in the expression 3x + ____ = 7x, one way to simplify this on a semi-abstract level would be to draw more than one x and use a process similar to the one used in Fig. 3.2. The bottom line is that you have three unknowns and you want to know how many more unknowns you will need to obtain seven unknowns. If you gave one elementary student three wooden Xs and another seven wooden Xs, would the problem be any different than the one using wooden blocks? One could write 3□ + ____ = 7□, where each □ represents a wooden box. Now the problem could be read, "I have three boxes and I need to know how many more boxes I need to have a total of seven boxes." The foundations of algebra begin in the elementary school.

The ALGEBRA FX-2.0 calculator developed by Casio provides the power of a calculator with the educational use of an algebraic tutorial. This technology allows the student to enter X + 3 = 7; with the push of a button, the calculator supplies the student with the solution for X. The FX-2.0 also provides an on-screen step-by-step process for solving even the simplest equations. For example, with X + 3 = 7, the first step shown by the calculator would be subtracting 3 from both sides producing X + 3 − 3 = 7 − 3. The next press of a button would simplify both sides of the equation yielding X = 7 on the screen. MathXpert (*www.mathxpert.com*) is another technology that reacts quite similar to the FX-2.0 in that it provides a statement and reason for each step taken as a problem is solved. Both of these technologies provide options for student solving with specific hints, general hints,

or they will automatically solve the problem for you. If a student (or teacher) wants to learn algebra, these technology pieces are invaluable.

Having Fun With Algebra

One way to gain mathematical enthusiasm is through number tricks. For example:

Pick any counting number.
Add the next highest counting number.
Add nine to the sum.
Divide the new sum by two.
Subtract five.
What did you get?

Try the same trick using a different counting number. What did you get? How did this work? If you try this for an entire class, you will love seeing the look of amazement on the children's faces when they find out that they each got the number with which they started. Of course, some of the students will make arithmetic mistakes. Ask them to try the process again. Many number tricks are algebraically based. For example, try this number trick:

Pick a counting number.
Multiply your number by two.
Add four to your new product.
Subtract 10 from your new sum.
Add six to your new number.
Now subtract your original number.
What did you get?

Looking at this problem algebraically reveals the answer. First, we picked a counting number that we call N.

Pick a counting number.
N

Multiply your number by two.

$$2 \times N = 2N$$

Add four to your new product.

$$2N + 4 = 2N + 4$$

Subtract 10 from your new sum.

$$2N + 4 - 10 = 2N - 6$$

Add six to your new number.

$$2N - 6 + 6 = 2N$$

Now subtract your original number.

$$2N - N = N$$

What did you get?

$$N$$

You will always get the number with which you started. Of course, we cannot expect most elementary students to do the algebra required to show that they will always get the number started with, but you might be amazed to see what would happen with upper elementary students if you gave them cubes and asked them to solve the problem. Figure 3.3 shows the same number trick solved using cubes.

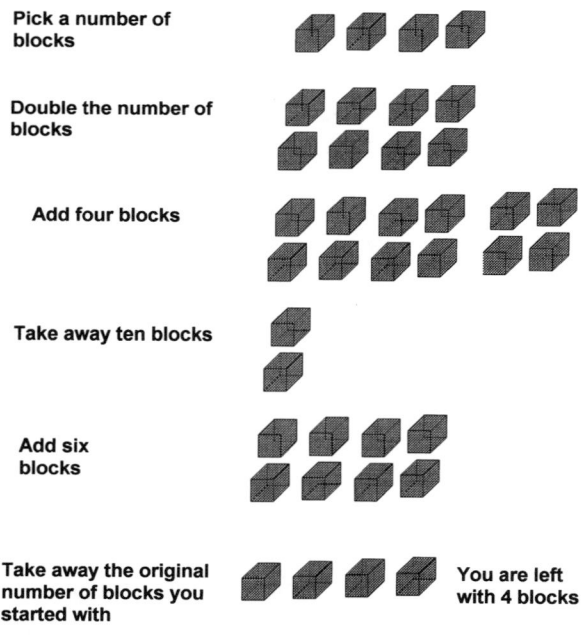

Pick a number of blocks

Double the number of blocks

Add four blocks

Take away ten blocks

Add six blocks

Take away the original number of blocks you started with — You are left with 4 blocks

FIG. 3.3.

Elementary students are able to follow along with blocks as the process is devel-

oped. You have the students working with algebraic concepts and they do not even know it. Even better is that they are having a good time playing with numbers and number tricks. Once again, you are laying the proper foundation for not only algebra, but for all mathematical concepts in the future.

INTEGRATING ALGEBRA IN THE ELEMENTARY CLASSROOM

Algebra should be infused throughout the mathematics curriculum. In your algebra class in high school, you learned to simplify expressions like $4y + 5y$. When learning to simplify expressions with variables, you were told to combine like terms. That really meant that you were only supposed to add or subtract the same letters, such as xs with xs and ys with ys. When dealing with $4y + 5y$, you combine the terms to get 9Y because you are adding four ys with five ys. In elementary school, students can complete similar tasks using manipulatives. For example, give a student two groups of blocks—one group containing four blocks and the other five blocks as shown in Fig. 3.4. Ask the student to combine the blocks and deter-

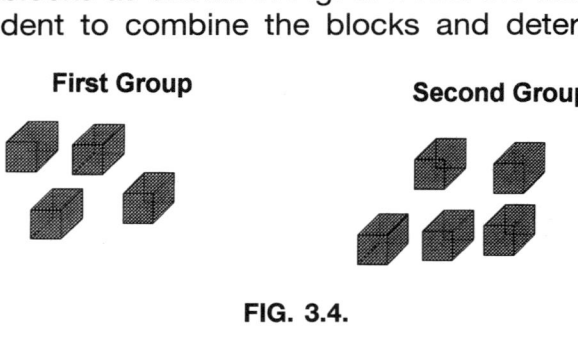

First Group   **Second Group**

FIG. 3.4.

mine the total number of blocks. Once again you have used blocks rather than x or y. Which problem is algebra? Is there really a difference?

As you learned to simplify more complicated expressions, you began to realize that you truly could not combine unlike terms. For example, when simplifying the expression 3x + 4y + 5x + 2y, you can only add the xs with the xs and the ys with the ys yielding 8x + 6y. By using pattern or attribute blocks at the elementary level, you can show why you cannot combine unlike terms. For this example, we use the squares and triangles from the pattern block set. Lay out the shapes as shown in Fig. 3.5.

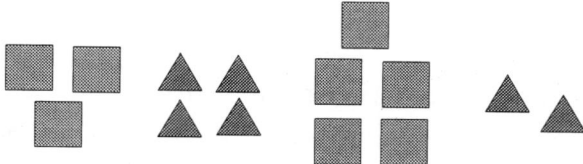

FIG. 3.5.

First ask the students to describe their blocks. Then suggest that the students arrange the blocks into like groups and determine how many are in each group. No matter how the blocks are arranged, there will still only be eight squares and six triangles. Ask the student how they arranged their groups. Can a square go into a triangle group? Can a triangle go into a square group? Why not? The same justifications hold true for letters. Once again, algebra has been integrated into the early elementary curriculum. The foundation for secondary mathematics is being developed. From this concrete stage, students can even move to a semi-concrete stage by using pictures of triangles and squares. The question you need to ask yourself is, "Would my secondary algebra class have been easier if the proper algebraic foundation had been established in elementary school?"

Read the following word problem: "Susan has three squares and four triangles and Amanda has five squares and two triangles. If they combined their blocks and arranged the shapes into like groups, how many would be in each group?" Now ob-

serve the expression 3□ + 4△ + 5□ + 2△. If a student was given shapes to concretely complete the problem, do you think it would make the previous expression easier to understand? With the expression 3□ + 4△ + 5□ + 2△, students can begin to make the connection that 3□ represents three squares, 4△ is four triangles, 5□ is five squares, and 2△ replaces two triangles. 3□ makes more sense to children than 3x. □ is a picture that is representative of the actual square pattern block. Many times it is extremely difficult for any age student, elementary or secondary, to make the connection that x represents a number. There is nothing to touch that would help make the connection. How often did you ever get to physically work with xs? Did you ever draw them on a semi-concrete level in algebra class? Do you think the expression 3x + 4y + 5x + 2y would have been easier to understand if it had been explained with concrete shapes first?

Exercises

253. List the algebraic concepts you feel could be introduced in an elementary school environment.

254. What manipulatives could have helped you learn algebra at the secondary level?

255. What manipulatives from the elementary program are best suited to introduce algebraic concepts?

In the section dealing with multiplying whole numbers, we discussed partial products and the connection with algebra. One problem we used there was:

```
   23
 × 4
   12   (from 4 × 3)
   80   (from 4 × 20—implies an understanding of
   92      place value)
```

We then transitioned to a parallel algebra problem with:

```
  2n + 3
 ×     4
      12    (4 × 3)
  8n        (4 × 2n)
 8n + 12.
```

Note the similarities between the two problems. The background established with the partial product multiplication easily transfers to a similar problem in algebra.

We also talked about using the Base 10 blocks as a tool to help students learn whole number multiplication and connected them to an algebraic basis as shown in Figs. 2.38 and 2.39. The shift between using the Base 10 blocks to do 12×14 and then dealing with $(x + 2)(x + 4)$ is quick and easy with the appropriate background. Once again, critical algebraic background can be established in the elementary program.

FORMULAS

Mathematical formulas are algebra based, and you see many of them in the elementary program. Although there will be several important formulas, we are not advocating that this list be completely memorized by the students. A formula provides helpful assistance in solving mathematical problems in the classroom as well as the real world. Algebra background helps develop a rationale and methods for using formulas in the elementary mathematics curriculum.

Teaching the Use of Formulas

How many formulas were you asked to memorize in your K–12 experience? A better question might be to ask you how many formulas you remember from your K–12 experience. Take a few minutes to write these formulas. Do not use any outside resources. Just produce them from memory. You need to *do* this *now*, please!

Children tend to remember more when they are active participants in their own learning. Think about the formulas you remembered. Did you use them often during your education? Do you use any now? What made you remember those specific formulas? Of course, many other factors affect how we remember particular formulas. The real question is not whether you memorized the formula, but rather whether you can effectively use and apply the formula to solve a mathematical problem.

Next to each formula you listed, describe what the formula is used to find or determine. Did you find that you remembered some formulas but have no inkling as to what they do? Why do you suppose you would remember a formula and yet not know its purpose? Are you beginning to get a message about formulas (no fair saying they are useless because that certainly is not the case).

Formulas are an integral part of the mathematics curriculum. As a teacher of mathematics, it is your job to teach several things when it comes to the use of formulas:

1. Teach students how to effectively determine which formula to use for a given situation.
2. Teach students how to effectively use the formula to solve a problem in mathematics.
3. Help students learn where to look for sources of formulas.
4. Help students learn processes that will lead to the ability to develop formulas if they cannot remember or find one (here is where the algebra comes in).

Notice that we did not include making students memorize a host of different formulas for a multitude of situations.

Exercises

256. Find an elementary textbook for a particular grade. Carefully go through the book and record each formula a child would encounter. Did the number of formulas surprise you? Were there more or fewer than you expected? Explain your reasoning.

257. After completing Exercise 256, which formulas would you omit from the text? Which formulas were not found in the text that you think should be added?

Discovering Formulas, Not Memorizing

If you want students to correctly apply the distance formula, try conducting a fun activity that requires the students to use this formula. The class can set up a speed trap. Begin by getting a linear measuring device such as a pedometer. Marking your starting point on a sidewalk beside a road, begin walking and make another mark on the sidewalk 528 feet (why would we pick 528?) from the first one. Have one student stand at the first mark. As a car passes, have the student raise or lower a hand exactly as a car passes by. The students will need to agree on what part of the car will be used because if one uses the front bumper and the other uses the back bumper, the data will be off by the car length. When the hand is raised or lowered, a student at the end mark begins the timing. Figure 3.6 shows a configuration for the speed trap. As the car passes the endpoint, the student stops the timing. Another student records the time it took for the car to travel the tenth of a mile. After allowing each student to take the stopwatch for at least one car as well as record the data, return to the classroom.

You now have the distance traveled for each car as well as the time it took to travel the distance. Select one piece of data. For example, suppose a car took 12 seconds to travel the tenth of a mile. How fast is the car traveling? We can introduce the distance formula, which states that the distance an object travels is determined by the product of the rate of the object and the time it takes to travel that distance or $d = rt$, where d is distance, r is rate, and t is time. In our example, we have the distance, 528 feet and the time, 12 seconds. Using the distance formula yields 528 feet = rate × 12 seconds. If we divide both sides by 12 seconds, we get $\dfrac{528 \text{ feet}}{12 \text{ seconds}}$ or 44 feet per second. The key to this activity is to show the students

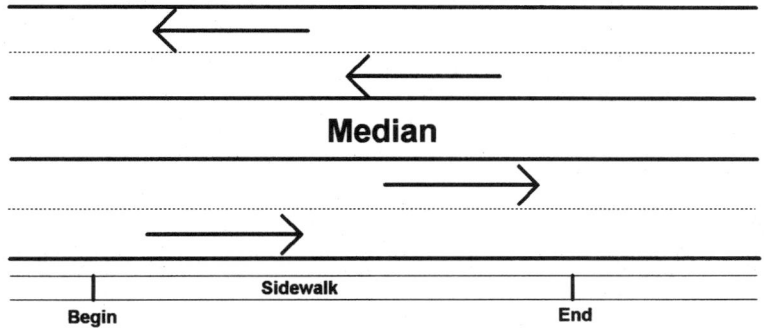

FIG. 3.6.

how to effectively utilize the distance formula to solve a real problem. In the process, they use a lot of algebra basics. Of course, the next step might be to get the children to convert from feet per second to miles per hour and, if the car is exceeding the speed limit, ascertain how much over the speed limit the car is going.

FORMULAS FOR ELEMENTARY MATHEMATICS

Area
    Circle
        πr^2 (r is radius)
    Rectangle
        l × w   (l is length, w is width)
    Square
        s^2 (s is side length)
    Trapezoid
        $\left(\dfrac{b_1 + b_2}{2}\right)h$ (b_1 is one base, b_2 is other base, h is height)
    Triangle
        $\dfrac{bh}{2}$ (b is base, h is height)
Distance formula
        d = rt   (d is distance, r is rate, t is time)
Mean
        $\left(\dfrac{\sum \text{ of scores}}{\text{number of scores}}\right)$
Volume
    Rectangular Prism (box)
        lwh   (l is length, w is width, h is height)
    Sphere
        $\dfrac{4}{3}\pi r^3$ ($\pi \approx 3.14$, r is radius)
    Right circular cylinder
        $\pi r^2 h$ ($\pi \approx \dfrac{22}{7}$, r is radius, h is height)

Perimeter of a rectangle
        2(L + W)(L is length, W is width)
Pythagorean Theorem
        $a^2 + b^2 = c^2$ (a and b are legs, c is hypotenuse of a right triangle)

You should have noticed that we used all capital letters in some formulas and all lowercase in others. You will see them written both ways, and there have been some lively discussions as to which is correct, preferred, easier for children to understand, and even easier to read. We cannot settle that debate here and would not presume to tell you which way is best for you. That is something you need to reflect on and arrive at a conclusion that makes sense to you so you can rationalize your position to your students.

Formulas come in many different shapes and sizes. We can teach our students how to apply these formulas to make the mathematical computations easier. Think about the pros and cons of memorizing a multitude of formulas. When your students eventually get a job in the real world, do you think their employer is going to demand that they have these formulas memorized? Most companies expect you to know where to find the needed formulas and, above all else, know when and how to effectively utilize the formula. Students need to learn the process.

The foundation of algebraic concepts is essential in a child's developmental process of learning mathematics. Algebra concepts have a proper place in the elementary classroom. As most of us would agree, we are far more advanced than the Babylonians of 4,000 years ago. If that is the case, then our children can begin to do the mathematics the Babylonians did such a long time ago. Of course, our students have the knowledge of a simpler number and place value system. Hopefully it is understood that algebra in its pure form will not be taught to most elementary school students. The ideas and concepts behind algebra can be integrated and introduced on a more concrete and semi-concrete level for easier comprehension and development. You might be surprised at the mathematics your students can learn.

REFERENCES

Eves, H. (1990). *An introduction to the history of mathematics* (6th ed.). Fort Worth, TX: Saunders College Publishing.

4

Geometry in the Elementary Classroom

FOCAL POINTS

- Building a Foundation
- When to Introduce Geometry in the Elementary Classroom
- Manipulatives and Geometry
- Using Technology to Teach Geometry

Children encounter and use concepts of geometry prior to entering your classroom. Even pre-K children work with basic concepts in the realm of geometry as they play. Toys often consist of a set of three-dimensional blocks such as cubes, prisms, and cylinders. Much of your students' prior knowledge of geometry came from playing with different objects. Many of the terms you refer to when teaching geometry, like calling a *block* a *cube*, may seem foreign to your students and quite possibly to even you.

BUILDING A FOUNDATION

"A *point* is the basic unit of geometry. It has no size. It is infinitely small. It has only location" (Serra, 1993, p. 72). How would you tell a child what a point is? Would you simply draw a dot on a chalkboard? Is that dot really a point?

A *line* is a straight arrangement of points. There are infinitely many points in a line. It has length but no thickness. It extends forever in two directions. A *line segment* con-

sists of two points and all the points between them that lie on the line containing the two points. (Serra, 1993, pp. 72–73)

The three previous definitions are important conceptual ideas for the foundation of geometry for elementary children. How will you explain these concepts? Figure 4.1 is something you might have seen when you

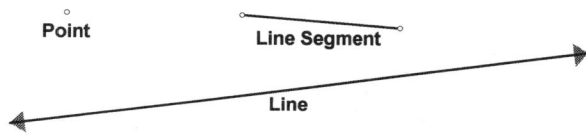

FIG. 4.1.

were introduced to these terms. Is Fig. 4.1 good enough for your students? Can you simply draw these items on a board and assume that the children will gain a true insight? Is the only difference between a line and a line segment the fact that the line has an arrow at each end of the drawing? Remember how important it is for children to be able to concretely interact with their learning. With yarn or string and aluminum foil, you can demonstrate these concepts very nicely. Cut a piece of string about 8 to 10 feet long. Have two students each tear a piece of aluminum foil. Ball the aluminum foil around the ends of the cut string. You have now formed two endpoints of aluminum foil on your string. Have two other students stand up and hold each aluminum foil endpoint of the string. Be sure to have the students pull the string taut. Remember that a line segment consists of two points and all the points between them on the line. The students can now see a line segment in space. The space happens to be the classroom. Ask two other students to take a piece of aluminum foil and make an aluminum wad around the center portion of the string. These pieces represent points on the line segment. Give two more pieces of aluminum foil to two other students. Be sure to give the students much larger pieces than the previous ones. These points will probably appear much larger on the line segment than the others. Are they still points? These pieces of foil are representations of points. In actuality, a point has no dimension. Using a thicker piece of string, repeat the activity with other students. Ask the students to compare the new line segment with the first one. How does the thickness of the string change the activity? A line segment has no thickness.

You have demonstrated a point and a line segment, but how about a ray and line? Take two balls of string tied together or, better yet, one long piece of string rolled from each end so there are two balls (representing endpoints) to work with. Take your students into a hallway where they have access to a door on each side of the hall. Move the class down the hall so they cannot see inside the two doors. Have a student hold each end ball of the string. The class should associate that with a representation of a line segment. Then ask one student to enter one of the rooms, moving out of site of the class.

Now the class can see one endpoint. The other end of the string is out of site. They do not know where the string ends inside the room. For all they know, the student could have gone out another door or window and is moving across the playground. This situation presents the idea of a ray because the class can see one end-

point, but the string appears to go on and on moving away from that point. Certainly there is an endpoint, but if the ball were *really big* or if more string were tied to it, it could appear to not have an end to the part that passed into the room. A similar experience could be created for a line, showing that there is no defined endpoint for the piece of string. These activities provide an excellent introduction to the symbol for a line segment, ray, or line and the reasoning for having arrows or points at the ends.

After making a big fuss about the definitions of line segments, rays, and lines, teachers often ask students to get out their lined paper and write the definitions. No wonder students get confused as we structure their learning environment. These terms are carefully defined and then an incorrect, but common, phrase is used in conjunction with the definitions. Lined paper is a part of our language, and we all understand what is meant by it. However, technically speaking, we should say line-segmented paper. It sounds strange, but it is correct.

Exercises

258. What other objects could you use to demonstrate terms like line segment and point?

259. Provide another activity that could possibly be used to demonstrate a line.

MANIPULATIVES AND GEOMETRY

As with most concepts in mathematics, manipulatives play an important role in the developmental process of geometry. Pattern blocks or attribute blocks, which come in several shapes and colors, provide a wonderful opportunity for understanding geometric shapes. We use the five shapes in Fig. 4.2. The color of each shape is written inside the shape. You should work with a set of pattern blocks while reading this chapter.

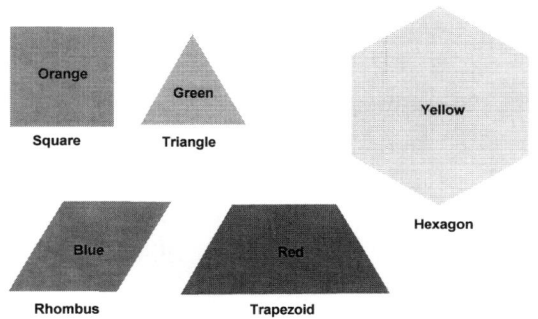

FIG. 4.2.

When working with geometric shapes, it is important for children to learn the characteristics of each shape. When you first introduce pattern blocks, it will be likely that the students do not know the names of each shape (you should be aware that the shape is only the outside edge of the block). Many children have heard of a square or triangle but may not truly know the characteristics of these shapes. Have the students answer the following questions individually:

Which shapes have three sides?
Which shapes have four sides?
Which shapes have five sides?
Which shapes have six sides?

After the students have answered these questions, have them pair up and compare their answers. Allow them to discuss discrepancies. You may find that many students only supplied one colored shape for shapes with four sides. A few students may have two, and even fewer will have three. One of the goals of these questions is to develop better reasoning and critical thinking skills. Check to see whether any students found a shape with five sides. Many students will try to find an answer

because they do not think the answer can be zero. Some children feel that if the teacher asks a question, there must be an answer (other than none).

After the students compare their results, ask them to tell you how the blue (rhombus) shape and orange (square) shape are similar. How are they different? This is a good time to explain that both shapes are quadrilaterals (four sides) and that all the sides for each shape are the same length. The major difference between the two shapes is that the edges of the orange square form right angles, while the edges of the blue shape do not. A rhombus is a quadrilateral with four sides that are the same length. A square is a quadrilateral with four sides the same length and four right angles. Does the square fit the description of a rhombus? Does the rhombus fit the description of the square? These are wonderful questions to build students' levels of understanding and logic, both of which enhance their problem-solving abilities. The orange square is a quadrilateral with all four sides the same length. Therefore, the orange square is also a rhombus. The blue rhombus is a quadrilateral with four equivalent sides, but its angles are not all equal. Therefore, a rhombus does not fit into the category of a square.

Exercises

260. Define a rectangle.
261. Is a rectangle a square? Is a square a rectangle? Explain why or why not.

Problem Solving and Geometry

Geometry and problem solving make a great pair. As your students learn basic geometric shapes such as triangles, squares, rectangles, rhombi, trapezoids, and hexagons, you can subtly integrate problem solving into the concepts of geometry. Have students pair up and take out one set of pattern blocks, a sheet of paper, and a writing utensil. The students need to determine who will be the recorder for their pair. Begin by asking the students to select one trapezoid. Ask the students to use any other pattern blocks to form a trapezoid the same size as the one selected. By working together, your students will probably determine one possible solution and perhaps more. The trapezoid can be formed by using three triangles and also by using one rhombus and one triangle as shown in Fig. 4.3.

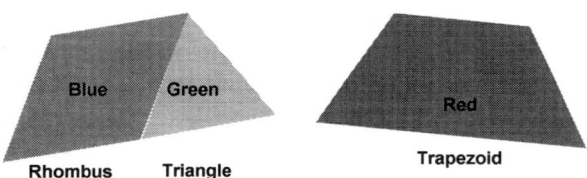

FIG. 4.3.

Have each pair compare their results with other pairs. This will help students who have only one solution see another possible method. This sharing process encourages students to learn from each other.

Next try the same activity using the hexagon. Ask your students to find different combinations of shapes that will construct a hexagon of the same size as the one in their pattern block set. Have the recorder for each pair of students construct a table similar to Table 4.1 and list their possible combinations. Ask the students how many

different combinations they found? Have someone demonstrate his or her combination of shapes to the class using a set of overhead pattern blocks and add their description, if different, to the table. This activity will encourage the entire class to participate in a discussion on geometric shapes and problem solving. The demonstrations get students to communicate their process to other students. The activity might encourage you as you observe an increase in mathematical self-esteem and confidence as students show their methods.

Exercise

262. Try the hexagon activity with pattern blocks. How many different combinations can be used to construct a trapezoid of the same size as the one in the pattern block set you have when using only the triangles, squares, rhombi, and trapezoids?

263. How many different combinations of pattern blocks can be used to construct any sized trapezoid using only the triangles, squares, rhombi, and trapezoids?

Tangrams, another useful geometry manipulative, consist of different sized isosceles triangles, a parallelogram, and a square. The Tangram shapes are used to construct specified figures, which might be a mathematical shape, an animal, or even a house. Figure 4.4 shows an object

TABLE 4.1
Building Shapes With Pattern Blocks

Selected Shape	Alternatives
Hexagon	Three rhombi
	Six triangles
	Two trapezoids
	Four triangles and one rhombus
	Two triangles and two rhombi
	Three triangles and one trapezoid

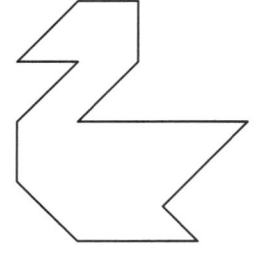

FIG. 4.4.

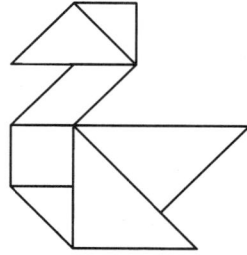

FIG. 4.5.

to construct using Tangrams, whereas Fig. 4.5 shows how a duck can be made using the manipulative. Students will get hours of enjoyment out of these puzzlelike manipulatives. Another way to utilize Tangrams is to have one student construct a figure using part or all of a set of Tangrams and trace around it. The paper is then given to another student, who tries to use Tangrams to determine which pieces were originally used.

Grandfather Tang's Story (Tompert, 1990) and Tangrams incorporate literature and mathematics. In this story, a grandfather tells a tale about two fox fairies who compete by changing into different shaped animals. As the teacher reads, the students use their Tangrams to duplicate the shapes of each animal the fox fairies become (the teacher would display something like Fig. 4.4.

Exercise

264. Develop an activity using Tangrams or pattern blocks for elementary students that can be used to introduce a concept of geometry.

INTEGRATING TECHNOLOGY INTO GEOMETRY

Integrating technology into the classroom has made discovering mathematics a reality for all students. Software such as *Ge-ometer's Sketchpad* by Key Curriculum Press (*www.keypress.com*) is a wonderful demonstration tool. Using computer technology for instruction is becoming extremely affordable. Suppose there are four computers in your classroom of 24 students, divided into three groups of eight. One group can work on the computers with students working in pairs. The second group can be working on a cooperative learning activity while the third group might get some extra small-group instruction from the teacher. Rotate the groups at an appropriate time or even the following day. The cooperative group could be working in pairs on an activity to identify the similarities and differences of scalene, isosceles, and equilateral triangles. Each pair would be given three activity sheets as shown in Figs. 4.6, 4.7, and 4.8. Each sheet would have four triangles. Students are to measure the side lengths

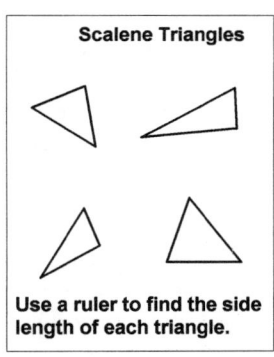

FIG. 4.6.

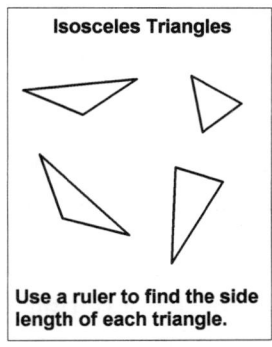

FIG. 4.7.

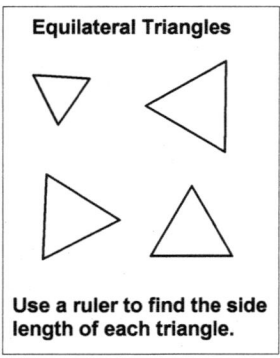

FIG. 4.8.

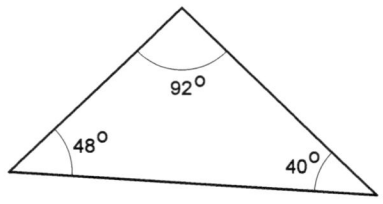

FIG. 4.9.

of each triangle and record the results. Then the students are to make a conjecture as to the definition of the triangles that are scalene, isosceles, and equilateral. Each pair is to compare their definitions with each other.

The second group could use software like *Geometer's Sketchpad* to discover that the sum of the measures of the interior angles of a triangle is 180 degrees. How were you introduced to this mathematical identity? Did you read it in a book? Did a teacher simply tell you this was true? Did you encounter several triangles on a worksheet and have to add their angles? Possibly, you used a protractor to measure the angles of a few triangles to find that the sum of the interior angles of a triangle is 180 degrees. If you did the last method, you actually participated in the discovery of the identity. A protractor is not usually used as a tool in the elementary mathematics curriculum. Using a tool like *Geometer's Sketchpad*, children can continue along their path to becoming self-learners by discovering this identity. When the students arrive at the computers, have a Sketchpad file opened with a triangle similar to Fig. 4.9. Notice that the angle measures appear on the screen. Have each pair of students add the angle measures for the triangle and record the result. Next, have one stu-

dent use the mouse to click on Point A and drag it to another place on the screen. Figure 4.10 shows that as Point A is moved, the angle measures dynami-

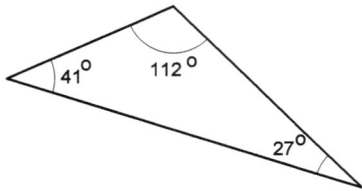

FIG. 4.10.

cally change. After Point A has been moved, have the students sum the angles again and record the result. Repeat by moving Point B and Point C. Have the students write a conjecture regarding their findings from this activity demonstrating that mathematics is not simply answers by numbers.

Using one computer as a demonstration tool, you can dynamically teach that the sum of the measures of the interior angles of a triangle is 180 degrees. Construct and animate something like Fig. 4.11. Animate Point B along segment DE,

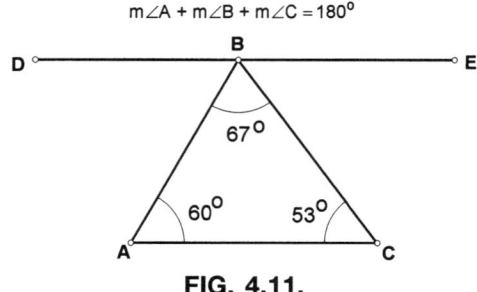

FIG. 4.11.

showing the students that each angle measure changes as Point B moves. Three of the animated triangles are shown

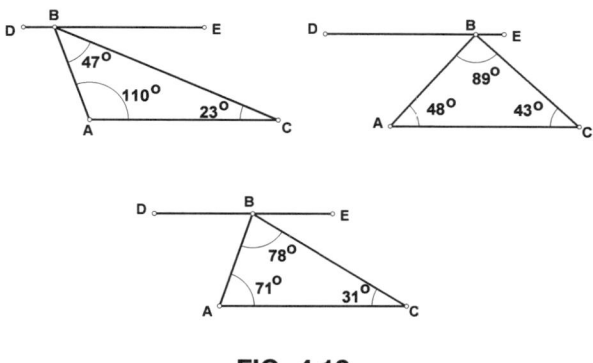

FIG. 4.12.

in Fig. 4.12. The students can see that the sum of the angles remains 180 degrees. If they do not believe it, stop the animation at any point and have them find the sum of the measures of the three angles.

Seeing is believing. This goes for children and adults alike. Too many times during mathematics instruction, teachers become the dispenser of knowledge by reading definitions. Many students believe their teachers are all-knowing mathematical beings and may just want to believe all that is told to them. This mentality prevents the student from gaining first-hand experience knowledge. Think about it! Memorizing information does not give you a complete understanding of mathematics.

The third group could have the opportunity to work with you, the teacher. This will give you the opportunity to gain extra diagnostic insights into the thinking of some students. Those students who are not having difficulty could help others who are.

Shapes

Through the elementary school years and beyond, children deal with shapes. Much of the work with shapes is subliminal and yet almost inescapable. It is imperative that a solid background be established for shapes. Shapes surround us in our world. Children become aware of shapes at an early age. There are several toys for young

children—put a shape in a hole that is similar—that begin to establish the concept of shape. As they move about their world, they learn to recognize shapes. When they come to the elementary school, they have had several casual experiences with geometric figures. Your task is to help them formalize their exposures and begin a classification process for the multitude of shapes they encounter.

Draw a rectangle (four-sided figure with opposite sides congruent and four right angles). As we discuss this drawing, you will learn some things about your own understanding of geometry. It is important that you draw the rectangle before reading on so the discussion is more meaningful. Once you have drawn your rectangle, color it.

STOP! Do not read on until you have drawn and colored your rectangle. More than likely, your rectangle will be drawn so that its sides are parallel to the sides of the paper (assuming you have a rectangular sheet of paper). It will probably either be tall and skinny or short and fat as shown in Fig. 4.13. The significance here is that you have drawn the sides of your rectangle so they are parallel to the sides of your paper. When one of the basic sides is parallel to the bottom of the page, board, screen, or line segments on a paper, the figure is said to be in standard position. This is very common, even more so if you use line-segmented paper.

The impact of consistently drawing rectangles (or any figure) in standard position is that children get the impression that another position cannot exist or that a rectangle in anything other than standard position is not truly a rectangle. Suppose you ask children which of a group of multiple-choice responses represents a rectangle as shown in Fig. 4.14. The num-

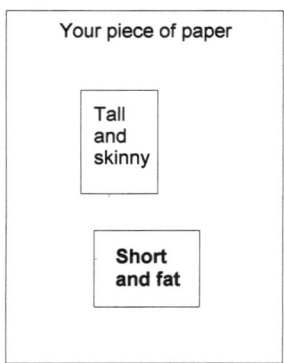

FIG. 4.13.

ber of students who select "None of these" as the correct response is amaz-

Which of these is a rectangle?

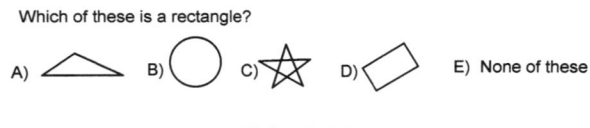

A) ◁ B) ○ C) ☆ D) ▱ E) None of these

FIG. 4.14.

ing. Many of them avoid using response D because they have only seen rectangles in standard position. Think of all the rectangles you have seen in books, magazines, papers, and drawn by others. How many of them have not been in standard position? What is the lesson you should glean from this discussion? Do not always draw figures in standard position. One way to help students see the impact of nonstandard positioning is to ask if one of them would be a different person while they were standing on their head. ☺

You were asked earlier to color your rectangle. More than likely, you created something similar to what is shown in Fig. 4.15, which is typical and incorrect. Figure 4.15 shows the interior of the rectan-

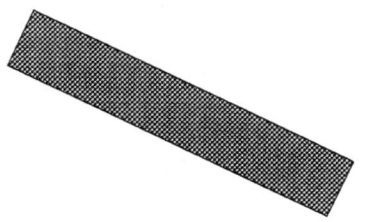

FIG. 4.15.

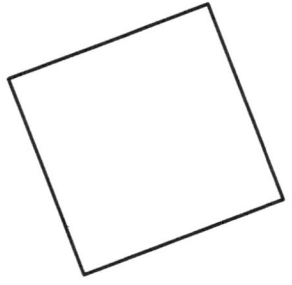

FIG. 4.16.

gle colored. Figure 4.16 shows the rectangle colored. Notice that when referring to a rectangle, you are only dealing with the edge, not the interior. Hopefully you noticed the use of nonstandard positioning in both cases. Do not worry if you colored the interior of the rectangle; almost everyone does. That little coloring lesson is designed to deliver a message to you about your knowledge of geometry and the impact you can have on children.

Finally, measure the length and width of the rectangle you drew. More than likely, one side will be about 1.5 times the length of the other. We do that naturally. Investigate the Golden Ratio and you will learn that this ratio you just created has been very common throughout the development of mathematics and construction since antiquity. Two useful Web sites on the Golden Ratio are:

http://math.rice.edu/~lanius/Geom/
golden. html

http://mathforum.org/dr.math/tocs/
golden.elem.html

Exercise

265. Research the Golden Ratio. Provide at least one example of where it shows up in ancient architecture and somewhere it can be found in nature today.

Asking you to make a rectangle and color it might have seemed unusual.

Actually it was done to help you become aware of your own readiness to deal with geometry. We implore you to strengthen your geometric underpinnings so you can adequately work with the children in your classes as they develop their understanding of shapes.

Diane van Hiele-Geldof and her husband, Pierre van Hiele, both did doctoral dissertations in 1984 that dealt with students learning geometry. Both dissertations dealt with the van Hiele assessment tool, which consists of five levels: visualization, analysis, informal deduction, formal deduction, and rigor. The van Hieles contend that students can be moved from one category to another via appropriate experiences. The following is a van Hiele-based test you should take to help assess your level of geometric understanding. Answer each of the following questions by choosing the answer that seems most correct. There is only one correct answer for each question.

1. Which of the shapes in Fig. 4.17 are squares?

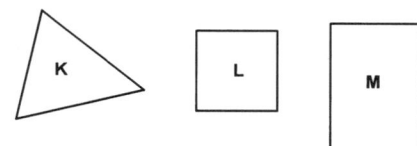

FIG. 4.17.

a. K only   b. L only   c. M only
d. L and M only   e. All are squares

2. Which of the shapes in Fig. 4.18 are triangles?

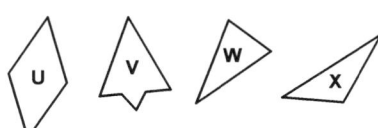

FIG. 4.18.

a. None   b. V only   c. W and X only
d. W only   e. V and W only

3. Which of the shapes in Fig. 4.19 are rectangles?

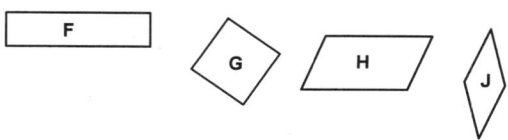

FIG. 4.19.

a. F only   b. F and G only
c. G only   d. H and J only
e. All are rectangles

4. Which of the shapes in Fig. 4.19 are squares?
a. None   b. G only   c. All
d. G and J only   e. F and G only

5. Which of the shapes in Fig. 4.17 are parallelograms?
a. L only   b. L and M only
c. K only   d. None   e. All

6. In Fig. 4.20, PQRS is a square. Which relationship is true of all squares?

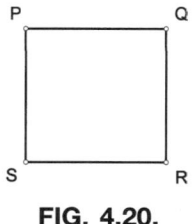

FIG. 4.20.

a. PR and RS have the same length.
b. QS and PR are perpendicular.
c. PS and QR are perpendicular.
d. PS and QS have the same length.
e. Angle Q is larger than angle R.

7. Figure 4.21 shows rectangle GHJK, where GJ and HK are the diagonals. Which in a–d is *NOT* true in *EVERY* rectangle?

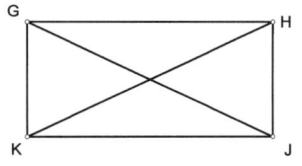

FIG. 4.21.

a. There are four right angles.
b. There are four sides.
c. The diagonals have same length.
d. The opposite sides have the same length.
e. All of a–d are true in every rectangle.

8. Figure 4.22 shows three examples of a rhombus (all four sides the same length). Which of a–d is *NOT* true in *EVERY* rhombus?

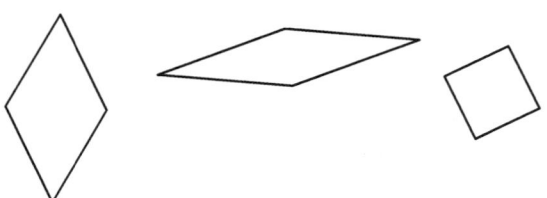

FIG. 4.22.

a. The two diagonals have the same length.
b. Each diagonal bisects two angles of the rhombus.
c. The two diagonals are perpendicular.
d. The opposites angles have the same measure.
e. All of a–d are true for every rhombus.

9. Figure 4.23 shows examples of isosceles triangles (two sides the same length). Which of a–d are true in every isosceles triangle?

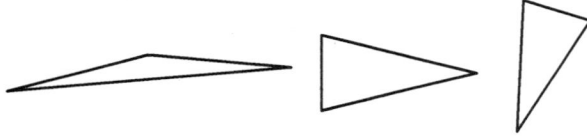

FIG. 4.23.

a. The three sides must have the same length.
b. One side must have twice the length of another side.
c. There must be at least two angles with the same measure.
d. The three angles must have the same measure.

e. None of a–d is true for every isosceles triangle.

10. Figure 4.24 shows examples of two circles with centers P and Q intersecting at R and S to form a four-sided figure PQRS. Which of a–d is *NOT* always true?

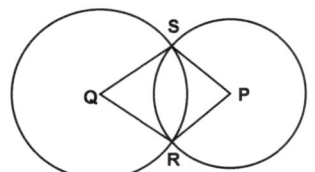 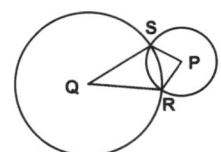

FIG. 4.24.

a. PQRS will have two pairs of sides of equal length.
b. PQRS will have at least two angles of equal measure.
c. The line segments PQ and RS will be perpendicular.
d. Angles P and Q will have the same measure.
e. All of a–d are true.

11. Given
Statement 1: Figure F is a rectangle.
Statement 2: Figure F is a triangle.
Which is correct?
a. If 1 is true, then 2 is true.
b. If 1 is false, then 2 is true.
c. 1 and 2 cannot both be true.
d. 1 and 2 cannot both be false.
e. None of a–d is true.

12. Given
Statement 1: ΔABC has three sides of the same length.
Statement 2: In ΔABC, ∠B and ∠C have the same measure.
Which is correct?
a. 1 and 2 cannot both be true.
b. If 1 is true, then 2 is true.
c. If 2 is true, then 1 is true.
d. If 1 is false, then 2 is false.
e. None of a–d is correct.

13. Which of the shapes in Fig. 4.25 are rectangles?

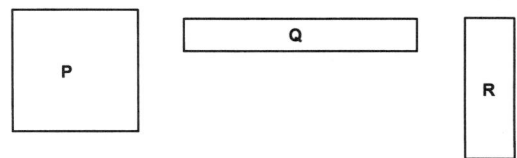

FIG. 4.25.

a. All   b. Q only   c. R only
d. P and Q only   e. Q and R only

14. Which is true?
a. All properties of rectangles are properties of squares.
b. All properties of squares are properties of rectangles.
c. All properties of rectangles are properties of parallelograms.
d. All properties of squares are properties of parallelograms.
e. None of a–d is true.

15. What do all rectangles have that some parallelograms do not have?
a. opposite sides equal
b. diagonals equal
c. opposite sides parallel
d. opposite angles equal
e. None of a–d is true.

16. Figure 4.26 shows right triangle ABC. Equilateral triangles ACE, ABF, and BCD have been constructed on the sides

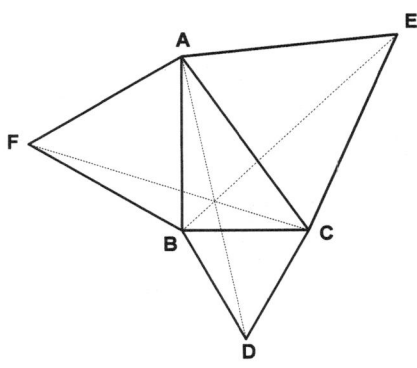

FIG. 4.26.

of ABC. From this information, one can prove that AD, BE, and CF have a point in common. What would this proof tell you?
a. Only in this triangle can we be sure that AD, BE, and CF have a point in common.
b. In some but not all right triangles, AD, BE, and CF have a point in common.
c. In every right triangle, AD, BE, and CF have a point in common.
d. In any triangle, AD, BE, and CF have a point in common.
e. In any equilateral triangle, AD, BE, and CF have a point in common.

17. Here are some properties of a figure:
Property D: It has diagonals of equal length.
Property S: It is a square.
Property R: It is a rectangle.
Which is true?
a. D implies S, which implies R.
b. D implies R, which implies S.
c. S implies R, which implies D.
d. R implies S, which implies D.
e. None of a–d is true.

18. Here are two statements:
1. If a figure is a rectangle, then its diagonals bisect each other.
2. If the diagonals of a figure bisect each other, then the figure is a rectangle.
Which is true?
a. To prove 1 is true, it is enough to prove 2 is true.
b. To prove 2 is true, it is enough to prove 1 is true.
c. To prove 2 is true, it is enough to find one rectangle whose diagonals bisect each other.
d. To prove 2 is false, it is enough to find one nonrectangle whose diagonals bisect each other.
e. None of a–d is correct.

19. In geometry:
a. Every term can be defined, and every statement can be proved true.
b. Every term can be defined, but it is necessary to assume that some statements are true.
c. Some terms must be left undefined, but every true statement can be proved true.
d. Some terms must be left undefined, and it is necessary to have some statements assumed to be true.
e. None of a–d is correct.

20. In Fig. 4.27, lines m and p are perpendicular and lines n and p are perpendicular. Which of the following sentences could be the reason that line m is parallel to line n?

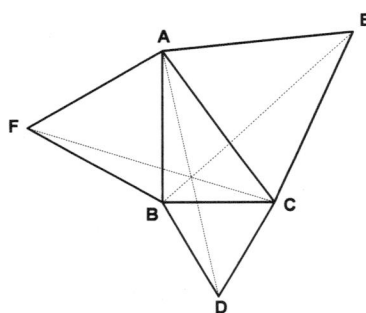

FIG. 4.27.

1. Two lines perpendicular to the same line are parallel.
2. A line that is perpendicular to one of two parallel lines is perpendicular to the other.
3. If two lines are equidistant, then they are parallel.
   a. 1 only   b. 2 only   c. 3 only
   d. either 1 or 2   e. either 2 or 3

21. In F geometry, one that is different from the one you are used to, there are exactly four points and six lines. Every line contains exactly two points. If the points are P, Q, R, and S, the lines are PQ, PR, PS, QR, QS, and RS. Here are how the words

intersect and *parallel* are used in F geometry. The lines PQ, RS, and RS are parallel because they have no point in common. From this information, which is correct?
a. PQ and RS intersect.
b. PR and QS are parallel.
c. QR and RS are parallel.
d. PS and QR intersect.
e. None of a–d is correct.

22. Trisecting an angle means to divide it into three parts of equal measure. In 1847, P. L. Wantzel proved that, in general, it is impossible to trisect angles using a compass and an unmarked straight edge. From his proof, what can you conclude?
a. In general, it is impossible to bisect angles using only a compass and straight edge.
b. In general, it is impossible to trisect angles using only a compass and straight edge.
c. In general, it is impossible to trisect an angle using any drawing instruments.
d. It is still possible that in the future someone may find a general way to trisect angles using only a compass and straight edge.
e. No one will ever be able to find a general method for trisecting angles using a compass and straight edge.

23. Given that there is a geometry in which it is true that the sum of the measures of the angles of a triangle is less than 180°, which of the following statements is correct?
a. A mistake was made in measuring the angles of the triangle.
b. A mistake was made in logical reasoning.
c. Someone had the wrong idea about what is meant by *true*.

d. Someone started with different assumptions than those in the usual geometry.

e. None of a–d is true.

24. Two geometry books define the word rectangle in different ways. Which is true?

a. One of the books has an error.

b. One of the definitions is wrong. There cannot be different definitions for a rectangle.

c. The rectangles in one book must have a different property than the rectangles in the other book.

d. The rectangle in one book must have the same properties as the rectangles in the other book.

e. The properties of the rectangles in the two books might be different.

25. Suppose you have proved Statements 1 and 2.

1. If p, then q.

2. If s, then not q.

Which statement follows from Statements 1 and 2?

a. If p, then s.   b. If not p, then not q.

c. If p or q, then s.

d. If s, then not p and if q, then p.

e. None of a–d is correct.

Your van Hiele level is determined by the highest group in which you correctly answer three or more questions. The classifications and question groups for van Hiele levels are:

Level 0—visualization: Questions 1–5;

Level 1—analysis: Questions 6–10;

Level 2—informal deduction: Questions 11–15;

Level 3—formal deduction: Questions 16–20;

Level 4—rigor: Questions 21–25.

Manipulatives for Shapes

Wire frames, cutouts, geoboards, Tangrams, attribute blocks, and logic blocks (the list goes on) all have shapes as a part of their existence. Any of them can be used to begin a discussion of shapes. Care must be taken to differentiate between the shape of the object being used and the interior of the shape. Remember, the shape is the outer boundary only. Any shape is going to be three-dimensional by virtue of its existence. That is unfortunate because a triangle, for example, is a closed figure made up of three line segments. That is a two-dimensional definition, and unless it is drawn, it is going to have a thickness. That is a limitation of our ability to model some things. Some argue that wire frame shapes are too expensive or difficult to locate or make. You could use drinking straws and pipe cleaners to build shapes. The pipe cleaners are used to form the joint between two straw ends. Toothpicks can be used for sides, and jellybeans, mini-marshmallows, Styrofoam, or clay could be used as a means of joining the toothpicks. Cut sections of coat hanger wire could be used as sides of a polygon, perhaps even making bends in the wire and creating a polygon out of one piece. Each child should have a set of shapes.

Tangrams shapes consist of seven pieces cut from an original square: one square, five triangles, and one square. Figure 4.28 shows that the square is cut so

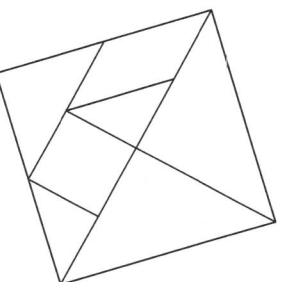

FIG. 4.28.

that each line segment meets the end or midpoint of another segment. One challenging puzzle is to re-create the original square using the seven separated pieces. Tangrams were also used as a storytelling tool as mentioned earlier in this text.

The geoboard is a versatile tool for teaching shapes. Geoboards vary in size, but usually are a square array of nails or pegs similar to Fig. 4.29. Rubber bands

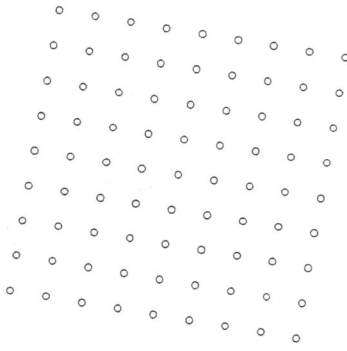

FIG. 4.29.

are stretched around the nails to form different shapes. Dot paper or even graph paper can be used as suitable substitutes for geoboards. Figure 4.30 shows some of the triangles that could be formed on a

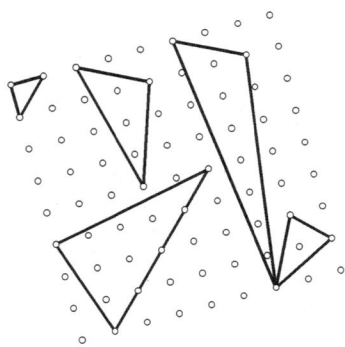

FIG. 4.30.

geoboard. Notice that each segment touches only the nails that are its respective endpoints. Younger children probably would construct triangles similar to the ones shown in Fig. 4.31, where a side of

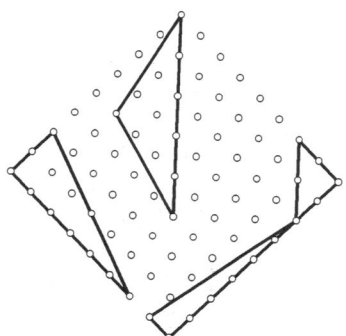

FIG. 4.31.

the triangle is collinear with a row or diagonal of nails on the geoboard.

Exercises

266. Create an argument for using the geoboard in the elementary classroom.

267. Create an argument against using the geoboard in the elementary classroom.

268. Present a lesson plan that would use the geoboard as a means to help children learn about shapes.

Two-Dimensional and Three-Dimensional Geometry

Ironically, all of the discussion so far has focused on two-dimensional geometry, and yet we live in a three-dimensional world. Students see three-dimensional objects all around them, so why do we focus on the two-dimensional aspects first? The answer is not so simple. One quick answer is that we have always done it that way. Why change? Historically, the need for measurement, area, perimeter, and so on forced the growth and development of geometry. The two-dimensional pieces become building blocks for the three-dimensional world. For example, a pyramid like those in Egypt has four isosceles triangles as faces and the bottom is a square. Those shapes are all two-dimensional, yet when put together they form the pyramid.

Elementary students can still study some three-dimensional aspects of geometry, however. Perspective drawings use the idea of a vanishing point. This technique makes things appear more realistic. Look at Figs. 4.32 and 4.33. They both show the same house, but Fig. 4.33 uses a vanishing point as part of the drawing technique.

FIG. 4.32.

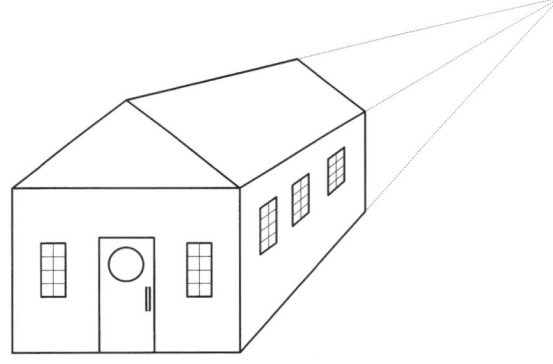

FIG. 4.33.

That vanishing point makes the picture appear to be more three-dimensional. Even if only at the rudimentary stages, any student who begins to employ this technique in drawing is showing an awareness of the differences between two- and three-dimensional geometry and should be encouraged to explore further. The foundations for real-world applications and career choices are being established even at this early age.

Another extension of two-dimensional geometry into the three-dimensional arena involves perspective drawings. Here again there is a career choice possibility. Drafting exercises often require drawing three different views of a three-dimensional object. From those views, you should be able to tell what the object is. What is

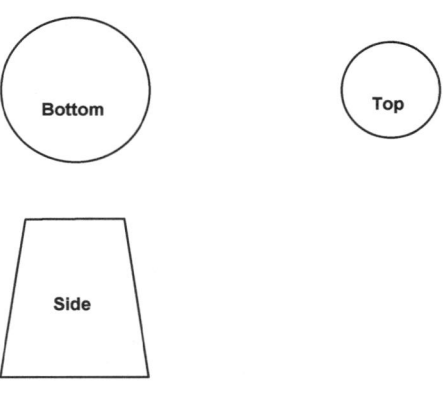

FIG. 4.34.

shown by Fig. 4.34? Figure 4.35 shows that it is a trash can placed upside down.

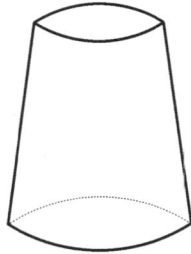

FIG. 4.35.

The interpretation of Fig. 4.34 requires flexible thinking and some good foundations in the basics of geometry.

Certainly the situations in drafting are much more complex, but this is a beginning. If you encourage your students to do these type of drawings to represent a three-dimensional object, you will be taking advantage of their inherent knowledge of objects and perhaps starting them along a career path at the same time.

What we have done here is only a rudimentary beginning. Shapes are one way to enter the wonderful world of geometry, where so many applications can be seen. We implore you to continue investigating shapes and geometry. You could find some interesting topics that could be used in an elementary school classroom.

Geometry is everywhere. It is important that we provide the activities and opportunities for children to make the connections of geometry and everyday life. Geometry also lends itself to endless hands-on explorations, which allow children to experience mathematics for themselves. These activities help create self-learners. The use of technology and the incorporation of literature can enhance the teaching and learning of mathematics in general and geometry in particular. This is evident when demonstrating the concepts of geometry that have been so abstract to students in prior years. Give your students the chance to experience geometry firsthand. Geometry can be an exciting topic to explore in mathematics.

REFERENCES

Serra, M. (1997). *Discovering geometry: An inductive approach* (2nd ed.). Berkeley, CA: Key Curriculum Press.

Tompert, A. (1990). *Grandfather Tang's story*. New York: Crown.

5
Measurement in the Elementary School

FOCAL POINTS

- Basic Measurement
- Readiness
- Need for Measurement
- Inch–Foot–Pound
- Metric
- Time
- Money
- Estimation and Measurement
- Area
- Perimeter
- Circumference
- Volume

BASIC MEASUREMENT

Children wake up to a type of measurement—time. The clock tells us how much time is left to complete our current project. A bowl of Cream of Wheat is made by using three tablespoons of Cream of Wheat and three fourths of a cup of hot water and then cooking it for a minute and a half. Measurement comes into play as the distance from home to school is considered. Lunch money (another measure) is collected at school. Measurement is an integral part of our lives. We need to prepare students to effectively handle a multitude of situations that involve measurement.

READINESS

Measurement should be integrated throughout all levels of the mathematics curricu-

lum. The developmental level of each individual determines the depth of inclusion of measurement in the curriculum. Exactly when measurement should be started is not something that can be assigned to a grade or age level. Readiness must be considered. Piaget did some interesting studies dealing with conservation. A classic one involves having a child establish that two lengths of material are the same. An example of how this would be done by the student is shown in Fig. 5.1. The individual conducting the study would alter the length of one of the objects to satisfy the child's desire to get both of them to be the same length. Once the child has agreed that the objects are the same length and while the child is watching, one of the objects is moved, as shown in Fig. 5.2. The child is again asked if the objects are the same length. If the child says they are, the indications are that the child is conserving length. If the

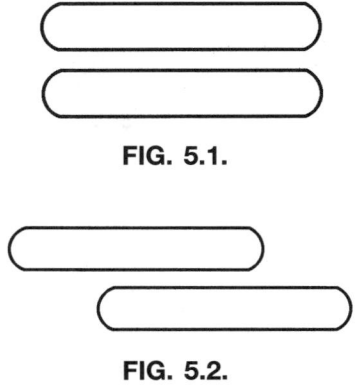

FIG. 5.1.

FIG. 5.2.

child says the objects are no longer the same length, then the indications are that the child is not conserving length. That result has a dramatic impact on that child's ability to perform measurement tasks involving linear measure.

If a student is not conserving length and we ask that something be measured, we essentially are asking that child to use a ruler that changes length when it is moved from one location to another. This contradicts the necessity for having a constant unit of measure, which is an essential feature of standard measurement systems. Use of measurement can show children a need for learning other concepts such as decimals and fractions.

NEED FOR MEASUREMENT

Ask your students to provide you with a list of tasks that they performed the previous day. Display several of these activities in the front of the room. Next to each activity, ask the students to identify what measurement was used. For example, if the students said they rode in a vehicle yesterday, how do you measure the distance the vehicle traveled? How do you know how long you traveled in the car? Suppose they had a soda. How much soda was in the container? How do you know? Looking at the container reveals a unit of measurement—fluid ounces or milliliters. Many cans or bottles look as if they would hold more liquid than others. Looks can be deceiving. Some of these containers have concave bottoms, which allow less fluid to be placed in a taller container.

To make your point, purchase five different sized juice drink containers of comparable volume. These tend to work well because they come in so many different shapes and sizes. Cover the units and

place the containers in front of the class. Ask the students to rank order the drinks from least amount of liquid to greatest. Ask how many students will look at the number of milliliters or fluid ounces in the future.

Exercises

269. Develop an exercise to show the use of measurement in children's everyday lives.

270. What is the difference between a fluid ounce and an ounce?

Nonstandard Units

With children who are being introduced to linear measure for the first time, arrange the class into pairs with one being the measurer and the other the recorder. Ask each pair to find the length of two items (length of a bulletin board, width of a student desk or table, length of a student's foot, etc.) in the room. Ask all of them to measure the width of the entrance door. They may use any unit to measure their selected objects. Some may decide to use a belt or possibly a shoelace. Others might use a pencil, hand width, or paper clip. Whatever object is selected to serve as the unit, the need for fractions is probably going to be evident. Even if the student's fraction skills are not well established, they will be able to participate in these activities.

When the class is finished, have each pair list the item they measured and their results. After all the measurements are listed, ask the students what the measurements mean. Why are they coming up with different measures for the width of the door? Each measurement is meaningless because no one knows the length of the unit used. The goal is for the students to understand the importance of having a standard unit when trying to measure.

Have all the students measure how many hands wide the top of their desk or table is using their own hands. Although they all use hands, their answers are sure to be different due to the different sizes of hands. This activity can lead to a wonderful discussion regarding the importance of using standard units.

271. What other nonstandard units will children possibly use in the previous activity?

272. Develop an activity that shows the difficulty associated with using nonstandard units.

INCH–FOOT–POUND (U.S. COMMON, U.S. STANDARD)

The earlier we introduce our most commonly used units of measurement the better, but the nonstandard unit measuring is a critical beginning step to build the need for a standard unit. Most of your students will have heard of inch, foot, and pound. The problem is that many of these students do not actually know how much an inch, foot, or pound actually measures. It is important to begin by planning activities that illustrate which unit is appropriate for which situation. Students need to distinguish between the ideal time to use inches and feet.

Arrange the students into groups of three. Provide each group with a 12-inch ruler. Somewhere in the curriculum, students need to understand that length is the distance between two points on a ruler. Many students end up counting the marks on the ruler, not the spaces between the marks. Ask them to record the

lengths of a set of items (one m&m®, one drinking straw, length of their desk, paper clip, height of a member of the group).

Ask each group whether they used inches or feet to measure each item and why. This is also a wonderful opportunity to discuss why some students have slightly different answers than others, even if they both used inches, for example. More than likely, some will give fractional answers, while others round to the nearest inch. This is an excellent opportunity to introduce an application of the concepts of rounding and estimation. For example, an m&m® is approximately one-half inch in diameter. How many students said one-half inch and how many said one inch? After the discussion, ask each student to write an essay describing 10 items that would be best measured using inches as the unit of measure and 10 items that would be best using feet. Be sure the reasoning is justified for each unit as a logical response that supports the answer.

The skills involved in using a ruler are quite complex. The last activity discussed had students measuring things with a 12-inch ruler. If they used the full length of the ruler, they probably were using about $12\frac{1}{4}$ inches because of how the ruler is made. Some rulers are calibrated to sixteenths of an inch for each inch. Others are calibrated to thirty-seconds for the first few inches, then to sixteenths for a few inches, and then to eighths for the rest. All of those little marks between the units can be very confusing. Which mark means what? The message is that you need to take great care in helping students understand the difference between each of the marks and why they represent what they do. It is imperative that they have a solid understanding of fractions. The weaker their ability with fractions, the simpler their rulers should be. That is, if the students understand only halves and fourths, you need to supply them with rulers that are calibrated only to fourths.

METRIC SYSTEM

In 1975, Congress decided that the United States should convert from the inch–foot–pound system of measurement to the metric system. All mathematics curricula were revised to include this new measurement system. As we know, this plan never fully materialized, and most U.S. people still use the inch–foot–pound system while the remainder of the world uses the metric system. The interesting part is that, although the country primarily does not use the metric system, it is still prevalent in many levels of elementary and secondary mathematics. One reason is due to the metric system's base 10 heritage. The metric system is an application topic when discussing things like exponents and place value.

The founding fathers of our country wanted to establish a decimally based measurement system and a decimally based monetary system. We have a modified decimal system with our money (penny, dime, dollar). The metric system has been an official measurement system in the United States for close to 200 years. We still use inch–foot–pound because, initially, most of our trade was with Canada and England, both of whom used inch–foot–pound measure.

Activities similar to the one used earlier when a 12-inch ruler was used should be inserted into your curriculum with metric rulers. Fraction interpretations are still necessary, but now each little mark will mean a tenth of something. As the lengths in these type activities are increased, the need to convert between units comes up. This is much more readily accomplished in the metric system because only multiplication or division by some integral power of 10 is involved. Certainly converting within the metric system is much easier than in the inch–foot–pound system. Students need to experience converting in both systems.

TIME

What time is it? Did you just look at your watch or a nearby clock? Maybe you have a digital watch and just read the numerals. Telling time is a skill that we tend to take for granted. It happens to be one of the most difficult concepts to teach as well as one of the more difficult ones for children to learn. Believe it or not, many fifth and sixth graders cannot read an analog clock accurately. Think about our time system.

60 seconds = 1 minute
60 minutes = 1 hour
24 hours = 1 day
365.25 days = 1 year

This does not make much sense to a child learning to tell time. One way to begin is to try to get students to have a better understanding of the concepts of seconds and minutes. Even as adults, we have trouble accurately using these terms. We tell each other, "I'll be there in a second." We might get there in 5 minutes. We might say, "I'll see you in a few minutes." We might get there in 20 minutes. These examples confuse students when learning about time.

Have each student close their eyes, telling them that when you say "go," you want them to wait until they think 1 minute has passed and raise their hands. Tell the students to keep their eyes closed when they raise their hands. When you say "go," begin timing the event. Talk out loud while timing. Ask them to recite their phone number, address, and name of their favorite animal while the timing is taking place.

This makes it difficult for the students to count in their head while they are waiting. When all students have raised their hands or after a couple minutes, have them put their hands down and open their eyes. Give the class the range of times they produced. You will be amazed at the disparity of times. The students will be surprised at their lack of the concept of a true minute.

Time can be taught in early grades in moderation. The more you use the concepts associated with time, the more familiar your students will become. You can introduce time by allowing students to measure time using only hours. Teach the student to tell time to the hour. This can be followed by half-hour intervals. As fractions are introduced, you can show students that the clock can be divided into fourths. This will provide an opportunity to round to the nearest quarter hour. Students can then make the association between half hour and 30 minutes and quarter hour and 15 minutes. As the sequence progresses, care must be taken to help the students that the numeral "1" on an analog clock really represents one set of 5 minutes. This is why when the minute hand is pointing at the "1" on the clock and the hour hand is just a little past the 3, we say 5 after 3 or "3 oh 5."

Exercises

273. Will you display a clock in your classroom? Why or why not? If you do, where will you place the clock in the room and why?

274. Do you advocate the use of a digital or analog clock for children? Support your response.

MONEY

Money can also be confusing for students. Unfortunately, the size and color of our coins and paper money do not help.

In many countries, the smaller the coin, the smaller the monetary value. Likewise, the larger the coin, the greater the value of the coin. In the United States, this is not the case at all. The dime is not the smallest valued coin.

The easiest way for students to become more adept at counting money is by using money manipulatives in class. It is important to give children an opportunity to use their money manipulatives to purchase merchandise similar to real life. One way to accomplish this is to establish a school store in your classroom. Set up a reward system. Pay students different amounts of money manipulatives based on accomplished goals or tasks in class. Perhaps they could purchase privileges like eating with a friend from another class, being line leader, using a special chair, taking shoes off (careful), and so on. Each morning before class begins, allow students to use their money to purchase items from your class store. These items could come from parents and local businesses. Items such as pencils, stickers, pens, erasers, and notebooks are just a few possibilities. Allow two different students each day to become the cashiers for the store. Make sure that the cashiers check each other's work when they collect payment and return change for a purchased item. Some places have a school-wide store and money as part of behavior modification programs. Activities such as these can be quite helpful in helping students establish money skills.

One of the more difficult skills for many students to learn is how to give change. You have probably been given change in the form of coins and bills for a purchase. Ideally the cashier would count your change to you as it is given. If the purchase cost $13.27 and you gave a $20 bill, the proper way to get your change would be to have the cashier say $13.27

(representing the cost), then $13.29, $13.30, $13.40, $13.50, $13.75, $14, $15, $20. This assumes you got back 2 pennies, 2 dimes, 2 quarters, 1 dollar, and 5 dollars. Certainly other combinations could have been used. The point is that you now know that the change give is correct because it was counted to you. Much earlier, we discussed the difficulty children have with the concept of counting on. Here is an application of the counting on principle. Regretfully, this is rarely done. One reason is that it takes too long, but another sad reason is that many of our graduates do not know how to count change properly.

Exercise

275. List different games that could be used to teach children about the concept of money.

Measurement is an important concept that needs to be introduced as early as kindergarten. Having students use a variety of measuring devices allows hands-on experiences with many different units of measure. Measurement can be incorporated into almost any area of the mathematics curriculum at any level, from addition to division and from algebra to geometry. Continually allow students to experience situations using real-life activities where measurement is needed and the students will develop a true sense of the importance of different units of measurement in the real world.

AREA

When developing the concept of area, it is important that students know the multiplication facts, be adept at basic multiplication, and know different units of measure-

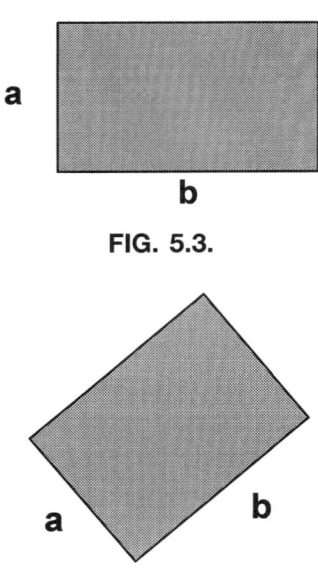

FIG. 5.3.

FIG. 5.4.

ment that can be associated with length. Is there a difference between the length and width of a rectangle? Observe Figs. 5.3 and 5.4. Which is the length in Fig. 5.3, side a or b? Which is width in Fig. 5.3, side a or b? Is the length always the longer side? Is the width always on the left or right side and the length on the top or bottom? If you think this makes it complicated, which is the length and width in Fig. 5.4, side a or b? The answer to the previous questions is that it does not matter which side is called the length or width. It is only necessary that the student define one side as the length and a side perpendicular to it as the width (base and height might be used).

What Is Area?

How would you define *area* to a child? The *American Heritage Dictionary of the English Language* defines *area* as the measure of a planar region or the surface of a solid. Does that definition make sense to you? Would a child understand this definition?

Ideally children learn about area by working with objects such as rectangles and triangles. When finding the area of a rectangle, many students are told to multiply the length by the width. Some argue that base and height should be used instead of length and width because those words are used with most other polygons. The area of the rectangle in Fig. 5.3 is the shaded region inside the boundary line segments. Stating that the area is a × b or ab does not really indicate whether a student understands the concept of the area of a rectangle. Observe Fig. 5.5. Without using a measuring device, which rectangle has the greater area? Can you tell?

FIG. 5.5.

Why or why not? What do you think a child would say?

One method of describing area is to divide the shaded region into a gridlike pattern as seen in Fig. 5.6. Count the number of squares that are contained in each rectangle. The grid was constructed so that

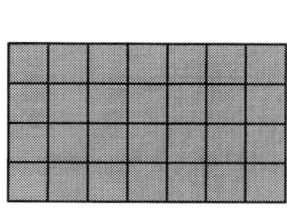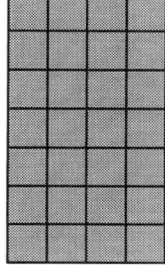

FIG. 5.6.

the squares in each rectangle have the same dimensions. Therefore, the distance

between the segments in each rectangle is the same. Each rectangle contains 28 squares. Because we do not know the actual length of the sides of each square, we say that the rectangle has an area of 28 square units. We do not need to know the size of the unit squares if we are trying to determine whether one rectangle has greater area than the other. It is important to know that the squares in each rectangle are congruent, however. That is, we want to determine the area of each rectangle using the same units. By using a pictorial representation of the area, the students can see why the areas are equal.

Exercises

276. Find a definition of area in three elementary textbooks. Do the texts state a definition of area or do they give the definition along with the picture of a rectangle?

277. Find three elementary textbooks. How does each text instruct the student to find the area of a rectangle? Do all three texts use length × width?

Arrange your students into pairs. Take your class into a hall or location that has a tiled floor. Establish a rectangular boundary around a section of the hall or floor. Ask the students to determine the area within the boundary. Most students will quickly realize that they can use the tiles as a unit of measure. Partial squares will have to be combined with other partial squares, so they might need to do some estimating. (This could help convince students of the need to accurately add fractions.) In some cases, students with excellent observation skills may look to the ceiling to find the area of the floor. Some school ceilings are made of square ceiling tiles. These tiles are usually 2′ × 2′ or 2′ × 4′ tiles. A good problem solver may realize that they need to add fewer ceiling tiles

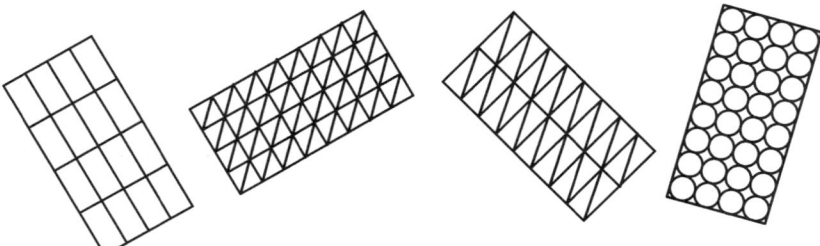

FIG. 5.7.

than floor tiles. This takes less time with less chance of a counting error. Other students may use different units of measure, such as sheets of paper or other objects. Originality has a chance to show during this activity.

Squares are typically used as a standard unit for measuring area. That has been an agreed on thing in mathematics mainly because of convenience of computation and estimation. You will see later that squares are used to find the area of triangles and circles. For some triangles, partial squares can easily be used to complete the area. That is not the case with circles. By the same token, sometimes triangles could easily be used to determine the area of some figures. We would need to adapt to different terminology because area would be reported in triangular regions rather than square units. That would sound strange to us—not because it is incorrect, but because we are not accustomed to hearing area expressed in terms other than square units. In fact, we could use standard sized circles to measure area. They certainly could fit well in some circles. Figure 5.7 shows a rectangle that could have its area measured in terms of rectangles, triangles, and circles.

Once students understand the idea behind finding the area of a rectangle, they usually graduate to finding the area of a triangle. As with finding the area of a rectangle, students are typically told that to

find the area of a triangle, you multiply half of the base by the height (remember some argue for base and height as opposed to length and width when dealing with rectangles). Then students are given 10 triangles and asked to find the area. Do students understand this new formula? Let us start over.

Observe rectangle ABCD in Fig. 5.8.

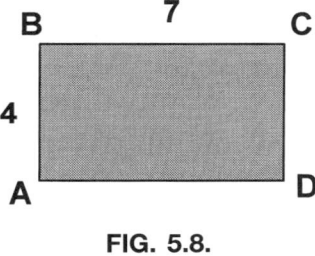

FIG. 5.8.

We will construct a diagonal AC for the rectangle as shown in Fig. 5.9. Because

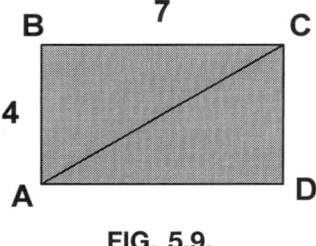

FIG. 5.9.

you find the area of a rectangle by finding the product of the length and the width, you can assign four as the width and seven as the length to determine the area as 28 square units. The diagonal divides the rectangle into two congruent parts as shown in Fig. 5.10.

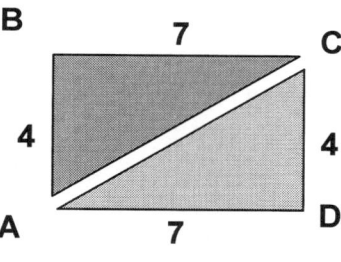

FIG. 5.10.

Because we know that each figure is half the area of the rectangle, each triangle must be the area of the rectangle divided by 2 or $\frac{bh}{2}$, which is also $\frac{1}{2}bh$. Now the students can see that the area of the triangles shown in Fig. 5.9 are actually half the area of the rectangle shown in Figs. 5.7 and 5.8. They should also see the connection between the area of a rectangle, which is the product of the rectangle's length (base) and width (height) and half the product of the triangle's base and height.

The diagonal of a rectangle divides it into two congruent parts. An easy way to show this with students is to have each child fold a rectangular-shaped piece of paper along the diagonal between opposite corners. Cut along that diagonal and one piece can be placed on top of the other to show they are congruent. Because the rectangle is cut into two congruent pieces, one of the triangles represents one of two equal sized pieces or one half of the area of the rectangle. Thus, the formula for the area of a triangle is one half the base times the height.

A geoboard could be used to show this conclusion a different way. Figure 5.11 shows a geoboard with triangles on it. Each of the triangles is surrounded by a rectangle that is congruent to each of the others. Triangles a and d are easily seen to be half of the area of the respective surrounding rectangle. Figure 5.12 shows an added segment that divides the initial

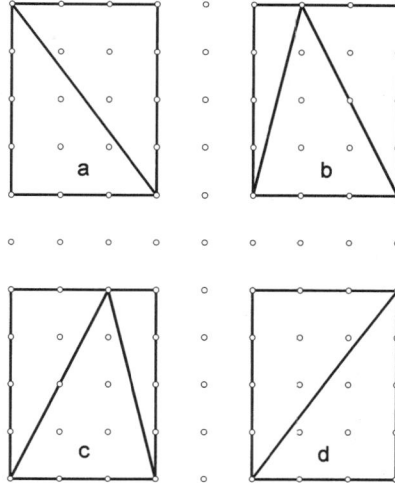

FIG. 5.11.

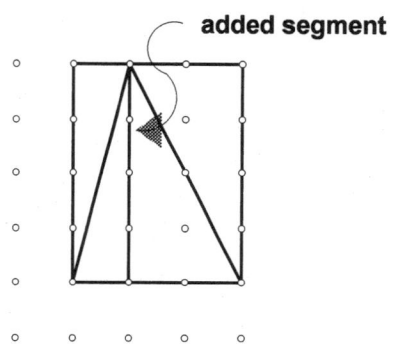

added segment

FIG. 5.12.

rectangle into two smaller rectangles. The areas of each of those smaller rectangles still sum to be the area of the initial rectangle. However, two of the sides of the triangle divide the smaller rectangles in half as before. When the half rectangular areas are added, the sum is the area of the triangle, which is still going to be half of the original rectangle.

Exercises

278. State the formula for finding the area of a parallelogram. Explain how you could model this to a child.

279. State the formula for finding the area of a rhombus. Explain how you could model this to a child.

280. Create a lesson that uses a geoboard to find the area of a triangle like Part c in Fig. 5.12.

281. Create a lesson that uses a geoboard to show how to find the area of any convex quadrilateral.

282. Describe in writing how Pick's Theorem can be used to find the area of any polygon on a geoboard. An introductory source can be found at http://mathforum.org/dr.math/problems/lindsay2.8.96.html.

Typically after students are provided with the formula for finding the area of a triangle, an accompanying worksheet with 20 different triangle area problems is provided. Each triangle has the base and the height listed. Therefore, the student has to find the product of the height and base and divide by two. Is the child really thinking or just acting on rote memorization skills? Many students still have trouble believing what they are truly seeing. For example, observe Fig. 5.13. Which triangle has the greater area? It is hard to

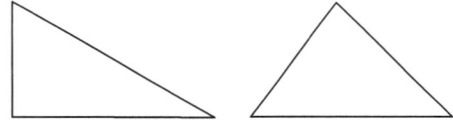

FIG. 5.13.

tell from the figure. When looking at Fig. 5.14, it may surprise you to find that the area of each triangle is the same. This is

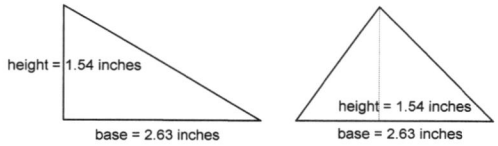

FIG. 5.14.

the case because the base and height of each triangle are identical. Unfortunately, it is still difficult to convince many children

that the area is the same because the triangles look so different.

When using dynamic geometry software such as Geometer's Sketchpad, students have the opportunity to become active learners through the discovery of properties by making their own conjectures and testing their logic. As seen in Fig. 5.13, it can be difficult to determine the difference between the areas of triangles. It is also hard for a student to understand why a particular formula works because their only validation comes from doing computational work to determine the solution. In Geometer's Sketchpad, the user can construct an animation that can open students' eyes to a new world of mathematics. For this next activity, you need a computer with a dynamic program like Geometer's Sketchpad and some type of projection device or connection to a large TV or monitor to display your computer to the entire class.

Create triangle ABC similar to Fig. 5.15.

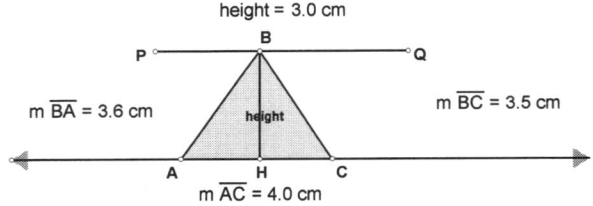

$$\text{Area} = \frac{1}{2} \cdot (m\,\overline{AC}) \cdot \text{height} = 6.00\ cm^2$$

FIG. 5.15.

Animate Point B along segment PQ and ask the students to share their observations. What is changing and what remains the same? Segments AB and BC have changing lengths, but segments AC (the base of the triangle) and BH (the height of the triangle) remain the same. Figure 5.16 shows a simulation of different triangles created by the animation of triangle ABC. Students should notice that the area is remaining the same even though the trian-

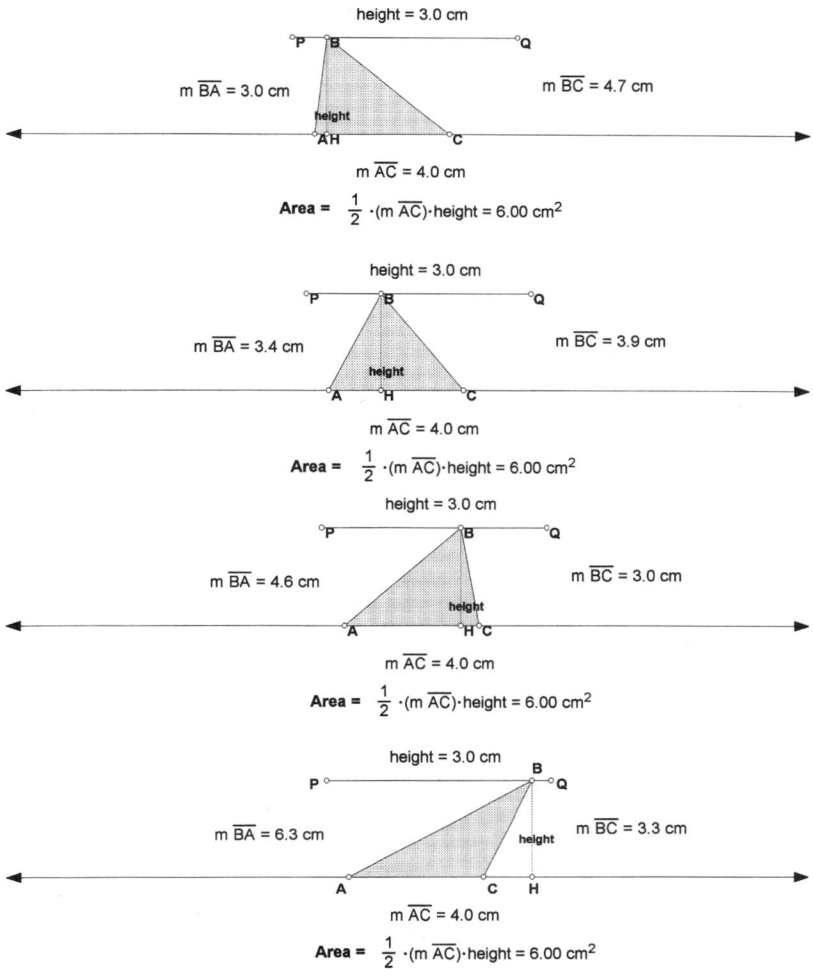

height = 3.0 cm

m $\overline{BA}$ = 3.0 cm   m $\overline{BC}$ = 4.7 cm

m $\overline{AC}$ = 4.0 cm

Area = $\frac{1}{2}$ ·(m $\overline{AC}$)·height = 6.00 cm²

height = 3.0 cm

m $\overline{BA}$ = 3.4 cm   m $\overline{BC}$ = 3.9 cm

m $\overline{AC}$ = 4.0 cm

Area = $\frac{1}{2}$ ·(m $\overline{AC}$)·height = 6.00 cm²

height = 3.0 cm

m $\overline{BA}$ = 4.6 cm   m $\overline{BC}$ = 3.0 cm

m $\overline{AC}$ = 4.0 cm

Area = $\frac{1}{2}$ ·(m $\overline{AC}$)·height = 6.00 cm²

height = 3.0 cm

m $\overline{BA}$ = 6.3 cm   m $\overline{BC}$ = 3.3 cm

m $\overline{AC}$ = 4.0 cm

Area = $\frac{1}{2}$ ·(m $\overline{AC}$)·height = 6.00 cm²

FIG. 5.16.

gle is moving. How can this be? Develop a class discussion to help the students observe that the area stays the same because the height and base remain constant. This allows students to discover and understand why the height and base of a triangle are used in the formula for area. Once again, children become active participants by discovering the mathematics behind the concepts.

PERIMETER

How many elementary students would understand the meaning of the word *perimeter*? If you ask for the perimeter of a rectangle, will the student incorrectly supply you with the area? Is it important for the child to know the formula for finding the perimeter of a rectangle? The perimeter is the distance around an object. When children hear the word *perimeter*, they should be thinking distance. To find the perimeter of a rectangle, what instructions would you give your students? How about, "find the sum of the lengths of all the sides." To find the perimeter of a triangle, find the sum of the lengths of all the sides. As a matter of fact, to find the perimeter of any polygon, don't you just find the sum of the lengths of all the sides?

Is there a need for a multitude of formulas? The fewer the number of formulas we ask students to memorize, the more we can expect them to retain. Because the perimeter is the distance around an object, that should be the concept we want the student to understand. What does the formula $P = 2L + 2W$ tell a child? Isn't it a shortcut to find the sum of two lengths and two widths of a rectangle. Would it be bad if a child were to use $P = L + L + W + W$?

Students are not ready for perimeter as soon as addition is encountered. They also need to have a handle on measuring distances and what lengths mean. Otherwise we are asking them to memorize a meaningless procedure. Incorporating activities and exercises involving perimeter provides an opportunity for children to practice addition and problem solving. Once the concept of perimeter is introduced, it can be a useful diagnostic topic for addition and problem-solving skills.

For example, provide Fig. 5.17 for the children. Ask them to find the perimeter of the object. All angles in Fig. 5.17 are right angles. While that may be meaningless to

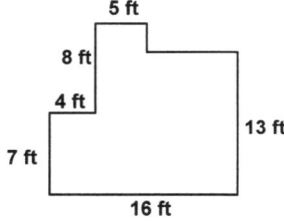

FIG. 5.17.

your students initially, you can use that information to reveal pertinent facts that could direct their future thinking. Be sure to have the students explain their work as they solve this problem. Notice that two of the side lengths are not provided in Fig. 5.17. There is enough information provided for many students to complete the task. You are possibly looking at three skills: addition facts, proper concept of perimeter, and problem-solving strategies. Solving this type of problem is difficult for

many students because they have to combine several pieces of information and then draw conclusions. In this example, looking at the left side of Fig. 5.17, there are vertical lengths of 7 and 8 feet, giving a total height of 15 feet. There are also two right vertical measurements on the right, but only one of them is known. Because all angles are right angles, the students can conclude that the missing height must be 15 feet − 13 feet, giving a missing length of 2 feet for x in Fig. 5.18. Similarly, information can be pieced together to determine the missing horizontal length to be 7 feet as shown in Fig. 5.18.

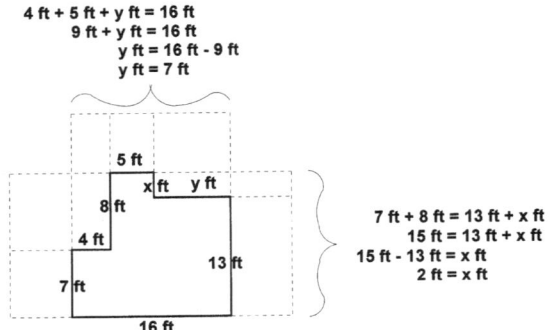

FIG. 5.18.

Confusing Perimeter With Area

If you ask a middle school class to answer the question in Fig. 5.19, how many would say A, B, C, or D? Many students will select A. Why do you think this is the case? There are several reasons. One possibility is the fact that area = L × W happens to be one of those memorized

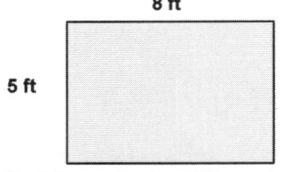

Find the perimeter of the rectangle.

A) 40 square feet   B) 13 feet   C) 26 feet   D) not A, B, or C

FIG. 5.19.

formulas that sticks in students' minds. Perhaps students recognize the rectangle in Fig. 5.19 because of having to repeatedly find the area of figures that looked just like it. Therefore, when they see a rectangle with only two side's lengths identified, they automatically think of using L × W. Typically, students do more problems dealing with finding the area of rectangles and that could become an overriding force as they look at the picture. The thought process could be, "I have seen this before and I multiplied the Length and Width." Many students find the area out of reflexive habit. No matter what the reason, it is apparent that elementary students need to work with the concept of perimeter more at earlier ages. When you think about it, finding the area requires multiplication while finding the perimeter can be done with only addition.

Exercises

283. Define *circumference*. When is this term used in mathematics?

284. Give an example of when the value of the area of a rectangle can equal the perimeter of a rectangle. Are other examples possible? Explain your answer.

285. Is it possible for the circumference and area of a circle to be equal? Explain your answer.

Children love to go on field trips. Have you ever thought of having a field trip on the school grounds—literally a trip around the school? The goal is for groups of students to measure the perimeter of the entire school. Be sure to check with the school administration before conducting this data-gathering experiment. You will need to get some other adults to assist with each group as you consider student safety and behavior.

Before beginning, explain which section of the building each group will be measuring. It is important to have a discussion on measuring techniques when using a tape measure. Measuring the base of each wall (if the ground is level) or along a brick seam will allow the best chances of horizontal measures, which will give the shortest length for each section. Decide on the unit of measure that would be used to make the tabulation of the data easier in the end. Be sure to discuss how the data are to be recorded.

When all groups have finished measuring their sections, return to the classroom to tabulate the data. If you have an aerial photograph of the school or a sketch of the base of the building, the class could label the dimensions of each part of the school. Have the students try to determine the section they measured. This is not always as easy as it sounds.

The class could construct a layout of the school on poster board, labeling points of interest. You could contact students in another school and ask them to do a similar activity. Which school has the greater perimeter? The opportunity for using these data is endless. List all of the lengths measured. What is the range of the lengths of the sides of the building? Median? Mean? Mode? What are the implications if the smaller perimeter belongs to the school with more people?

CIRCUMFERENCE

To find the perimeter of a given polygon, you find the sum of the lengths of all its sides. If this is the case, how do you find the perimeter of a circle, since a circle is not a polygon? It does not have sides. It has one continuously curved side. The perimeter of a circle is called the circumference. Because you do not have multiple sides to add, the process for finding the circumference is a little different. If you simply want to tell a student the method for obtaining the circumference of a circle, it is determined by finding the product of the circle's diameter (or twice the radius) and the constant Pi (π). Therefore, the formula is $C = \pi d$ (or $2\pi r$), where C is the circumference and d is the circle's diameter. Some elementary textbooks simplify the process by saying the circumference is approximately three times the diameter. Unfortunately, neither formula gives any insight into how the circumference is determined or the derivation of π.

Arrange the students into pairs. Each pair needs a measuring device (ruler, meter, or yard stick), string, calculator, and four or five different sized round objects. An inherent assumption for this activity is that the students possess the appropriate skills in using the measurement tools. It is best if each pair has a variety of round objects. Ask the class how they could measure the distance around one of the circular objects using a ruler. One way would be to wrap a part of the string around the object. Take that section of string and stretch it along the ruler to determine its length. Another approach is to mark a spot on the object where it touches a smooth flat surface, roll it along the surface until that spot again touches the surface, mark that spot, and then measure the distance between the spots. This works well with right circular cylinders. Have each pair find the circumference of each circular object they were given and record it.

Next, have each pair use their string or measuring device to determine and record the diameter of each object. This is not as easy as it sounds. Care must be taken to record the greatest distance across the circle. One interesting way to do this is to have two known right angles (shoe boxes work well). Place the round object between the two boxes as shown in Fig. 5.20. Measure the distance be-

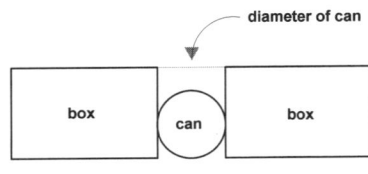

FIG. 5.20.

tween the two boxes (along a line parallel to the top of the can) and you have the diameter of the can.

Now have the students compute (wonderful time to use calculators) the circumference of each object divided by its respective diameter. This missing factor is the ratio of the circle's circumference to its diameter. Tell the students to round the quotient to the nearest hundredth and record this information with the circumference and diameter of each object. What similarities and differences do they notice? Many of the calculations will be between 3.10 and 3.20. Some may get close to 3.14, which is a common approximation of π. It is important for the students to notice that the ratios are all very close to each other even though the diameters could vary significantly. If π is always the same, why did the ratios slightly differ from each other and from π? It is important to discuss the errors that can occur when measuring (human error and lack of precision). This activity promotes discovery learning.

Exercise

286. Does $\frac{22}{7} = \pi$? Explain your reasoning.

VOLUME

Take a look inside your refrigerator. Is there a lot of excess space for you to put additional groceries in there if you went shopping tomorrow? Do you have a lot of leftovers taking up space? Do you sometimes wish you had a bigger refrigerator? Do you think that you have a small or large refrigerator right now? How would you know if your refrigerator is large or small? You could just compare it to a friend's. Obviously, you cannot simply take your refrigerator over to their house and check them out side by side. What would you do? Would you measure both units? Does the taller one hold more food or possibly the wider one? One dilemma is that some refrigerators have a top freezer and bottom refrigerator and some are side-by-side models. Therefore, you could not simply use only height or width.

When checking out a refrigerator's size, you typically want to know how much food the unit can store. Therefore, you are looking for the interior space or volume of the refrigerator. Volume is the three-dimensional measurement that shows how much space is inside the refrigerator. Therefore, to determine which refrigerator is larger, we need the volume of each unit. The question is how do we determine volume? By the way, one easy way is to get the owners manual or maybe check on the unit. It might give you the volume. We have to be careful to discuss this idea with students. If students think of looking in the refrigerator's owner's manual for the answer, they could easily become convinced that mathematics was invented to make their lives more miserable.

To begin discussing the concept of volume, we take another look at area. Figure 5.21 displays a rectangle (two-dimensional polygon) and a right, rectangular-based

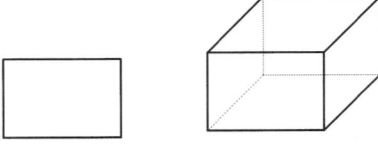

FIG. 5.21.

prism (three-dimensional object) or box. The rectangle has length and width—two dimensions. The rectangular prism has length, width, and height—three dimensions. When describing the area to children, we sectioned off the rectangle into square units. By counting them, we could determine the area of the rectangle as shown in Fig. 5.22. The volume of a three-dimensional object is determined by finding the number of cubic units in the ob-

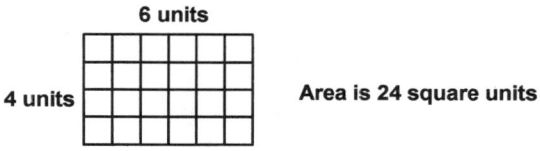

FIG. 5.22.

ject. Figure 5.23 displays a box as cubic units are constructed to fill the volume of

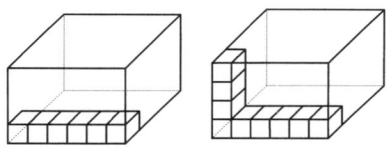

FIG. 5.23.

the box. The object is for students to understand that volume is measured by filling the box with cubic units.

A child can count the number of square units in the rectangle to find its area. Eventually, the student discovers that, by finding the product of the length and width, you can obtain the same value as counting the square units. The student discovers that multiplication can be much quicker. How many cubic units would be in the rectangular prism that is four units wide, six units long, and three units high? Manipulatives such as unifix cubes provide excellent hands-on experiences when learning about volume. These cubes connect together, allowing the student to make a rectangular prism with the specified dimensions. Children have numerous options when constructing their boxes. They can make unifix towers of three cubes and then connect four towers together. This will take 12 cubes as shown in Fig. 5.24. Then by constructing and

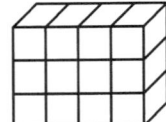

FIG. 5.24.

connecting six more configurations, the student will have a box that is three cubes high, four cubes wide, and six cubes long as simulated in Fig. 5.25. Counting the cubes yields 72 cubic units.

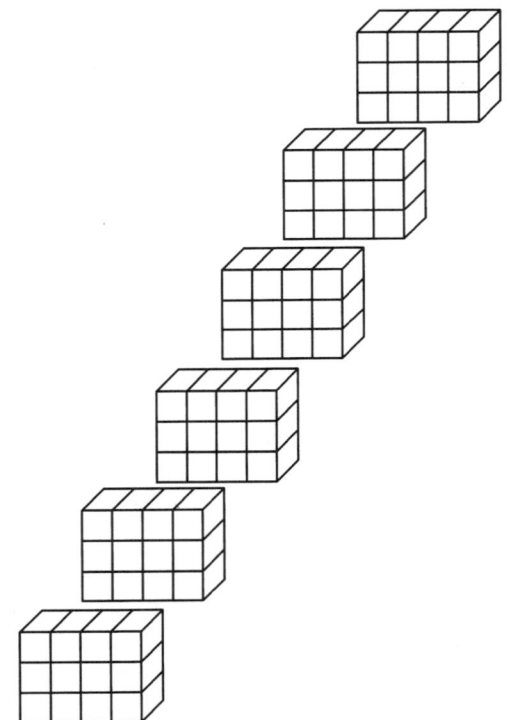

FIG. 5.25.

Exercises

287. Other than unifix cubes, what other types of manipulatives could you use to demonstrate volume?

288. What real-world things are measured using volume?

Children sometimes need some extra hands-on activities to understand mathematical concepts. When dealing with volume, children can still be a little foggy on what they are actually looking for. Volume represents how much something holds. Initially volume could be expressed in terms of how many paper clip boxes a larger box will hold, assuming the paper clip boxes are carefully placed into the larger box. Eventually, there is a need to express volume in terms of standard units of measure. The inside of a refrigerator is an example, but it may not be a good enough example because elementary students are not usually in the market for a new refrigerator. The following activity might help students begin to grasp the holding capacity (volume) of objects.

Divide the class into groups of three or four students. Provide each group with four different sized containers that can hold water, many paper towels, a larger basin, and a plastic pitcher of water. Each container should vary in height and width. Ask the students to arrange the containers in order from the container that will hold the least amount of water to the one that will hold the greatest. Then have them place the container they believe will hold the least amount of liquid in the basin (to catch any overflow water). Fill the container with water. Place the next larger container into the basin. Pour all the water from the first container into the second. If all the water fits into the second container without any overflow, then their assumption as to which container is the smallest appears correct. Fill the remaining portion of Container two with water and repeat the process with Container three. If all the water fits into the third container from the second without any overflow, then their assumption again appears correct and they move to the final container. If there is an overflow, the group has to reorder their containers because that would mean that a perceived larger container holds less water then the previous one. Students should begin to realize that the taller object does not necessarily hold more—or in other words, have a greater volume.

Technology can allow teachers to demonstrate mathematical concepts and principles that cannot be performed adequately using a piece of chalk. Figure 5.26 displays a rectangular prism constructed using Geometer's Sketchpad. Notice that this prism shows a length and width of the base of the prism along with its height. The software also allows the user to measure the lengths of selected objects, calculate the area of the base (Length × Width), and display the value in the proper units. There are several important features that we consider in the beginning of the exercise. First, notice that the length is 1.37 inches and the width is 1.22 inches. The product of the length and the width should be 1.6714 in^2, but the software yields 1.67 in^2 because it was set to round to the nearest hundredth of an inch. Measurements given for calculations are not as precise as they sometimes seem.

You would need to construct Fig. 5.26 before the lesson and display this construction so the entire class could view the image. As you click and drag Point E

down, notice what happens to the value of the height and volume. Figures 5.27 and 5.28 display two views of the prism with Point E dragged down the screen to

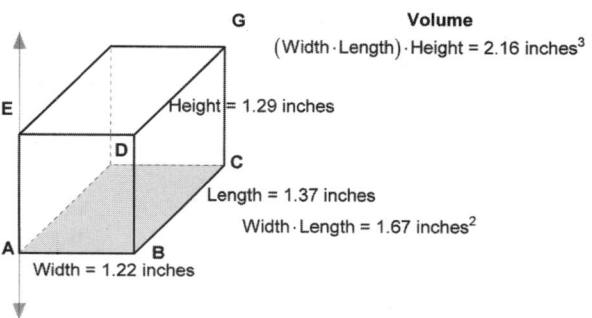

FIG. 5.27.

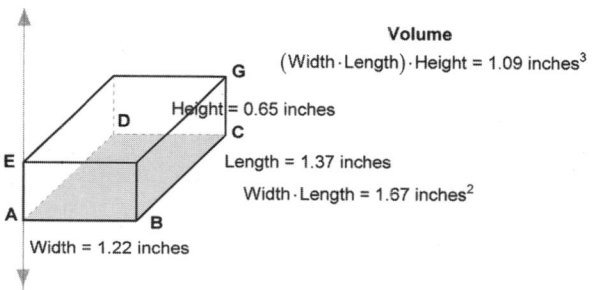

FIG. 5.28.

different locations. Ask your students what things are changing and what things are staying the same on the screen as you move Point E. Notice that the height and volume are changing, while the length and width of the base remains constant. What is the volume of this box dependent on? The answer is the height. When you take another look, you are trying to find the area of the prism's base first. To find the volume of the prism, you find the product of the area of the base and the height of the rectangular prism. This can be reinforced when you move Point E on top of Point A as shown in Fig. 5.29. Notice what happens. The height is now zero, causing the volume to be zero. Ask a student to explain why the volume is now zero. Because there is no height, the

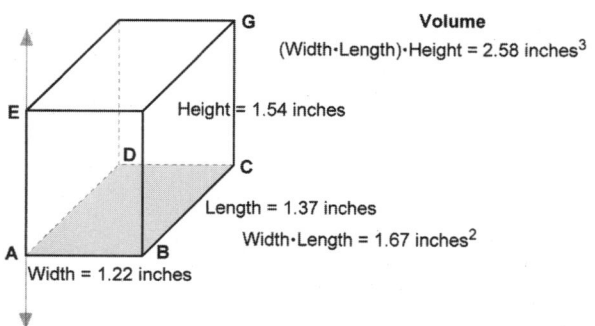

FIG. 5.26.

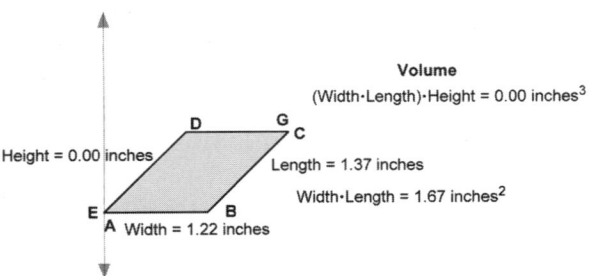

FIG. 5.29.

prism has become a two-dimensional figure. In student terms, it cannot hold anything because the box has become flat. We have gone from three dimensions to two dimensions. The best part about this activity is that the students can actually see the process as it occurs.

After seeing enough examples, the students will begin to realize that finding the area of the base is an excellent beginning for finding the volume of an object. Once the area of the base is known, determine the height and multiply them to get the volume. Figure 5.30 shows a right triangular

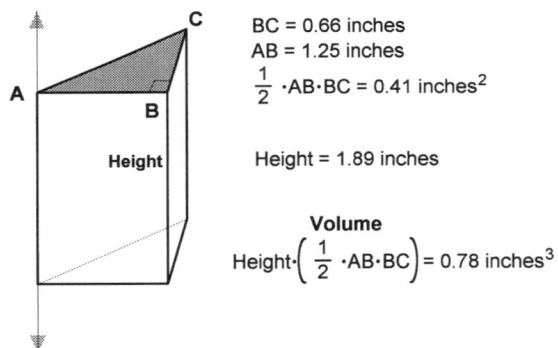

FIG. 5.30.

prism, which is another example of where students can find the volume by finding

the product of the area of the base of the prism and the height. The base for the triangular prism is a triangle. As Point A is moved, the height of the prism will change along with the volume, but the area of the base triangle will remain the same.

Exercises

289. For what other solids can you find the volume by multiplying the area of the base by the height? What solids will not work using that method?

290. Use a dynamic geometry software package to demonstrate how to find the volume of a right circular cylinder.

291. Will the formula Bh (B = area of the base) work for finding the volume of any prism? Did you consider only right prisms? Explain your answer.

By allowing students to play with manipulatives and use dynamic geometry software, they can gain a deeper conceptual understanding of area and volume. Technology allows the student and teacher to construct geometric figures that cannot be effectively drawn on paper or a board. Allow students to learn and see how mathematics is done in the 21st century.

REFERENCES

Gardella, F. J., Fraze, P. R., Meldon, J. E., Weingarden, M. S., & Campbell, C. (1992). *Mathematical connections: A bridge to algebra and geometry*. Boston, MA: Houghton-Mifflin.

Maganzini, C. (1997). *Cool math*. New York: Price Stern Sloan.

6
Data Analysis and Probability

FOCAL POINTS

- Gathering Data
- Interpreting the Results
- Fun Activities for Gathering Data
- Statistics
- Probability
- Integrating Literature With Probability

GATHERING DATA

One of our tasks in today's society is to sift through the abundance of data and retrieve the useful information. Every time you use the radio, TV, or newspaper, you are supplied with collected data. Commercials provide you with information stating, "four out of five doctors recommend. . . ." Newspapers and magazines present graphs representing data that have been collected from various sources. These graphs present a plethora of information in a small space. A graph is a picture, and a picture is worth a thousand words.

"When mathematical ideas are also connected to everyday experiences, both in and out of school, children become aware of the usefulness of mathematics" (NCTM, 1989, p. 32). We know that the more interesting and enjoyable the topic, the greater the students' attention. Teachers of mathematics should try to make connections between mathematics and things of interest in our student's lives. One difficulty is finding out what interests students.

An Interest Inventory can be used to determine what fascinates students. The information collected can be fun for the students, help you get to know them, and be used throughout the year. Questions could vary, but some could be:

1. When is your birthday?
2. How many pets do you have?
3. What is your favorite flavor of ice cream?
4. How many telephones do you have in your house?
5. How many brothers and sisters do you have?
6. What is your favorite color m&m candy?

Exercises

292. List three topics that can be used to make mathematics more meaningful to elementary children.
293. Construct an interest inventory that could be used in a class. Be sure to identify the grade level for this interest inventory.

Another effective means of collecting real data is to allow students to conduct their own surveys. Have each student come up with a topic of interest using one or two questions associated with that topic. Consider the colors of m&ms® candy. You are making the connection between mathematics and things that are meaningful to the students. A student can use the following questions:

What is your favorite m&ms®, plain or peanut?
What is your favorite color m&m®?

Students might survey their classmates or other students in the school. It is important that students record their survey responses. Figures 6.1 and 6.2 show sample data sheets students could use to record information. Tally marks would be a way for students to record the survey responses. When the survey is completed, each student should total the responses for each question and record the total number of participants. One objective of a survey such as this is to get the students to draw some conclusions from their survey data.

Graphs (bar graph or pie chart) are ways for students to display collected data. When using a bar graph or histogram, students can display the results of their collected data by showing the quantity of one response versus other responses. A sample bar graph of class responses for the question, "What is your favorite type of m&m® candy, plain or peanut?", is shown in Fig. 6.3. Notice that the bar graph clearly shows that one response was selected over the other. This may seem trivial to you, but it is a clear visual representation that plain m&m®s are preferred over peanut ones in the survey. Graph paper, rulers, and color pencils or markers are use-

What is your favorite m&m® candy, plain or peanut?

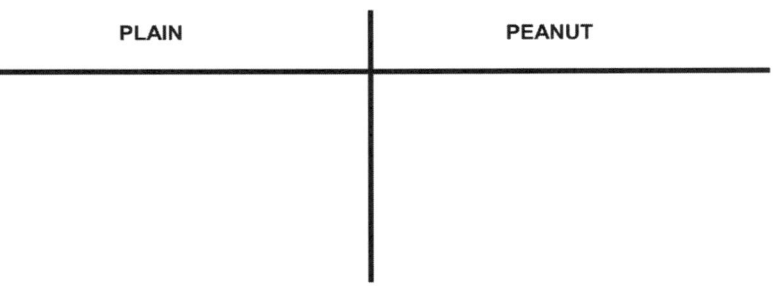

PLAIN	PEANUT

FIG. 6.1.

What is your favorite color m&m® candy?

Color	Number of Responses
Red	
Blue	
Brown	
Yellow	
Green	

FIG. 6.2.

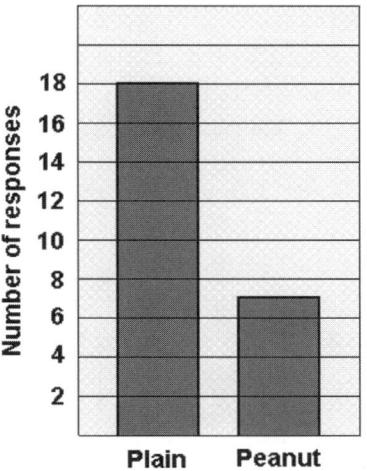

FIG. 6.3.

ful tools as students make their own bar graphs. Interpretation of the presented data, which is an important step in this process, is discussed later.

Figure 6.3 helps student determine that plain m&m®s are more popular than peanut ones. Pie charts also summarize collected data. The responses to Question 2 in the sample m&m® survey are shown in Fig. 6.4, which displays a label (m&m® color) as well as a percentage next to the

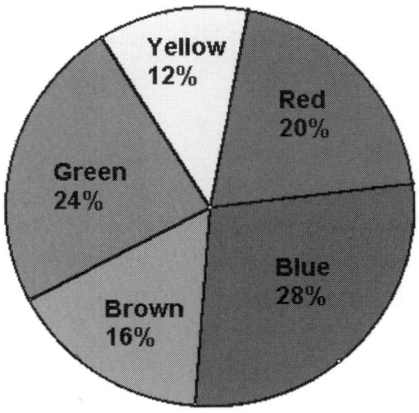

FIG. 6.4.

piece of the pie it represents. The percentage is found by dividing the number of responses by the total number of responses

for the class. If students are going to make pie charts by hand, it is important to begin with a close approximation of a circle and caenter of that circle. A good foundation of fractions and percentages is helpful. For example, Fig. 6.4 shows that green was selected 24% of the time. Because pie charts can be a little bit more complicated, have students create bar graphs prior to attempting pie charts.

Exercise

294. Name five other topics on which students can conduct a survey. Supply at least two questions that could be asked for each topic.
295. What mathematical concepts do students have to master prior to using bar graphs?
296. What mathematical concepts do students have to master prior to using pie charts?

Interpreting the Results

Collecting data using topics that interest children can increase enthusiasm for mathematics. Displaying the data by using bar graphs and pie charts can be fun, hands-on activities for children of all ages. Although the last two statements are true and provide justifiable reasons to conduct surveys and collect data, the true goal is for students to draw inferences, interpret the collected data, and draw some type of conclusion. Our goal with the use of data is to get the students to think and use analytical skills.

Look at Fig. 6.3. What conclusions can be drawn? More students like plain m&m®s than peanut ones. There is more information in the graph. Not only do more students like plain m&m®s, but more than twice the number of students prefer plain m&m®s over peanut m&m®s. That is significant. Furthermore, 18 out of 25 students preferred plain m&m®s over peanut. That is close to 75% of the class. Because approximately 75% of the students in the class prefer plain m&m®s over peanut, this would be a great time to make the connection between 75%, or three fourths of the students, which could be represented by the ratio of three out of every four students. One could also conclude that only 7 out of 25 students would rather have peanut m&m®s over plain ones. That is a little more than 25% of the students. Based on this information, you could ask students to make a projection or hypothesis about students in their school. Have students write an essay describing what percentage of students prefer plain m&m®s over peanut and explain their reasoning.

Look at Fig. 6.4. What conclusions can be made? Can you determine which color m&m® is the most popular in the class? Can you determine which color m&m® is the least favorite in the class? You can determine that more than half the class prefers either blue or green m&m®s because 28% of the students voted for blue and 24% picked green.

Exercise

297. What other inferences can be made from the pie chart displayed in Fig. 6.4?

Fun Activities for Gathering Data

Although we used the m&m® survey as a sample activity, there are alternatives for collecting and interpreting data in the classroom. With each activity, some supplies need to be purchased outside the classroom. These supplies can be used as real-world data. Give each student a

package of Skittles®. Divide the class into groups making sure that every group has three bags of Skittles®. Before the activity begins, ask each student to write the answers to the following questions:

1. What color do you think will occur the most in your bag?
2. Do you think this color will represent the greatest number of Skittles® in every bag?
3. What color do you think will occur least often in your bag?
4. Do you think this color will represent the least number of Skittles® in every bag?

Have each student open one bag and sort the Skittles® by color. Then write the true answers to Questions 1 and 3 beside their original answers. Next, have each group combine their Skittles®, again sorting by color. Have one student construct a data sheet and another record the number of each color of Skittles®. Have each group create a Skittles® bar graph on construction paper using the Skittles® to represent the bars similar to Fig. 6.5. Have the students compare and contrast their original guesses. Ask each group to make some conclusions about the color of Skit-

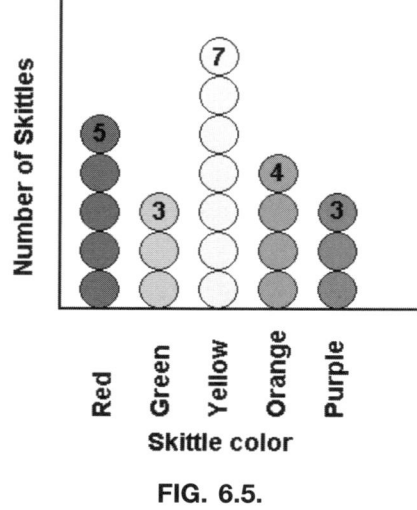

FIG. 6.5.

tles® in a single bag. Add some questions of your own. This activity also works extremely well with pie charts.

You could use the fun size (or small size) of five different types of candy bars that are approximately the same size for an interesting activity. You need enough candy for the entire grade at your school. You need to discuss this project with your administration as well as coordinate the activity with other teachers in your grade. At a specified time, have certain students take a bag of candy bars, scissors, and napkins into another class. Each student in that class is to select one candy bar from the collection. When they make the selection, the student from your class clips off the end of the wrapper and slides the candy bar onto a napkin. Your students must retain the wrapper for the activity while the students in the other class get to eat the candy bar. Your students return to your classroom with the empty wrappers. Your class project is to make a bar graph for displaying the five candy bar preferences for your grade. The unique part of this activity is that you can use the wrappers of candy bars to make a giant bar graph. This graph can be displayed outside your classroom for all students to see. You might want to take a picture of your class in front of the graph. Have your students write an essay describing the process they went through to complete the activity. Also, have the students draw some conclusions about their graphs. Finally, have the class write letters to the headquarters of the candy bar companies describing their project. Be sure to include the photograph. Who knows what they may send back!

Another activity will require a microwave and microwave popcorn packages from several different brands. Begin this activity by having each student in the class answer these questions:

1. Which brand of popcorn will have the most popped pieces? Why?
2. Which brand of popcorn will have the most unpopped kernels? Why?
3. Which brand of popcorn does your family eat at home if any? Why?

Divide your class so that each group gets one bag of popcorn. Pop each bag in the microwave. Follow the directions carefully so the popcorn does not burn. Be sure to allow the popcorn to cool before you give the bags to the respective groups. One person in each group should make a data sheet with two columns: popped popcorn and unpopped kernels. One person should be in charge of recording the data. Have the rest of the group begin counting the popped and unpopped kernels. Have each group construct a pie chart to represent the data. Be sure to have the students include the percentages on the pie chart. This allows the students to see which brand had the greatest percentage of popped popcorn, the greatest percentage of unpopped kernels, the smallest percentage of popped popcorn, and the smallest percentage of unpopped kernels. Have the students compare pie charts. Have the students answer the following questions after they review all of the pie charts in the class:

1. Which is the first brand of popcorn you would buy and why?
2. Which is the last brand of popcorn you would buy and why?
3. If the brand had the most pieces of popped popcorn in it, does that make it the best popcorn to buy? Why or why not?

Add a few of your own questions as well. The students will love this activity because they get to eat the data at the end! Once again, you might have your students write letters to the companies including copies of all the pie charts and results from the class activity.

Collecting and interpreting data can lead to exciting and fun activities. Bar graphs and pie charts are used constantly in advertising. Bar graphs are quite easy to make using stick notes and allowing children to place them on a larger sheet of paper. For example, place the 12 months of the year across the bottom of a poster and then have each student place a stick note over the month of their birth, being careful that the bottom of their stick note is touching the top of the last one placed in their respective column. Having students conduct surveys that involve the collection of real data allows children to actively participate in real mathematics. Sending the results of student surveys to different companies may generate a corporate response. Most important, your students see how mathematics is used in the real world.

STATISTICS

How many commercials are in a 1-hour TV show? How many pages contained an advertisement in the last magazine you read? How many billboards did you pass the last time you went into a city? Advertisements are part of our everyday life.

Companies use statistics to convince us to purchase products. How many toothpaste commercials say, "Four out of five dentists recommend our toothpaste." This statement says that 80% of the dentists surveyed recommend this product. Students are targeted by commercials too. Providing our children with a background in basic statistics can help them become informed consumers. Data to be analyzed by elementary students should have some interest for them.

Ask a police officer to give your class a talk about how a car's speed impacts its ability to stop. Either you or the officer should ask the class if many cars speed past the school when students are not present. Ask the officer to bring a speed-detection unit to measure the speeds of cars in the school zone. While the students watch, have the officer use the speed-detection device to monitor the speed of all the cars passing by the school. As each car passes the school, each student should have an opportunity to read the speed and record it on their data sheet. The more data the students collect, the more effective the subsequent class activity is likely to be. Many police departments have a special radar device that is in the form of a large sign that displays a car's speed before passing the sign. This device would be even better for the activity because the students would be able to effectively view each car's speed from a safe distance from the road.

Exercises

298. Contact a principal. Ask about the policy and proper procedure for conducting an onsite field trip learning activity such as the prior speeding activity.

299. Contact a local law enforcement agency and ask about possible learning activities that officers conduct on a regular basis. Also ask about any education materials or programs for the classroom that are available.

On returning to the classroom after the speed study, the introduction of statistics begins. Have the students organize the speeds from least to greatest. Ask the students to determine the range (difference between the least and greatest values) of speeds produced by the cars that passed by the school. Ask the students to record slowest speed, fastest speed, and the range.

Have the students construct a frequency chart on another sheet of paper. The frequency tells the students how many times a particular speed or measure occurred. Figure 6.6 shows an example of a frequency chart. To construct the frequency chart, have students begin with the lowest speed and provide a space for each possible measure within the range. Speeds that do not occur get a frequency of zero. Once a frequency chart is complete, it is easy to identify the mode, which is the speed that occurs most often. In Fig. 6.6, the mode is 34 mph.

Speeds	Frequency
25	1
28	1
30	1
32	2
33	1
34	5
35	1
36	3
39	2
40	2
43	1
44	1
45	2
48	1
49	1

FIG. 6.6.

Mode is one of the measures of central tendency. Be sure the students do not think that most of the cars traveled at 34 mph because that was the mode. There were 21 other cars in the survey that traveled at other speeds. It would be beneficial to know the median (another measure of central tendency) or middle speed. The median is the score that is in the middle of a list arranged from largest to smallest or smallest to largest. It is easy for children

to associate the median of the road with this term. The median is the middle number that would balance all of the scores somewhat as if the same number of scores were on each side of the fulcrum of a see-saw. One method of finding this speed is to systematically cross out first and last measures until one is left (assuming there is an odd number of scores). For example, in Fig. 6.6, you could cross off 25 and 49 as a pair. Then 28 and 48 would be crossed out because they are the new lowest and highest speeds. The next pair would be 30 and one of the 45s. Next would be one of the 32s and the other 45. This process is repeated with the remaining speeds. If there is an odd number of measures, the median will be the one remaining speed not crossed out. If the number of speeds is even, the median is determined by halving the sum of the last two speeds crossed out (or finding the average of the two center speeds). Use an odd number of speeds when introducing the concept of median. Once the students grasp the idea, introduce an even number of data.

Because we found the median to be 36 mph, it can be said that the same number of cars traveled faster than 36 mph compared with those traveling slower than 36 mph. Have the students record the median. Have the students write an explanation on whether most of the cars traveled faster or slower than the speed limit posted on the road. If the posted speed limit is lower than the median, most of the cars were speeding. If the speed limit is greater than the median, then most of the cars were not traveling over the limit.

We have found the median and mode speed for the data gathered. Another measure of central tendency is the mean (also called the arithmetic mean), which is commonly referred to as the average. What does average mean to most students?

Synonyms for average are medium, mediocre, fair, middling, indifferent, run-of-the-mill, so-so, and tolerable (Morris, 1976). How many of these synonyms would an elementary student understand? Are they synonymous with the concept of average in a mathematical setting? Mathematically stated, the mean is calculated by dividing the sum of the measures by the number of measures. In the speeding activity, the mean would be

$$\frac{\text{Sum of speeds}}{\text{Number of cars monitored}} = \frac{925}{25} = 37.$$

As a teacher of elementary mathematics, you must be careful when using the term average. Many students have heard the word average if only from averaging their grades. Have each student write an essay describing the measures of central tendency (mean, median, and mode) for the speeding activity. They should explain the important information each measure of central tendency provides. This discussion should provide a detailed frequency chart, each measurement of central tendency, and what recommendations the class might suggest if possible changes are needed.

Exercises

292. Find the mean, median, and mode of the number of years it has been for everyone in the class since they started college. Which measure of central tendency best describes the class data?

293. Can you have more than one mode in a set of data? Site your source to justify your answer.

Range, frequency, mean, median, and mode can also be incorporated into the data-gathering experiences. How many total m&ms® come in a 3.14-ounce bag? How many red m&ms® come in a 3.14-ounce bag? Is it always the same number? Earlier each student in the class sorted some m&ms®. Reclaim these data or reproduce the activity. Ask each student to record the total number of m&ms® in their bag on the board. After all bag counts have been displayed, ask the students to identify the range of the number of m&ms® in a 3.14-ounce bag. Have each student determine the median number of m&ms® in a 3.14-ounce bag. Have each student construct a frequency chart to determine the mode number of m&ms® in a 3.14-ounce bag. Finally, ask them to calculate the mean number of m&ms® found in the bags. After the exercise is completed, hold up an unopened bag of m&ms®. Ask each student to predict the number of m&ms® in the unopened bag. Have the students justify their prediction. It would be prudent to have a class discussion on which measure of central tendency would best describe the data that the class collected for the m&ms®. The fun begins when the bag is opened!

This activity can be taken one step farther. Have each student sort the m&ms® by color. Construct an m&ms® chart on the board displaying the student's name and how many of each color were in their bag. With these data, the students can now calculate the mean, median, and mode for each color in a bag of m&ms®. Once again, on completion of the calculations, show students an unopened bag of m&ms®. Have students predict the quantity of each color m&m® in the unopened bag. Be sure to have the students justify their predictions. Before you open the bag, begin a discussion on which measure of central tendency students used. Maybe the student who comes closest to all colors should win the unopened bag!

When teaching data collection and statistics in the elementary curriculum, remember what concepts you are teaching.

Although students will be using all four basic numeric operations, the goal is to effectively teach data-collection techniques and introductory methods of statistics. The students need to understand the meaning of mean, median, and mode and what these values represent in a given situation. Technology could be used to increase speed and accuracy. We want the child to be focused on interpreting the significance of the measures of central tendency. Requiring them to do calculations by hand detracts from learning the statistical concepts. If you want to drill the students on their ability to do arithmetic operations, then provide the drill in a different format. You do not want to taint their impression of statistics by clouding the issue with arithmetic drill and practice.

Exercise

294. Look at a newspaper. Highlight as many uses of measures of central tendency that you can find.

The introduction to statistics can play an integral role in the art of data collecting in the elementary curriculum. The more interest a student has in the data, the greater the level of enthusiasm in the activity. We want to encourage students to learn more about statistics because so much of the real world revolves around the interpretation of this area of mathematics.

PROBABILITY

Some of the earliest mathematics books dealt with gambling. Trying to make money by gambling has been around for centuries. Over the years, some people used their mathematical backgrounds to better their odds of winning. Mathematics became extremely useful because the science could be used to enhance the chances of turning

a profit. The mathematics used in gambling involves mastering the odds or probability.

Probability is a number expressing the likelihood of occurrence of specific effect (Morris, 1976). In other words, we use probability to determine the likelihood that something might happen. Much of the weather forecast is based on probability. For example, when listening to the weather forecast, you hear there is a 30% chance of rain for the day. One method of determining that figure is to look at the past 100 years on that day. If it rained 30 days out of the past 100 years on that given day of the year, then there will be a 30% chance that it will rain somewhere in the considered area on that given day this year.

The likelihood that an event will happen is calculated by dividing the number of times an event occurred by the total number of possible occurrences. This yields a probability from zero to one. You will need a one-pound bag of plain m&ms®. Open the bag and ask six students to sort the m&ms® by color, assigning each student a specific color. Have each student record the total number of m&ms® for their color on the board in a chart similar to the one in Fig. 6.7. After all the colors have been tabulated, place all the m&ms® in a container that does not let the student see the colors

Color	Quantity
Red	100
Blue	59
Yellow	117
Orange	27
Brown	163
Green	57
Total	523

FIG. 6.7.

of the m&ms® in it. Mix the m&ms® thoroughly and have each student write the answer to each of the following:

1. If we select one m&m® out of the container, which color do you think it will be? Explain your reasoning.
2. If we take two m&ms® out of the container, what color do you think the first one will be? What do you think the color of the second one will be? Explain your reasoning.
3. If we take five m&ms® out of the container, how many do you think will be red, blue, yellow, orange, brown, or green? Explain your reasoning.
4. If we take 10 m&ms® out of the container, how many do you think will be red, blue, yellow, orange, brown, or green? Explain your reasoning.

Now comes the moment of truth. Have a student select one m&m® out of the container. Write the numbers 1 to 10 on the board and put the color of the first m&m® next to 1. Ask to see a show of hands for the students who chose the color that was selected as the first m&m®. Repeat the process for the second m&ms®, then the fifth m&ms®, and finally tenth.

The table you display should be similar to Fig. 6.8. You could also provide a column using fractions. Try the example yourself. We did! Which m&ms® color do you think occurred most often? How many m&ms® do you think are in a one-pound bag? We opened two 1-pound bags of m&ms®, and Fig. 6.9 displays our results. The m&ms® were sorted and counted by 13-year-old Tommy Miller of Portland, Oregon.

Exercises

295. Other than the weather, give two examples of where students encounter the use of probability.

Color	Quantity	Probability of Picking that Color (approximation)
Red	100	0.191 or 19%
Blue	59	0.113 or 11%
Yellow	117	0.224 or 22%
Orange	27	0.052 or 5%
Brown	163	0.312 or 31%
Green	57	0.109 or 11%
Total	523	

FIG. 6.8.

296. Give an example of where probability can help your students or their families in their daily routines.

When the class has compared their answers with the results tabulated after counting the m&ms® in a one-pound bag, it is time to discuss how probability can help predict the outcome of an event. Why would you select brown as the first possible m&m® to be selected from the con-

Color	Quantity Bag 1	Quantity Bag 2
Red	100	100
Blue	59	61
Yellow	117	110
Orange	27	16
Brown	163	184
Green	57	68
Total	523	539

FIG. 6.9.

tainer? The probability that you will select a brown m&m® is approximately 0.31. In other words, there is a 31% chance that a brown m&m® will be selected out of the container. As students observe Fig. 6.8, they can see that brown yields the greatest chance of being selected.

A difficult concept for many students is trying to understand that you should have also selected brown as the second m&m® to be drawn. Many of your students will think that yellow should be next because it has the second highest probability of being selected, but brown actually has a greater chance of being the second m&m® taken. Drawing a chart next to your original chart will help students to see the picture more clearly. Each time an m&m® is selected, the number of pieces of that color is reduced by one and so is the total number of m&ms®. Demonstrate this concept by selecting a brown m&m® out of the container. Ask the students how many brown m&ms® are left? Ask the students how many total m&ms® remain in the container. Because one brown has been removed, the container would have 162

brown m&ms® and a total of 522 m&ms®. Now create a second table next to your first one using 162 for brown and 522 for the total. Be sure to calculate the associated probabilities as well and note the changes. Figure 6.10 shows both tables side by side. Ask the students to observe the second table. They should notice that the probabilities are almost identical. Ask the students to identify which color has the greatest chance of being selected in the second table. Of course the brown m&ms® still have the greatest chance of being selected. Ask the students to explain why this is so. Some of the students should notice that the probability of picking a brown is still greater than any other color, whereas other students will notice that their number of browns still exceeds the quantity of the other colors. The students should begin to see the connection to the number of m&ms® for each color and the probability of selecting that color. Once this connection is established, ask the class which color is least likely to be selected and why? Again, the students need to make the connection between the fact

Color	Before removing a brown m&m® Quantity	Probability of Picking that Color (approximation)	Before removing a brown m&m® Quantity	Probability of Picking that Color (approximation)
Red	100	0.191 or 31%	100	0.192 or 19%
Blue	59	0.113 or 11%	59	0.113 or 11%
Yellow	117	0.224 or 22%	117	0.224 or 22%
Orange	27	0.052 or 5%	27	0.052 or 5%
Brown	163	0.312 or 31%	162	0.310 or 31%
Green	57	0.109 or 11%	57	0.109 or 11%
Total	523		522	

FIG. 6.10.

that the orange m&ms® have the least probability of being selected because orange represents the fewest number of all the colors.

Estimation skills are stressed in the NCTM standards. How can probability help increase a student's power of estimation? A day or two after your class has completed the activity using a one-pound bag of m&ms®, bring in two king size bags of m&ms® (3.14 ounce). Place the table your class constructed like Fig. 6.8 on the board before you begin this new lesson. Ask the students to answer the following questions:

1. How many m&ms® will be in each king size bag?
2. How many of each color will be in each king size bag?

Have students explain their answers to each question. Group the students and have each group construct a table similar to Fig. 6.7 with their predictions. After all tables are completed, open each bag of king size m&ms®. Which group was closest? How could the groups have used probability to estimate their answers? How could the students determine the number of m&ms® in the king size bag?

The one-pound bag is equivalent to 16 ounces of m&ms®. The king size bag contains 3.14 ounces. Set up a proportion to estimate the number of m&ms® in the king size bag:

$$\frac{\text{Number of ounces in a king size bag}}{\text{Number of ounces in a one} - \text{pound bag}} =$$

$$\frac{\text{Number of m\&m's in a king size bag}}{\text{Number of m\&m's in a one} - \text{pound bag}}$$

$$\frac{3.14}{16} = \frac{?}{523}$$

$$3.14 \cdot 523 = 16 \cdot ?$$

$$1642.22 = 16 \cdot ?$$

$$102.63875 = ?$$

You would expect about 103 m&ms® in a king size bag. Another way to estimate this problem is to notice that the number of ounces in a king size bag is about one fifth or 20% of a one-pound bag. The students could divide the number of m&ms® in a one-pound bag by five to estimate the number of m&ms® in a king size bag. We asked Tommy Miller to again do a little counting for us. He found exactly 103 m&ms®. Will all king size bags contain exactly 103 pieces of candy? Explain your reasoning.

Exercises

297. Find a 1.69-ounce bag of m&ms®. Before opening the bag, estimate how many m&ms® are in the bag.

298. Find a 1.69-ounce bag of m&ms®. Before opening the bag, estimate how many of each color you think you will find.

Earlier we discussed mathematics books and gambling. Most of your students only hear about the glory of potentially winning lots of money as individuals gamble on lotteries. They rarely hear about all the money that is lost. Although gambling is forbidden in schools, discussing probability allows demonstrations on how unlikely it is to win when gambling, especially with a lottery.

Many lotteries have the player select 6 numbers out of 50 or so. Consider a game that allows the player to select a three-digit number. You need a means of generating a three-digit number. One way is to use the Casio FX-55 fraction calculator, which randomly produces a three-digit decimal number between 0 and 1. For example, when you press the RAN# key, the calculator displays a number such as 0.235 on the screen. Use the 235 portion to simulate the random selection of numbers.

Each student gets 20 m&ms® to be used as money. Ask each student to place one m&m® at the top of their paper and then write a three-digit number on the first line. You will then press the RAN# on the calculator to produce a three-digit number. Using an overhead calculator for this activity also adds excitement because the students can then see the numbers on the screen. A student can win m&ms® in two ways. First, if their number matches the number on your calculator exactly (in the same order), they win 250 m&ms®. If they have the same three digits as your display but in different places, they win 50 m&ms®. Repeat this activity at least 20 times. You will be amazed at the results and so will your students. Each time a student does not match your number, take away an m&m®. After 20 trials, your students will be out of m&ms®. They will have lost all of their candy. Have each student answer the following questions:

1. How many m&ms® did you begin with?
2. How many m&ms® did you lose?
3. How many m&ms® did you win?

The next day, try the activity again. Give each student 20 m&ms®. Tell them that they can choose not to play or quit playing the game at any time. If they have any m&ms® left over, they may eat them. Play the game for 20 trials and have the students answer the following questions:

1. How many m&ms® did you begin with?
2. How many m&ms® did you lose?
3. How many m&ms® did you win?
4. How many m&ms® did you eat?
5. If you did stop playing the game, explain why you did so.

Use these questions to generate a class discussion. The object is for the students to see that gambling does not pay. Remember that probability is the number of outcomes compared to the possible number of outcomes. To match the number exactly, the student picks one three-digit number. There are 1,000 possible outcomes from 000 to 999. There is a 1 in 1,000 (or 0.001 or 0.1%) chance of matching the number exactly. Matching the three digits in any order requires some additional thought. Suppose the number is 257. A winning selection would consist of 257, 275, 527, 572, 725, or 752. There are six possible winners out of 1,000 different possible three-digit numbers—not a very good opportunity for winning. After discussing this activity, hopefully students will begin to understand how unlikely winning a lottery is.

Integrating Literature With Probability

The children's novel *The Twenty-One Balloons* by William Penn Dubois (1947) tells the story of a man who finds a remote Pacific island filled with diamonds. He decides to select 21 families to live with him permanently on the Island of Krakatoa. This tale is unique because the man only selects families with a mother, father, and exactly one son and one daughter. In the article "From the Giver to the Twenty-One Balloons: Explorations with Probability" (Lawrence, 1999), Ann Lawrence provides a wonderful lesson that incorporates hands-on experiences with the concepts of probability. Have each student select a manipulative that can simulate the selection of a boy or a girl such as a two-color chip. For example, if one side is red and the other is blue, designate blue to represent boys and red for girls. The students now have an instrument that can be used to predict gender. Arrange the students in

TABLE 6.1
Gender Probability in a Family

Older Child	boy	boy	girl	girl
Younger Child	boy	girl	boy	girl

pairs, each having one chip. Ask the students to predict the probability of a family with exactly two children, one boy and one girl. You will find that many of the students will suggest 0.33 or 33%. Although the solution is incorrect, it is the result of good logical thinking. Your students think that there are three possibilities for families with two kids: two boys, two girls, or one of each. Have each pair of students begin flipping their chips. Tell them that they are trying to determine the gender of 20 separate families. In other words, when they flip two chips, they need to record the results. If the chips both land blue facing up, then the children are both boys; if the chips both land red facing up, then the children are both girls; and if the chips land one blue and one red facing up, then you have one boy and one girl. Have the students complete and record for 20 different trials and compare their results with their classmates. Then have each pair answer the following questions (Lawrence, 1999):

1. How did the results of the experiment compare with your prediction? Why do you think this happened?
2. Show all the possibilities for a family with two children.
3. Write two paragraphs below this activity.
   What we found . . .
   What I learned . . .

The goal is for the students to find that the actual probability is 0.5. This can be displayed by listing the children as older child and younger child in Table 6.1. Notice that there are four possible outcomes for families with two children and that two of those outcomes contain one boy and one girl. Therefore, the probability of exactly one boy and one girl is 0.5.

Teaching probability is a wonderful opportunity to incorporate hands-on learning activities in the elementary curriculum as well as provide added enjoyment and enthusiasm for students in mathematics. The drive to learn more about probability has been around for hundreds of years. Now we have the opportunity to show our students probability outside the classroom in the real world. Have fun and allow the students to explore this area of mathematics.

REFERENCES

Dubois, W. (1976). *From the giver to the twenty-one balloons.* New York: Viking-Penguin.

Lawrence, A. (1999, May). Explorations with probability. *Mathematics Teaching in the Middle School, 8,* 504–509.

Morris, W. (Ed.). (1976). *The American Heritage Dictionary of the English Language.* Boston, MA: Houghton-Mifflin.

National Council of Teachers of Mathematics. (1989). *Curriculum and evaluation standards for school mathematics.* Reston, VA: Author.

7
Problem Solving

Problem solving is enjoying a renewed emphasis. Some educators are treating it like a new idea, whereas others feel problem solving has been an essential ingredient since the beginnings of the formal development of mathematics. For example, Newman (1956) indicated that it is generally accepted that the ancient Egyptians invented geometry (geo meaning Earth, metry meaning measure) to restore land boundaries swept away by the flooding Nile River. New or old, problem solving holds wonderful opportunities for you and your students to learn mathematics and see its applications.

SEQUENCE FOR STUDENT DEVELOPMENT

In some areas of mathematics, a definite sequence for learning exists. Unfortunately, problem solving is not one of them. About all that can be said as far as a sequence for problem solving is that you should start early and do it often. There are some essential factors about problem solving that should not be neglected.

You need to have a problem-solving plan. Problem solving could be introduced as a separate entity, but it is better to blend it into the topics being covered. Care needs to be taken to ensure that the degree of difficulty of the problem being presented is not too great for the students or beyond their skill and readiness levels. If it is, they will become discouraged about solving problems and mathematics as well. However, if the problem is too easy, the students can get the impression that there are few challenges in mathematics. There is a delicate balance between hard and easy and between ready or not when considering problem solving. That balance can be achieved and you and your students will be the benefactors.

HISTORY OF PROBLEM SOLVING

The history of mathematics is rich with problem-solving situations that can be used to attract student attention, connect mathematics with other disciplines, show applications, and provide challenges for individuals. The "Seven Bridges of Konigsberg" is a classic problem that Euler proved impossible (Newman, 1956). This problem can be the basis for an enthralling lesson.

As the story is told, the German town of Konigsberg (now Kallningrad, Russia) faced a difficult dilemma each year. The people planned an annual parade through their village and wanted the parade to follow a path that would march the procession across each of the town's bridges only once. The citizens of Konigsberg did not want the parade to pass any of its landmarks more than once. A diagram of the town, which is on the Pregel River, is shown in Fig. 7.1. This seemed like such a

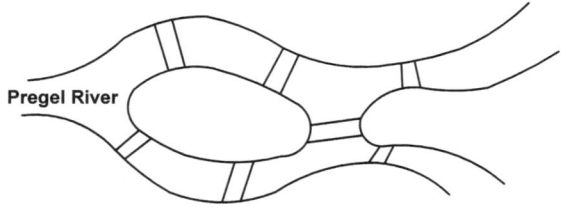

Pregel River

FIG. 7.1.

simple task, yet no one was able to plot a course for the parade to cross each bridge in the town once and only once. Try placing this drawing or one similar on a poster or overhead transparency for the class. Also, make copies of the diagram for students to work with at their desks. Tell the perplexing story of the Bridges of Konigsberg. Ask your students to try to trace a course that would cross each bridge once and only once.

After the students have attempted to solve the problem, tell them that the famous mathematician Leonard Euler showed it was impossible to complete the task as defined. Your students might surprise you by continuing to try the problem even after being told that Euler proved it impossible. Your students will willingly doing mathematics as they increase their problem-solving skills. Searching for a path for the bridges of Konisberg led to the development of a branch of mathematics called topology.

Another historic problem students can work with was solved by Gauss, who intuitively "discovered" how to sum consecutive counting numbers while in his early school years (Beck, Bleicher, & Crowe, 1969). The teacher assigned the task of finding the sum of the first 100 consecu-

tive counting numbers to Gauss, who quickly determined the sum to be 5,050. This idea can be an interesting challenge for some students, perhaps beginning with a smaller set of numbers. A lesson could be built around it in the following manner. (T represents a teacher comment and S stands for something a student might say).

T: What is the sum of the first three consecutive counting numbers?
S: 6.
T: What is the sum of the first four consecutive counting numbers?
S: 10.
T: What is the sum of the first five consecutive counting numbers?
S: 15.
T: What is the sum of the first six consecutive counting numbers?
S: 21.
T: What is the sum of the first 100 consecutive counting numbers? (You might do a few more numbers before asking for such a large value.)
S: That is too big to try (although some might work at it).
T: Is there a pattern we can look for?

Students could say a variety of things here. They could say yes or no to the pattern question and perhaps make suggestions about what to look for. Eventually you will need to lead the class in the following type of discussion.

T: Look at $1 + 2 + 3 = 6 = \dfrac{3 \times 4}{2}$.

T: $1 + 2 + 3 + 4 = 10 = \dfrac{4 \times 5}{2}$.

T: $1 + 2 + 3 + 4 + 5 = 15 = \dfrac{5 \times 6}{2}$.

T: $1 + 2 + 3 + 4 + 5 + 6 = 21 = \dfrac{6 \times 7}{2}$.

T: Do you see a pattern?

S: Take half of the product of the largest addend and the next biggest counting number.

T: Explain that, please.

S: In 1 + 2 + 3 + 4, the sum is 10, which is half of 4 times 5. Four is the largest addend and 5 is the next biggest counting number.

T: What is the sum of the first 100 consecutive counting numbers?

S: It has to be $\dfrac{100 \times 101}{2} = 5050$.

These two sample lessons provide insight into the history of mathematics and hold a wealth of potential problem-solving situations. Other lessons could be developed around the Egyptians measuring land after floods. Consider a herder who could not count, but could keep track of sheep by moving stacks of pebbles as the sheep came or went. We have calculators, but so did the ancients in the form of the abacus. Piles of stones, papyrus, an abacus, and calculators are all tools that have been used to help solve problems. The important thing to note is that a problem presented itself and somehow it got solved. That is a spirit you need to instill in your students.

It is difficult to discuss problem solving without mentioning George Polya, who wrote *How to Solve It* (Polya, 1945/1973). Polya presented four steps for problem solving: (a) *understand* the problem, (b) make a *plan* for solving the problem based on data and ideas given, (c) *carry out* the plan, and (d) *look back* at the solution. The literature on problem solving contains several outlines of steps to use to solve problems. Examination of the steps shows that almost all of them are extensions of the ones presented by Polya.

More recently, National Council of Teachers of Mathematics (2000) listed problem solving as 1 of 10 standards that describe a connected body of mathematical understandings and competencies saying that problem solving is an integral part of all mathematics learning. The basic Problem Solving Standard says:

> Instructional programs from prekindergarten through grade 12 should enable all students to—
>
> > build new mathematical knowledge through problem solving;
> >
> > solve problems that arise in mathematics and in other contexts;
> >
> > apply and adapt a variety of appropriate strategies to solve problems;
> >
> > monitor and reflect on the process of mathematical problem solving. (p. 52)

Problem-solving situations spring from within the study of mathematics. As students mature mathematically, they can encounter dilemmas from their world and use their mathematical skills to solve them just like ancient mathematicians.

Exercises

299. The *Seven Bridges of Konigsberg*, a discussion of Gauss, and the Egyptians using geometry to measure flooded ground were given in the text as examples of historical topics that could be inserted into the elementary classroom. Find a different historical topic appropriate for elementary students. Give all appropriate bibliographic information and create a lesson plan that would incorporate your topic.

300. Find a list different from the four steps Polya presents for problem solving. Describe the similarities and differences between the list you found Polya's.

301. Read the parts in NCTM's *Principles and Standards for School Mathematics* pertaining to problem solving. Reflect on what the publication says and write

your feelings about their position on problem solving in the elementary curriculum.

PHILOSOPHICAL APPROACHES TO PROBLEM SOLVING

Effective problem solving requires open-minded approaches from teachers and students. That sounds so easy to say and yet it is so difficult to accomplish. We all have our preconceived notions. What is a problem-solving problem? Krulick and Rudnick (1987) gave a list of four essentials to determine whether something is a problem-solving problem:

1. A nonroutine solution is necessary,
2. A challenge is presented,
3. An individual accepts the challenge, and
4. A positive attitude about problem solving is fostered.

If a problem is routine, the challenge is missing. You will encounter many problem-solving problems, some of which you will opt to do. It is not expected that you solve every problem you see. However, you are not at liberty to continually say that each problem you see has no challenge for you. If you are to be an effective teacher of problem solving, you have to be a problem solver. As you solve problems, your attitude will change.

Exactly what is a problem-solving problem? "A toy costs $1.98. How much would three toys cost, excluding tax?" Is that a problem-solving problem for *you* given the previous description? The answer is no because it offers no challenge for you. You have done problems like that before. The cost was different, the item name was something else, and you got more or fewer of them, but the problem involves the same ideas.

Would purchasing the toys be a problem-solving problem for a first grader? You probably said, "Of course." You might even question whether first graders could do the problem. A typical first grader would not be able to do the problem abstractly (notice decimals, regrouping in addition, and money), but it is possible some of them could do it concretely by using money.

So buying the toys is not a problem-solving problem for you, but it is for a first grader. It might be a problem-solving problem for average second and third graders too. Somewhere along the continuum, it ceases to be a problem-solving problem because it is like others that have been solved. As an individual solves appropriate problem-solving problems, a good feeling should occur and that generates a positive attitude about problem solving and mathematics.

Take a sheet of notebook paper and fold it in half. Fold it in half a second time. Fold it in half a third time. If you could continue folding it in half 50 times, how high would the stack of paper be? This is a classic that might be a problem-solving problem for you.

Exercises

302. In the "fold the paper in half again and again problem," physically, how many times can the paper be folded in half?

303. In the "fold the paper in half again and again problem," does the size of the paper being used matter?

304. In the "fold the paper in half again and again problem," how high is the stack after 50 folds?

The following should be a problem-solving problem for you, and it can serve as an outline of a problem-solving lesson you could do. One thing you need to remember is that, as problems are solved, ideas are bantered about, either with others or in your own mind. As you are doing that, you are *thinking*, which is essential to any learning. The ability to generate ideas as you think is important to the overall process of becoming a problem solver.

Suppose the class is given the set of shapes shown in Fig. 7.2. Each shape is made up of five congruent squares. The teacher is thinking of a particular question, and the students' task is to determine the question the teacher has in mind. Each question that is generated could stimulate class discussion and serve as the basis for a lesson. One question could relate to the area of each figure. Because each figure is made up of five congruent squares, all the areas will be the same. That might not be so obvious to all of your students, and a short lesson could help them understand.

As soon as area is mentioned, perimeter is almost a reflexive companion question. Many students assume that, because the areas are the same for all figures, the perimeter will be also. Are they? Investigation of the perimeter presents an interesting consideration. What is the minimum perimeter of a shape made up of five congruent squares? What is the maximum perimeter of a shape made up of five congruent squares? See Fig. 7.3 for a picture of both the maximum and minimum perimeter. These perimeter questions provide the opportunity for students to manipulate sets of unit squares. The process can stimulate concrete and abstract thoughts while offering a means to deal with different ability levels. One problem associated with finding perimeters of figures made up of squares is that students sometimes mistakenly count squares to get perimeters. Clear understanding of the definitions is essential.

FIG. 7.2.

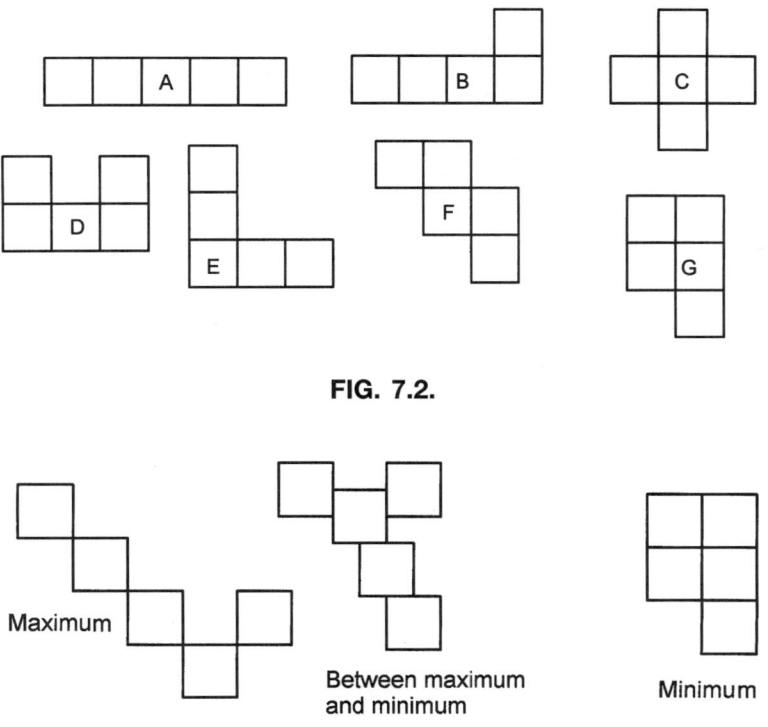

FIG. 7.3.

One of the outgrowths of the manipulation can be something like the "Between maximum and minimum" part of Fig. 7.3. As you do problem solving, you need to be careful to avoid self-imposed restrictions. Typically students will say they did not think of using part of a side to join the shapes.

Exercises

305. Create a higher order thinking question from the shapes in Fig. 7.2. Discuss a potential lesson development to answer your question.

306. The maximum perimeter of the shapes in Fig. 7.3 is 20 units and the minimum is 10 units. Explain why this is the case.

307. Can five squares be arranged to give any perimeter between 10 units and 20 units? Why or why not?

A heuristic is "a method of education . . . in which the pupil . . . proceeds along empirical lines, using rules of thumb, to find solutions or answers" (Neufeldt, 1996, p. 634). In the definition, the "rules of thumb" could be the focal point. If Polya's four steps are expanded, the result is a set of heuristics. The following explanation is not the only possible one, but it should give you a good idea of things to do as you solve problems. Each entry could be expanded to a paragraph or two as details and examples would be provided.

Understand the problem

Read carefully.
Do all the words make sense?
Paraphrase the problem.
What is given?
What are you asked to find or do?
Is there adequate information given?

Is unnecessary information given?
Have you worked a similar problem?
Have you overlooked assumptions?

A farmer had 26 cows. All but 9 died. How many lived?

Make a *plan* for solving the problem based on data and ideas given. (You would probably not use all of the ideas stated in this section.)

Is there a pattern?
Will a picture help?
Can the problem be simplified?
Have you worked a similar problem?
Can you guess and check?
Is there a formula that could be used?
Did you list all pertinent facts and conclusions about the information?
Will a table or chart help?
Can you make different cases?

A uniform log can be cut into three pieces in 12 seconds. Assuming the same rate of cutting, how long would it take a similar log to be cut into four pieces?
Carry out the plan

Does your strategy work?
Can you see a course of action?
Is there a need to reexamine the problem?
Will another strategy work better?

Look back at the solution.

Check your work.
Is there an easier way to do the problem?
Can the solution be generalized?

This discussion is only part of the problem-solving picture. Additional ideas are presented in other sections of this book. There are different steps for solving problems. The list of heuristics might be altered in another source. The bottom line is that problem solving can be fun for you and your students. All you have to do is try.

Exercises

308. A farmer had 26 cows. All but 9 died. How many lived?

309. A uniform log can be cut into three pieces in 12 seconds. Assuming the same rate of cutting, how long would it take a similar log to be cut into four pieces?

310. How many different ways can you add four odd counting numbers to get a sum of 10?

TEACHING PROBLEM SOLVING

Why teach problem solving? For many, mathematics is problem solving. One thing problem solving can do is connect the classroom to real life. It also provides an opportunity to join different mathematical topics. Suppose a student is asked to use 100 feet of fence to provide a maximum play area for a dog. Figure 7.4 shows some of the possible shapes and areas. The student learns that when a perimeter is fixed, the maximum area comes from a circle. In the process of investigating, a useful generalization is developed.

If you are going to be teaching problem solving, you have to be a problem solver. As stated earlier, you do not need to do every problem, but you do have to practice what you preach. As you talk the talk and walk the walk of problem solving, your excitement will spill over into other teaching areas. Your class cannot be constantly problem solving. You and your students need time for explaining, discussing, elaborating, generalizing, algorithm building, and practicing known mathematical content.

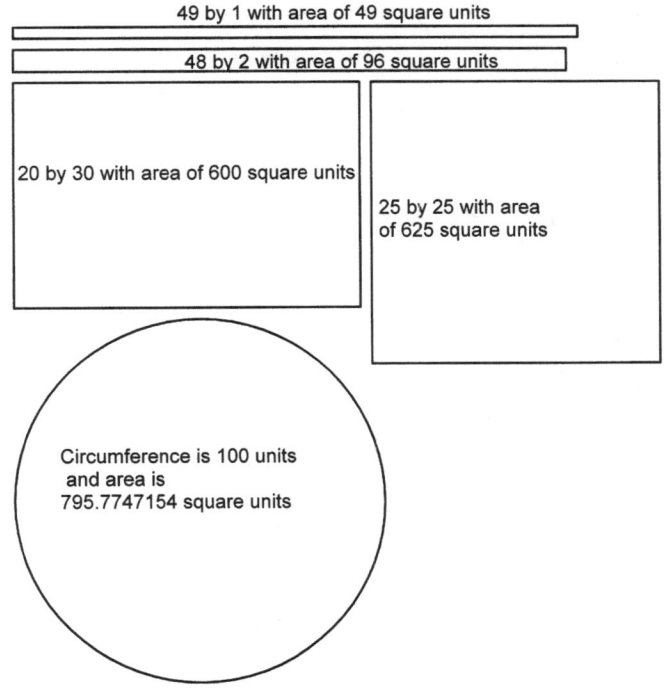

49 by 1 with area of 49 square units

48 by 2 with area of 96 square units

20 by 30 with area of 600 square units

25 by 25 with area of 625 square units

Circumference is 100 units and area is 795.7747154 square units

FIG. 7.4.

There are several things to keep in mind as you integrate problem solving into your curriculum. First and foremost, do it consistently. As you do it, pose problems appropriate for all levels of your students. Keep textbook problems in perspective. (Your textbook is not the only source of problem-solving problems.) Put a premium on thinking and creative solutions. Consider posting the work of a student who has produced an exceptionally clear or innovative solution. It is not just how much you know that counts. It is how you use what you know, when you need it. Sometimes in problem solving, that can be difficult. Problem solving should lead to more mathematics and stimulate a need for mathematics. Your plan for problem solving should start with reasonably easy problems and build toward more difficult ones to avoid discouraging students.

The key word approach to problem solving is popular. A student who focuses on the word *sum* in the problem, "Some of these numbers are odd: 1, 5, 3, 2, 4, 7, 8, 9, 13, 16, 19," would be just as lost as the student who focuses on the word *some* if the problem were stated, "The sum of the odd numbers in the list 1, 5, 3, 2, 4, 7, 8, 9, 13, 16, 19 is ?" Key words are not enough in many problem-solving situations. You need to know the entire story. Consider the problem where Person A weighs 160 pounds, Person B weighs 108 pounds, and Person C weighs 26 pounds more than B. What is the average weight of all three people? The key words are often listed as *average* and *more than*. *More than* is often overlooked and C's weight is given as 26 pounds. Do not construe this discussion to say that the key word approach should not be used. You should give careful consideration to this strategy and approach. Remember, multiple strategies work for multiple learners.

How do you spot a good problem solver? Certainly we are not all equally ad-

ept at doing everything and that includes problem solving. It is a struggle for some and easy for others. Problem solving is a valuable skill, so it is important to encourage those who are good at it. One indicator is that the individual is willing to try problems. Another involves persistence. Many times a good problem solver is able to skip steps as a situation develops, generally reflecting a clear understanding of what is happening. Finally, good problem solvers frequently talk to themselves. In the process, they learn what questions are helpful to ask and what to do with the answers they derive.

REAL-WORLD PROBLEMS AND APPLICATIONS

You will read a lot about real-world problems and applications. Proceed with caution here. We as adults talk about real-world problems for students, but the problems are often not relevant for the world as students see it. Many mathematics texts discuss a student wanting to redecorate a bedroom. The mathematics involves finding areas and computing how much paint, carpet, or wall paper is needed to do the job. Many students know the carpet person will be able to tell exactly, and that information would be easily obtained in the carpet store, for example. Thus, even if the student is interested in the idea of redecorating, more than likely the student would not be overly thrilled at having to do all the associated computations in the mathematics class when the information is so readily available in another venue.

This is only the beginning of a discussion on problem solving. You need to become a problem solver. The literature abounds with many successful problem-solving examples from various classrooms. It is your responsibility as a professional to learn problem solving and to lead by example. Solve on!

The exercises in the TAG section for this book are problems that have been solved by elementary age students from around the world. Do not let them fool you. Some of these challengers are not easy. It is not necessary to do all of them, but you should do some. Remember, the more you do, the more of a practitioner you are, and, as such, you set a better example.

REFERENCES

Beck, A., Bleicher, M. N., & Crowe, D. W. (1969). *Excursions into mathematics*. New York: Worth.

Eves, H. (1967). *An introduction to the history of mathematics* (rev. ed.). New York: Holt, Rinehart & Winston.

Krulick, S., & Rudnick, J. A. (1987). *Problem solving: A handbook for teachers* (2nd ed.). Boston: Allyn & Bacon.

Microsoft Corporation. (1994). *Encarta*. Redmond, WV: Microsoft Corporation.

National Council of Teachers of Mathematics. (2000). *Principles and standards for school mathematics*. Reston, VA: Author.

Newfeldt, V. (Ed.). (1996). *Webster's New World College Dictionary*. Cleveland, OH: Simon & Schuster.

Newman, J. R. (1956). *The world of mathematics* (Vol. 1). New York: Simon & Schuster.

Polya, G. (1973). *How to solve it* (2nd ed.). Princeton, NJ: Princeton University Press. (Original work published 1945)

8
Reasoning and Proof

WHY PROVE THINGS?

Any time you say "Why?" you are asking for some explanation of the actions behind an event. To some extent, you are asking for a proof. As you teach, you want students to ask why. That is the beginning of their ability to investigate things beyond the surface. As you ask them why or they ask you why, they start to think of a proof.

Ask most people what they think of when you say the word *geometry* and they will tell you proof. In our curriculum, geometry is typically the first course where students deal with proof in any sort of a regular manner. Regretfully, some students believe that their high school geometry course was one of the saddest periods in their academic life primarily due to those proofs. The classic geometry class is essentially a year-long exercise in inductive and deductive reasoning using classical proofs to justify mathematical theorems and concepts. Unfortunately, many people feel it was not a pleasant experience. The reality is that the geometry course is probably the first time most students encounter proofs at any depth beyond a superficial level.

What a shame! The curriculum is loaded with places where the idea of proof can be introduced. We have provided examples of proving things throughout this text. There is a message here. We have been working them into your curriculum, much as we would ask you to do with your students. Refer to these as examples of proofs we have discussed:

the sum of the first n consecutive counting numbers is $\dfrac{n(n+1)}{2}$ (see Gauss in the index),

the sum of the interior angles of a triangle is 180° (see Fig. 4.9),

how Tangram shapes can be used to construct some of the forms the fox fairies adopted in *Grandfather Tang's Story* (Tompert, 1990; see Fig. 4.4),

Casio's FX-2.0 and MathXpert giving statements and reasons for each step made in an algebra problem being solved,

that 10 units are equivalent to one 10 in place value (see Fig. 2.7), etc.

The question is not whether you should introduce reasoning and proof to your students, but when and where. The answer is simple: as often as possible and throughout the curriculum.

NCTM has identified Reasoning and Proof as one of the Standards we should be inserting throughout the curriculum saying:

Instructional programs from prekindergarten through grade 12 should enable all students to—

> recognize reasoning and proof as fundamental aspects of mathematics;
>
> make and investigate mathematical conjectures;
>
> develop and evaluate mathematical arguments and proofs;
>
> select and use various types of reasoning and methods of proof. (National Council of Teachers of Mathematics, 2000, p. 56)

The overlap between problem-solving characteristics and proof is significant.

INFORMAL PROOFS

"Mathematics does not grow through a monotonous increase of the number of indubitably established theorems but through the incessant improvement of guesses by speculation and criticism, by the logic of proofs and refutations" (Lakatos, 1976, p. 5). We know there is a need to have proofs in the study of mathematics. Without them, we may arrive at incorrect conclusions. Proof convinces one that a discourse and its associated conclusion are factual. Proven things could be replicated and do not contradict something else known to be true. Depending on the setting, the dialogue takes on a variety of approaches. A young child, talking with another, may attest to the proof of something being true because "someone said so." Here the child yields to authority. Eventually, as the youngster gets a little older, the route to proof might turn to a less acceptable process: something like saying, "I am tougher than you are and will beat you up to prove it." The associated fisticuffs, although undesirable, do show advancement in the development of proof.

Eventually the need for more exactness in proof develops. An immediate question becomes how to express the proof. The classic geometric two-column demonstration is certainly one method. In middle-grade mathematics, pre-algebra, and algebra courses, the two-column proof does not appear very often. A structured approach to establishing the validity of an argument follows a clearly established sequence of steps, leading to a result that is checked to ensure the correctness of the answer. The paragraph proof, where the development of convincing evidence is put into words, can be the forte of some students. Really, the manner used for the proof is not critical. What is most important is that a coherent, logically correct discussion is presented. Although elementary students are not going to be overly formal in their beginning proofs, the reasoning and verification of things is an essential developmental skill.

TEACHER RESPONSIBILITY IN DEVELOPING REASONING AND PROOF

How do we convince students of the need for proof? One way would be to create situations that appear to be true, but in reality are not. Lead the students to make false conjectures and then help them see the error of their ways. Earlier we talked of adding fractions using Cuisenaire Rods or egg cartons to generate a set of problems and answers like

$$\frac{1}{3} + \frac{1}{4} = \frac{7}{12}$$
$$\frac{1}{2} + \frac{1}{3} = \frac{5}{6}.$$
$$\frac{1}{2} + \frac{1}{7} = \frac{9}{14}$$

Some enterprising student concluded that the denominator of the answer is the product of the denominators in the problem and the numerator in the answer is the sum of the denominators in the problem. A reasonable follow-up question is, "Will this always work?" We know the answer is, "No." Students may not know that. Essentially a false conjecture has been made. You would then continue the discussion by asking them to do a problem like $\frac{2}{3} + \frac{1}{4}$ and help students correct their misconceptions.

Young children often get the idea that they know the biggest number in the world. Usually they will give it, whatever it is. You can make a game out of the situation and ask the children to add 1 to their number. Then ask if this new sum is the biggest number in the world. After a few rounds of that, children realize there is no biggest

number. Not only has a false conjecture been corrected, but the children have also participated in a level of reasoning that establishes the basics of proof.

"Seeing is believing" is often accepted as proof. Optical illusions such as the ones shown in Figs. 8.1, 8.2, and 8.3 could be used to attract students' attention while establishing the need for some more explanation. Figure 8.1 has been around a

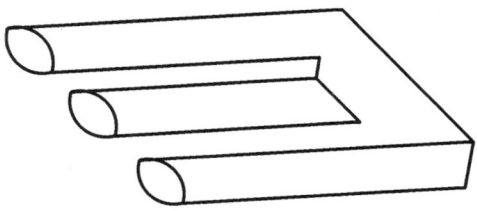

FIG. 8.1.

long time and always stimulates a good discussion. Depending on how you look at it, you get different interpretations of

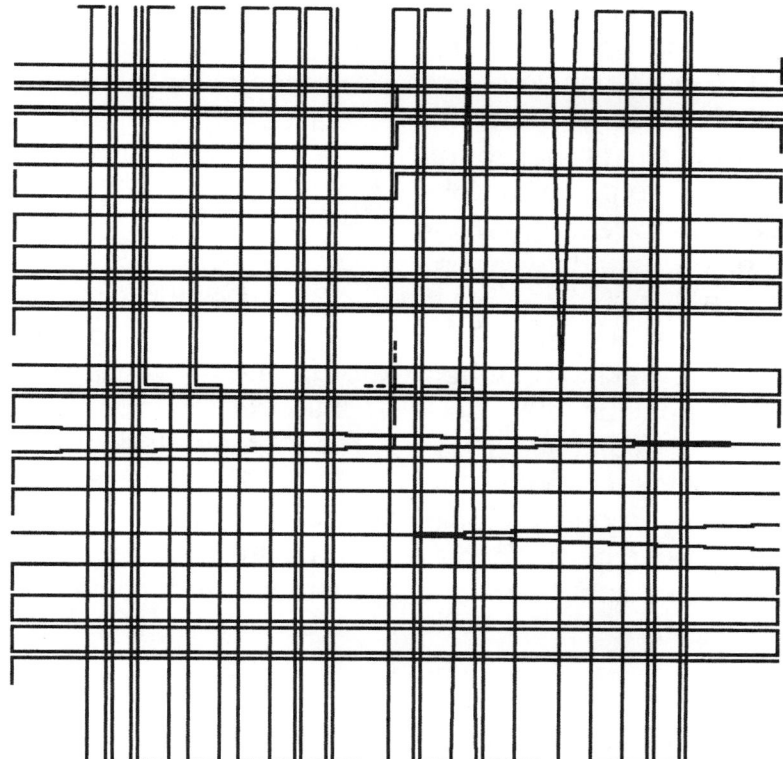

FIG. 8.2.

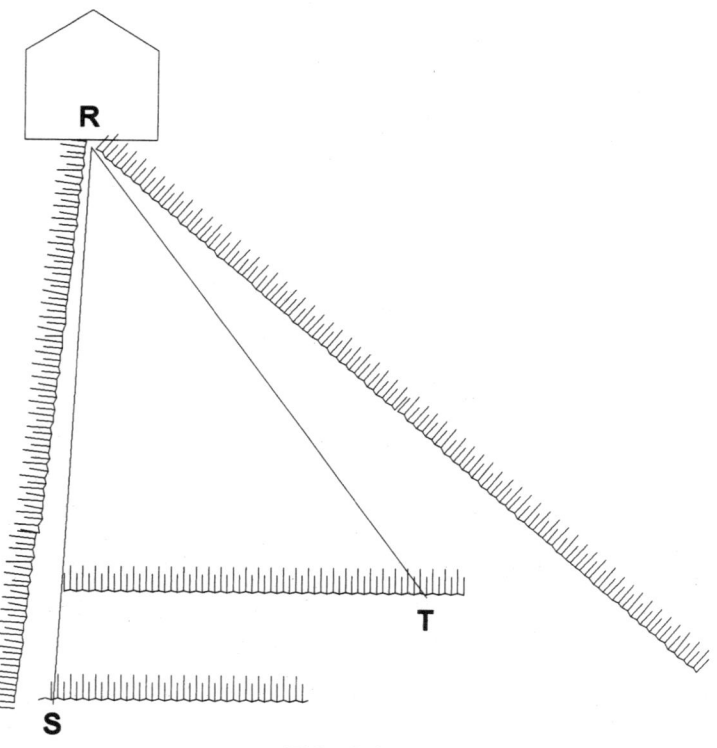

FIG. 8.3.

what is there. Figure 8.2 contains the same message twice, with one printed at a 90-degree rotation and put on top of the other. Even knowing that, you probably will not be able to read the message. Hold the page on a plane that is almost horizontal and a few inches below your line of sight and you should be able to read it. Which line segment, $\overline{RS}$ or $\overline{RT}$, is longer in Fig. 8.3? Measure them and see. ☺

So maybe seeing is not believing. Paulos (1988) described firewalking on a bed of hot coals. When an individual performs this feat (pun intended), the discussion centers on the ability to control the mind and exclude the associated pain that should go with walking on hot coals. The walk is observed, and spectators are convinced that the described process of mind over matter works because of what they have seen. The event is based on a little known fact that dehydrated wood has an extremely low heat content and is a poor heat conductor. A person walking

quickly across the coals feels little of the apparent heat. Of course, the mind over matter routine sounds much more glamorous. Seeing is not always believing. Investigation will yield a proof.

Exercises

311. Describe a situation similar to the biggest number idea that would be appropriate as a means of building a foundation in reasoning and proof for a primary grade student.

312. Find an optical illusion like the ones in Figs. 8.1, 8.2, and 8.3 that you feel would be appropriate to present to an elementary student as a means to discuss reasoning, explaining, or proving.

Earlier in this book, we talked about Hutchings' (1976) Low Stress Addition of whole numbers. The students see a different way of adding that seems to work all the time. A question that students ask in situations like that is, "Does this always work?" WOW! You were just asked to prove something. The point is that the students saw something and then asked how it works.

Number tricks hold a wealth of opportunity for developing reasoning and proof. Two things are accomplished at the same time in many number tricks: Mathematical skills are practiced and students ask why they work. Tell someone you are going to add five digits where they pick two of the addends and you pick three and the answer will be 24. Suppose you are given 7 and 4. You select 2, 5, and 6. Most people reflexively ask how you did it (request for explanation or proof). Although the sum could vary, using 24 at least the second time is fun, particularly with students, because they assume that if they change their choices, you will get a different answer. (Remember the part about them needing to learn to make conjectures?) Suppose you are given 1 and 5. You select 8, 4, and 6. Multiple examples can be used to show how the problem works:

7	1	5	1	3	0
4	5	6	2	6	9
6	6	3	7	4	7
5	4	4	8	5	2
+2	+8	+6	+6	+6	+6
24	24	24	24	24	24

In the list of examples of addition columns, the double underscore indicates the addends selected by the person. The two examples on the left were discussed earlier. There are several clues in the set that students might notice. The bottom addend is the same in the last four problems. Notice that 6 is two greater than the ones digit of the sum and there is at least one 6 in each of the six problems. In the

third problem and fourth problems, the second and third addends have a sum of 9. In the fifth problem, the first two addends and the second two addends each have a sum of 9. Focus on the fifth problem. Rather than seeing 3 + 6 + 4 + 5 + 6, look at it as 9 + 9 + 6 or two 9s plus 6. Two nines and the 6 is *two* more than the ones digit in the sum. Also, the tens digit of the sum is 2. Finally, if the students do not see how the addition is done by doing the first five problems, encourage either a 0 or 9 as an addend. That helps students see the "sums of 9." In all six examples in the set, 6 is the *magic number*. It is not paired with another addend to make a sum of 9. Because 6 is the magic number, it determines the ones digit of the sum.

Exercises

313. Extend the addition number trick to include seven addends and then nine addends with you being given three addends and four addends, respectively. Have 8 be the magic number in all examples you do with either seven or nine addends. You should see a pattern.

314. Extend the addition number trick to adding five 2-digit addends with the magic number being 47. You should see a pattern. This idea can be extended to any number of addends and any number of digits in the addends with some restrictions. How would you generalize the trick?

Some students enjoy doing problems like
E L F
+ E L F, where each letter represents a
F O O L
digit and is unique within the problem. That is, F has the same value within the problem. With a four-digit sum and two addends, F must be 1 because the largest value E could take is 9 and 9 + 9 = 18. Similarly, E must be at least 5 or there

would be no regrouping. Shift the focus from E to F. Because F is 1, L must be 2. If L is 2, O must be 4. But if O is 4, then E must be 7 because 7 + 7 = 14, which fits with the regrouping idea discussed earlier. So, the problem is

$$
\begin{array}{r}
721 \\
+721 \\
\hline
1442.
\end{array}
$$

The ELF problem requires reasoning to solve it. As students work through the solution, they are beginning to develop the skills required for proofs. That reasoning development is an essential part of the development of the ability to construct proofs.

Proofs help answer the question "Why?" Students need to be encouraged to ask why something acts as it does, if it always works, if there is a pattern, whether there are exceptions, and so on. In the process, they are beginning to ask for proofs. The degree of formality may change, but the basis is there. As stated earlier, reasoning and proof should start early in the curriculum. It is your responsibility to help your students raise those questions. It is inappropriate to say, "Because the book says so." It is acceptable to say, "I don't know, but I will find out." All of this is a mosaic that goes together to develop reasoning and proof skills.

REFERENCES

Hutchings, B. (1976). Low-stress algorithms. In D. Nelson & R. E. Reys (Eds.), *Measurement in school mathematics, 1976 yearbook* (pp. 218–239). Reston, VA: National Council of Teachers of Mathematics.

Lakatos, I. (1976). *Proofs and refutations*. Cambridge, England: Cambridge University Press.

National Council of Teachers of Mathematics. (2000). *Principles and standards for school mathematics*. Reston, VA: Author.

Paulos, J. A. (1988). *Innumeracy: Mathematical illiteracy and its consequences*. New York: Hill & Wang.

Tompert, A. (1990). *Grandfather Tang's story*. New York: Crown.

9
Communication

"I know what I want to say, but I can't find the words." Has anyone ever said that to you or have you ever said that to anyone? How frustrating it is to know something and yet not be able to put that knowledge into a neat, concise package of words. Sometimes a words-only message simply does not communicate what we want. Generally we do not just use words to communicate. We use gestures, body language, objects we hold and point to, things we refer to, and a host of other means, all designed to get our message across.

CLARITY OF THOUGHT

Undoubtedly, you have studied different learning modalities as a part of your education program. It is your responsibility to know the primary modality of your students. They are not all auditory learners. You will have visual, kinesthetic, and who knows what other kinds of learners in your class. As you work through a lesson with a class, it is imperative that you periodically focus on the visual learners and say something like, "Look at . . ." or "Pick up . . . and place it. . . ." By doing that, you are not assuming that the different modalities will pick out their respective clues as needed. You are focusing on the specific learning modality of each student

and enhancing understanding of the topic at hand.

The traditional mathematical world can hold few clues for students who do not learn by demonstrated example. Typically the teacher shows how to do a problem by example, often saying, "Put this number here, that number there, then do. . . ." Please read this next sentence carefully. We are *not* saying that a teacher should never teach by showing examples. Much of the mathematics that has been learned over time has been learned by mimicking demonstrations of someone else. That is an effective means of instruction for some students. However, it is not a practical method for all learners, and it is not the only way to teach mathematics. Somehow many people seem to have assumed it is.

Part of that assumption is based on history. Most of us have been taught mathematics by observing demonstrations by the teacher. Perhaps that is one reason that things like Cuisenaire Rods, Base 10 blocks, geoboards, dynamic software, and models seem so foreign to us. It is common to rationalize that, if I learned it that way, why can't everyone? Knowledge of different learning modalities clearly indicates that everyone cannot effectively absorb information via the teacher-telling mode. Throughout this text, we have been giving you examples of different ways to present things. Certainly there are many places where teacher telling is an appropriate method of instruction. Yet, it is not the only way. You are responsible for teaching all students in your classroom. You do not have the privilege of saying that if a child does not get it the way you present it, then you do not have time to work with that child.

WAYS OF EXPRESSING WHAT YOU KNOW

So how do you communicate with each child? Certainly the different learning modalities are part of the picture. In addition, it is imperative that you know what you are talking about. You respond to that statement saying, "I know elementary school mathematics," but that is only part of the story. What if a child does not understand your explanation? The following vignette will help make the point. A teacher is explaining something to a class. After the presentation is completed, the teacher asks for questions. The dialogue between the two is:

S: I don't get it.
T: (the teacher is quite patient with all such questions) The explanation is repeated almost verbatim from the first one.
S: (after the repeated explanation is completed) I still don't get it.
T: The explanation is repeated again, still calmly and patiently, again, almost verbatim.
S: I still don't get it.
T: Exasperation is beginning to show but patience persists and again, the material is covered, almost verbatim.
S: I still don't get it.
T: Finally pushed beyond the limit, looks at the student and says, "Haven't you been listening?"

Hopefully that type of scenario does not occur, but you get the point. The teacher

is failing miserably when it comes to communication. Perhaps a verbatim explanation is in order the first time the student asks for clarification. However, after that, it should be clear to the teacher that a communication gap is present. One solution is to explain the material a different way. That mandates that you understand mathematics. Do you see now why we have been presenting so many different ways of approaching topics? Perhaps there is something missing from the child's readiness package for the topic. Maybe there is a need to recycle to one of the concrete, semi-concrete, or semi-abstract prestages. Something different needs to be done. The teacher has the knowledge and is responsible for portraying that knowledge to the student in a manner that is understandable to the student. Teacher telling is not necessarily equivalent to student learning.

Before leaving that vignette, there is one more important factor to consider. We were mighty hard on the teacher as we went through the discussion. At the same time, the student bears some responsibility to communicate too. "I don't get it" is not helpful or specific for the teacher. We can guide students to better communicate by trying to elicit a more specific comment from them. You can help them by asking things like: "At what step do you begin to get confused?" "What part do you understand?" "Tell me what you do understand." These questions begin to force the student to think about what is going on and express a more specific idea. In the process, you, the teacher, are more able to assist them as they strive to grow and learn.

Back when you were in precollege and the teacher was generating a mathematics discussion in class, how many times did you hear a student answer by saying, "You know what I mean." Sometimes that teacher is actually an incredible seer and can read a child's mind. However, this obviously is not always the case, nor is it how we want our students answering questions and explaining the mathematics they know. How can we promote mathematical communication in our students? You can begin by asking children to explain the mathematics they are doing on paper. For example, when finding the sum of one third and one half, students may be quick to determine that you need to find a common denominator for each fraction. Ask the students to provide a written explanation for determining the common denominator. You might be surprised at the responses. Some students will correctly find the least common denominator (LCD) without realizing they found the least common multiple (LCM) of the two denominators. Ask a child to explain how to find the LCM or GCF of two given numbers. Student explanation of the concepts is essential in the learning of mathematics. Promoting communication must be an ongoing process and expectation inside your classroom. It cannot be a one-time shot during a test at the end of a chapter. Continually ask students for verbal and written explanations and class demonstrations of concepts throughout the year. You need to ask them to explain, and they need to learn how to ask elaborating questions.

There are several ways to help children learn how to ask questions. One that also incorporates literature at the same time comes out of the Stories With Holes series by Nathan Levy. Each booklet in the series contains several stories often one paragraph long. A situation is described and the child is to determine what information is missing by asking questions that can be answered only with a yes or no. One situation from Volume 5 in the series has a person living on the 20th floor of an apartment building. The person

leaves the building by riding the elevator to the first floor. The person returns, taking the elevator to the 15th floor, and walks the rest of the way. The question is, "Why?" Ultimately the students determine that the individual is tall enough to only reach the 15th floor button on the panel. Therefore, the elevator ride ends on the 15th floor. Notice how this is a blend of literature, problem solving, reasoning, and questioning skills, and, in this case, the objective is to build communication skills.

Earlier we mentioned Gauss' procedure for finding the sum of the first 100 consecutive counting numbers. This solution is well known in mathematical circles and is often referred to in textbooks. One such reference can be found in the Grade 5 Guidebook for MathLand. There is a discussion of how Gauss supposedly solved the problem, but there are some questions that could be used to help you and your students learn how to communicate about mathematics. We suggest that you refer to the Teacher's Guide and supplemental materials that come with your textbook. You might be amazed by the hints that help you learn to investigate mathematics and communication.

The world of mathematics is loaded with tradition. Teacher telling as a means of instruction is one of them. Yet, teacher telling is not the only way to teach mathematics. Discovery has a place. That is why we have talked so much about investigation of patterns. Many things can be extracted from a set of numbers when a pattern is spotted, sometimes even going to the point of generating a formula that works for all similar situations. That is really one of the things mathematics is all about—reducing a set of experiences to a formula or rule that makes the solving of similar problems simple. Although discovery has a place in the mosaic that is becoming your teaching style, it is not the only way to help your students learn. It would not be practical to have your students discover everything. You need to find an acceptable level between no discovery and total discovery. That point will vary with grade level, student readiness, teacher preference, time, available materials, high-stakes testing pressures, and a host of other variables. Still, somewhere between none and total means exactly that. None is not a reasonable option.

That last discussion could be repeated for any other point you want to present: lecture, constructivism, self-paced, back to the basics, and so on. Each of those points has a place in the curriculum. Have a potpourri of methods ready in your teacher *bag of tricks* so you are ready to help all students. You need to learn to blend all of them into your curriculum because that is how you are going to effectively communicate with all students.

Another tradition is inherent in the world of mathematics. Ask someone what they think of when you say *mathematics* and most people will say numbers, arithmetic, or formulas. Think back over the mathematical instruction you had in the K to 12 environment. More than likely most of it involved expressing things in terms of numbers. How many times did you write an explanation of how to do a problem type? Had you heard of a paragraph proof before the section on Proof and Reasoning?

There is a whole new mathematical world out there waiting for you. It can be exciting. The thrill you will get from learning to communicate mathematics to your students will be unlike any other. It feels good!

REFERENCE

Levy, N., & Gordon, J. A. (Ed.). (2000). *Stories with holes* (Vol. 5). St. Paul, MN: Trend Enterprises.

10
Connections

FOCAL POINTS

Many students see mathematics as a collection of independent events. That is not good for a couple of reasons. First and foremost, mathematics in not a collection of separated topics. Individuals who visualize mathematics as a bunch of unrelated events are laboring under false pretenses. Second, seeing mathematics as a collection of independent events hampers a student's growth to mathematical maturity.

How do individuals conclude that mathematics is not interconnected? One culprit is our curriculum and how we present it to students. It is common for students to see mathematics as a collection of topics that have no apparent connection. Do you remember how you learned your multiplication facts? Was there any discussion about how 3 × 5 is a shortcut method of working with 5 + 5 + 5? That connection is using the repeated addition definition for multiplication. Although there are other ways to define multiplication, the repeated addition method makes a connection to prior work. One of the strongest methods for teaching any subject is to take a new topic and relate it back to something studied earlier. The reference relaxes the student by making the new work sound familiar, and therefore the assumption is that it is not going to be too hard. As the connections between the topics are made, often the student sees a shortcut that can be made

and will abandon the prior information in favor of the new approach to the topic. Many students would not see much advantage to abandoning 5 + 5 + 5 in favor of 3 × 5, but few students would like to do 9 × 47 in repeated addition form (47 + 47 + 47 + 47 +47 + 47 + 47 + 47 + 47). If you find a student who prefers doing 9 × 47 via repeated addition, be careful not to chastise that student too much. You asked for the product and the student gave you the answer. Maybe the student did not use the method you would have preferred, but the student did get the answer. That student can be convinced to change methods of solving the problem types if you continue to provide problems that are more conveniently solved with multiplication as opposed to being done by repeated addition. Ultimately, the student is going to be asking for an easier way to do the problem. You will now help that student understand the world's slickest, quickest way to do the problem—multiplication. Mission accomplished and connection made.

Stick with multiplication for a little longer. The problem 3 × 5 could be solved via the array method with something like Fig. 10.1. The squares could be counted so the total number of unit squares would be known. The discussion would focus on three sets of five or three fives giving 15. There is a verbal transition that helps make the connection between addition and multiplication. When we were discussing multiplication of whole numbers, we talked about connecting the repeated addition model from the number line with the array model, also built from the number line, and the commutative property of addition on the set of whole numbers. Look at the connections that have been made throughout this text. We have been doing that with you throughout our discussions. Only now are we calling the idea to your attention. We did that on purpose. We wanted to show you how easily connections can be inserted into the curriculum. Figure 10.1 can be used to extend that idea. It could have been built

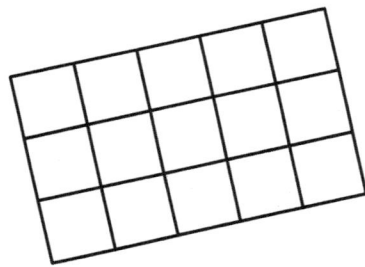

FIG. 10.1.

much like we constructed Figs. 2.33 and 2.34, but our emphasis is different now. We are going to connect multiplication to the concept of area.

Figure 10.1 shows the area of a rectangle that has a base 5 of units and a height of 3 units (or is that a length of 3 and a width of 5?). Yet Fig. 10.1 looks a lot like one part of Fig. 2.34 with different dimensions. How is it that the pictures are so similar and yet we are talking multiplication in one situation and area of a rectangle in another? Surprise! Connections! Hold on, we are not done. Almost any two-factor multiplication problem is going to result in a product that could be expressing the area of a rectangle. Suppose one dimension is 3.5 and the other is 6 units. Figure 10.2 shows the situation. Sure, there are partial squares, but two of the six partial squares can be put together to make another square because each partial square is a half of an original

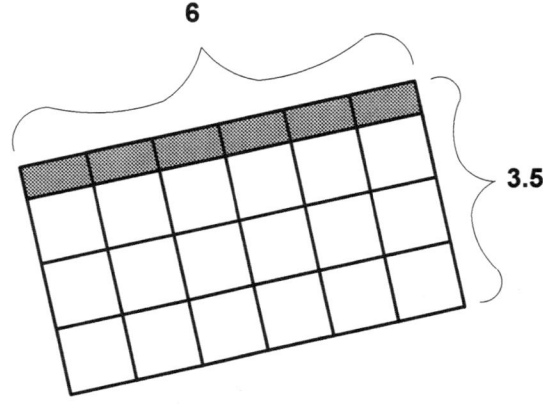

FIG. 10.2.

square. Do that three times and you end up with a total of 21 squares. What is the product of 6 and 3.5? It better be 21. By the way, the results are the same if you multiply $3\frac{1}{2}$ or $\frac{7}{2}$ by 6. The numbers can be switched to look a lot more complex, but the story is the same—you end up with an area when you do a two-factor multiplication problem. Now you have another connection—from repeated addition through multiplication to areas of rectangles. You could also connect between decimals, improper fractions, and mixed numbers in multiplication from our discussion. Those connections abound in mathematics. You only have to learn to recognize them. Few mathematical concepts can be taught in total isolation.

Exercise

315. Will all two-factor multiplication problems give a product that is an area? Provide a written explanation to defend your answer.

Continuing with the array definitions of *multiplication* and *area* shows another connection too. We have said that the dimensions were 3.5 units by 6 units. Yet we did not extend that to the product of 21. An important part of learning about area involves helping the students under-

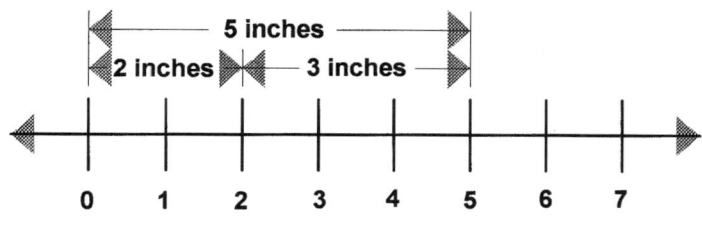

FIG. 10.3.

stand what is happening with the units. Initial comprehension of work with units can be established by considering what happened when the students learned addition facts and combined three blocks and two more blocks to give five blocks. That verbiage is fairly natural, and many students say it reflexively as they do the problem or answer the question. Extend that to the idea of finding the sum of 3 inches and 2 inches. For some reason, there is a temptation to omit the inches part as the sum of 5 is given. Recording the answer as 5 inches is a significant factor and should not be overlooked. The connection is fairly easy for students to make if they are working with something like Fig. 10.3. A key element of the discussion is to discuss the length of the new segment, which is the sum of the two shorter ones. When the answer is given as 5, a reflexive question from you or the students should be "5 what?", and the units are emphasized.

A similar discussion can be developed when doing area (grid paper could come in handy here). The readiness skill for dealing with units comes out of the discussion used with Fig. 10.3. When doing area, the unit is a little square rather than a length of a segment. So the area is expressed in terms of how many little squares it takes to cover the shape. The central discussion issues become: How many little squares? What is the length of one side of one of the squares? If the length of the side is an inch, the discus-

sion can be built around a "square with an inch long side," which can be verbally transitioned to a "square inch." You now have connected the "little square" to "square inch," the unit for area discussions (except "inch" might be "meter," "foot," "centimeter," or the generic "unit," which comes later developmentally). Initially the students might write the area as 15 square inches. Eventually they will write that as 15 inches^2 or even 15 in^2, but only after the concept of exponents has been developed.

Some students struggle to understand how squares can be used to express the area of a triangle. Connecting the area of a triangle to the area of a rectangle helps. Suppose the triangle has a base of four units and a height of three units. Assuming the students have worked with the area of rectangles already, start with a rectangle. In fact, start with a sheet of rectangular paper. Fold the paper along the diagonal as shown in Fig. 10.4. Cutting along the fold and rotating one piece

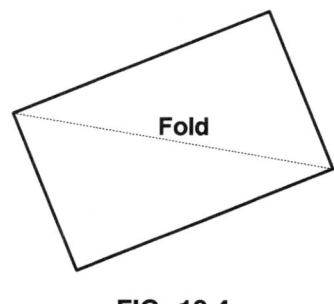

FIG. 10.4.

shows that the two triangles have the same area. Thus, one of the triangles has an area that is half of the area of the original rectangle, and the formula $\frac{base \times height}{2}$ or $\frac{bh}{2}$ is established. Certainly the formula does not come as quickly as it took to read those last two sentences, but it can be developed. Still some students will struggle to see how the little squares fit in a triangle. Figure 10.5 might help. Scene 1 shows a rectangle (all squares are rectangles), and Scene 2 shows the diagonal, which would fold the rectangle in half. Scene 3 shows the little triangles (half unit squares) shaded. The other half of the square is removed in Scene 4 to make it easier to see the triangle being used in the example. Some student could mentally visualize the little triangles being paired together to make squares and, in the process, conclude that the area of the triangle is eight square units. Scene 5 might help some students. Scene 5 is interesting in that it might help clarify the situation for some students and confuse others because the triangle has been transitioned to a rectangle. All of the pieces are unchanged in size—they are merely moved around. A discussion based on Scene 5 of Fig. 10.5 might prove rather interesting. Scene 5 shows the final figure giving an area of eight square units. There are a lot of connections being made in Fig. 10.5.

Exercise

316. Describe how an isosceles trapezoid can be transitioned to a rectangle to demonstrate the development of the formula for the area of a trapezoid, $\frac{(b_1 + b_2)h}{2}$.

In the multiplication of whole numbers section of this text, we discussed partial products. That was extended into algebra, another connection. We discussed patterns in the early childhood section as well as several other places and ended with extensions into the work of Gauss. More connections. They are everywhere; all you have to do is notice them. You might find that you will actually get excited about some of the connections you see. That excitement is contagious and will spill over into your teaching. Your students might actually start getting excited about some of the mathematics they are learning and seeing in their world. Aaaahhhhhh, connections, they really are everywhere!

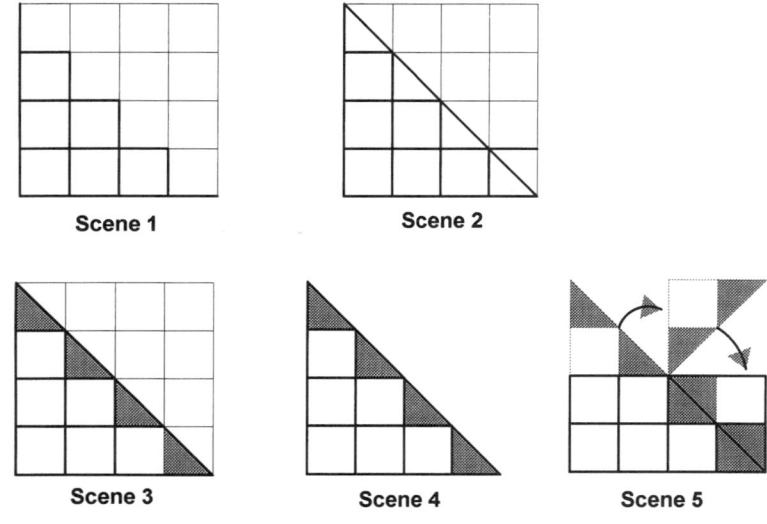

Scene 1   Scene 2

Scene 3   Scene 4   Scene 5

FIG. 10.5.

11
Representation

FOCAL POINTS

- Different Ways of Saying the Same Thing

I am one of the authors of this book. My name is Douglas Kent Brumbaugh. I have been addressed as Doug most of my life. In my younger days, if I was not behaving as well as I should have been, I heard Douglas. If I was more out of line, I heard Douglas Kent. If I was pushing the envelope to the limit, I heard Douglas Kent Brumbaugh. My dad and grandfather wanted to name me Mike, but they lost that discussion. Undaunted, they called me Mike. My friends awarded several different nicknames to me. Over the years, I have answered to all of them. I am still me no matter what I am called.

DIFFERENT WAYS OF SAYING THE SAME THING

Representations are something like that.

> The term representation refers both to process and product—in other words, to the act of capturing a mathematical concept or relationship in some form and to the form itself. ... Moreover, the term applies to processes and products that are observable externally as well as to those that occur "internally," in the minds of people doing mathematics. All these meanings of representation are important to consider in school mathematics. (National Council of Teachers of Mathematics, 2000, p. 67)

Figure 11.1 shows how a child was described in the prior quote as showing her age to be 5 and one half. It appears as if the girl has begun to establish a feel for the idea of a half by how she writes the second part of her age. Her style seems strange and yet she seems to have established that she is 5 and some more. She apparently knows that that *some more* is a half, and she seems to be attempting to convey that message by writing half of the numeral 5. It makes sense, doesn't it, and yet we would write 5.5 or $5\frac{1}{2}$.

Representation consistently moves from concrete to abstract as new concepts are encountered and understood. The ultimate goal is to have students function abstractly with their mathematical understandings because that is the most convenient and accepted way to communicate about such things. Yet the main idea is to communicate the idea at hand. If the work of a student reflects understanding of the concept, we can help that student progress to a more sophisticated or acceptable representation of the idea.

Young children represent numbers of objects via sets. They then move on to using pictures of the sets, tally marks to

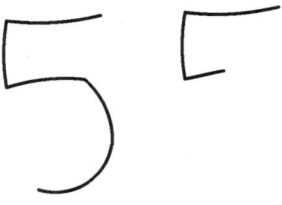

FIG. 11.1.

represent the pictured objects to represent the objects, and finally a numeral, which is known to be a shortcut way to show the tally marks representing the pictured objects that represent the objects themselves. That last sentence describes parallel developments that might take years to accomplish depending on the complexity of the concept being considered. Think back through the things covered in this text. You should be able to conjure up ideas that show the development of the different representations.

Technology comes into play as a means to represent ideas too. Consider fractions. Many calculators express three fourths as 3/4 (did you get the idea represented in number words and also as a fraction?). Some calculators show three fourths as 3⌐4, whereas a few show its *pretty print* form of $\frac{3}{4}$. You become comfortable with one way, but generally easily gravitate to another because you understand that all those forms are different ways of saying the same thing. That is where we want our students to get. More than likely, you have been visualizing something like Fig. 11.2 to depict what was being discussed as three fourths of something. Those are only some of the ways to represent $\frac{3}{4}$, and it is not the end of the fraction line of development.

Not all fractions are less than one. Fractions also represent the concept of a ratio, and we even sometimes use fractions to mean division.

Throughout this text, we have used manipulatives and technology to depict or model different mathematical situations. Those have all been representations. We did it to you again ☺. We gave you examples of representations and did not tell you we were doing it. Now as you look back over the semester, you should be able to see a variety of representations of different concepts.

Howard Eves and Peter Hilton, both personal friends of the authors and world class mathematicians, have said, "If you have algebra without geometry you have answers to questions nobody would ask, and if you have geometry without algebra you have questions you cannot answer." You might be asking why we would discuss algebra and geometry in an elementary text (which we have done throughout), but we also ask you to recall the last statement in our introduction: "So, let the adventure begin."

You have now reached the end of this text. However, this is not the end of your learning mathematics, how to teach mathematics, about students, about how to communicate with students, about different interpretations, and so much more. You are about to enter a profession where you will be learning for the rest of your career. With that in mind, we leave you with a statement we have used before: So, let the adventure begin.

—Linda, Michelle, David, & Doug/Mike ☺

REFERENCE

National Council of Teachers of Mathematics. (2000). *Principles and standards for school mathematics*. Reston, VA: Author.

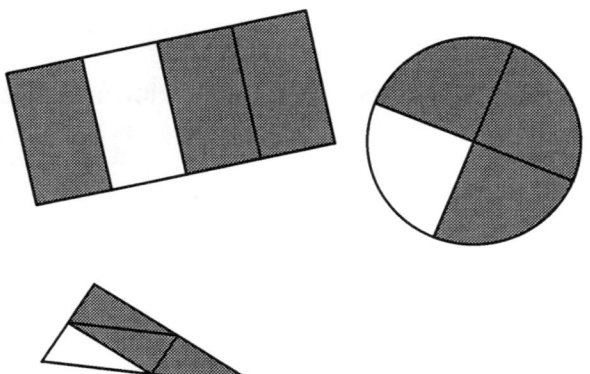

FIG. 11.2.

Index

Solutions Manual

1. Do each of the problems listed here (the left one first, the one to its right second, etc. to the last one). The italic numbers are those supplied by the student. A new hint is given as you move to the right in the problems. What is the secret to doing the trick?

24	89	65	16	33	00
46	52	23	*83*	*66*	*99*
67	14	*76*	36	11	44
75	*85*	*34*	63	88	*55*
+*53*	+*47*	+53	+62	+48	+93
265	287	251	260	246	291

Subtract each "student selected" addend from 99 and that missing addend becomes one of the numbers you pick. In the leftmost problem, a student picked *53*. 99 − *53* = 46, one of the numbers you select. Similarly, 99 − *75* = 24. The only remaining number is your choice of 67, or the magic number. The 67 is two more than the 65 part of the sum. Notice also that the 2 appears in the hundreds place of the sum.

2. Explain how the trick in Exercise 1 of this section works.

Each sum of 99 can be expressed as (100 − 1). The left problem of
24 + 46 + 67 + **75** + **53** = 265 becomes
(100 − 1) + (100 − 1) + 67 or (200 − 2) + 67 or
200 + 67 − 2, which is 267 − 2 or 265.

3. Do a trick similar to the one in Exercise 1 of this section using seven 4-digit addends. Describe the general answer and explain your conclusions.

Answers may vary. The idea is similar except that the seven addends indicate that the leftmost digit of the sum will be a 3. The four-digit addends indicate the 3 will be in the ten-thousands place. The magic number will be 3 greater that the remaining four digits of the sum because the three student-selected numbers plus your three obtained by subtracting from 9999 will give
(10,000 − 1) + (10,000 − 1 + (10,000 − 1) or
(30,000 − 3).

4. Find another number trick that involves addition. Do the trick with a class of elementary students who have the appropriate background. Describe the reaction of the students.

Answers may vary. Pick a number. (17) Multiply it by 6. [(17)(6) = 102] Add 24 to the product. (102 + 24 = 126) Divide by 6.

$$\left(6\overline{)126}^{\ 21}\right) \text{ Subtract the original number}$$

(21 − 17 = 4). Everyone should have 4. Although this trick involves other operations, addition is getting practiced too.

5. Locate a Web site that lists problem solving problems appropriate for elementary school students. Provide the name of the site, the address, and a brief description of the site.

Answers may vary.

Name: BRAIN TEASER OF THE WEEK CONTEST
Address: http://www.olemiss.edu/mathed/brain/
Description: A problem appropriate for elementary students is posted every week. Names of students correctly solving the problem are listed on the site. A Casio calculator is

randomly awarded to one participant who correctly solves the problem each week.

6. Present an appropriate problem-solving problem you found on a Web site to a group of elementary students and describe their reactions.

Answers may vary. Usually students react positively and enthusiastically.

7. Locate a Web site that lists games, tricks, activities, or technology appropriate for elementary school students. Provide the name of the site, the address, and a brief description of the site.

Answers may vary.

8. Present an appropriate game or trick you found on a Web site to a group of elementary students and describe their reactions.

Answers may vary. Usually students react positively and enthusiastically.

9. Locate a resource that is appropriate for a student needing special assistance in learning mathematics. List the resource and briefly describe what "is claimed to be done" for the student who uses it. Reflect on the manufacturer's claim and state why you agree or disagree.

Answers may vary.

10. Locate a resource that is appropriate for a mathematically talented student. List the resource and briefly describe what "is claimed to be done" for the student who uses it. Reflect on the manufacturer's claim and state why you agree or disagree.

Answers may vary.

11. Is it feasible that a resource could be used for students of all ability levels? Why or why not? If possible, cite an example.

Answers may vary.

12. Examine the problem sections of an elementary mathematics textbook. How many of the problems come from the world as viewed by a student? Of all the problems, how many are designed to appeal to girls?

Answers will vary.

13. What are the major characteristics you would ascribe to a positive mathematics classroom? Which of these would you control? Which would be dependent on your students? Which of these would depend on administration?

Answers will vary.

14. Was the mathematics learning environment you experienced in your secondary school years constructivist based? Describe your experiences to amplify your selection.

Answers will vary.

15. Describe your mathematics classroom of the future.

Answers will vary.

16. Is it reasonable to have a test of major proportions at some point during the school year? Why or why not? Describe the impact on the curriculum.

Answers will vary.

17. Should you teach in the sequence that the material is presented in the text? Why or why not?

Answers will vary.

18. Why do new teachers tend to teach mathematics in the sequence presented in the text?

Answers will vary.

19. Examine several textbooks for a given mathematics concept. Describe their similarities. Are there any significant differences? Is there a text that is notably different from the rest? If there is a different text, rationalize why it should or should not be available for adoption. If there is no different text, discuss why they are all similar.

Answers will vary.

20. Should you, the teacher, as the local authority on your class solely determine the material to be covered? If yes, why? If no, how much outside influence should be acceptable and why?

Answers will vary.

21. Do you think the teaching of mathematics in the elementary school should be different as compared with when you were in elementary school? Why or why not?

Answers will vary.

22. Have you read the Standards? Will you? Do you need to read them before you begin your teaching career? Why or why not?

Answers will vary.

23. Select a vignette from the Professional Standards that you believe to be a description of a good classroom situation. Highlight the strong points of the vignette and describe your impression of the strengths.

Answers will vary.

24. Should your lessons follow the structure of the text? Why or why not?

Answers will vary. Generally, the text will provide a basic outline. However, your lesson should be influenced by the ability level of the students, their readiness, and state or local standards. If your experience has shown that a different way is more effective with the students, then you should use that one. Be aware that using a method different from the one in the text can lead to confusion.

25. Should two teachers in the same grade, with students of the same ability, in the same school, follow the same lesson plans? Why or why not?

Answers will vary. Generally, no. Although students possess similar abilities, their personalities and learning modalities might be quite different.

26. If you cannot finish the curriculum, how do you decide what to sacrifice? What are the ramifications of eliminating some topics? Is there a way this dilemma can be resolved?

Answers will vary. Local and state assessment programs could have a dramatic impact on this response. In today's high-stakes test environment, many curricular sacrifices may be made to enhance the student's abilities to score well on the test.

27. Determine the error pattern the student made in each of the following problems:

$42 + 71 = 491$

$34 + 28 = 368$

$29 + 37 = 2127$

$76 + 54 = 7114$

Describe the error the student is making. List the steps you would employ to assist the student in learning how to do the problem correctly and avoid repeating the same error. Could this error have been caused because the students are not accustomed to seeing addition problems written horizontally?

The student is writing the first digit of the problem as the hundreds digit of the sum, adding the second and third digits of the problem, using that sum as the tens digit in the sum, and writing the last digit of the problem as the ones digit in the sum. The likelihood is great that this error is a result of unfamiliarity with writing problems horizontally. Sequencing answers will vary. Perhaps there is a need to return to the Base 10 blocks. Before doing that, however, ascertain whether the problem can be done correctly when written in vertical format.

28. Determine the error pattern the student made in each of the following problems:

4567	389	2468	3421
+7968	+964	+3517	+2476
14635	1453	7085	5897

The student is adding from right to left. When a regrouping occurs, the student is placing a 1 in each column to the left of the place where the regrouping occurs. Consider the example 389 + 964. 4 + 9 = 13 so the 3 is written in the sum and then a 1 is placed over each of the tens and hundreds columns. Then the tens are added; 6 + 8 = 14 plus the 1 regrouped from the ones gives 15. The 5 is recorded as the tens digit in the sum and the 1 is regrouped to the hundreds column. When the hundreds are added, the student gets 9 + 3 = 12 plus the 1 regrouped from the units column and the second 1 regrouped from the tens column, giving a total of 14.

29. Define an error pattern you think a student would make. State the grade level. Provide sufficient examples. Give your error pattern to a peer to solve. Describe your discussions with your peer about the error pattern and how to correct it.

Answers will vary.

30. Summarize and react to one article dealing with the use of calculators in a mathematics classroom. Include all bibliographic information.

Answers will vary.

31. Should calculators be used in the elementary setting? Why or why not?

Answers will vary. Research can be found to support both sides of the issue. Our position is that an informed decision must be made. That means that each prospective teacher of elementary school mathematics must become informed on the use of calculators, their

impacts, and the many opinions on when and where the calculator should be used. Compiling all that information leads to an informed decision.

32. Name a mathematical concept that would be hindered by the use of calculators and one that would benefit from the use of calculators. Rationalize your position in both instances.

Answers will vary.

33. How would you convince a student that memorization of basic fact tables is a necessity?

Answers will vary. One way is to split the class into those who prefer to use a calculator for answers to fact problems and those who have memorized them. The calculator group **must** use their calculators for this activity. Challenge the two groups to have a race to do some problems. When they are ready, project five fact problems. As each individual finishes the problems, they are to stand at their seat and say, "I am done." Those who do the problems from memory will probably all be done before the calculator person has finished one problem.

34. Devise a set of problems that could be used as a basis to teach the order of operations for addition, subtraction, multiplication, and division on the set of counting numbers.

Answers will vary.

35. Is there any value to using larger numbers for the entries in the problem sets given to students as they are discovering the aspects of order of operations with their calculators? Why or why not?

Answers will vary.

36. Discuss the advantages or disadvantages of selecting a sequence of exposures that lead students from excess in division being expressed as remainders, then fractions, and finally decimals.

Answers will vary.

37. The two major microcomputer platforms are PC and Mac. Which one will you use in your classroom and why?

Answers will vary. Generally, you use what is provided.

38. If your school's computer platform is different from the one you prefer, what will you do?

Answers will vary. Usually you have to learn the new platform and use the available software. If there is no appropriate software on that platform, then perhaps there is a need to lobby to change platforms.

39. Select a child who is at the beginning school age and conduct a conservation of number activity. Describe the results of your experiment.

Answers may vary. The assumption is that conservation tasks have been discussed during a session on educational research in a foundations class where it is likely you have studied about individuals such as Jean Piaget. If that has not occurred, it is assumed that you will do some individual research on conservation tasks.

40. Observe a kindergarten or first-grade student who is placed in an unusual environment. Describe how the child reacts.

Answers may vary. The description should contain information about the child's independence, flexibility, and originality.

41. Describe a plan you could implement to help your students' parents view mathematics in a more positive light.

Answers may vary. The description should include comments that encourage applications, extensions beyond rote memorization, investigations, multiple approaches to the same problem, and so on.

42. What do you think would happen if you used pennies, dimes, and quarters (or other different size objects) at the same time?

Answers may vary. Perhaps younger children would be bothered by the size differences.

43. How could the penny flashing activity be used for another operation?

Answers may vary. Addition could be a response if the pennies are grouped into two sets.

44. Give a similar example to the money and the briefcase where children see inappropriate uses of numbers in real life.

Answers may vary. Children are frequently told to "Wait a minute." The actual time they wait may be much longer than a minute.

45. Would it be appropriate to bring a stack of $100 bills in class to show students how ridiculous the ransom requests are in movies? Why or why not?

Answers may vary. Most teachers would probably not do this. First, most teachers will not have $100.

46. Describe three other ways students could group pattern blocks?

Answers may vary. Color, number of sides, shapes, and so on.

47. Name two other manipulatives that younger students could use to sort and classify. Explain how the manipulatives could be used.

Answers may vary. They could describe a different set of pattern blocks or even just a box of buttons. The objects are not as important as the idea of having something that can be sorted by students in some fashion.

48. Describe how you would help a student learn that the whole numbers are not closed for division.

Answers may vary. Give any problem where the answer is not a whole number $(\frac{5}{4})$.

49. Is there ever a time when there would be a distributive property of multiplication over subtraction on the set of counting numbers?

Answers may vary. It is always true that $a \times (b - c) = (a \times b) - (a \times c)$. If the value of c is greater than the value of b, the result would be negative, but it would be negative in both instances. Merely picking whole numbers does not guarantee a whole number as the answer.

50. Select one number property that has not had some idea for presentation given in this text, and describe how you would present it to a class having the appropriate readiness skills.

Answers will vary.

51. When will four-digit place value need to be discussed in the addition sequence and why?

Place value needs to be discussed before the sum goes over 1,000 to ensure that the students know how to deal with four-digit numbers.

52. Complete the prior addition sequence until all three-digit + three-digit examples are done. Do an example with each entry.

Examples will vary. (3D means three-digit) 3D + 3D (with regrouping) out of tens only; 3D + 3D out of both ones and tens; 3D + 3D out of hundreds only; 3D + 3D out of ones and hundreds only; 3D + 3D out of tens and hundreds only; 3D + 3D out of ones, tens, and hundreds.

53. Some elements of the 2D + 2D and 3D + 3D sequences given earlier could be switched around. Which ones and why?

Answers may vary. 3D + 1D with no regrouping could be inserted into the 2D sequence in several places. If the children are struggling with regrouping in addition, the 3D + 1D might be an easy type for them to do

and still continue learning about addition of whole numbers.

54. If set A is your copy of the text for this class and set B is another copy of the same text (same edition), are sets A and B disjoint?

Answers may vary. It can be argued that the books are using different sheets of paper and thus are not the same. Most people would probably say they are the same.

55. Describe how you would use the Base 10 blocks to teach an addition fact. Explain each stage, beginning with the concrete and going through the abstract level where the fact is memorized. Your explanation could be a series of pictures, like in Fig. 2.9, a verbal description of what you would do, or a combination of words and pictures.

Answers may vary. In 3 + 4, the concrete description would describe forming a set of three unit blocks and a set of four unit blocks, which would then be combined and counted to be seven unit blocks. The rest of the sequence would be similar to that in Fig. 2.10, and the final step would be to say, "The fact is memorized by the student."

56. Describe how you would use the Base 10 blocks to teach finding the sum of two addends where there is regrouping out of all three place values. Explain each stage, beginning with the concrete and going through the abstract level where the algorithm is used. Your explanation could be a series of pictures like in Fig. 2.11, a verbal description of what you would do, or a combination of words and pictures.

Answers may vary. The concrete description would describe forming sets to represent the addends, which would then be combined and counted to be a representation of the sum. The rest of the sequence would be similar to that in Fig. 2.11, and the final step would be an algorithmic depicting of the problem.

57. A *doubles* addition fact has both addends being the same. How many *doubles* addition facts are there?

10.

58. How many addition facts are known once the student knows zero is the additive identity in the addition of whole numbers?

19. There are 10 facts where zero is the first addend and 9 more where zero is the second addend. 0 + 0 would not be double counted.

59. How many addition facts are known once the student realizes that adding one to a number will give the next consecutive counting number?

19. There are 10 facts where one is the first addend and 9 more where one is the second addend. 1 + 1 would not be double counted.

60. Assuming the student is aware that zero is the additive identity in addition of whole numbers and that adding one to a number gives the next consecutive counting number, how many addition facts are known?

36. 19 facts are done with the additive identity. 19 more are done with the role of 1 in addition. However, 0 + 1 and 1 + 0 were already counted with the additive identity in addition of whole numbers.

61. Based on the pictures in Fig. 2.13, define a train as used with Cuisenaire Rods.

Answers may vary. A train is two or more rods placed end to end in a straight line segment.

62. Describe what you would accept from a student using the Cuisenaire Rods to confirm that blacK = 7 when White is the unit.

Answers may vary. The blacK rod is the same length as a train consisting of seven White rods.

63. Describe how you would use the Cuisenaire Rods to teach an addition fact. Explain each stage, beginning with the concrete

and going through the abstract level where the fact is memorized. Your explanation could be a series of pictures like in Fig. 2.15, a verbal description of what you would do, or a combination of words and pictures.

Answers may vary. In 3 + 4, the concrete description would describe forming a Lime–Purple train, which would then be represented by the blacK rod. The rest of the sequence would be similar to that in Fig. 2.15, and the final step would be to say, "The fact is memorized by the student."

64. Do 25 + 9 using the Cuisenaire Rods, and show the result with pictures.

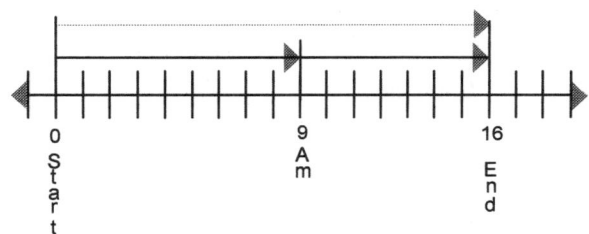

65. Do 9 + 7 on the number line using the procedure described in this text.

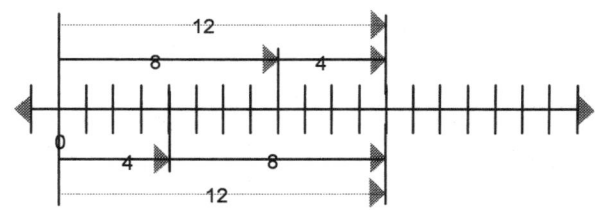

66. Show that 8 + 4 = 4 + 8 on the number line using the procedure described in this text.

67. Discuss how you would use the number line to introduce 20 + 30, assuming that the students have used the number line to learn their addition facts.

Answers may vary. Part of the discussion should deal with 2 + 3 being two steps and then three more, and 20 + 30 is like taking two

"10-step jumps" followed by three more. The students should conclude that 20 + 30 is just like 2 + 3 except there is a zero in the one's place.

68. Do 967 + 579 + 418 using the partial sum method.

```
      9 6 7
      5 7 9
   +  4 1 8
      1 4 0
    1 8 0 0
        2 4
    1 9 6 4
```

69. Do 967 + 579 + 408 using the scratch method.

```
      9 6 5
      5 7 9
   +  4 0 8
    1 8 3 2
      9 5
```

70. Do 687 + 579 + 498 using the Low Stress method.

```
    2   2          (regroups)
    6   8   7
      8 1 0
    5   7   9
  1 3   7 1 6      (fact sums)
  + 4   9   8
        1   1      (10s from fact sums)
  _____
  1   7   6   4
```

71. Explain the scratch method to someone who does not know how to add that way.

Answers may vary. The person will usually express an interest in seeing the new method done a few times. After that, they frequently opt to say they prefer the old way.

72. Explain the Low Stress method to someone who does not know how to add that way.

Answers may vary. The person will usually express an interest in seeing the new method done a few times. They usually ask why no one ever showed them that way earlier in their addition careers. After that, they frequently opt to say they prefer the old way.

73.

	4689	538	9681
	5794	721	4032
	+ 157	+ 746	+ 6195
	9420	1995	19708

No regroupings are considered or listed. Perhaps a comment like "You forgot the regroupings" will correct the situation. If not, a few simpler problems with the Base 10 blocks should make the error apparent. After that, you might be able to skip to partial sum addition and then back to the algorithm.

74.

	4689	538	9681
	5794	721	4032
	+ 157	+ 746	+ 6195
	14420	2095	21708

All regroupings are added to the leftmost column only. A few simpler problems with the Base 10 blocks should make the error apparent. After that, you might be able to skip to partial sum addition and then back to the algorithm.

75.

	4689	538	9681
	5794	721	4032
	+ 157	+ 746	+ 6195
	14840	2105	21908

stack regroups on each to left

Any regrouping is listed in each and every successive column to the left. A few simpler problems with the Base 10 blocks should make the error apparent. After that, you might be able to skip to partial sum addition and then back to the algorithm.

76. Explain to an individual just beginning subtraction how to do take-away subtraction using a set of objects. Describe the reaction and advantages or disadvantages of the approach you used.

Answers may vary. Assuming the student is aware of numberness, this should be fairly easy. This model is advantageous when small values are involved.

77. Explain to an individual just beginning subtraction how to do comparison subtraction using a set of objects. Describe the reaction and advantages or disadvantages of the approach you used.

Answers may vary. Assuming the student is aware of numberness, this should be fairly easy. This model is advantageous when small values are involved.

78. Do 13 – 6 with the Cuisenaire Rods. Try not to *cheat* by doing it mentally. Rather, *pretend* you do not know how to subtract and randomly place the rods as if you had no idea what to do until you find the right one. Describe your thoughts after you complete that process.

Answers may vary. There should be a small AHA with the thought about limits.

79. Do 57 – 26 with the Cuisenaire Rods. Describe your thoughts after you complete the problem.

Answers may vary. The length of the trains should be one comment. There could be a comment about emphasizing place value with trains made out of Orange rods. Individual sets do not have enough Orange rods to do this problem.

80. Do 13 – 6 on the number line. Describe your thoughts after you complete that process.

Answers may vary. The process is similar to that of the Cuisenaire Rods except you only need to count the spaces to determine the missing addend.

81. Do 57 – 26 on the number line. Describe your thoughts after you complete the problem.

Answers may vary. The process is similar to that of the Cuisenaire Rods except you only need to count the spaces to determine the missing addend. Even at that, this is not easy to do on the number line because of the size of the numbers.

82. Discuss the similarities and differences between the Cuisenaire Rods and the number line for doing subtraction facts. Which would you prefer to use with children and why?

Answers may vary. Except for finding the rod or counting the spaces for the missing addend, they are the same. Most people probably prefer the number line because it seems easier to use due to the lack of learning all the colors and values.

83. Use the Base 10 blocks to do 357 – 198. Describe with pictures and scenes, words, or a combination of the two how a student would transition through the concrete, semi-concrete, and semi-abstract stages to the standard algorithm.

Answers may vary.

84. Use letter names for Base 10 blocks to do 3001 – 1469. Discuss the advantages of a concrete approach to this particular problem.

Answers may vary. The big advantage is that a variety of error patterns can be avoided by showing the proper regroupings.

85. Outline how you would convince a colleague to use Base 10 blocks to teach subtraction of whole numbers.

Answers may vary. With the concrete, the student can see the regroupings. This should assist in understanding the algorithm when the time comes.

86. Do 67953 – 18076 using the borrow–payback method. Describe your thought process as you do it.

49877. Answers may vary. Confusion (due to lack of practice). "Neat." "Why didn't my teachers show me this?"

87. Do 67953 − 18076 using integer subtraction. Describe your thought process as you do it.

49877. Answers may vary. Confusion (due to lack of practice). "Neat." "Why didn't my teachers show me this?"

88. Do 5007 − 2345 by renaming 5007 as 4999 + 8. Do you think this is a good method to show students? Why or why not?

Answers may vary. "Neat." "Why didn't my teachers show me this?"

89. Do 5007 − 2345 using the scratch method for subtraction. Do you think this is a good method to show students? Why or why not?

49877. Answers may vary. Confusion (due to lack of practice). "Neat." "Why didn't my teachers show me this?"

90.

4361	5231	63421	653
−1879	−1879	−21879	−128
3518	4648	42458	535

little from big

91.

4361	5231	63421	653
−1879	−1879	−21879	−128
532	1462	12652	435

regroup from far left

92.

4361	5231	63421	653
−1879	−1879	−21879	−128
3592	4462	42652	525

don't account for regroup

93.

4361	5231	63421	653
−1879	−1879	−21879	−128
382	1252	9442	325

regroup out of each

94. Reflect on the idea of introducing multiplication before subtraction. Summarize your thoughts in writing.

Answers may vary. The thought is so foreign to most people that there is considerable resistance. However, many do conclude that it does make sense.

95. Of the three multiplication models mentioned in the text, which appeals the most to you and why?

Answers may vary. Each has advantages and disadvantages that are often related to students' background exposures.

96. Investigate an elementary mathematics textbook that introduces multiplication. Which model is used? Is the appropriate concrete background established before the students are moved to the pictorial and abstract level of dealing with multiplication?

Answers may vary. The major outcome should be an awareness of the presence or absence of concrete beginnings.

97. Would you use the number line to show that 4 × 1 = 4? Why or why not?

Answers may vary. Some will like it because it is easy to work with in that there are no pieces to distribute to students.

98. Use the number line to show (2 × 3) × 4 = 2 × (3 × 4).

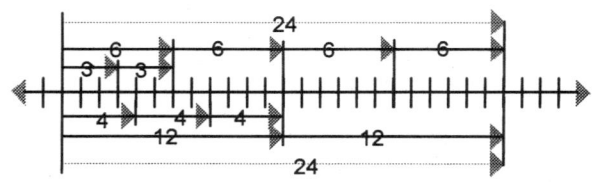

99. Use the array model to show (2 × 3) × 4 = 2 × (3 × 4).

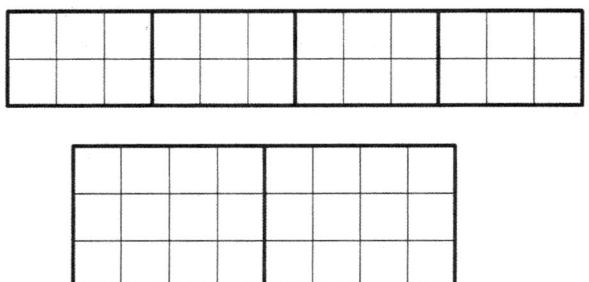

100. Use the cross method to show 7 × 8 with the Cuisenaire Rods.

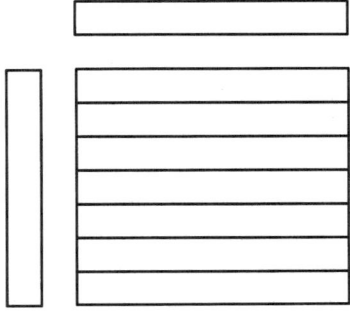

101. Use the bordered rectangle method to show 7 × 8 with the Cuisenaire Rods.

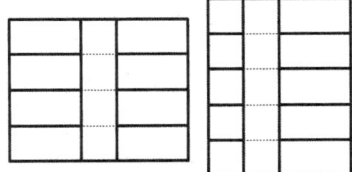

102. Show that 5 × 4 = 4 × 5 with the Cuisenaire Rods. Is one configuration more advantageous than the other? Why or why not?

103. Compare the Russian peasant method with lattice multiplication approach. Which do you prefer and why?

Answers may vary. Most will probably prefer lattice.

104. Compare lattice multiplication with the partial product method. Which do you prefer and why?

Answers may vary. Most will probably prefer partial product.

105. The partial product method for multiplication is a modification of "Napier's

Bones." Describe Napier's Bones and how they would be used to do 45 × 73.

Napier's Bones were the precursor of lattice multiplication. Each digit and its multiples (0–9) are placed vertically on a rod (bone). In this case, the 7 bone would be placed left of the 3 bone and the index rod (0–9) is placed to the left of that. Use the 4 and 5 row of the index rod to determine the array for the product. From that point on, the process is exactly like that of lattice multiplication.

106. Using Russian peasant multiplication to do 106 × 37, which factor would you select as the one to be halved and why?

Answers may vary. Most people select 106 because it is even. The desirable choice is 37 because, in halving to get to 1, the smaller factor gets to 1 in fewer steps.

107. Create a three-digit times two-digit problem and do it using partial product, lattice, and Russian peasant multiplication.

Answers may vary.

108.

45	69	387
× 28	× 74	× 59
320	246	2723
90	423	1505
1220	4476	17773

No regroupings

109.

45	69	387
× 28	× 74	× 59
360	276	3483
90	483	1935
450	759	5418

Right justify

110.

45	69	387
× 28	× 74	× 59
360	276	3483
130	513	2695
1660	5406	30433

Add all regroupings

111.

45	69	387
× 28	× 74	× 59
640	366	13563
100	843	4055
1640	8796	54113

Add regroup first, then multiply

112.

45	69	387
× 28	× 74	× 59
360	246	3483
90	483	1935
1260	4006	12733

No regroupings in addition

113. List the advantages and disadvantages of using *divisor*, *dividend*, and *quotient* as opposed to *factor*, *product*, and *missing factor*. Which set of words do you prefer and why?

Answers may vary. Most people elect to stay with divisor, dividend, and quotient because they are familiar with them. The objective is to do what will make things easier for the elementary student to learn and understand.

114. Do you think the idea of a division problem being a rectangle where one dimension is known and you are looking for the other one is a reasonable approach to introducing division? Why or why not?

Answers may vary. Typically college students tend to say it is not reasonable because they are not familiar and comfortable with it.

115. Is it reasonable to think of having your students attempt division of whole numbers before they are well founded in the skills related to multiplication? Why or why not?

Answers may vary. Most college students agree.

116. Did you notice there is no comma in $78\overline{)541554}$, whereas in place value we teach students the comma should be there. Is this a potential distraction for students? Why or why not?

Answers may vary. Most people do not notice the absence of commas in the product until it is called to their attention. By the same reasoning, it may not be a distraction for elementary students. It should be discussed, however, because they are told in most number theory sections that a comma is required for more than a four-digit whole number. At least you could tell them the commas make the numbers easier to read. Many parts of the world use spaces between sets of three digits in a number like we use commas.

117. Finish the discussion started in the text that deals with potential sources of errors when doing $78\overline{)541554}$. Explain in general terms why long division is difficult for students.

Answers may vary. The discussion will focus on such a large variety of potential locations for errors.

118. Complete the problem $2\overline{)68}$, but do it in the format $2\overline{)60 + 8}$. Describe your impressions as you complete the problem.

Answers may vary. Generally, students say it is strange because it is such an unfamiliar routine.

119. Do $68\overline{)8000 + 300 + 60 + 4}$ by rounding 68 to 70. Describe your impressions as you complete the problem.

Answers may vary. Generally, students say it is strange because it is such an unfamiliar routine.

120. Is it necessary to differentiate between problem types like $68 \div 2$ and $36 \div 2$? Why or why not?

Answers may vary. Usually students who have thought about the process see the advantage of the more precise development of the continuum.

121. Show how 35 ÷ 7 could be developed using the Cuisenaire Rods.

Answers may vary.

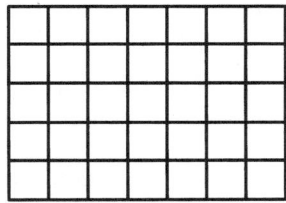

122. Show how 35 ÷ 7 could be developed using an array.

Answers may vary.

123. Show how 169 ÷ 13 could be developed using an array.

Answers may vary.

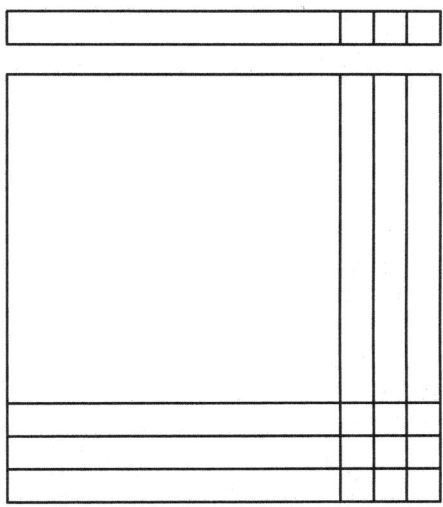

124. Is there value in using manipulatives with division of whole numbers? Why or why not?

Answers may vary. Manipulatives should be used to assist students in seeing what is happening

125. Multiply a two-digit number by a one-digit number. Use the product and the one-digit factor to create a division problem, making the two-digit factor become the missing factor. Now do the division problem using the repeated subtraction approach. *You may not estimate accurately!* Give a low estimate for both the ones value and the tens value (see Fig. 2.45 for a model of how to estimate low) so you get a feel for how repeated subtraction division works.

Answers may vary.

126. Multiply a two-digit number by a three-digit number. Use the product and the two-digit factor to create a division problem, making the three-digit factor become the missing factor. Now do the division problem using the repeated subtraction approach. *You may not estimate accurately!* Give a low estimate in the ones, tens, and hundreds values so you get a feel for how repeated subtraction division works.

Answers may vary.

127. Write a summary of your impressions on the advantages and disadvantages of repeated subtraction division.

Answers may vary. The advantage is the ability to estimate low and the disadvantage is length.

128. Describe or write a short story that uses division of whole numbers as an integral part of its development.

Answers may vary.

129. Describe a number trick that involves division.

Answers may vary.

130. Use egg cartons to show $\frac{2}{3} = \frac{4}{6}$.

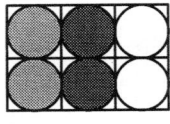 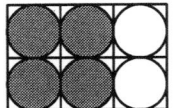

$\frac{2}{3}$ $\frac{4}{6}$

131. Use egg cartons to show $1\frac{5}{12} = \frac{17}{12}$.

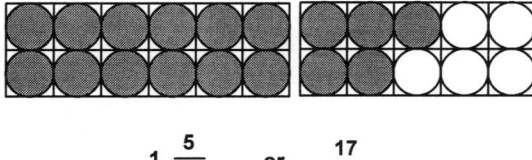

$1\frac{5}{12}$ or $\frac{17}{12}$

132. Use the Cuisenaire Rods (or a suitable substitute) to show that if Green is the unit, $\frac{2}{3} = \frac{4}{6}$.

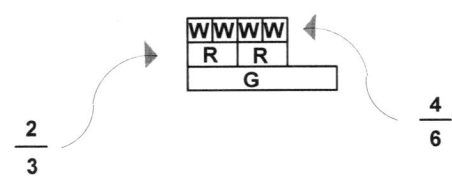

$\frac{2}{3}$ $\frac{4}{6}$

133. Use the Cuisenaire Rods (or a suitable substitute) to show that if the Orange–Red train is the unit, $\frac{1}{2} = \frac{2}{4} = \frac{3}{6} = \frac{6}{12}$.

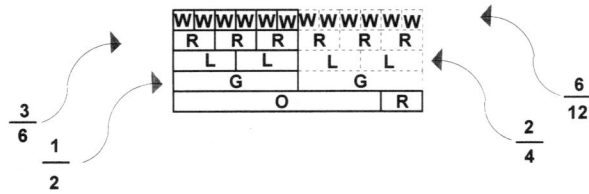

$\frac{3}{6}$ $\frac{1}{2}$ $\frac{6}{12}$ $\frac{2}{4}$

134. Use the strip of paper routine to establish a unit divided into sevenths.

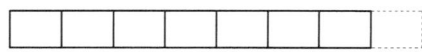

Fold strip in half, then half again, and that in half still again. That will give 8 equal sized segments. Remove one of the end sections leaving a strip divided into 7 equal sized segments, each of which is one-seventh.

135. Use the strip of paper routine to establish a unit divided into fifths.

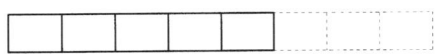

Fold strip in half, then half again, and that in half still again. That will give 8 equal sized segments. Remove 3 of the end sections leaving a strip divided into 5 equal sized segments, each of which is one-fifth.

NOTE - - You could do thirds and then fold that set in half, giving sixths. Having done that, remove one of the end sections and you have fifths.

136. Is it reasonable to expect young children to be able to say divide out common factors and understand what they mean?

The answer depends on the age, maturity, background, and readiness of the children. Basically, the expectation is not realistic for many elementary age children.

137. Show someone who is not in your class how to reduce a fraction by making it smaller and describe their reaction.

Most people will laugh, but an opportunity to discuss mathematics has been created.

138. Should students be expected to express fractions where the greatest common factor between the numerator and denominator is one? Why or why not?

Yes. One of their initial exposures to fractions will be $\frac{1}{2}$, and these two numbers are relatively prime (their greatest common factor is one). Expecting students to deal with situations where the numerator and denominator are not relatively prime is not realistic initially because they do not have the ability to divide out common factors.

139. Describe another way Fig. 2.58 could be shown. Is there an advantage to the way you show it as opposed to the one shown in the text? Why or why not?

Both the shadings could begin in the upper left corner. The advantage would be that this is a more typical (and probably common) way to show the product. The one done in the text is intended to promote divergent thinking.

140. What could be a major difficulty for students who do $\frac{2}{3} \times \frac{3}{4} \times \frac{4}{5} \times \frac{6}{7} \times \frac{7}{8}$ by first finding $2 \times 3 \times 4 \times 6 \times 7$ and $3 \times 4 \times 5 \times 7 \times 8$?

The products are large by young child standards. Assuming the students are required to express the product in simplest terms, the opportunity for arithmetic errors is increased significantly.

141. Describe how you would help a student see the advantage of dividing out common factors first in problems like $\frac{2}{3} \times \frac{3}{4} \times \frac{4}{5} \times \frac{6}{7} \times \frac{7}{8}$.

Answers will vary. The major points should be faster, easier, and fewer chances for arithmetic errors.

142. Explain the similarities between Figs. 2.58 and 2.60.

Both methods show an array of overlapping squares. The shaded unit squares represent the numerator, and the total number of unit squares (shaded or not) represent the denominator.

143. Explain the differences between Figs. 2.58 and 2.60.

The method for determining the dimensions of the numerator and denominators is different. In the array model, the two dimensions of the rectangle is subdivided and the appropriate shading is inserted. The overlapping shaded unit squares represents the numerator, whereas all unit squares represent the denominator. For the Cuisenaire Rods, the numerator and denominator rods are established to form a boundary for the product. The layers of rods are interpreted in terms of White rods to give the values for the numerator and denominator.

144. Discuss the advantages or disadvantages of doing multiplication with either the array method or Cuisenaire Rods (remember there are two different ways with the Rods).

Answers will vary. The major advantage is that the product can be seen in either format. The major disadvantage is that as the size of the fractions increases, the time required to create the product with the Cuisenaire Rods increases as well. With larger fractions, the array model is quicker.

145. Use egg cartons to show the sum $\frac{1}{2} + \frac{1}{3}$. Describe the process necessary to determine the LCD. Remember, if the LCD can be determined abstractly, there is no need to use the egg cartons. Assume you do not know how to find the LCD abstractly and role-play using egg cartons to gain insight into what your students will experience.

The unit is a 6-holer.

N-holer	Accept	Reason
1-holer	No	Can't find $\frac{1}{3}$ or $\frac{1}{2}$
2-holer	No	Can find $\frac{1}{3}$, but not $\frac{1}{2}$
3-holer	No	Can find $\frac{1}{2}$, but not $\frac{1}{3}$
4-holer	No	Can't find $\frac{1}{3}$ or $\frac{1}{2}$
5-holer	No	Can't find $\frac{1}{3}$ or $\frac{1}{2}$
6-holer	YES	Can find $\frac{1}{2}$ and $\frac{1}{3}$

With the 6-holer unit, 5 of the 6 holes will be filled (3 for a half, 2 for a third), giving $\frac{1}{2} + \frac{1}{3} = \frac{5}{6}$ as shown below.

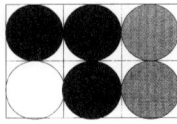

146. Use egg cartons to show the sum $\frac{2}{3} + \frac{1}{4}$.

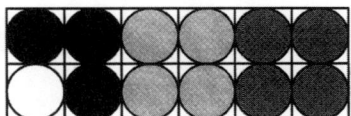

147. Use egg cartons to show the sum $\frac{4}{5} + \frac{2}{3}$. Explain your answer.

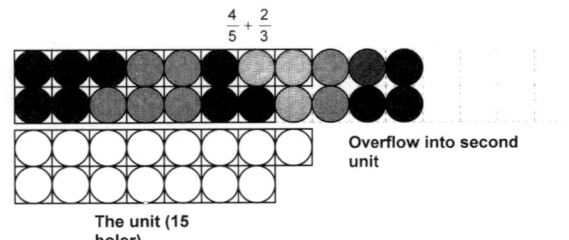

One 15-holer unit is filled and then 7 more holes of another unit are also filled. That is interpreted as one unit and $\frac{7}{15}$ more, giving a sum of $1\frac{7}{15}$ or $\frac{22}{15}$. Notice that this is actually a concrete explanation for converting between mixed numbers and improper fractions.

148. Use Cuisenaire Rods to show the sum $\frac{1}{2} + \frac{1}{3}$. Describe the process necessary to determine the LCD. Remember, if the LCD can be determined abstractly, there is no need to use the Cuisenaire Rods. Assume you do not know how to find the LCD abstractly and role-play using Cuisenaire Rods to gain insight into what your students will experience.
    The unit is the Green rod.

Rod	Accept	Reason
White	No	Can't find $\frac{1}{3}$ or $\frac{1}{2}$
Red	No	Can find $\frac{1}{3}$, but not $\frac{1}{2}$
Lime	No	Can find $\frac{1}{2}$, but not $\frac{1}{3}$
Purple	No	Can't find $\frac{1}{3}$ or $\frac{1}{2}$
Yellow	No	Can't find $\frac{1}{3}$ or $\frac{1}{2}$
Green	YES	Can find $\frac{1}{2}$ and $\frac{1}{3}$

With the Green rod unit, 5 of the 6 White equivalents will be used (3 for a half, 2 for a third), giving $\frac{1}{2} + \frac{1}{3} = \frac{5}{6}$ as shown below.

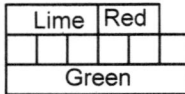

149. Use Cuisenaire Rods to show the sum $\frac{2}{3} + \frac{1}{4}$.

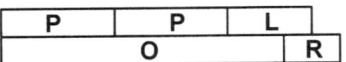

150. Use Cuisenaire Rods to show the sum $\frac{4}{5} + \frac{2}{3}$. Explain your answer.

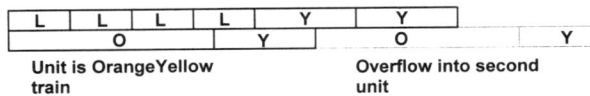

Unit is Orange Yellow train   Overflow into second unit

151. Suppose a student says $\frac{2}{3} + \frac{1}{8} = \frac{3}{11}$. Describe how you would use egg cartons to establish the actual sum of $\frac{19}{24}$.

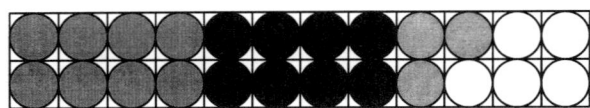

The key to this answer lies in determining the unit and then establishing the size of each of the fractional pieces.

152. Suppose a student says $\frac{2}{3} + \frac{1}{2} = \frac{3}{5}$. Describe how you would use Cuisenaire Rods to establish the actual sum of $\frac{7}{6}$ (or $1\frac{1}{6}$).

Red	Red	Lime
W		
Green		

The key to this answer lies in determining the unit and then establishing the size of each of the fractional pieces. Discussion may or may not deal with converting from an improper fraction to a mixed number.

153. Define an error pattern for adding fractions that is different from placing the sum of the numerators over the sum of the denominators of the addends. Describe how you would help a student correct such an error.

Answers may vary. For example, $\frac{2}{3} + \frac{1}{5} = \frac{4}{7}$ might be seen. In this case, the student was adding the numerator of the first addend to the denominator of the second addend, making it the denominator of the sum. Similarly, the denominator of the first addend was added to the numerator of the second addend to give the numerator of the sum. The direction of addition was followed to determine where each sum was placed in the answer (2 + 5 goes from upper left to lower right so that sum becomes the denominator). Discussion with the student revealed that cross-multiplication (to determine whether two fractions were equivalent) had been done recently and caused the confusion.

154. Create a sequence for subtracting fractions starting with two unit fractions with the same denominator and ending with mixed numbers with quasirelated denominators.

Answers may vary.

$$\frac{4}{7} - \frac{1}{7} \qquad \frac{5}{7} - \frac{2}{7} \qquad 18\frac{5}{7} - 6\frac{2}{7}$$

$$\frac{1}{7} - \frac{1}{14} \qquad \frac{6}{7} - \frac{3}{14} \qquad 19\frac{6}{7} - 11\frac{3}{14}$$

$$\frac{1}{5} - \frac{1}{7} \qquad \frac{4}{5} - \frac{3}{7} \qquad 8\frac{4}{5} - 6\frac{3}{7}$$

$$\frac{1}{4} - \frac{1}{6} \qquad \frac{5}{6} - \frac{3}{4} \qquad 9\frac{5}{6} - 7\frac{3}{4}$$

This sequence avoids situations that involve dividing common factors out of the numerator and denominator of the missing addend. Further, none of the examples shows a fraction that could be reduced, which should be a consideration. How can you justify insisting that your students divide out all common factors from the numerator and denominator if you do not do so in the examples you give them?

155. As the addition of fractions sequence was developed, some discussion focused on providing steps that were not listed in the table. For example, $\frac{1}{7} + \frac{2}{7}$ was listed as a poten-

tial entry between $\frac{1}{7} + \frac{1}{7}$ and $\frac{2}{7} + \frac{3}{7}$. Does the subtraction sequence you created allow for such detail or would it need to be added?

Answers may vary. In the sequence provided, one item that could be added would be subtracting one unit fraction from another where the denominators are the same. With similar problems, a generalization—that subtracting one unit fraction from another when one denominator is twice the other will yield a missing addend equaling the addend—could be established.

156. Create a subtraction problem with related denominators and describe how to solve it concretely with egg cartons. Include an account of how to determine the LCD in your discussion.

Answers may vary. If the problem is $\frac{5}{6} - \frac{3}{4}$, the LCD can be determined using the process described earlier. The figure below shows 10 holes shaded and all but 1 is dark. The two white holes were not considered as part of the subtraction. The 10 filled holes represent $\frac{5}{6}$, and the 9 dark holes represent $\frac{3}{4}$. The one light-shaded hole represents $\frac{5}{6} - \frac{3}{4}$, and this one hole is 1 out of 12 available or $\frac{1}{12}$.

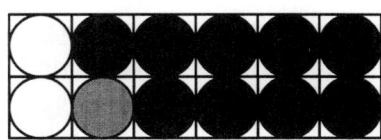

157. List at least three subtraction problems with unrelated denominators and specify the conclusion they could generate.

Answers may vary. $\frac{1}{5} - \frac{1}{7} = \frac{2}{35}$, $\frac{1}{3} - \frac{1}{4} = \frac{1}{12}$, and $\frac{1}{4} - \frac{1}{7} = \frac{3}{28}$ would be one set. Here the generalization would be that the denominator of the missing addend is the product of the denominators in the problem, and the numerator of the missing addend is the larger denominator minus the smaller.

158. Suppose you asked your students to do a series of problems like $\frac{1}{4} - \frac{1}{12}, \frac{1}{5} - \frac{1}{15}, \frac{1}{6} - \frac{1}{18}$, and so on. What generalization could they be expected to develop?

Answers may vary. If the students do not divide out common factors, they should notice that the answer is always 2 over the LCD.

159. If the problems from the last exercise were followed by sets of problems like $\frac{1}{4} - \frac{1}{16}$, which would be followed by problems like $\frac{1}{4} - \frac{1}{20}$, which would be followed by problems like $\frac{1}{4} - \frac{1}{24}$, and so on for as long as necessary, what generalization could students be expected to develop?

Answers may vary. If the students do not divide out common factors, they should notice that the answer is always 3 over the LCD, followed by 4 over the LCD, and so on. A generalization could be a unit fraction minus a unit fraction with a denominator that is a multiple of the original unit fraction gives a fraction, where the numerator of the answer will be one less than the multiple number and the denominator is the larger denominator.

160. Create a subtraction problem with related denominators, and describe how to solve it concretely with Cuisenaire Rods. Include an account of how to determine the LCD in your discussion.

Answers may vary. If the problem is $\frac{5}{6} - \frac{3}{8}$, the unit will be equivalent to a train of 24 White rods. The LCD can be determined with the process described earlier. The figure below shows one way to determine the LCD and the missing addend of $\frac{11}{24}$ with dashed segments.

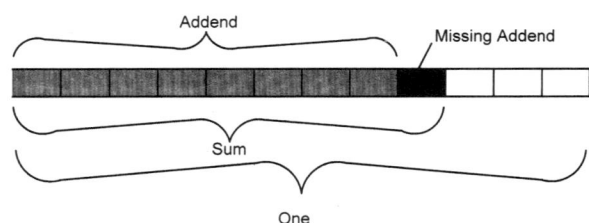

Determining the LCD for sixths and eighths

161. Do $\frac{3}{4} - \frac{2}{3}$ on a paper number line.

162. Describe your reaction to doing fraction subtraction problems on a paper number line.

Answers may vary. Most people do not care to use the paper number line because of the time consumption and potential inaccuracies related to the fan folding.

163. Define an error pattern for subtraction of fractions. Create three subtraction fraction problems using the error pattern. Give those three problems to another person in your class and ask them to describe the error pattern. Assess the description. Note that if you create multiple-choice tests and include error patterns such as this, you can gather additional information about your students. It takes time to create the questions, but the gains are significant.

Answers may vary. $\frac{3}{4} - \frac{2}{3} = \frac{1}{7}, \frac{5}{6} - \frac{2}{7} = \frac{3}{13}$, and $\frac{4}{5} - \frac{3}{4} = \frac{1}{9}$. The error is complex in that the second numerator is subtracted from the first to give the numerator of the missing addend, and the sum of the denominators is the denominator of the missing addend.

164. Describe how you would correct the error you just created.

Answers may vary. The best response would be to list the stages for solving the problem beginning with a concrete method and ending abstractly. The erring student would then be appropriately placed in the sequence of stages.

165. List at least one other problem type that should be done with students before they encounter $\frac{1}{2} \div \frac{1}{8}$.

Answers may vary. Nonunit fractions should be developed. One example could be $\frac{3}{4} \div \frac{3}{20}$. The significance of these types is that the missing factor is still a counting number.

166. Do $\frac{7}{8} \div \frac{3}{4}$ with the Cuisenaire Rods and explain why the answer is $1\frac{1}{6}$.

Answers may vary. The question is, "How many $\frac{3}{4}$s are in $\frac{7}{8}$?" The figure below shows that there is one White more than $\frac{3}{4}$ in $\frac{7}{8}$. Because the $\frac{3}{4}$s is the basis for comparison, the answer is one whole $\frac{3}{4}$s and a White more. However, because it takes six White rods to make $\frac{3}{4}$, White must be $\frac{1}{6}$ and the answer is 1 $\frac{1}{6}$.

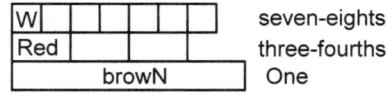

W	seven-eighths
Red	three-fourths
browN	One

167. Do $\frac{3}{4} \div \frac{7}{8}$ with the Cuisenaire Rods and explain why the answer is $\frac{6}{7}$.

Answers may vary. The question is, "How many $\frac{7}{8}$s are in $\frac{3}{4}$?" The figure below shows that $\frac{3}{4}$s is one White too short to make $\frac{7}{8}$. Be-

cause the $\frac{7}{8}$s is the basis for comparison, the answer is one White short of $\frac{7}{8}$. Because it takes seven White rods to make $\frac{7}{8}$, White must be $\frac{1}{7}$, and the answer is six Whites or $\frac{6}{7}$.

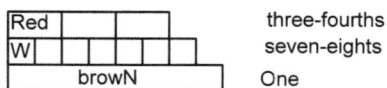

Red	three-fourths
W	seven-eighths
browN	One

168. Do $\frac{3}{4} \div \frac{4}{5}$ with the Cuisenaire Rods and explain why the answer is $\frac{15}{16}$.

Answers may vary. The verbal explanation would be similar to that found with the answers to the last two exercises. The figure below shows the solution with the Cuisenaire Rods.

Purple	Purple	Purple	Purple	four-fifths
Yellow	Yellow	Yellow		three-fourths
Orange		Orange		

169. Do $\frac{4}{5} \div \frac{3}{4}$ with the Cuisenaire Rods and explain why the answer is $\frac{16}{15}$.

Answers may vary. The verbal explanation would be similar to that found earlier in this section. The figure below shows the solution with the Cuisenaire Rods.

Yellow	Yellow	Yellow		three-fourths
Purple	Purple	Purple	Purple	four-fifths
Orange		Orange		

170. Do $\frac{7}{8} \div \frac{4}{5}$ using the equivalent fraction process. Make up at least two more fraction division problems where the denominators are unrelated and do them using the equivalent fraction process. After you have done at least those three problems, describe your feelings of the equivalent fraction division process.

Answers may vary.

$$\frac{4}{5}\bigg)\frac{7}{8} = \frac{32}{40}\bigg)\frac{35}{40}\quad\begin{array}{r}1\frac{3}{32}\\[2pt]\overline{\smash{\big)}\,35}\\[-2pt]\end{array}$$

$$\begin{array}{r}\dfrac{32}{40}\\[6pt]\dfrac{3}{40}\end{array}\text{ or }$$

$$\begin{aligned}\frac{4}{5} \div \frac{7}{8} &= \frac{35}{40} \div \frac{32}{40}\\[4pt] &= \frac{35 \div 32}{40 \div 40}\\[4pt] &= \frac{35 \div 32}{1}\\[4pt] &= \frac{35}{32}\text{ or }1\frac{3}{32}.\end{aligned}$$

171. Find a student (or adult not in your class) with the appropriate background to be dividing fractions and demonstrate equivalent fraction division. Describe their reaction to what you show them.

Answers may vary. Generally, individuals who know how to divide fractions by inverting the second fraction and multiplying think this is an interesting and easy way to do fraction division.

172. Discuss an error pattern different from those described in the text. Explain how you would help a student learn to avoid the error.

Answers may vary. Occasionally a student will not invert either fraction in a division problem and merely multiply the two fractions as they are given, essentially ignoring the division requirement. They would say $\frac{7}{8} \div \frac{3}{5} = \frac{21}{40}$. Correction of this might be as easy as ensuring that the student knows what division involves by asking the student to do $\frac{7}{8} \times \frac{3}{5}$. If that fails, you will need to proceed backward through the sequence of fraction division development, perhaps all the way to the concrete beginnings to determine where the lack of understanding begins.

173. Find an example of a fraction divided by a fraction—something like $3 \div \frac{1}{2}$. For this assignment, dividing something in half would be like dividing by $\frac{2}{1}$, which is not acceptable.

Answers may vary. Suppose you have 3 feet of ribbon and want to know how many half-foot pieces that makes. The question is, "How many $\frac{1}{2}$ foot pieces are in 3 feet?" The problem is $3 \div \frac{1}{2}$ or 3×2, which is 6.

174. Create a lesson plan using the calculator in a manner that will help students discover that fractions like $\frac{3}{10} = 0.3$.

Answers may vary. The lesson plan needs to include a set of problems for the students to do, followed by questions about use of the F<->D key and the results it generates. The problems should be grouped by their denominators, and they should not all have denominators of 10.

175. What happens when you enter 0.700 in your calculator and touch =, Enter or EXE? Do this activity with a friend and explain the result.

Answers may vary. Most calculators will return 0.700 = 0.7, and the explanation would be that the two are equivalent. It might include a discussion about $\frac{7}{10}$ and $\frac{700}{1000}$.

176. Create a lesson plan to help students realize that 0.32 = 0.320 = 0.3200 = ...

Answers may vary. One way to accomplish this is to relate the different values to their fractional equivalent. Another might be to enter them into a calculator and observe the results. That is, enter 0.32000 and then touch =. Most calculators will give 0.32 as the result.

177. Suppose you have several students who struggle with addition of whole numbers. How do you rationalize asking them to add decimals?

Answers may vary. One would be that the curriculum standards for the grade level call for that knowledge. Perhaps the treatment of the concept could be delayed until the students are more ready.

178. Do you think writing a decimal at the end of a sentence would cause problems for students? For example, find the sum of 43.6 and 9.2. Defend your position in writing.

Answers may vary. Many will probably not have thought of the situation. On consideration, the situation could be avoided with careful wording.

179. Do you agree that the statement "Calculators: Don't leave home without them" applies to you?

Answers may vary.

180. Do you agree that the statement "Calculators: Don't leave home without them" applies to your students?

Answers may vary.

181. Explain why your answers to Questions 7 and 8 in this section were the same or different.

Answers may vary. Hopefully they are not saying it is permissible for the teacher but not their students to use a calculator.

182. Describe how you would use the Base 10 blocks to show 1.69 + 0.7 + 4.5.

Answers may vary.

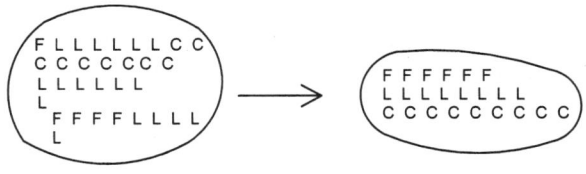

183. Would you use the number line to demonstrate that the sum of 1.69, 0.7, and 4.5 is 6.89? Why or why not?

Answers may vary. It is cumbersome and thus unappealing as a means to show addition of decimals. However, it does work.

184. Show how to do 6.86 + 0.94 + 7.35 using the scratch method for addition.

```
  6 . 8 6
  0 . 9 4
+ 7 . 3 5
1 3 . 0 5
    5   1
```

185. Describe how you would relate the Base 10 blocks to the partial sum method for adding 6.86 + 0.94 + 7.35

Answers may vary.

```
  6 . 8 6
  0 . 9 4
+ 7 . 3 5
      1 5    start with 15 Cs, but trade
                 for 1 L, leaving 5 Cs
    2 0      start with 20 Ls, but trade
                 for 2 Fs, leaving 0 Ls
  1 3        start with 13 Fs, but trade
                 for 1 Block, leaving 3 Fs
  _____
  1 5   1 5
```

186. Suppose a student consistently gives the sum of problems like:

3.2 + 0.98 + 4.657 as 47.87

2.178 + 4.6 + 0.35 as 22.59 and

0.46 + 1.3 + 5.278 as 53.37. Describe the error being made, including how the decimal is being placed in the answer.

Answers may vary. The student is lining up the last digit. The decimal is placed by averaging (taking 6 decimal places and dividing by 2).

187. Outline how you would correct the error in the problems given in Exercise 186.

Answers may vary. Base 10 blocks would help.

188. Describe how you would suggest introducing the addition of decimals to help avoid errors such as the one described in Exercise 186.

Answers may vary. Base 10 blocks should be used in the introduction. Help students conceptualize the idea of lining up the ones and using 0.4 for four tenths.

189. Suppose a student consistently gives the sum of problems like:

3.2 + 0.98 + 4.657 as 883.7

2.178 + 4.6 + 0.35 as 712.8 and

0.46 + 1.3 + 5.278 as 703.8. Describe the error being made, including how the decimal is being placed in the answer.

Answers may vary. The student is adding correctly, including lining up the ones and adding correctly. The decimal is counted from the right and the units alignment is ignored.

190. Develop a sequence for subtraction of decimals that incorporates all concepts from the basics through complete mastery.

Answers may vary. Problems like 0.80 − 0.50 should be evident as should discussions about place value when an additional place is introduced.

191. Show how to do 0.71 − 0.58 on the number line.

Answers may vary.

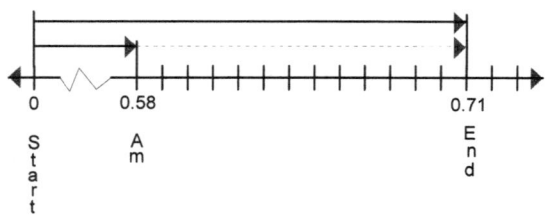

192. Show how to do 0.71 − 0.58 with the Base 10 blocks.

Answers may vary.

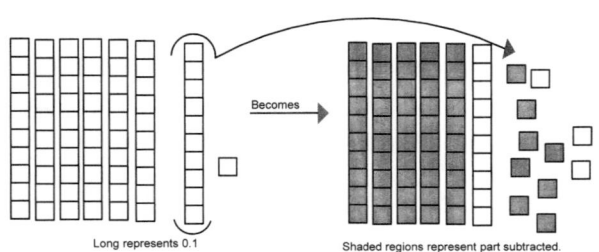

193. By now you should have formulated an opinion of which manipulative you prefer to use. Discuss why you have prioritized them as you have. Rationalize why it is necessary to be able to develop a concept using more than one manipulative.

Answers may vary. It is necessary to be able to use more than one manipulative to reach different learning modalities. Furthermore, if a student does not understand the concept of using one manipulative, it is still necessary to provide the concrete exposure through another one.

194. Should more than one manipulative be used to develop a concept?

Answers may vary. We think the answer is generally no. A teacher selects a favorite manipulative and uses it as a primary source of explanation. However, it is imperative that other manipulatives remain in the collection of usable tools in case some student needs a different approach.

195. Describe whether you feel a calculator is a valuable tool for teaching the subtraction of decimals and why.

Answers may vary.

196. Describe how you would use a calculator to help students do a problem like 5.2 − 1.679.

Answers may vary. The discussion should include comments about adding the necessary zeros after the 2.

197. Show how to do 4 × 0.6 on the number line.

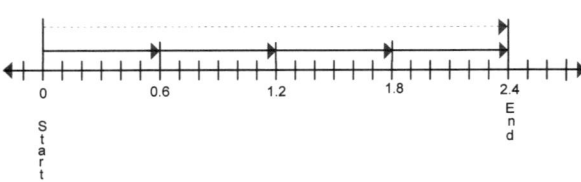

198. Show how to do 12 × 0.3 with the Base 10 blocks.

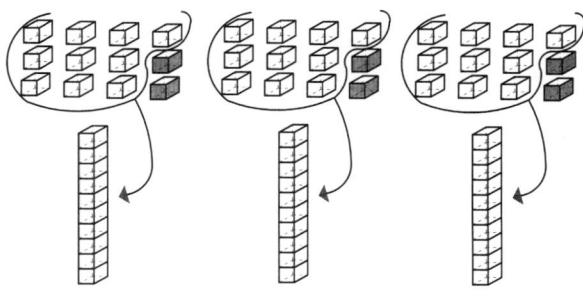

199. Show how to do 0.2 × 0.4 on an array.

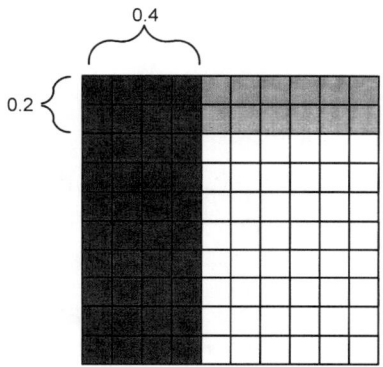

200. Using Russian peasant multiplication to do 1.06 × 3.7, which factor would you select as the one to be halved and why?

Answers may vary, but 3.7 should be selected because it will result in getting to 1 most quickly.

106	37
~~212~~	~~18.5 but drop the half, leaving 18~~
424	9
~~848~~	~~4.5 but drop the half, leaving 4~~
~~1696~~	~~2~~
3392	1

Decimal point placement puts it between the two 3s.

201. Create a three-digit (hundredths) times two-digit problem (tenths) and do it using partial product, lattice, and Russian peasant multiplication.

Answers may vary.

202. Provide a written defense of your position on what is an appropriate problem type to permit students to use calculators when doing decimal division problems.

Answers may vary. Reason dictates that calculators should be permitted early in the sequence of decimal division. This assumes that the ability to do long division exists. The number of negative affective factors in mathematics instruction is so great, and this is one place where some of them can be eliminated or reduced with no harm to the student's mathematical abilities.

203. Assume that your position for permitting the use of calculators in decimal division differs from that of your department, school, district, or state standards. What do you do and why?

Answers may vary. This is a difficult dilemma particularly for the beginning teacher. Suppose the beginner wants to approve calculator use in a situation that has essentially banned them. Adopting the opposing position like this can cost the individual their job. Now the question becomes one of how much one is willing to compromise personal standards to keep a job.

204. Make up a problem involving a whole number divided by a decimal. Explain how to convert your problem to one where it is a whole number divided by a whole number.

Answers may vary. One example would be $\dfrac{73554}{0.78} = \left(\dfrac{73554}{0.78}\right)\left(\dfrac{100}{100}\right) = \dfrac{7355400}{78}$.

205. Make up a problem involving a decimal divided by a decimal. Explain how to convert your problem to one where it is a whole number divided by a whole number.

Answers may vary. One example would be $\dfrac{73.554}{0.78} = \left(\dfrac{73.554}{0.78}\right)\left(\dfrac{1000}{1000}\right) = \dfrac{73554}{780}$.

206. Is it necessary to convert all problems involving a decimal divided by a decimal to one involving a whole divided by a whole? Why or why not?

Answers may vary. One example would be $\frac{73.554}{0.78} = \left(\frac{73.554}{0.78}\right)\left(\frac{100}{100}\right) = \frac{7355.4}{78}$. It is only necessary to have the factor be a whole number. Making the factor a whole number properly locates the decimal point in the product as well as the missing factor.

207. Describe your impression of the concept of addition of integers at this point. Include a discussion of whether you think it is hard or easy to learn and why you hold that position.

Answers may vary. Most people will say they do not like it and it is confusing.

208. What do you think about the idea that we have students adding positive numbers in the early grades, then insist that they insert the signs, and later tell them not to worry about the signs?

Answers may vary. Most students do not think it makes much sense.

209. Describe two different ways you would introduce the idea of negative numbers to your students. Include a discussion about why you feel your selections would be good to use with students.

Answers may vary.

210. Create a set of problems that you would use to teach students that when adding numbers of like signs, they add and give the sum the common sign. Develop an outline of the lesson that would be used with the problem set.

Answers may vary. The plan should focus on generalizing from having done several problems. The discussion of comparing the operation to normal addition without the signs should be evident.

211. Create a set of problems you would use to teach students that, when adding numbers of unlike signs, they subtract the smaller absolute value from the larger absolute value and give the answer the sign of the larger absolute value. Develop an outline of the lesson that would be used with the problem set.

Answers may vary. The plan should focus on generalizing from having done several problems. The discussion of comparing the two problem types should be evident to show the idea of changing the sign of the operation and then subtracting the smaller absolute value from the larger absolute value.

212. How could absolute value be explained to your students?

Answers may vary. Look at the distance from zero on the number line and ignore the direction.

213. Describe how the calculator could be used to help develop generalizations about adding signed numbers.

Answers may vary. Let the students play with different integer problems and encourage them to generalize.

214. Do $^{+}7 + {}^{+}3 = {}^{+}10$ on a number line and write a lesson plan to introduce your students to finding the sum of two positive integers.

Answers may vary. The plan should include a number line explanation of the problem and the expectation that students do some problems on the number line. After several problems are done, they should conclude that the absolute values (they may not use that term) are added and the answer gets the common sign.

215. Do $^{-}7 + {}^{-}3 = {}^{-}10$ on a number line and write a lesson plan to introduce your students to finding the sum of two negative integers.

Answers may vary. The plan should include a number line explanation of the problem and the expectation that students do some problems on the number line. After several problems are done, they should conclude that the absolute values (they may not use that term) are added and the answer gets the common sign.

216. Describe how you would use problems like $^+7 + {}^+3 = {}^+10$ and $^-7 + {}^-3 = {}^-10$ along with the number line to help your students generalize that, when adding two integers with the same signs, add the absolute values and give the answer the common sign.

Answers may vary. The generalizations developed should be discussed and the similarities stressed. The students should be encouraged to generalize the generalizations into one rule for adding numbers with like signs.

217. Do $^+9 + {}^-3 = {}^+6$ on a number line and write a lesson plan to introduce your students to finding the sum of a positive and a negative integer.

Answers may vary. The plan should include a number line explanation of the problem and the expectation that students do some problems on the number line. After several problems are done, they should conclude that the smaller absolute value (they may not use that term) is subtracted from the larger and the answer gets the sign of the larger absolute value.

218. Do $^-9 + {}^+3 = {}^-6$ on a number line and write a lesson plan to introduce your students to finding the sum of a negative and a positive integer.

Answers may vary. The plan should include a number line explanation of the problem and the expectation that students do some problems on the number line. After several problems are done, they should conclude that the smaller absolute value (they may not use that term) is subtracted from the larger and the answer gets the sign of the larger absolute value.

219. Describe how you would use problems like $^+9 + {}^-3 = {}^+6$ and $^-9 + {}^+3 = {}^-6$ along with the number line to help your students generalize that, when adding two integers with opposite signs, subtract the smaller absolute value from the larger and give the answer the sign of the larger absolute value.

Answers may vary. The generalizations developed should be discussed and the similarities stressed. The students should be encouraged to generalize the generalizations into one rule for adding numbers with unlike signs.

220. Create a problem set to help students generalize a rule for dealing with problems like $^+8 - {}^+3 = {}^+5$ and $^-8 - {}^-3 = {}^-5$. State the generalization you expect them to generate from these problems.

Answers may vary. The set should include several problems dealing with a positive minus a positive and several more involving a negative minus a negative. Some should be like $^+3 - {}^+8 = {}^-5$. The generalization should discuss changing the sign of the second number and following the rule for addition of integers.

221. Create a problem set to help students generalize a rule for dealing with problems like $^+8 - {}^-3 = {}^+11$ and $^-8 - {}^+3 = {}^-11$. State the generalization you expect them to generate from these problems.

Answers may vary. The set should include several problems dealing with a positive minus a negative and several more involving a negative minus a positive. The generalization should discuss changing the sign of the second number and following the rule for addition of integers.

222. Explain how the two generalizations developed in Questions 220 and 221 can be stated as one generalization for the subtraction of one integer from another.

Answers may vary. The discussion should be rather limited because both generalizations will be similar, if not the same.

223. Do ⁻8 – ⁻3 = ⁻5 on the number line and explain your answer.

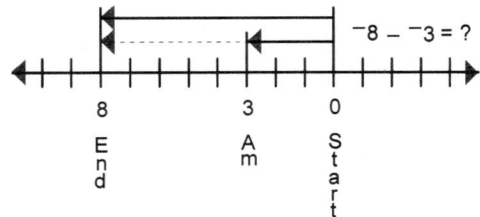

224. Do ⁻5 – ⁺8 = ⁻13 on the number line and explain your answer.

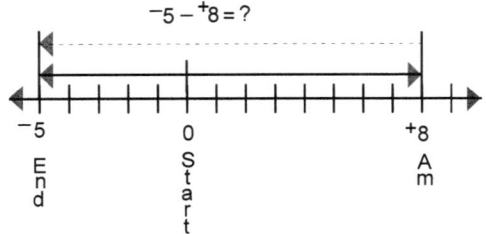

225. Describe how you would lead a class to the generalization for changing the sign of the second number and following the rules for addition when dealing with the subtraction of integers.

Answers may vary. The discussion should include examples done on the number line and generalizations drawn from the examples that lead to the idea of changing the sign of the second number and following the rule for addition when subtracting integers.

226. Create a lesson plan covering each of the four problem types for subtracting integers represented by colored chips or by the number line. Be sure to include detailed examples and questions that would lead to the desired generalizations.

Answers may vary. The plan should include descriptions similar to those given in the chapter as well as questions designed to lead the students to the appropriate generalizations.

227. Outline a lesson on how to introduce a problem like [(⁻3 × ⁻4) × ⁻5] × ⁺2 = ?

Answers may vary. Find the product of two factors. Use that answer as a factor and multiply it by a third factor. Use this product as a factor times the fourth factor. With each product, the sign will be determined by those of the factors used.

228. Do the sequence of problems with students that started with ⁻6 × ⁺6 = ⁻36 and ended with ⁻6 × ⁻1 = ⁺6 with someone. As you do it, focus on their reaction to the comments that are made as any problem is compared with the preceding one. Write your reflections to their responses and actions.

Answers may vary. Assuming they are not familiar with the sequence, they should sound bored and perhaps even question why they have to do so many. Continue through ⁻6 × ⁻1 = ⁺6, when they should see the reason for the activity.

229. Describe how you would convince students that ⁻7 × ⁺4 = ⁻28.

Answers may vary. Some reference needs to be made to the commutative property of multiplication on whole numbers and that, because the other properties from whole numbers have held for addition, we have every reason to expect that the same would be true of multiplication.

230. Describe how you would convince students that the product of two factors with the same sign is positive.

Answers may vary. Problem pairs like ⁻7 × ⁻4 = ⁺28 and ⁺7 × ⁺4 = ⁺28 should help get the point across. (Positive factors should probably be listed first since they are more comfortable for the students.)

231. Describe how you would convince students that the product of two factors with opposite signs is negative.

Answers may vary. Problem pairs like ⁺7 × ⁻4 = ⁻28 and ⁻7 × ⁺4 = ⁻28 should help get the point across.

232. Do $^+3 \times {}^+5 = {}^+15$ on the number line.

Answers may vary.

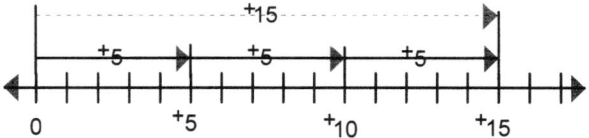

233. Do $^+3 \times {}^-5 = {}^-15$ on the number line.

Answers may vary.

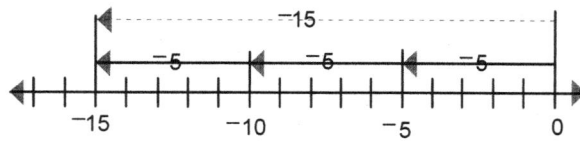

234. Outline a lesson that would use the calculator to help students generalize that if the signs of two factors are the same, the product is positive.

Answers may vary. The lesson should include problems demonstrating each of the two possibilities: (+)(+) and (–)(–). There should be a generalization that when the factors have the same sign, they yield a positive product.

235. Outline a lesson that would use the calculator to help students generalize that if the signs of two factors are different, the product is negative.

Answers may vary. The lesson should include problem demonstrating each of the two possibilities: (+)(–) and (–)(+). There should be a generalization that when the factors have different signs, they yield a negative product.

236. Create a lesson plan covering each of the four problem types for multiplying integers represented by colored chips. Be sure to include detailed examples and questions that would lead to the desired generalizations.

Answers may vary. The plan should include descriptions similar to those given in the chapter as well as questions designed to lead

the students to the appropriate generalizations.

237. Create a lesson plan that includes a pair of problem sets for division where the signs of the two numbers involved in the division are the same. Describe in the lesson plan how the problem sets could be used within a class period to lead the students to this conclusion: When the signs of the numbers in a division problem are the same, the missing factor is positive.

Answers may vary. There should be two distinct problem sets: one with both signs positive and one with both signs negative. The lesson plan should have the students doing the first set, generalizing, and then doing the second set and generalizing. Finally, the two generalizations should be blended into one.

238. Create a lesson plan that includes a pair of problem sets for division where the signs of the two numbers involved in the division are opposite. Describe in the lesson plan how the problem sets could be used within a class period to lead the students to the conclusion that when the signs of the numbers in a division problem are opposites, the missing factor will be negative.

Answers may vary. There should be two distinct problem sets: one with both signs positive and one with both signs negative. The lesson plan should have the students doing the first set, generalizing, and then doing the second set and generalizing. Finally, the two generalizations should be blended into one.

239. Create a lesson plan covering each of the four problem types for dividing integers represented by colored chips. Be sure to include detailed examples and questions that would lead to the desired generalizations.

Answers may vary. The plan should include descriptions similar to those given in the chapter as well as questions designed to lead the students to the appropriate generalizations.

240. At what grade level should children begin to use calculators?

Grade levels will vary—usually after basics facts are mastered and a strong conceptual understanding of the four operations.

241. If you are in an interview for your first teaching position and a principal asks you for your position on the use of calculators, what will you say?

Answers will definitely vary.

242. When should technology not be used in the elementary curriculum?

Answers will vary and probably spawn a lively discussion.

243. Outline an idea for a learning center that would promote the concepts of standard and expanded notation.

Answers will vary.

244. Make a list of inexpensive replacements for Base 10 blocks.

Examples are popsicle sticks and beans, plastic lattice used for needle point, and straws bundled together with rubber bands.

245. Show why 5^0 is one.

When multiplying factors such as $5^6 \cdot 5^2 = 5^8$, the rule established shows that you can add exponents when multiplying factors with like bases. For division such as $\frac{5^6}{5^2} = 5^4$, the rule established shows that you can subtract exponents when dividing like bases. Because this is true, $\frac{5^6}{5^6} = 5^{6-6} = 5^0 = 1$. Because anything other than zero divided by itself equals 1, then $5^0 = $.

246. Is anything to the zero power one?

No, zero to the zero power is not one, it is zero.

247. What mathematical content could be covered in the Pete–Repeat example?

Write equations and expressions. Use of table to show rate of change. Pattern interpretation. Variables. Evaluation of expressions. Constant rate of change. Direct variation. Multiple representation an idea (words, graphs, tables, equations). Proportional reasoning.

248. What pedagogy could be covered with the Pete–Repeat example?

Group work. Discovery learning. Real-world mathematics. Inquiry method. Communication (explaining what happened).

249. What NCTM Standards 2000 are covered in the Pete–Repeat example?

Number and Operation. Algebra. Measurement. Geometry. Data analysis and probability. Problem Solving. Reasoning and proof. Communication. Connections. Representation. (all of them)

250. Have some early elementary students solve 15 problems: 5 in the form of 3 + 4 □ with a box as a missing addend, 5 in the form of 3 + □ = 7 with the box as the second addend, and 5 in the form of □ + 4 = 7 with the box as the first addend. Which problem type was easiest for the students? Which did the students find the hardest? Why do you suppose this occurred?

Answers will vary.

251. Look at the table of contents of an Algebra 1 textbook. What concepts could possibly be introduced in the elementary classroom using manipulatives?

Answers will vary.

252. Have some early elementary students solve 15 addition problems: 5 in the form of in the form of 3 + 4 = □ with a box as a missing addend, 5 in the form of 3 + □ = 7 with the box as the second addend, and 5 in the form of □ + 4 = 7 with the box as the first addend. Which type of problem did the students find the easiest? Which did the students find the hardest? Why do you suppose this occurred?

Students will generally have an easier time when the box is the sum and the most difficult time when the box is the first addend. The box as the sum is most representative of all the addition facts they are asked to master. The box as the first addend tends to be the more difficult problem-solving situation because you are introducing an abstract (variable) quantity first.

253. List the algebraic concepts you feel could be introduced in an elementary school environment.

Answer may vary. Combining like terms, solving simple expressions, use of a variable to replace a value, and linear graphs are some of the ones that should be there.

254. What manipulatives could have helped you learn algebra at the secondary level?

Answer may vary. Hopefully the student will investigate to determine what manipulatives are available for algebra. In the process, they should discover
algebra lab gear™© *or something like that* and algebra tiles™© *or something like that.*

255. What manipulatives from the elementary program are best suited to introduce algebraic concepts?

Answers may vary. Base 10 blocks are probably the dominant force here particularly because of the similarities between them and some of the algebra manipulatives used today.

256. Find an elementary textbook for a particular grade. Carefully go through the book and record each formula a child would encounter. Did the number of formulas surprise you? Were there more or fewer than you expected? Explain your reasoning.

257. After completing Exercise 256, which formulas would you omit from the text? Which formulas were not found in the text that you think should be added?

258. What other objects could you use to demonstrate terms line segment and point?

Styrofoam balls and fishing line are one possibility.

259. Provide another activity that could possibly be used to demonstrate a line.

Power lines are a possibility because you usually cannot see the ends of the lines.

260. Define a rectangle.

A parallelogram is a quadrilateral with opposites sides parallel. A rectangle is an equiangular parallelogram. A rectangle is a quadrilateral with four right angles and whose opposite sites are parallel. A rectangle is a quadrilateral with four right angles whose opposite sides are the same length.

261. Is a rectangle a square? Is a square a rectangle? Explain why or why not.

A square is a rectangle because opposite sides are the same length and all angles are right angles. A rectangle is a square unless all sides are the same length.

262. Try the hexagon activity with pattern blocks. How many different combinations can be used to construct a trapezoid of the same size as the one in the pattern block set you have when using only the triangles, squares, rhombi, and trapezoids?

7 Ways
2 trapezoids
1 trapezoid, 1 rhombus, 1 triangle
1 trapezoid, 3 triangles
3 rhombi
2 rhombi, 2 triangles
1 rhombi, 4 triangles
6 triangles

263. How many different combinations of pattern blocks can be used to construct any sized trapezoid using only the triangles, squares, rhombi, and trapezoids?

Infinite many hexagons of any size.

264. Develop an activity using tangrams or pattern blocks for elementary students that can be used to introduce a concept of geometry.

Answers will vary.

265. Research the Golden Ratio. Provide at least one example of where it shows up in ancient architecture and somewhere it can be found in nature today.

Answers may vary. "The Golden Mean is a ratio that is present in the growth patterns of many things—the spiral formed by a shell or the curve of a fern, for example. The Golden Mean or Golden Section was derived by the ancient Greeks. Like "pi", the number 1.618 . . . is an irrational number. Both the ancient Greeks and the ancient Egyptians used the Golden Mean when designing their buildings and monuments. The builders of Paestum used the Golden Mean in their temples. Artists as diverse as Leonardo da Vinci and George Seurat used the ratio when constructing their paintings. These artists and architects discovered that by utilizing the ratio 1 : 1.618 . . . , they could create a feeling of order in their works. Even today, artists are still using this proportion in their works, and scientists, like Roger Penrose are discovering new things about the Golden Mean and its place in science, mathematics, and nature." (http://tony.ai/KW/golden.html)

266. Create an argument for using the geoboard in the elementary classroom.

Answers may vary. Discussion could focus on the versatility of being able to change shapes by merely moving rubber bands.

267. Create an argument against using the geoboard in the elementary classroom.

Answers may vary. One point that causes concern for some people is the sharpness of the ends of the nails or pins. Concern centers on scratching or puncturing the skin of children.

268. Present a lesson plan that would use the geoboard as a means to help children learn about shapes.

Answers may vary. One possible response could be found at http://forum.swarthmore.edu/trscavo/geoboards/geobd6.html. Select right triangles at the bottom of the page (http://forum.swarthmore.edu/trscavo/geoboards/geobd6.html) for a lesson plan on searching out all right triangles on a 5 × 5 geoboard.

269. Develop an exercise to show the use of measurement in children's everyday lives.

Answers will vary. Additional ideas are activities that would incorporate weight. Purchase five different bags of potato chips. Cover up the weight and place the bags in front of the class. On individual sheets of paper, ask the students to rank order the potato chips from least amount of chips to greatest. Reveal the actual weight to the students. Determine how many students were correct. Ask how many students will look at the number of ounces on the bag in the future.

270. What is the difference between a fluid ounce and an ounce?

A fluid ounce measures the volume the liquid takes up (displaces). An ounce measures the weight of the object. For example, 12 fluid ounces of water may weigh less than 12 fluid ounces of maple syrup. A fluid ounce is 29.573 milliliters.

271. What other nonstandard units will children possibly use in the previous activity?

Answers will vary. Some may include shoes, pencils, paper, pens, string, and coat sleeve.

272. Develop an activity that shows the difficulty associated with using nonstandard units.

Answers will vary.

273. Will you display a clock in your classroom? Why or why not? If you do, where will you place the clock in the room and why?

Answer will vary. Many rooms will come with clocks mounted on the walls. If a teacher does not want to have the students constantly watching the clock, the teacher will probably have to rearrange the students in the class before the clock.

274. Do you advocate the use of a digital or analog clock for children? Support your response.

Answers will vary.

275. List different games that could be used to teach children about the concept of money.

Answers will vary. Monopoly and Life are excellent choices for a game day in class.

276. Find a definition of area in three elementary textbooks. Do the texts state a definition of area or do they give the definition along with the picture of a rectangle?

Most texts will define the area of an object, but not the term *area*.

277. Find three elementary textbooks. How does each text instruct the student to find the area of a rectangle? Do all three texts use length × width?

Area can also be thought of as base × height. Using base × height can help students better understand the logic behind using base and height when finding the area of a triangle.

278. State the formula for finding the area of a parallelogram. Explain how you could model this to a child.

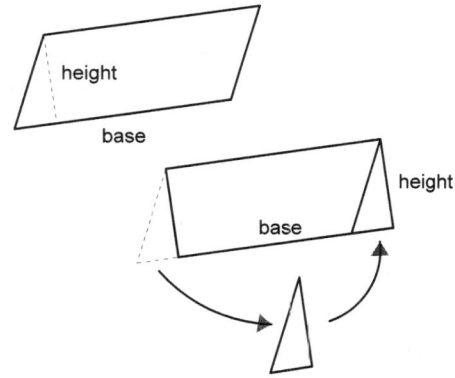

The product of the base of the parallelogram and the height yield the area. You are really finding the area of the rectangle. Show the student how you could remove the triangle end and attach it to the opposite side to form a rectangle using the parallelogram's base and the triangle's height.

279. State the formula for finding the area of a rhombus. Explain how you could model this to a child.

A rhombus is a special parallelogram. The same formula can be used. The only difference is that all the sides are congruent. Therefore, you can substitute any side for the base.

280. Create a lesson that uses a geoboard to find the area of a triangle like Part c in Fig. 5.12.

Answers will vary.

281. Create a lesson that uses a geoboard to show how to find the area of any convex quadrilateral.

Answers will vary.

282. Describe in writing how Pick's Theorem can be used to find the area of any polygon on a geoboard. An introductory source can be found at http://forum.swarthmore.edu/dr.math/problems/lindsay2.8.96.html.

Answers will vary.

283. Define circumference. When is this term used in mathematics?

Circumference is the distance around a circle. This term is used to find the perimeter of a circle. The formula for finding the circumference of a circle is C = d, where C is circumference and d is the diameter of the circle and is the constant 3.1415926 . . . that represent the ratio of the circle's circumference to its diameter.

284. Give an example of when the value of the area of a rectangle can equal the perimeter of a rectangle. Are other examples possible? Explain you answer.

One example is a 3 × 6 rectangle. The area is 18 square units and the perimeter is 18 units. Another possibility is a square with side lengths of 4 units. Remember, a square is a special rectangle. The area is 16 square units and the perimeter is 16 units.

285. Is it possible for the circumference and area of a circle to be equal? Explain your answer.

Yes, when the radius is 2. For a circle, $A = \pi^2$ and $C = 2\pi r$, where A is area and C is circumference. You want to find where A = C. Therefore, find where $\pi^2 = 2\pi r$. Divide both sides of the equation by πr, yielding r = 2.

286. Does $\frac{22}{7} = \pi$? Explain your reasoning.

No. $\frac{22}{7}$ is a close approximation for π. $\frac{22}{7} \approx 3.1428571$, whereas $\pi \approx 3.1415926$. Notice there is a significant difference after the second decimal place.

287. Other than unifix cubes, what other types of manipulatives could you use to demonstrate volume?

Algebra blocks, Legos, Cuisenaire Rods, and Base 10 blocks

288. What real-world things are measured using volume?

Sand, potting soil, water, soda, lemonade, salt, pepper, rice, spaghetti sauce, ice cream, helium, and the list goes on!

289. For what other solids can you find the volume by multiplying the area of the base by the height? What solids will not work using that method?

Right circular cylinder, pentagonal prism, hexagonal prism, and so on. Spheres, pyramids, and cones will not work and many more.

290. Use a dynamic geometry software package to demonstrate how to find the volume of a right circular cylinder.

Activities will vary.

291. Will the formula Bh (B = area of the base) work for finding the volume of any prism? Did you consider only right prisms? Explain your answer.

Yes. When you deal with nonright prisms, the height still exists as the perpendicular distance between the two bases. This value times the area of the base will provide the volume of the figure.

292. List three topics that can be used to make mathematics more meaningful to elementary children.

Answers will vary. Various athletics and hobbies work extremely well. Food is also an appealing topic to children.

293. Construct an interest inventory that could be used in a class. Be sure to identify the grade level for this interest inventory.

Answers will vary.

294. Name five other topics on which students can conduct a survey. Supply at least two questions that could be asked for each topic.

Answers will vary.

295. What mathematical concepts do students have to master prior to using bar graphs?

Addition facts.

296. What mathematical concepts do students have to master prior to using pie charts?

Addition facts, division facts, decimals, and percentages. If students are still having difficulty with division facts and decimals, it might be prudent to allow the use of a calculator. After all, you are trying to teach the students how to interpret collected data, not reteach basic facts.

297. What other inferences can be made from the pie chart displayed in Fig. 6.4?

Answers will vary. Almost three fourths of the students preferred blue, green, or red to the other three colors—light brown, yellow, and dark brown. Brown is not a popular color for m&m®.

298. Contact a local principal in your area. Ask the policy and proper procedure for conducting an onsite field trip learning activity such as the prior speeding activity.

Answers will vary.

291. Contact a local law enforcement agency and ask about possible learning activities that officers conduct on a regular basis. Also ask about any education materials or programs for the classroom that are available.

Answers will vary.

292. Find the mean, median, and mode of the number of years it has been for everyone in the class since they started college. Which measure of central tendency best describes the class data?

Answers will vary.

293. Can you have more than one mode in a set of data? Site your source to justify your answer.

Yes. If two or more measures occur most often, you will have more than one mode.

294. Look at a newspaper. Highlight as many uses of measures of central tendency that you can find.

Answers will vary. Try the sports page. For example, in basketball, a player's statistics usually shows their average points per game, which is the mean.

295. Other than the weather, give two examples of where students encounter the use of probability.

Playing games and sports.

296. Give an example of where probability can help your students or their families in their daily routines.

Answers will vary.

297. Find a 1.69-ounce bag of m&ms. Before opening the bag, estimate how many m&ms are in the bag.

Answers will vary.

298. Find a 1.69-ounce bag of m&ms. Before opening the bag, estimate how many of each color you think you will find.

Answer will vary.

299. The *Seven Bridges of Konigsberg*, a discussion of Gauss, and the Egyptians using geometry to measure flooded ground were given in the text as examples of historical topics that could be inserted into the elementary classroom. Find a different historical topic appropriate for elementary students. Give all appropriate bibliographic information and create a lesson plan that would incorporate your topic.

Answers may vary. A beginning source of information to start with is http://aleph0.clarku.edu/~djoyce/mathhist/webresources.html.

300. Find a list different from the four steps Polya presents for problem solving. Describe the similarities and differences between the list you found and Polya's.

Answers may vary. Read, reread, restate; List information; Plan solution; Work out solution; Check; Generalize.

301. Read the parts in NCTM's *Principles and Standards for School Mathematics* pertaining to problem solving. Reflect on what the publication says and write your feelings about their position on problem solving in the elementary curriculum.

Answers may vary. The assumption is that the comments will be positive and include statements about not having thought about problem solving that way.

302. In the "fold the paper in half again and again problem," physically, how many times can the paper be folded in half?

Answers may vary. It is either seven or eight depending on interpretation of a fold.

303. In the "fold the paper in half again and again problem," does the size of the paper being used matter?

No.

304. In the "fold the paper in half again and again problem," how high is the stack after 50 folds?

2^{50} times the paper thickness = 1125899906842624 times the thickness of the paper. If the paper is 0.003 of an inch thick, the stack is $\dfrac{422212465065984}{125}$ inches thick = $\dfrac{35184372088832}{125}$ feet thick = $\dfrac{1099511627776}{20625}$ miles high = 53,309,654.64 miles, which is about $\dfrac{2}{3}$ of the distance to the sun. That is a fair sized stack!

305. Create a higher order thinking question from the shapes in Fig. 7.2. Discuss a potential lesson development to answer your question.

Answers may vary. One interesting question is, "How many of the shapes can be folded to make a box without a lid?" The lesson development could have students cutting out the shapes and folding them. Many students will be able to visualize shape C making

a box, but will struggle with shape F and the folding process will help.

306. The maximum perimeter of the shapes in Fig. 7.3 is 20 units and the minimum is 10 units. Explain why this is the case.

Answers may vary. The maximum exists because each square in the shape has all four sides fully exposed. The minimum exists because the fewest number of sides are exposed or the maximum number of sides is shared.

307. Can five squares be arranged to give any perimeter between 10 units and 20 units? Why or why not?

Yes. In Fig. 7.3, suppose the "Between maximum and minimum" shape has one square's corner being at the midpoint of the side of another square in all cases, which gives a perimeter of 16 units. If the overlap is $\dfrac{1}{4}$ of a unit, then the overhang in each case would be $\dfrac{3}{4}$ of a unit and the perimeter would be 18 units. Adjusting the overlap will yield any perimeter desired between 10 units and 20 units.

308. A farmer had 26 cows. All but 9 died. How many lived?

9.

309. A uniform log can be cut into three pieces in 12 seconds. Assuming the same rate of cutting, how long would it take a similar log to be cut into four pieces?

Three pieces means two cuts in 12 seconds or six seconds per cut. At that rate, four pieces would take 8 seconds. A creative solution is 12 seconds, making the first cut parallel to the length of the log and the second perpendicular to the length of the log cutting the two long parts at once.

310. How many different ways can you add four odd counting numbers to get a sum of 10?

Answers may vary. An initial assumption frequently is that the four addends must be different. They don't. A question is whether or not a counting number can be used more than once. Yes. Does order matter? You would decide that. 1 + 1 + 1 + 7 = 10. 1 + 3 + 3 + 3 = 10. 1 + 1 + 3 + 5 = 10.

311. Describe a situation similar to the biggest number idea that would be appropriate as a means of building a foundation in reasoning and proof for a primary grade student.

Answers will vary.

312. Find an optical illusion like the ones in Figs. 8.1, 8.2, and 8.3 that you feel would be appropriate to present to an elementary student as a means to discuss reasoning, explaining, or proving.

Answers will vary. The Fig. 8.2 message is "THIS IS COOL—REALLY COOL." $\overline{RS}$ and $\overline{RT}$ are the same length in Fig. 8.3.

313. Extend the addition number trick to include seven addends and then nine addends with you being given three addends and four addends, respectively. Have 8 be the magic number in all examples you do with either seven or nine addends. You should see a pattern.

With seven addends, the sum will be 35 because there are three sets of addends giving a sum of 9. With nine addends, the sum will be 44 because there are four sets of addends giving a sum of 9. The ones digit of the answer is the magic number minus the number of sets of addends giving a sum of 9. The tens digit of the answer is the number of sets of addends giving a sum of 9. Suppose the sets of addends giving a sum of 9 are 4 + 5, 2 + 7, and 1 + 8, or 9 + 9 + 9, which could be written as 10 − 1 + 10 − 1 + 10 − 1. That is really 30 − 3, but the magic number (8 in this case) has not been added. The whole problem is reexpressed as 30 − 3 + 8, giving a sum of 35. With nine addends, the problem would be 40 − 4 + 8, giving a sum of 44. Expressing the 9s as 10 − 1 makes it easier to see what is happening. You also have an informal discussion of proving how the trick works.

314. Extend the addition number trick to adding five 2-digit addends with the magic number being 47. You should see a pattern. This idea can be extended to any number of addends and any number of digits in the addends with some restrictions. How would you generalize the trick?

The discussion in Exercise 283 gives most of the generalization foundations. Rather than describing a sum of 9, you generalize to strings of 9s, which could be 99, 999, and so on. The number of 9s in a string is determined by the number of digits in the addends. For the example in the text, the addends were digits so the string of 9s was only one 9. For this problem, the addends had two digits so the strings of 9s would be 99. The total number of addends must be odd because each choice given you is paired with another number to give a string of 9s sum. That pairing suggests an even number. There is still the magic number, however, making the total an odd number of addends.

315. Will all two-factor multiplication problems give a product that is an area? Provide a written explanation to defend your answer.

No. If one of the factors is negative, there is no area because a negative length is undefined.

316. Describe how an isosceles trapezoid can be transitioned to a rectangle to demonstrate the development of the formula for the area of a trapezoid, $\dfrac{(b_1 + b_2)h}{2}$.

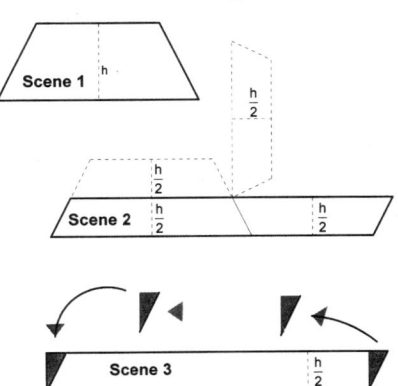

Tag Activities

TAG stands for TRICKS, ACTIVITIES, and GAMES. This is a support set of activities to accompany the text. There are no direct references to the TAG activities within the text and yet many of them could be used to supplement the chapters. Any or all of these could be used as activities for you, the elementary education major, to do while you are using this text in your course. We have used each TAG activity listed here with elementary students. The students enjoyed doing them and frequently presented the TAG questions to friends and family members.

TAG

TAG 1.1

We are going to add five two-digit numbers. You will pick two of them and I will pick three of them. When we are done, the sum will be 247. For now, do not repeat the digits within an addend.

TAG 1.2

Form a magic triangle (place one value in each circle to get the same sum on each side of the triangle) using 23, 34, 45, 56, 67, and 78 similar to TAG Figure 1.1.

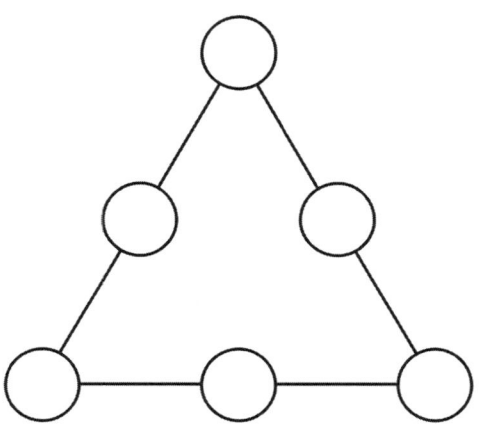

TAG FIG. 1.1.

TAG 1.3

Give each pair one calculator. Have the first student enter 50 into the calculator. Have the next student press the subtraction key and 1, 2, 3, 4, or 5, followed by the = key. The second student then presses the subtraction key followed by 1, 2, 3, 4, or 5 and the = key. The students continue to take turns. The winner is the student that gets 0 after pressing the = key.

TAG 2.1

You can determine whether children recognize the number of elements in a set by showing a number of objects in a set. Each child should have a series of cards with one numeral on each. When the objects are shown, each child would sort through the cards and hold up the card they believe represents the number of objects. This allows you to quickly determine who has grasped the concept and who has not. At the same time, you can gather evidence on who needs additional help.

TAG 2.2

Assuming the group possesses conservation of length, have them measure some distance in terms of their hand span (define it however you want for the class). The results will vary. Discuss why the variations exist, and guide the conversation toward the need for a standard unit of measurement.

TAG 2.3

Given the following information, where would the Z go and why?

```
A       E F  H I   K L M N                 T  V W X Y
     B C D     G       J         O P Q R S  U
```

TAG 2.4

Use jump rope rhymes and bouncing balls for counting, skip counting, coordination, and fun for individuals, partners, and the whole group in unison.

RHYME 1
I love stories and I love reading
How many books will I be needing?
1, 2, 3, 4, . . . (or 2, 4, 6, 8, . . .)

RHYME 2
Teacher, teacher
Hear me count.
Will I reach the greatest amount?
5, 10, 15, 20, . . . (vary the count)
(Brumbaugh, p. 15)

TAG 2.5

The game board is shown in TAG Fig. 2.1. Initially two copies of the game board are made, at least one of which should be on one inside face of a file folder. The second game board has all the sums entered in the appropriate squares. The sum board is cut into small squares with one sum per square.

These pieces will be placed appropriately on the game board during play. Any values to serve as addends may be listed across the top and down the left column. The playing pieces are placed face down on the table, and each player (no more than four is best) draws five. The objective is to be the first person to play all five pieces. The first player is randomly selected, and play goes around the table in a clockwise direction. If a piece cannot be placed, that player passes. TAG Fig. 2.2 shows two playing pieces on the board. The options available to the next player are indicated by Xs. Diagonal touches may or may not be permitted. As you can see, with only two pieces played, a large part of the game board is available for use. Larger game boards increase the degree of difficulty.

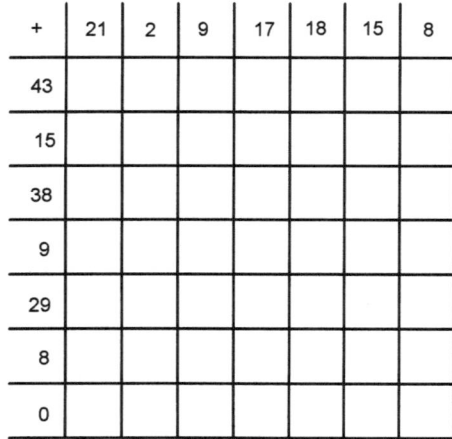

+	21	2	9	17	18	15	8
43							
15							
38							
9							
29							
8							
0							

Game Board

+	21	2	9	17	18	15	8
43	64	45	52	60	61	58	51
15	36	17	24	32	33	30	23
38	59	40	47	55	56	53	46
9	30	11	18	26	27	24	17
29	50	31	38	46	47	44	37
8	29	10	17	25	26	23	16
0	21	2	9	17	18	15	8

Playing Pieces

TAG FIG. 2.1.

+	21	2	9	17	18	15	8
43							
15		X	X	X			
38		X	47	X	X		
9		X	X	26	X		
29			X	X	X		
8							
0							

TAG FIG. 2.2.

TAG 2.6

Each student should have a copy of TAG Fig. 2.3 and you should have one to project at the same time. The students are told to loop any value on the board and eliminate every other value in the row and column containing the selection (shown by a single strike through in TAG Fig. 2.3). One of the remaining values is looped and the other numerals in that row and column are eliminated (shown by a double strike through in TAG Fig. 2.3). One of the remaining values is looped and the other numerals in that row and column are eliminated (shown by an underscore in TAG Fig. 2.3). The one remaining value should be looped. Find the sum of

~~18~~	~~35~~	~~33~~	(49)
~~31~~	(48)	~~46~~	~~62~~
(12)	~~29~~	27	~~43~~
27	~~44~~	(42)	~~58~~

TAG FIG. 2.3.

the looped values. In this case, the sum is always 151.

TAG 2.7

Dominoes can be used to practice addition. For young children, have them make an addition equation based on the spots showing on the two parts of one domino. As they get older, they could randomly draw two dominos, find the total number of spots, add the number of spots on a third domino to that sum, and so on.

TAG 2.8

Use the cards from a standard playing deck (Ace through 10 only) where the Ace represents one. Shuffle the deck and distribute them so that each player has the same number of cards. The respective stacks are placed face down on the table. When told, each player turns over one card and places it so all players can see it. The first player to give the correct sum of all the cards in a round wins a point. Those cards are set aside and the cycle is repeated until all the cards are gone, at which time the deck could be reshuffled and the game repeated.

TAG 2.9

Choose any number with more than one digit. Add the digits used in the selected number. Subtract that sum of the digits from the original number. If the missing addend is not a single digit number, repeat the process.

TAG 2.10

Pick four different digits from 0 to 9. Arrange them to make the largest possible number. Rearrange them to make the smallest possible number. Subtract the smaller value from the larger. Next rearrange the digits of that missing addend to make both the largest and smallest possible values and again subtract the smaller from the larger. Repeat the process until you get 6174. Try 8753 − 3578.

TAG 2.11

Prepare a set of cards large enough so that anyone in the room can see the numeral on each one. Each card should have a unique numeral on it. The student who starts the game selects a second student and they both stand at the front of the room. They both reveal their cards to the class whose task it is to find the missing addend by subtracting the smaller value from the larger. The student holding the card with the missing addend then gets to select another student and the process is repeated. For example, if the two revealed cards are 12 and 7, the missing addend is 5. The student holding the 5 card would then select another person, and those two cards would become the subtraction problem the class is to do.

TAG 2.12

Instruct each student to write the number of members of their family. Add 14. Subtract 7. Add 93. Call on a student to give the result of the computation.

TAG 2.13

Have the class form a ring. One person starts counting with one and then the next person says two, the next three, and so on around the loop. Rather than saying four, the next person would say *buzz*. Similarly, *buzz* is substituted for any multiple of four. Thus, the counting would be 1, 2, 3, *buzz*, 5, 6, 7, *buzz*, 9, 10, 11, *buzz*, 13, ... A player who misses is eliminated. The count could continue from the miss or start back at one. It is interesting to insert a time limit into the game. As the numbers get higher, the pace slows.

Some players will recognize the pattern that after every three numbers, *buzz* is used.

TAG 2.14

This is an extension of buzz. Now when a multiple of a digit is encountered, *buzz* is used. If the number contains the chosen digit, *beep* is the proper response. Suppose the magic number is 3. When they get to 3, they would say *buzz-beep* because 3 is a multiple of three and also contains a 3. The count would be 1, 2, *buzz-beep*, 4, 5, *buzz*, 7, 8, *buzz*, 10, 11, *buzz*, *beep*, 14, *buzz*, 16, . . . This gets quite interesting when they get to the 30s.

TAG 2.15

Use the buzz-beep rules with one alteration, which makes things rather difficult even for adults. When either *buzz* or *beep* is said, the direction around the ring reverses. If 6 is used, the count would be 1, 2, 3, 4, 5, *buzz-beep* (**reverse direction**), 7, 8, 9, 10, 11, *buzz* (**reverse direction**), 13, 14, 15, *beep* (**reverse direction**), 17, *buzz* (**reverse direction**), 19, 20, . . . This variation can get a little loud!

TAG 2.16

Use a standard deck of cards with the Jacks, Queens, and Kings removed. Ace is interpreted as one. Shuffle the deck. Deal an equal number of cards to each player (at first start with only two players). Each player turns up one card. The first player to express the correct product of the exposed cards wins the cards. These cards are turned face down and placed at the bottom of that player's stack. Play another round. Using three or more players for one deck increases the degree of difficulty rapidly.

TAG 2.17

The Doorbell Rang is a book about cookies that have been baked. As the number of people increases, the number of cookies available for each individual decreases. This is a good example of blending mathematics with literature.

Hutchins, P. (1996). *The doorbell rang*. New York: Greenwillow Books.

TAG 2.18

One Hundred Hungry Ants discusses different ways ants can walk so that the same number of ants is in each row and column. This is another example of blending mathematics with literature.

Pinczes, E. (1993). *One hundred hungry ants*. New York: Scholastic.

TAG 2.19

Pick a number.
Double it.
Add 4.
Divide by 2.
Subtract your original number.

What did you get? Repeat this with different numbers. What do you get each time? Why does that work? Select different number values within the directions for variety.

TAG 2.20

Write any three-digit number (485). Repeat that number making a six-digit number (485,485). Divide the six-digit number by seven. Divide the answer from that division problem by 11. Divide the answer from *that* division problem by 13. What did you get? Try it with a different original number. Why does that work?

TAG 2.21

How can a nonhard-boiled egg be dropped 3 feet over a concrete floor without breaking? (no props permitted)

TAG 2.22

What is 10 divided by a half?

TAG 2.23

The Loch Ness monster is 20 feet plus half its own length. How long is the creature?

TAG 2.24

A ping-pong ball weighs about a tenth of an ounce. How many ping-pong balls are needed to have a pound of ping-pong balls?

TAG 2.25

Work with a partner. Each player must add a hundredths decimal that has a non-zero ones digit. No tens digits are permitted in any addend. Keep a running total. The player getting a sum less than 40, forcing the next player to exceed 40 wins.

TAG 2.26

Make a chart similar to the one shown in TAG Fig. 2.5. Students work in pairs. Each student creates a list of five numbers that have a maximum value expressed by a digit in the tens place and a minimum of a value expressed by a digit in the thousandths place. The lists are exchanged and the receiving student is to correctly place the number in the chart. Sample numbers to be listed: 3 and 58 hundredths; $14\frac{672}{1000}$; 0.9.

Tens	Ones	Tenths	Hundredths	Thousandths

TAG FIG. 2.5.

TAG 2.27

Each student is given several 10 × 10 sections of graph paper representing one unit. Thus, each little square represents 0.01. They are to add hundredths only to achieve a given sum and show each addend by coloring the appropriate number of squares. For example, if the desired sum is 0.42, the first student could color 0.09. The second student could color 0.07 more, giving a total of 0.16, which should be represented by one compete row (or column) and six squares in the next one. The original player would add no more than 0.09 (remember, hundredths only). Play would continue until the desired sum is achieved. This amplifies the idea of regrouping in addition of decimals.

TAG 2.28

Create a spinner like shown in TAG Fig. 2.6. Arrange three or four students in a group. One player spins the dial and all students record the value shown. The dial is spun a second time and the object is to add the two values. The fastest student gets a point. The first student to get five points wins that round. You might consider permitting calculators. It should not take long for students to realize that the sums can often be found quicker without a calculator.

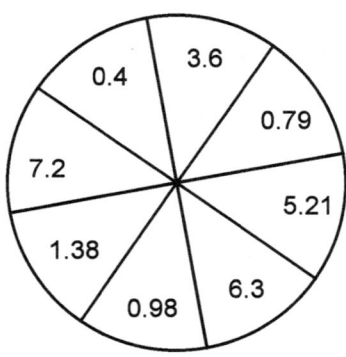

TAG FIG. 2.6.

TAG 2.29

Create a collection of cards with one decimal value on each. A pair of players will use a deck by turning them face down on the table. The top two cards are exposed, and the first player to find a nonintegral value between the two is awarded a point. Play continues with the next two cards in the stack. The game can end when the bottom of the stack is reached, or the cards can be reshuffled and the game continued until a specified number of points is achieved by one of the players.

TAG 2.30

Create a deck of cards with one decimal value on each. A pair of players will use a deck by turning them face down on the table. The top two cards are exposed, and the first player to subtract the smaller from the larger is awarded a point. Play continues with the next two cards in the stack. The game can end when the bottom of the stack is reached, or the cards can be reshuffled and the game continued until a specified number of points is achieved by one of the players.

TAG 2.31

A pair of players start with a 3 × 3 grid. The first player writes a nonintegral decimal in any one of the cells. The second player then writes a different decimal in another cell. Play continues with the ultimate objective of using all values in a row, diagonal, or column, to give a sum of zero. The player correctly completing any row, column, or diagonal is awarded two points. If the correct completion of two of a row, column, or diagonal is accomplished with one placement, the player is awarded two points for the first one and three more for the second one. Play continues to a specified number of points.

TAG 2.32

Provide a 5 × 5 array similar to the one shown below. The objective is to route through the table from the start at the top left to the exit at the bottom right with the smallest value. Movement must be right, down, or diagonally down to the right, and no value may be passed through or jumped over. For each move, the new value is subtracted from the previous. For example, $9.1 - 6.4 = 2.7$. Then, $2.7 - 4.5 = -1.8$. And so on. Not all values on the grid will be used. The answer is going to be a negative decimal.

Start	9.1	7.2	5.3	3.4	1.5	
	7.3	6.4	4.6	3.2	1.4	
	6.8	5.7	4.5	2.9	1.2	
	4.9	4.7	3.6	1.3	0.9	
	4.6	3.1	1.3	0.7	0.2	End

TAG 2.33

Find a pattern for the following set of numbers: 0.5, 0.677, 0.6003, 0.66033, 0.6273135, . . . In this case, a listed value is between the two preceding values. In each instance, the last value is multiplied by some value that gives the necessary result. The students should be encouraged to generate similar examples and have their colleagues solve them.

TAG 2.34

Give the students a statement like $0.34N + 7.2 = ?$ along with a value for N. They are to compute the result using the given value(s). For example, if N is 5.8, then $0.34N + 7.2 = 9.172$. Using 18.94 for N, $0.34N + 7.2 = 13.6396$. Students could make up the statements or values to be used, perhaps so that the new situation will yield a result larger or smaller than the previous one. Scoring could be based on the number of correct responses.

TAG 2.35

A player rolls three probability cubes (dice). Two of the three values are to be used as a base number expressed in terms of hundredths. The third value serves as an exponent. Suppose 3, 5, and 6 is rolled. That could yield, among other things, $(0.56)^3$, which is 0.175616. However, the player could have used $(0.63)^5$, which is 0.0992436, or $(0.35)^6$, which is 0.0018382. Different arrangements of the values rolled could provide alternate responses. The goal could be to generate a value larger or smaller than the previous one, with a point awarded for a correct answer. Play would continue until a player could not meet the stated objective, at which time a new round would be started. Interesting variations could be added by using either a negative base or exponent.

TAG 2.36

Two, three, or four players use the same two spinners similar to the ones in TAG Fig. 2.7. A digit is generated on each spinner board and placed appropriately in a factor. The first player to correctly find the product of all the factors in a round is awarded a point. Play continues to a specified number of points.

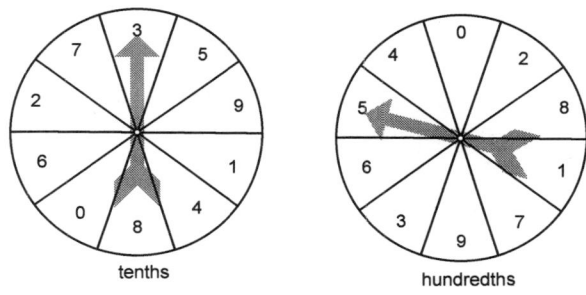

TAG FIG. 2.7.

TAG 2.37

Create a deck of cards with one decimal value on each. A pair of students uses the deck by placing the cards face down on the table. The top two cards are exposed, and the first student to find a value halfway between two wins a point. Play continues with the next two cards in the stack. The game can end when the bottom of the stack is reached, or the cards can be reshuffled and the game continued until a specified number of points is achieved by one of the players.

TAG 2.38

Each student should write a measurement on a piece of paper and state the precision of the measurement. Select two students to list their measurements and precision on the board. Students at their seats should determine the accuracy for each of the listed measurements (precision divided by measurement), listing each result as a decimal value. The seat students should then determine whether their accuracy is between the two listed on the board.

TAG 2.39

Give the students a statement like 0.34 ÷ N + 7.2 = ? along with a value for N. They are to compute the result using the given value(s). For example, if N is 5.8, then 0.34 ÷ N + 7.2 = 7.2586207. Using 18.94 for N, 0.34 ÷ N + 7.2 = 7.2179514. Students could make up the statements or values to be used, perhaps so that the new situation will yield a result larger or smaller than the previous one. Scoring could be based on the number of correct responses.

TAG 2.40

Two players select some nonintegral value, expressing it as a decimal. The objective is to list a decimal closest to the average of the two initial values without actually equaling the average. The closest person would gain one point and a new pair of numbers would be created. Play continues to a specified point total. An interesting variation would be to add the

correct value to the winner's total; after a preannounced number of rounds, the highest (or lowest) total wins.

TAG 2.41

Two players use a pair of dice (different colors) designating one to represent positive and one to be negative. Roll the dice. The first player to correctly name the sum of the top faces gets a point. Play to a total of 10 points. One die could be used: The first roll defined as positive and the second as negative.

TAG 2.42

With the Ace representing one, use all the nonface cards from a standard deck. Shuffle the deck and distribute an equal number to each of four players. The cards are placed face down in front of each player. When signaled, each player turns the top card face up. Reds are positive and blacks are negative. The first player to correctly give the sum of all four cards takes them all. The cards are put face down under that player's stack. Play continues until one player has all the cards or time is called.

TAG 2.43

TAG Fig. 2.8 shows a variety of signed numbers in a grid. The objective is to traverse from the word *start* to the word *fin-*

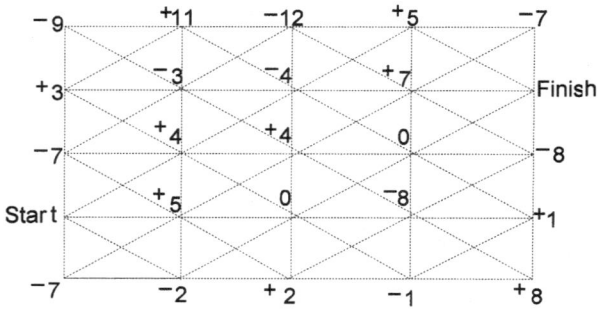

TAG FIG. 2.8.

ish, moving diagonally, horizontally, or vertically and get a sum closest to zero. The move must always be away from the word *start* or toward the word *finish*.

TAG 2.44

Two players use a 4 × 4 grid. They take turns placing an integer in a cell of their choosing. The objective is to have the sum of a row, column, or major diagonal be zero. If placement completes a row and column at the same time, double points are generated. If placement completes a row, column, and major diagonal at the same time, triple points are awarded. The player with the most points wins.

TAG 2.45

Two players use a calculator. The first player enters an addend and hands the calculator to the second player. The first player announces a desired sum (within established limits). The second player is to enter the addend that, when added to the first addend, will give the desired sum. The calculator is used to provide immediate feedback.

TAG 2.46

This is a home-made board game where each player moves a token from start to finish. There is a stack of problem cards (in this case involving subtraction of integers); a player draws a card and must solve the problem on it. The other players check the result. If it is correct, the player's token is moved an assigned number of spaces found on the card. The first one to finish is the winner.

TAG 2.47

On index cards, write an open sentence on one side and an integer on the other. For example, on one side, you write ⁻5 – ⁺8; on the other side you write ⁻2. The number is not the missing addend of the open sentence on the other side of the card. Each student in the class gets an index card. Each card has a different open sentence. The backs of the cards are the missing addends for one of the other problems. Have one student stand up and say, "Who has the missing addend for ⁻5 – ⁺8 = ?" The person who has ⁻13 stands up and says, "I have ⁻13. Who has the missing addend of (the open sentence on their card)?" This continues until the entire class has played. Remember to make the cards so that each open sentence has a corresponding answer.

TAG 2.48

This card game can be played in pairs with a regular deck of 52 playing cards. Place the deck between the two students. Each red card is negative and each black is positive. The first player turns over two cards and must correctly subtract the second card from the first. It is Player 2's job to check Player 1's subtraction. A calculator can be used to check the results. If they are correct, the player keeps the two cards and Player 2 turns over two more cards. If they are incorrect, the cards are placed off to the side. When all cards have been turned over, the missed cards are shuffled and replayed. When all cards have been taken, the person with the most cards is the winner.

TAG 2.49

Pick a whole number.
Subtract 2 from your number.
Multiply the result by 3.
Add 12 to your new product.
Divide your new sum by 3.
Add 5 to your result.

Now subtract your original number from your last sum.

What did you get?

Repeat the process and begin with a negative integer.

What was your result?

TAG 2.50

Three players are involved. The first player selects an integer. The second player must select an integer that divides the first integer. The third player is to determine the missing factor (answer) when the first player's number is divided by the second player's number. Once the answer is stated, a calculator could be used to verify it.

TAG 2.51

Assume that a videotape or movie can be made. The tape or movie must be capable of being played in reverse as well as forward. The students are filmed walking forward while indicating the direction of their walk by holding one arm so it points forward (ball caps with peaks pointing forward could also be used). After several variations of the students walking forward (in a row, column, or circle), repeat the procedure with them walking backward. Then have them walk forward without indicating their direction. Finally, have them walk backward without indicating their direction.

Playing the movie for the students can be a fun experience. Forward walking is defined as positive and backward walking is negative. The motion of the projector is defined as positive if it is running in forward and negative if it is in reverse. Finally, the motion on the screen is positive or negative depending on whether it is forward or backward, respectively. The stu-dent will see how a negative motion coupled with the machine running in a negative direction causes a positive result.

TAG 2.52

This is a board game consisting of player markers, one die, one spinner, a stack of problem cards, and the board. Each player's marker is put on the start location. The problem cards are placed face down on the board. The first player turns up a problem card and then uses the spinner twice. The spinner is divided into two parts: positive and negative. The first spin indicates the sign of one number in the problem, and the second spin shows the sign of the other number in the problem. A positive answer means the player moves forward that number of spaces. A negative answer means the player moves back that number of spaces. The first player to reach the finish location wins. Sample problems would be: $12 \div 3$, $6\overline{)18}$, $36\overline{)18}$, $80 \div 40$, and so on.

TAG 2.53

Use three nines and each operation sign ($+$, $-$, $\times$, $/$) once and only once to write an expression equal to 1.

TAG 2.54

What sound might you hear if you were at the North Pole? To find out, use a calculator to find $0.161616 \div 4$. Turn the calculator upside down to determine the answer.

Direction when walking	Direction of projector	Result on screen
Forward (positive factor)	Forward (positive factor)	Forward (positive result)
Back (negative factor)	Forward (positive factor)	Back (negative result)
Forward (positive factor)	Back (negative factor)	Back (negative result)
Back (negative factor)	Back (negative factor)	Forward (positive result)

TAG 2.55

What do many people do to occupy their spare time? To find out, use a calculator to find $127^3 + 4,618,283 - 1,347,862$. Turn the calculator upside down to determine the answer.

TAG 2.56

Have you lived 10^9 seconds yet?

TAG 3.1

Conduct a formula scavenger hunt. Have the students find places within the school grounds where formulas are posted.

TAG 3.2

Conduct a formula scavenger hunt. Have the students search for Internet sites for formulas they could understand.

TAG 3.3

Have the students conduct a survey of adults they encounter, asking for formulas that are used in the workplace.

TAG 3.4

Have the students conduct a survey of adults they encounter, asking for formulas used in nonwork environments.

TAG 3.5

Pick any counting number.
Add the next highest counting number.
Add 9 to the sum.
Divide the new sum by 2.
Subtract 5.
What did you get?

TAG 3.6

Pick a counting number.
Multiply your number by 2.
Add 4 to you new product.
Subtract 10 from your sum.
Add 6 to your new number.
Now subtract your original number.

What did you get?

TAG 3.7

Pick a number greater than 6.
Add 11 to your number.
Multiply that sum by 6.
Subtract 3 from that product.
Divide the missing addend by 3.
Subtract a number that is six less than your original number.
Subtract a number that is one more than your original number.
Divide that missing addend by 2.
What did you get?

TAG. 4.1

How many squares are on a checkerboard?

TAG 4.2

There is a pond, 100 feet in diameter. Dead in the center of the pond, on a lily leaf, is a frog. If the average leap of a frog is 2 feet and there are plenty of other lily pads to jump on, what is the minimum number of leaps it will take for the frog to jump out of the pond?

TAG 4.3

Why are manhole covers round?

TAG 4.4

How can you plant 10 trees in five rows, having only 4 trees in each row?

TAG 4.5

Symmetry can be investigated with shapes. If you limit yourself to line segments, how many lines of symmetry are there for a square?

TAG 4.6

Segments can be used to divide a given figure into two congruent shapes. How many different line segments can be used to divide a square into two congruent shapes?

TAG 4.7

Describe the shapes seen in your classroom.

TAG 4.8

The artist M. C. Escher used congruent or similar shapes in many of his works. Find an example of Escher's work.

TAG 5.1

How much dirt is in a hole 2 feet deep, 2 feet wide, and 2 feet long? What unit of measurement is required?

TAG 5.2

A train is traveling 60 mph. The train is 1 mile long. The train approaches a tunnel that is 1 mile long. How long will it take the train to travel completely trough the tunnel?

TAG 5.3

If an empty barrel weighs 20 pounds, what can you put in that barrel to make it weigh less?

TAG 5.4

Do you know how many feet are in a yard?

TAG 5.5

Which is worth more, a new ten dollar bill or an old one?

TAG 5.6

When does 10 + 3 = 1?

TAG 5.7

How can you arrange for two people to stand on the same piece of newspaper, yet not be able to touch each other?

TAG 5.8

David has three piles of dirt and Doug has four piles of dirt. If they combined their piles of dirt together, how many piles of dirt do they have?

TAG 5.9

How many 3-cent stamps are there in a dozen?

TAG 5.10

Use a geoboard to show at least seven different triangles with the same area with the surrounding rectangle.

TAG 5.11

Here is an tidbit of trivia from Christy Maganzini's (1997) *Cool Math*. Spelling bees have become a common contest in schools across the globe. Some schools hold another type of contest, a Pi Contest. The object is to correctly state π to the most decimal places. The current record holder is Hideaki Tomoyori of Japan. How many decimal places did he correctly recite π?

TAG 5.12

Here is π calculated to 20 decimal places: 3.14159265358979323846. If we continued typing out π on an endless amount of paper so that the number stretched horizontally across the paper continuously for 1 billion decimal places, how long would this number be?

TAG 5.13

Pick a counting number less than 10. Multiply that number by 9. Now multiply that product by 12,345,679. What is the result? Try it with a different number. What is the result?

TAG 5.14

You have a three-gallon, five-gallon, and an eight-gallon bucket. You need to put exactly seven gallons of water in the eight-gallon bucket. You only use these three buckets. Describe your process to accomplish the task.

TAG 6.1

Give each student in the class a package of Skittles®. Divide the class into groups of three students. If one group has only two students, make sure that every group has three bags of Skittles®. Before the activity begins, ask the students to write the answers to the following questions:

1. What color do you think will occur the most in your bag?
2. Do you think this color will represent the greatest number of Skittles® in every bag?
3. What color do you think will occur least often in your bag?
4. Do you think this color will represent the least number of Skittles® in every bag?

Have each student open their bag and group the Skittles® by color. Then write the true answers to Questions 1 to 4 beside their answers. Next, have each group combine their Skittles® and group the Skittles® by color. Be sure to have one student construct a data sheet and another record the number of each color of Skittles®. Have each group create a Skittles® bar graph on construction paper using the Skittles® to represent the bars similar to TAG Fig. 6.1. Have the students compare and contrast their original guesses. Ask each group to make some conclusions about the color of Skittles® in a single bag. Add some questions of your own. This activity also works extremely well with pie charts. That will allow the students to display the percentages of each color in their group of Skittles®.

TAG 6.2

This is a great activity for an entire class around Halloween. You will need the fun size (or small size) of five different candy bars. Try to get brands that are approximately the same size. You will need enough candy for the entire grade at your school. You will need to discuss this project with your administration as well as coordinate the activity with other teachers in your grade. At a specified time, have certain students take a bag of candy bars, scissors, and napkins into another class. Each student in that class is allowed to select one favorite candy bar from the bag. When they make the selection, the students from your class clip off the end of the wrapper and slide the candy bar onto a napkin. Your students must retain the wrapper for the activity, whereas the students in the other class get to eat the candy bar. Your students return to your classroom with the empty wrappers. You class project is to make a bar graph for displaying the five candy bars preferences for your grade. The unique part of

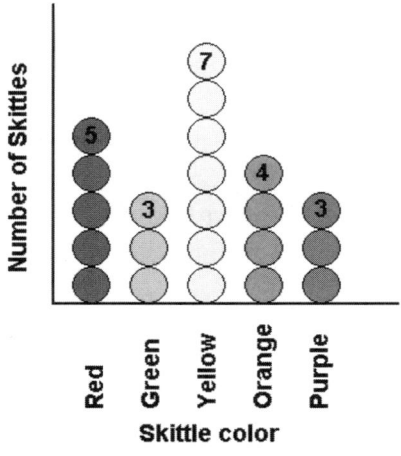

TAG FIG. 6.1.

this activity is that you can use the wrappers of candy bars to make a giant bar graph. This graph can be displayed outside your classroom for all students to see. When completed, take a picture of your class in front of the graph. Have your students write an essay describing the process they went through to complete the activity. Also, have the students draw some conclusions about their graphs. Finally, have the class write letters to the headquarters of the candy bar companies describing their project. Be sure to include the photograph. Who knows what they may send back!

TAG 6.3

This activity requires a microwave and microwave popcorn packages from several different brands. Begin this activity by having each student in the class answer the following questions:

1. Which brand of popcorn will have the most popped pieces? Why?
2. Which brand of popcorn will have the most unpopped kernels? Why?
3. Which brand of popcorn does your family eat at home if any? Why?

Divide your class so that each group gets one bag of popcorn. For example, if you have six brands and 24 students, each group will have four children. Pop each bag in the microwave. Keep a close eye on the time so the popcorn does not burn. Once that burned popcorn smell gets out, it will permeate the school! Be sure to allow the popcorn to cool before you give the bags to the respective groups. One person in each group should make a data sheet with two columns: popped popcorn and unpopped kernels. One person should be in charge of recording the data. Have the rest of the group begin counting the popped and unpopped popcorn.

Have each group construct a pie chart to represent the data. Be sure to have the students include the percentages on the pie chart. This will allow the students to see which brand had the greatest percentage of popped popcorn, the greatest percentage of unpopped kernels, the smallest percentage of popped popcorn, and the smallest percentage of unpopped kernels. Have the students compare each other's pie charts. Have the students answer the following questions after they review all of the pie charts in the class:

1. Which is the first brand of popcorn you would buy and why?
2. Which is the last brand of popcorn you would buy and why?
3. If the brand had the most pieces of popped popcorn in it, does that make it the best popcorn to buy? Why or why not?

Add a few of your own questions as well. The students will love this activity because they get to eat the data at the end! Once again, you might have your students write letters to the companies including copies of all the pie charts and results from the class activity.

TAG 6.4

Have students bring in newspapers from home. Give each student a section of the newspaper. Ask each student to find an example of the use of a measure of central tendency. Have the student highlight the use with a marker. Post on an interactive bulletin board in the room.

TAG 6.5

Give each student a die. Ask the student to roll it 100 times and record the value on the top face each time. What is the mode value? Are most of the values close to being equal? Why do you think that is so?

TAG 6.6

Combine all the results for the whole class from the TAG 6.5 activity. Do the results change? Why would there be an expected change?

TAG 6.7

Supply each student with a paper drink cup (getting some for a variety of fast food restaurants can provide some added interest). Each student should drop the cup 25 times, recording whether it lands on its top, side, or bottom as shown in TAG Fig. 6.2. Ask the students to predict which of the three options they feel will be the most prevalent, and ask them to defend their position in writing. Have them do a frequency distribution of the three possibilities. Would the results vary if all the data were compiled? Why or why not?

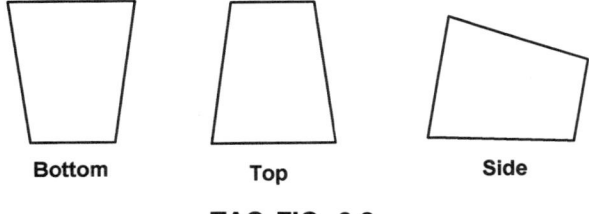

Bottom　　　　**Top**　　　　**Side**

TAG FIG. 6.2.

TAG 6.8

Have each student flip a coin 50 times, recording the number of heads and tails. What is the class average for heads?

TAG 6.9

Each student should list their top five preferred records, tapes, CDs, movies, TV shows, and so on. Have them compile the results, making a frequency distribution for the class information and list the most popular title. Ask the class which measure of central tendency represents the most popular title? Would the other measures of central tendency be appropriate in this situation?

TAG 6.10

Have each student record the amount of rain or snow at their home over a given period of time. Compile the results and determine the different measures of central tendency. Why could it be that different students would have different data for the same time period?

TAG 6.11

Have the students use the sports section of a paper to determine the batting average, average goals per game, yardage gained per carry, points scored per game, and so on of their favorite player in some sport. Find the salary figures for these individuals, and determine how much they make per hit, goal, point, yard, and so on. What is the average income of professional athletes? Is it reasonable for children to aspire to become professional athletes? Why or why not?

TAG 6.12

What is the probability of 2 students in a class of 30 having the same birthday (month and day only)? What would the chance be if there were 40 students in the class?

TAG 7.1

What is the sum of the first 100 consecutive counting numbers?

TAG 7.2

Take an ordinary sheet of paper and fold it in half. Fold it in half a second time. Fold it in half a third time. If you could continue folding it in half 50 times, how high would the stack of paper be? Take an ordinary sheet of paper and fold it in half. Fold it in half a second time. Fold it in half a third time. If you could continue folding it in half 50 times, how high would the stack of paper be?

TAG 7.3

Suppose the class is given the set of shapes shown in TAG Fig. 7.1. Each shape is made up of five congruent squares. What possible questions could be generated from these shapes?

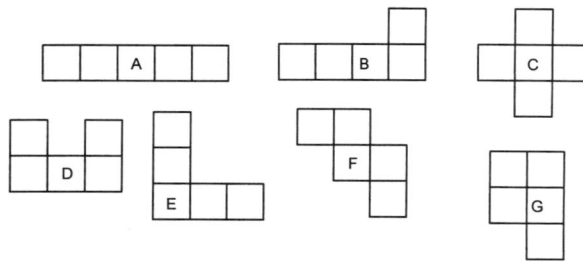

TAG FIG. 7.1.

TAG 7.4

A farmer had 26 cows. All but 9 died. How many lived?

TAG 7.5

A uniform log can be cut into three pieces in 12 seconds. Assuming the same rate of cutting, how long would it take a similar log to be cut into four pieces?

TAG 7.6

How many different ways can you add four odd counting numbers to get a sum of 10?

TAG 7.7

How many cubic inches of dirt are there in a hole that is 1 foot deep, 2 feet wide, and 6 feet long?

TAG 7.8

How many squares are there in a 4 × 4 grid?

TAG 7.9

A little green frog is sitting at the bottom of the stairs. She wants to get to the tenth step, so she leaps up two steps and then back one. Then she leaps another two steps and back one. How many leaps will she have to take if she follows this same pattern until she reaches the tenth step?

TAG 7.10

If there are 7 months that have 31 days in them and 11 months that have 30 days in them, how many months have 28 days in them?

TAG 7.11

There are exactly 11 people in a room, and each person shakes hands with every other person in the room. When A shakes with B, B is also shaking with A. That counts as *one* handshake. How many handshakes will there be when everyone is finished?

TAG 7.12

TTTTTTT9 What number does this represent?

TAG 7.13

There are nine stalls in a barn. Each stall fits only one horse. If there are 10 horses and only nine stalls, how can all the horses fit into the nine stalls without placing more than one horse in each stall? Explain how you got your answer.

TAG 7.14

You are given five beans and four bowls. Place an odd number of beans in each bowl. Use all beans.

TAG 7.15

You are to take a pill every half hour. You have 18 pills to take. How long will the pills last?

TAG 7.16

If you got a 40% discount on a $150 pair of sport shoes and 20% of a $200 set of roller blades, what was the percent discount on the total purchase (assuming no taxes are involved)?

TAG 7.17

How old would you be in years if you lived 1,000,000 hours?

TAG 7.18

A kid has $3.15 in U.S. coins, but only dimes and quarters. There are more quarters than dimes. How many of each coin does the kid have? Explain how you got your answer.

TAG 7.19

There are three children in a family. The oldest is 15. The average of their ages is 11. The median age is 10. How old is the youngest child?

TAG 7.20

A famous mathematician was born on March 14, which could be written 3.14. This date is the start of a representation for pi. It is interesting that this mathematician was born on "pi day." Give his name.

TAG 7.21

What is the next number in the 10, 4, 3, 11, 15, ? sequence and why?

A) 14, B) 1 C) 17 D) 12

Notice how questions can be asked in a multiple-choice format.

TAG Solutions Manual

TAG 1.1

We are going to add five two-digit numbers. You will pick two of them and I will pick three of them. When we are done, the sum will be 247. For now, do not repeat the digits within an addend.

Answer: Pair one of your selected numbers with one chosen by the students so the sum is 99. Do the same thing with the second number. Your third choice will be two greater than the tens and ones digit of the sum. That fifth number you pick will be preceded by a 2, giving your three-digit sum. In this example, your third number (the one not paired with the ones selected by the students would have been 49). This trick can be altered to include more addends and a different number of digits used for the addends.

TAG 1.2

Form a magic triangle (place one value in each circle to get the same sum on each side of the triangle) using 23, 34, 45, 56, 67, and 78.

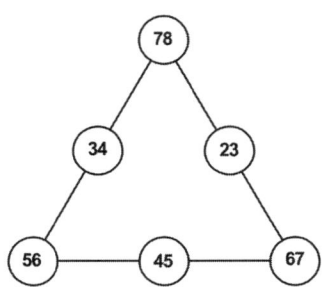

TAG FIG. 1.2.

TAG 1.3

Give each pair one calculator. Have the first student enter 50 into the calculator. Have the next student press the subtraction key and 1, 2, 3, 4, or 5, followed by the = key. The second student then presses the subtraction key followed by 1, 2, 3, 4, or 5 and the = key. The students continue to take turns. The winner is the student who gets 0 after pressing the = key.

TAG 2.1

You can determine whether children recognize the number of objects in a set by showing a number of objects in a set. Each child should have a series of cards with one numeral on each. When the objects are shown, each child would sort through the cards and hold up the card they believe represents the number of objects. This allows you to quickly determine who has grasped the concept and who has not. At the same time, you can gather evidence on who needs additional help.

TAG 2.2

Assuming the group possesses conservation of length, have them measure some distance in terms of their hand span (define it however you want for the class). The results will vary. Discuss why the variations exist, and lead the conversation toward the need for a standard unit of measurement.

TAG 2.3

Given the following information, where would the Z go and why?

```
A        E F  H I   K L M N              T  V W X Y
  B C D      G    J          O P Q R S  U
```

ANSWER: Z goes above the segment. Straights are above and curves are below.

TAG 2.4

Use jump rope rhymes and bouncing balls for counting, skip counting, coordination, and fun for individuals, partners, and the whole group in unison.

RHYME 1
I love stories and I love reading
How many books will I be needing?
1, 2, 3, 4, . . . (or 2, 4, 6, 8, . . .)

RHYME 2
Teacher, teacher
Hear me count.
Will I reach the greatest amount?
5, 10, 15, 20, . . . (vary the count)
(Brumbaugh, p. 15)

TAG 2.5

The game board is shown in TAG Fig. 2.1. Initially two copies of the game board are made, at least one of which should be on one inside face of a file folder. The sec-

+	21	2	9	17	18	15	8
43							
15		X	X	X			
38		X	47	X	X		
9		X	X	26	X		
29			X	X	X		
8							
0							

TAG FIG. 2.2.

ond game board has all the sums entered in the appropriate squares. The sum board is cut into small squares with one sum per square. These pieces will be placed appropriately on the game board during play. Any values to serve as addends may be listed across the top and down the left column. The playing pieces are placed face down on the table, and each player (no more than four is best) draws five. The objective is to be the first person to play all five pieces. The first player is randomly selected, and play goes around the table in a clockwise direction. If a piece cannot be placed, that player passes. TAG Fig. 2.2 shows two playing pieces on the board.

+	21	2	9	17	18	15	8
43							
15							
38							
9							
29							
8							
0							

Game Board

+	21	2	9	17	18	15	8
43	64	45	52	60	61	58	51
15	36	17	24	32	33	30	23
38	59	40	47	55	56	53	46
9	30	11	18	26	27	24	17
29	50	31	38	46	47	44	37
8	29	10	17	25	26	23	16
0	21	2	9	17	18	15	8

Playing Pieces

TAG FIG. 2.1.

The options available to the next player are indicated by Xs. Diagonal touches may or may not be permitted. As you can see, with only two pieces played, a large part of the game board is available for use. Larger game boards increase the degree of difficulty.

Solution: Answers may vary.

TAG 2.6

Each student should have a copy of TAG Fig. 2.3, and you should have one to project at the same time. The students are told to loop any value on the board and eliminate every other value in the row and column containing the selection (shown by a single strike through in TAG Fig. 2.3). One of the remaining values is looped and the other numerals in that row and column are eliminated (shown by a double strike through in TAG Fig. 2.3). One of the remaining values is looped and the other numerals in that row and column are eliminated (shown by an underscore in TAG Fig. 2.3). The one remaining value should be looped. Find the sum of the looped values. In this case, the sum is always 151.

Solution: Answers will vary as the numbers in the table are changed. The answer will always be 151 in this example because the addends across the top (4, 21, 19, 35, respectively) and down the left

side (14, 27, 8, 23, respectively) are hidden in TAG Fig. 2.3, but they were used to create the table. The sum of 14, 21, 19, 35, 14, 27, 8, and 23 is 151. When 48 is looped, the addends 27 and 21 are taken and will not be used by any other sum in the table because their row and column are eliminated. Thus, each looped numeral eliminates two of the eight available addends as shown in TAG Fig. 2.4. Change the addends and the secret sum will change.

	4	21	19	35
14	~~18~~	~~35~~	~~33~~	(49)
27	~~31~~	(48)	~~46~~	~~62~~
8	(12)	~~29~~	<u>27</u>	~~43~~
23	<u>27</u>	~~44~~	(42)	~~58~~

TAG FIG. 2.4.

TAG 2.7

Dominoes can be used to practice addition. For young children, have them make an addition equation based on the spots showing on the two parts of one domino. As they get older, they could randomly draw two dominos, find the total number of spots, add the number of spots on a third domino to that sum, and so on.

Solution: Answers may vary.

TAG 2.8

Use the cards from a standard playing deck (Ace through 10 only) where the Ace represents one. Shuffle the deck and distribute them so that each player has the same number of cards. The respective stacks are placed face down on the table. When told, each player turns over one

~~18~~	~~35~~	~~33~~	(49)
~~31~~	(48)	~~46~~	~~62~~
(12)	~~29~~	27	~~43~~
<u>27</u>	~~44~~	(42)	~~58~~

TAG FIG. 2.3.

card and places it so all players can see it. The first player to give the correct sum of all the cards in a round wins a point. Those cards are set aside and the cycle is repeated until all the cards are gone, at which time the deck could be reshuffled and the game repeated.

Solution: Answers may vary.

TAG 2.9

Choose any number with more than one digit. Add the digits used in the selected number. Subtract that sum of the digits from the original number. If the missing addend is not a single digit number, repeat the process.

Answer: Eventually the sum of the digits will be 9.

TAG 2.10

Pick four different digits from 0 to 9. Arrange them to make the largest possible number. Rearrange them to make the smallest possible number. Subtract the smaller value from the larger. Next rearrange the digits of that missing addend to make both the largest and smallest possible values and again subtract the smaller from the larger. Repeat the process until you get 6174. Try 8753 − 3578.

Answer: Eventually you get 6174.

TAG 2.11

Prepare a set of cards large enough so that anyone in the room can see the numeral on each one. Each card should have a unique numeral on it. The student who starts the game selects a second student and they both stand at the front of the room. They both reveal their cards to the class, whose task it is to find the missing addend by subtracting the smaller value from the larger. The student holding

the card with the missing addend then gets to select another student and the process is repeated. For example, if the two revealed cards are 12 and 7, the missing addend is 5. The student holding the 5 card would then select another person, and those two cards would become the subtraction problem the class is to do.

TAG 2.12

Instruct each student to write the number of members of their family. Add 14. Subtract 7. Add 93. Call on a student to give the result of the computation.

Answer: Subtract 100 and you have the number of people in that family.

TAG 2.13

Have the class form a ring. One person starts counting with one and then the next person says two, the next three, and so on around the loop. Rather than saying four, the next person would say *buzz*. Similarly, *buzz* is substituted for any multiple of four. Thus, the counting would be 1, 2, 3, *buzz*, 5, 6, 7, *buzz*, 9, 10, 11, *buzz*, 13, . . . A player who misses is eliminated. The count could continue from the miss or start back at one. It is interesting to insert a time limit into the game. As the numbers get higher, the pace slows. Some players will recognize the pattern that after every three numbers, *buzz* is used.

TAG 2.14

This is an extension of buzz. Now when a multiple of a digit is encountered, *buzz* is used. If the number contains the chosen digit, *beep* is the proper response. Suppose the magic number is 3. When they get to 3, they would say *buzz-beep* because 3 is a multiple of three and also contains a 3. The count would be 1, 2, *buzz-beep*, 4, 5, *buzz*, 7, 8, *buzz*, 10, 11, buzz, beep, 14, buzz, 16, . . . This gets quite interesting when they get to the 30s.

TAG 2.15

Use the buzz-beep rules with one alteration, which makes things rather difficult even for adults. When either buzz or beep is said, the direction around the ring reverses. If 6 is used, the count would be 1, 2, 3, 4, 5, buzz-beep (**reverse direction**), 7, 8, 9, 10, 11, buzz (**reverse direction**), 13, 14, 15, beep (**reverse direction**), 17, buzz (**reverse direction**), 19, 20, . . . This variation can get a little loud!

TAG 2.16

Use a standard deck of cards with the Jacks, Queens, and Kings removed. Ace will be interpreted as one. Shuffle the deck. Deal an equal number of cards to each player (at first start with only two players). Each player turns up one card. The first player to express the correct product of the exposed cards wins the cards. These cards are turned face down and placed at the bottom of that player's stack. Play another round.

Discussion: Using three or more players for one deck increases the degree of difficulty rapidly.

TAG 2.17

The Doorbell Rang is a book about cookies that have been baked. As the number of people increases, the number of cookies available for each individual decreases. This is a good example of blending mathematics with literature.

TAG 2.18

One Hundred Hungry Ants discusses different ways ants can walk so that the same number of ants is in each row and column. This is another example of blending mathematics with literature.

TAG 2.19

Pick a number.
Double it.
Add 4.
Divide by 2.
Subtract your original number.

What did you get? Repeat this with different numbers. What do you get each time? Why does that work? Select different number values within the directions for variety.

Answer: You should get 2 each time. Let x be the chosen number. Doubling gives 2x. Adding 4 gives 2x+4. Dividing by 2 gives x+2. Subtracting the original number gives x+2-x or 2. Trying different values works the same way. For example, triple your choice, add 12, divide by 3 and you will always get 4.

TAG 2.20

Write any three-digit number (485). Repeat that number making a six-digit number (485,485). Divide the six-digit number by seven. Divide the answer from that division problem by 11. Divide the answer from *that* division problem by 13. What did you get? Try it with a different original number. Why does that work?

Answer: 485,485 = 485(1001).
         7 × 11 × 13 = 1001.

TAG 2.21

How can a nonhard-boiled egg be dropped 3 feet over a concrete floor without breaking? (no props permitted)

Hold it more than 3 feet from the floor and drop it. It will travel 3 feet before it breaks.

TAG 2.22

What is 10 divided by a half?

20. Did we get you?! $10 \div \frac{1}{2} = 10 \times \frac{2}{1} = 20$

TAG 2.23

The Loch Ness monster is 20 feet plus half its own length. How long is the creature?

40 feet. $x = 20 + \frac{x}{2}$, where x is the length of the monster.

TAG 2.24

A ping-pong ball weighs about a tenth of an ounce. How many ping-pong balls are needed to have a pound of ping-pong balls?

160 ping-pong balls. There are 10 ping-pong balls in one ounce and 16 ounces in a pound. Therefore, there are 10 × 16 or 160 ping-pong balls in a pound.

TAG 2.25

Work with a partner. Each player must add a hundredths decimal that has a non-zero ones digit. No tens digits are permitted in any addend. Keep a running total. The player getting a sum less than 40, forcing the next player to exceed 40 wins.

TAG 2.26

Make a chart similar to the one shown in TAG Fig. 2.5. Students work in pairs. Each student creates a list of five numbers that have a maximum value expressed by a digit in the tens place and a minimum of a value expressed by a digit in the thousandths place. The lists are exchanged and the receiving student is to correctly place the number in the chart.

Tens	Ones	Tenths	Hundredths	Thousandths

TAG FIG. 2.5.

Sample numbers to be listed: 3 and 58 hundredths; $14\frac{672}{1000}$; 0.9.

TAG 2.27

Each student is given several 10 × 10 sections of graph paper representing one unit. Thus, each little square represents 0.01. They are to add hundredths only to achieve a given sum and show each addend by coloring the appropriate number of squares. For example, if the desired sum is 0.42, the first student could color 0.09. The second student could color 0.07 more, giving a total of 0.16, which should be represented by one compete row (or column) and 6 squares in the next one. The original player would add no more than 0.09 (remember, hundredths only). Play would continue until the desired sum is achieved. This amplifies the idea of regrouping in addition of decimals.

TAG 2.28

Create a spinner like shown in TAG Fig. 2.6. Arrange three or four students in a group. One player spins the dial and all students record the value shown. The dial is spun a second time and the object is to add the two values. The fastest student gets a point. The first student to get five points wins that round. You might consider permitting calculators. It should not take long for students to realize that the

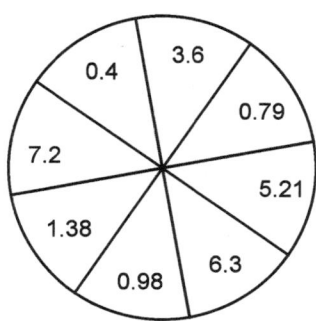

TAG FIG. 2.6.

sums can often be found quicker without a calculator.

TAG 2.29

Create a collection of cards with one decimal value on each. A pair of players will use a deck by turning them face down on the table. The top two cards are exposed, and the first player to find a non-integral value between the two is awarded a point. Play continues with the next two cards in the stack. The game can end when the bottom of the stack is reached, or the cards can be reshuffled and the game continued until a specified number of points is achieved by one of the players.

TAG 2.30

Create a deck of cards with one decimal value on each. A pair of players will use a deck by turning them face down on the table. The top two cards are exposed, and the first player to subtract the smaller from the larger is awarded a point. Play continues with the next two cards in the stack. The game can end when the bottom of the stack is reached, or the cards can be reshuffled and the game continued until a specified number of points is achieved by one of the players.

TAG 2.31

A pair of players start with a 3 × 3 grid. The first player writes a nonintegral decimal in any one of the cells. The second player then writes a different decimal in another cell. Play continues with the ultimate objective of using all values in a row, diagonal, or column, to give a sum of zero. The player correctly completing any row, column, or diagonal is awarded two points. If the correct completion of two of a row, column, or diagonal is accomplished with one placement, the player is awarded two points for the first one and three more for the second one. Play continues to a specified number of points.

TAG 2.32

Provide a 5 × 5 array similar to the one shown below. The objective is to route through the table from the start at the top left to the exit at the bottom right with the smallest value. Movement must be right, down, or diagonally down to the right, and no value may be passed through or jumped over. For each move, the new value is subtracted from the previous. For example, $9.1 - 6.4 = 2.7$. Then, $2.7 - 4.5 = -1.8$. And so on. Not all values on the grid will be used. The answer is going to be a negative decimal.

Start	9.1	7.2	5.3	3.4	1.5	
	7.3	6.4	4.6	3.2	1.4	
	6.8	5.7	4.5	2.9	1.2	
	4.9	4.7	3.6	1.3	0.9	
	4.6	3.1	1.3	0.7	0.2	End

TAG 2.33

Find a pattern for the following set of numbers: 0.5, 0.677, 0.6003, 0.66033, 0.6273135, . . . In this case, a listed value is between the two preceding values. In each instance, the last value is multiplied by some value that gives the necessary result. The students should be encouraged to generate similar examples and have their colleagues solve them.

TAG 2.34

Give the students a statement like $0.34N + 7.2 = ?$ along with a value for N.

They are to compute the result using the given value(s). For example, if N is 5.8, then $0.34N + 7.2 = 9.172$. Using 18.94 for N, $0.34N + 7.2 = 13.6396$. Students could make up the statements or values to be used, perhaps so that the new situation will yield a result larger or smaller than the previous one. Scoring could be based on the number of correct responses.

TAG 2.35

A player rolls three probability cubes (dice). Two of the three values are to be used as a base number expressed in terms of hundredths. The third value serves as an exponent. Suppose 3, 5, and 6 is rolled. That could yield, among other things, $(0.56)^3$, which is 0.175616. However, the player could have used $(0.63)^5$, which is 0.0992436, or $(0.35)^6$, which is 0.0018382. Different arrangements of the values rolled could provide alternate responses. The goal could be to generate a value larger or smaller than the previous one, with a point awarded for a correct answer. Play would continue until a player could not meet the stated objective, at which time a new round would be started. Interesting variations could be added by using either a negative base or exponent.

TAG 2.36

Two, three, or four players use the same two spinners similar to the ones in TAG Fig. 2.7. A digit is generated on each

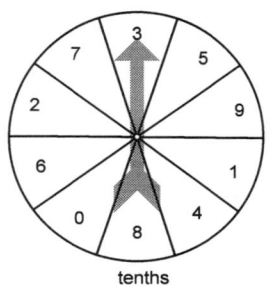 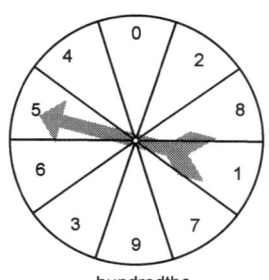

tenths   hundredths

TAG FIG. 2.7.

spinner board and placed appropriately in a factor. The first player to correctly find the product of all the factors in a round is awarded a point. Play continues to a specified number of points.

TAG 2.37

Create a deck of cards with one decimal value on each. A pair of students uses the deck by placing the cards face down on the table. The top two cards are exposed, and the first student to find a value halfway between two wins a point. Play continues with the next two cards in the stack. The game can end when the bottom of the stack is reached, or the cards can be reshuffled and the game continued until a specified number of points is achieved by one of the players.

TAG 2.38

Each student should write a measurement on a piece of paper and state the precision of the measurement. Select two students to list their measurements and precision on the board. Students at their seats should determine the accuracy for each of the listed measurements (precision divided by measurement), listing each result as a decimal value. The seat students should then determine whether their accuracy is between the two listed on the board.

TAG 2.39

Give the students a statement like $0.34 \div N + 7.2 = ?$ along with a value for N. They are to compute the result using the given value(s). For example, if N is 5.8, then $0.34 \div N + 7.2 = 7.2586207$. Using 18.94 for N, $0.34 \div N + 7.2 = 7.2179514$. Students could make up the statements or values to be used, perhaps so that the new situation will yield a result larger or smaller than the previous one. Scoring could be based on the number of correct responses.

TAG 2.40

Two players select some nonintegral value, expressing it as a decimal. The objective is to list a decimal closest to the average of the two initial values without actually equaling the average. The closest person would gain one point and a new pair of numbers would be created. Play continues to a specified point total. An interesting variation would be to add the correct value to the winner's total; and after a preannounced number of rounds, the highest (or lowest) total wins.

TAG 2.41

Two players use a pair of dice (different colors) designating one to represent positive and one to be negative. Roll the dice. The first player to correctly name the sum of the top faces gets a point. Play to a total of 10 points. One die could be used: The first roll defined as positive and the second as negative.

TAG 2.42

With the Ace representing one, use all the nonface cards from a standard deck. Shuffle the deck and distribute an equal number to each of four players. The cards are placed face down in front of each player. When signaled, each player turns the top card face up. Reds are positive and blacks are negative. The first player to correctly give the sum of all four cards takes them all. The cards are put face down under that player's stack. Play continues until one player has all the cards or time is called.

TAG 2.43

TAG Fig. 2.8 shows a variety of signed numbers in a grid. The objective is to tra-

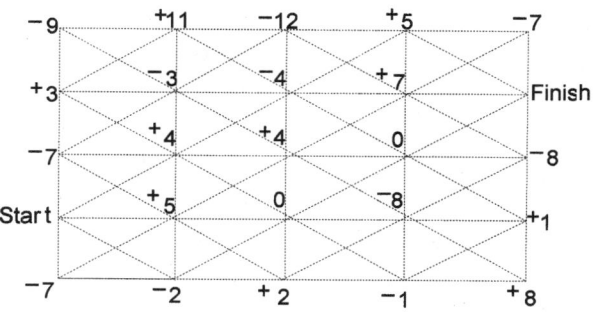

TAG FIG. 2.8.

verse from the word *start* to the word *finish*, moving diagonally, horizontally, or vertically and get a sum closest to zero. The move must always be away from the word start or toward the word finish.

TAG 2.44

Two players use a 4 × 4 grid. They take turns placing an integer in a cell of their choosing. The objective is to have the sum of a row, column, or major diagonal be zero. If placement completes a row and column at the same time, double points are generated. If placement completes a row, column, and major diagonal at the same time, triple points are awarded. The player with the most points wins.

TAG 2.45

Two players use one calculator. The first player enters an addend and hands the calculator to the second player. The first player announces a desired sum (within established limits). The second player is to enter the addend that, when added to the first addend, will give the desired sum. The calculator is used to provide immediate feedback.

TAG 2.46

This is a home-made board game where each player moves a token from start to finish. There is a stack of problem cards (in this case involving subtraction of integers); a player draws a card and must solve the problem on it. The other players check the result. If it is correct, the player's token is moved an assigned number of spaces found on the card. The first one to finish is the winner.

TAG 2.47

On index cards, write an open sentence on one side and an integer on the other. For example, on one side, you write $^-5 - {}^+8 = $; on the other side, you write $^-2$. The number is not the missing addend of the open sentence on the other side of the card. Each student in the class gets an index card. Each card has a different open sentence. The backs of the cards are the missing addends for one of the other problems. Have one student stand up and say, "Who has the missing addend for $^-5 - {}^+8 = $?" The person who has $^-13$ stands up and says, "I have $^-13$. Who has the missing addend of (the open sentence on their card)?" This continues until the entire class has played. Remember to make the cards so that each open sentence has a corresponding answer.

TAG 2.48

This card game can be played in pairs with a regular deck of 52 playing cards. Place the deck between the two students. Each red card is negative and each black is positive. The first player turns over two cards and must correctly subtract the second card from the first. It is Player 2's job to check Player 1's subtraction. A calculator can be used to check the results. If they are correct, the player keeps the two cards and Player 2 turns over two more cards. If they are incorrect, the cards are placed off to the side. When all cards have been turned over, the missed cards are shuffled and replayed. When all cards have been taken, the person with the most cards is the winner.

TAG 2.49

Pick a whole number.
Subtract 2 from your number.
Multiply the result by 3.
Add 12 to your new product.
Divide your new sum by 3.
Add 5 to your result.
Now subtract your original number from your last sum.
What did you get?
Repeat the process and begin with a negative integer.
What was your result?

TAG 2.50

Three players are involved. The first player selects an integer. The second player selects an integer that divides the first integer. The third player is to determine the missing factor (answer) when the first player's number is divided by the second player's number. Once the answer is stated a calculator could be used to verify it.

TAG 2.51

Assume that a videotape or movie can be made. The tape or movie must be capable of being played in reverse as well as forward. The students are filmed walking forward while indicating the direction of their walk by holding one arm so it points forward (ball caps with peaks pointing forward could also be used). After several variations of the students walking forward (in a row, column, or circle), repeat the procedure with them walking backward. Then have them walk forward without indicating their direction. Finally, have them walk backward without indicating their direction.

Playing the movie for the students can be a fun experience. Forward walking is defined as positive and backward walking is negative. The motion of the projector is defined as positive if it is running in forward and negative if it is in reverse.

Direction when walking	Direction of projector	Result on screen
Forward (positive factor)	Forward (positive factor)	Forward (positive result)
Back (negative factor)	Forward (positive factor)	Back (negative result)
Forward (positive factor)	Back (negative factor)	Back (negative result)
Back (negative factor)	Back (negative factor)	Forward (positive result)

Finally, the motion on the screen is positive or negative depending on whether it is forward or backward, respectively. The students will see how a negative motion coupled with the machine running in a negative direction causes a positive result.

TAG 2.52

This is a board game consisting of player markers, one die, one spinner, a stack of problem cards, and the board. Each player's marker is put on the start location. The problem cards are placed face down on the board. The first player turns up a problem card and then uses the spinner twice. The spinner is divided into two parts: positive and negative. The first spin indicates the sign of one number in the problem, and the second spin shows the sign of the other number in the problem. A positive answer means the player moves forward that number of spaces. A negative answer means the player moves back that number of spaces. The first player to reach the finish location wins. Sample problems would be: $12 \div 3$, $6\overline{)18}$, $36\overline{)18}$, $80 \div 40$, and so on.

TAG 2.53

Use three nines and each operation sign ($+$, $-$, $\times$, $/$) once and only once to write an expression equal to 1.

$9^{(9-9)}$ $16666666\frac{2}{3}$ $9^{9-9} = 9^0 = 1$

TAG 2.54

What sound might you hear if you were at the North Pole? To find out, use a calculator to find $0.161616 \div 4$. Turn the calculator upside down to determine the answer.

hohoho—a laugh from Santa Claus

TAG 2.55

What do many people do to occupy their spare time? To find out, use a calculator to find $127^3 + 4{,}618{,}283 - 1{,}347{,}862$. Turn the calculator upside down to determine the answer.

hOBBIES

TAG 2.56

Have you lived 10^9 seconds yet?

10^9 seconds is 1,000,000,000 seconds, which is $16666666\frac{2}{3}$ minutes. This is approximately 277777.7778 hours, which is approximately 11574.07408 days and 31.699 years. We have lived that long, have you?

TAG 3.1

Conduct a formula scavenger hunt. Have the students find places within the school grounds where formulas are posted.

Answers will vary.

TAG 3.2

Conduct a formula scavenger hunt. Have the students search for Internet sites for formulas they could understand.

Answers will vary.

TAG 3.3

Have the students conduct a survey of adults they encounter, asking for formulas that are used in the workplace.

Answers will vary.

TAG 3.4

Have the students conduct a survey of adults they encounter, asking for formulas used in nonwork environments.

Answers will vary.

TAG 3.5

Pick any counting number.	N
Add the next highest counting number.	N + (N + 1)
Add 9 to the sum.	2N + 1 + 9
Divide the new sum by 2.	N + 5
Subtract 5.	N
What did you get?	

The number you started with.

TAG 3.6

Pick a counting number.	c
Multiply your number by 2.	2c
Add 4 to you new product.	2c + 4
Subtract 10 from your sum.	2c − 6
Add 6 to your new number.	2c
Now subtract your original number.	c
What did you get?	

The number you started with.

TAG 3.7

Pick a number greater than 6.	x
Add 11 to your number.	x + 11
Multiply that sum by 6.	6x + 66
Subtract 3 from that product.	6x + 63
Divide the missing addend by 3.	2x + 21
Subtract a number that is six less than your original number.	x + 27
Subtract a number that is one more than your original number.	26
Divide that missing addend by 2.	13
What did you get?	

Should always get 13.

TAG 4.1

How many squares are on a checkerboard?

204. You have one 8 × 8 square, four 7 × 7 squares, nine 6 × 6 squares, sixteen 5 × 5 squares, twenty-five 4 × 4 squares, thirty-six 3 × 3 squares, forty-nine 2 × 2 squares, and sixty-four 1 × 1 squares. $1 + 4 + 9 + 16 + 25 + 36 + 49 + 64 = 204$.

TAG 4.2

There is a pond, 100 feet in diameter. Dead in the center of the pond, on a lily leaf, is a frog. If the average leap of a frog is two feet and there are plenty of other lily pads to jump on, what is the minimum number of leaps it will take for the frog to jump out of the pond?

Zero. The frog is DEAD!

TAG 4.3

Why are manhole covers round? Are there other shapes that will be effective as manholes?

Answer: Manhole covers are round to prevent the lid from falling down the hole. An equilateral triangle will not work because the altitude is less than the length of its sides. If the altitude line were held parallel to the plane of the hole while the lid was held close to one edge, the lid would fall to the bottom of the hole. A similar explanation can be generated for almost any polygon. In the process of exploring altitudes of these polygons, a broad coverage of geometry is generated.

There are other shapes that will work. It is assumed that the lid and hole are similar shapes with the lid being slightly larger than the hole. A Rouleau triangle is shown in TAG Fig. 4.1. The dashed segments represent sides of an equilateral triangle. Arcs are made so the radius is the side length of the triangle, with the arcs terminating at the verticies opposite the vertex serving as the center. In a Rouleau triangle, each point on any arc is equidistant from the opposite vertex. Thus, the lid could not fall down the hole. Any regular polygon with an odd number of sides will generate a Rouleau figure that will work.

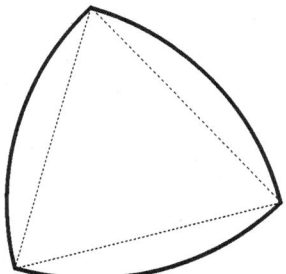

TAG FIG. 4.1.

The Rouleau triangle is an integral basis of Mazda's rotary engine.

TAG 4.4

How can you plant 10 trees in five rows, having only 4 trees in each row?

Plant the trees in the shape of a five-pointed star. The trees are planted at the intersecting points of each segment. The shaded squares mark each tree.

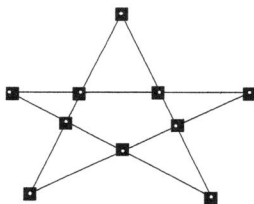

TAG 4.5

Symmetry can be investigated with shapes. If you limit yourself to line segments, how many lines of symmetry are there for a square?

Four. Two diagonals and two segments joining the midpoints of opposite sides.

TAG 4.6

Segments can be used to divide a given figure into two congruent shapes. How many different line segments can be used to divide a square into two congruent shapes?

Infinite. Suppose the side length of the square is 4 inches. Move 1 inch from a vertex and also move 1 inch along the parallel side from the diagonally opposite vertex. You now have two right trapezoids that are similar as shown. Rather than moving 1 inch, move 1.5 inches. This process could result in an infinite number of options.

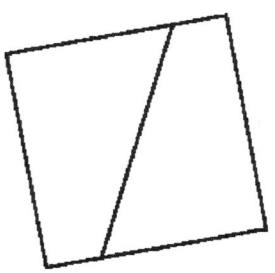

TAG 4.7

Describe the shapes seen in your classroom.

Answers may vary. Rectangles abound with boards, walls, doors, windows, desks, books, floor, ceiling, and so on.

TAG 4.8

The artist M. C. Escher used congruent or similar shapes in many of his works. Find an example of Escher's work.

Answers may vary. Maurits Cornelis Escher (1898–1972, Holland) did a lot of work with tessellating the plane. One of the many examples can be found at *http://www.enchantedmind.com/escher.htm*.

TAG 5.1

How much dirt is in a hole 2 feet deep, 2 feet wide, and 2 feet long? What unit of measurement is required?

None, there is no dirt in a hole. No unit of measurement is needed. The amount of dirt removed is 8 cubic feet. The unit of measurement is cubic feet, which measures volume.

TAG 5.2

A train is traveling 60 mph. The train is 1 mile long. The train approaches a tunnel that is 1 mile long. How long will it take the train to travel completely trough the tunnel?

Two minutes. A train traveling 60 mph travels 1 mile in 1 minute. The front of the train enters the tunnel and takes 1 minute to reach the end. When the front reaches the end of the tunnel, the end of the train is just beginning the tunnel. The end of the train will take another minute to reach the end of the tunnel for a total of two minutes.

TAG 5.3

If an empty barrel weighs 20 pounds, what can you put in that barrel to make it weigh less?

Put holes in the barrel. Then you have removed some of the material to make the barrel weigh less.

TAG 5.4

Do you know how many feet are in a yard?

It depends on how many people or animals are in the yard.

TAG 5.5

Which is worth more, a new ten dollar bill or an old one?

Any ten dollar bill is worth more a one dollar bill.

TAG 5.6

When does 10 + 3 = 1?

When you are talking about time. If you add 3 hours to ten o'clock, you will get one o'clock.

TAG 5.7

How can you arrange for two people to stand on the same piece of newspaper, yet not be able to touch each other?

Place the newspaper on the floor under a closed door. Have each person stand on opposite sides of the closed door.

TAG 5.8

David has three piles of dirt and Doug has four piles of dirt. If they combined their piles of dirt together, how many piles of dirt do they have?

One pile of dirt. If you combine the piles together, you would have one big pile.

TAG 5.9

How many 3-cent stamps are there in a dozen?

There are twelve 3-cent stamps in a dozen.

TAG 5.10

Use a geoboard to show at least seven different triangles with the same area with the surrounding rectangle idea demonstrated in TAG Fig. 5.1 and TAG Fig. 5.2.

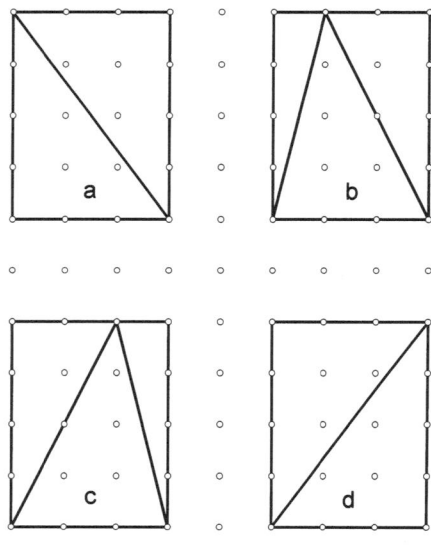

TAG FIG. 5.1.

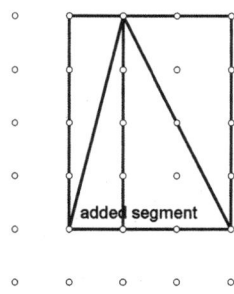

TAG FIG. 5.2.

TAG 5.11

Here is an tidbit of trivia from Christy Maganzini's (1997) *Cool Math*. Spelling bees have become a common contest in schools across the globe. Some schools hold another type of contest, a Pi Contest. The object is to correctly state to the most decimal places. The current record holder is Hideaki Tomoyori of Japan. How many decimal places did he correctly recite?

40,000 decimal places, which took him 17 hours.

TAG 5.12

Here is π calculated to 20 decimal places: 3.14159265358979323846. If we continued typing out on an endless amount of paper so that the number stretched horizontally across the paper continuously for 1 billion decimal places, how long would this number be?

Using Ariel font size 12, there are 12 decimal places per 1 inch. Therefore,

1,000,000,000 ÷ 12 = 83,333,333.33 inches

83,333,333.33 ÷ 12 = 6,944,444.444 feet

6,944,444.444 ÷ 5280 = 1315.23569 miles

TAG 5.13

Pick a counting number less than 10. Multiply that number by 9. Now multiply that product by 12,345,679. What is the result? Try it with a different number. What is the result?

The result will be a repetition of your original number. For example, if your number is 3, then find the product of 3 and 9, which is 27. Next multiply 27 by 12345679. The result is 333333333.

TAG 5.14

You have a three-gallon, five-gallon, and an eight-gallon bucket. You need to put exactly seven gallons of water in the eight-gallon bucket. You only use these three buckets. Describe your process to accomplish the task.

Answers will vary. One solution is to fill the five-gallon bucket. Then fill the three-gallon bucket with water from the five-gallon bucket. That would leave two gallons of water in the five-gallon bucket. Pour the two gallons into the eight-gallon bucket. Then fill the five-gallon bucket with water again. Empty the five gallons into the eight-gallon bucket, which will yield seven gallons in the eight-gallon bucket.

TAG 6.1

Give each student in the class a package of Skittles®. Divide the class into groups of three students. If one group has only two students, make sure that every group has three bags of Skittles®. Before the activity begins, ask the students to write the answers to the following questions:

1. What color do you think will occur the most in your bag?
2. Do you think this color will represent the greatest number of Skittles® in every bag?
3. What color do you think will occur least often in your bag?

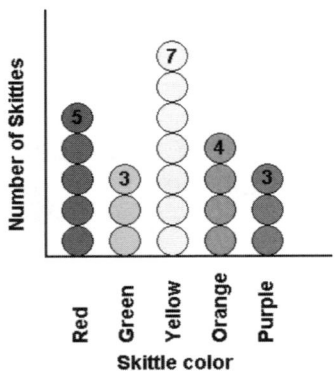

TAG FIG. 6.1.

4. Do you think this color will represent the least number of Skittles® in every bag?

Have each student open their bag and group the Skittles® by color. Then write the true answers to Questions 1 to 4 beside their answers. Next, have each group combine their Skittles® and group the Skittles® by color. Be sure to have one student construct a data sheet and another record the number of each color of Skittles®. Have each group create a Skittles® bar graph on construction paper using the Skittles® to represent the bars similar to TAG Fig. 6.1. Have the students compare and contrast their original guesses. Ask each group to make some conclusions about the color of Skittles® in a single bag. Add some questions of your own. This activity also works extremely well with pie charts. That will allow the students to display the percentages of each color in their group of Skittles®.

TAG 6.2

This is a great activity for an entire class around Halloween. You will need the fun size (or small size) of five different candy bars. Try to get brands that are approximately the same size. You will need enough candy for the entire grade at your school. You will need to discuss this proj-

ect with your administration as well as coordinate the activity with other teachers in your grade. At a specified time, have certain students take a bag of candy bars, scissors, and napkins into another class. Each student in that class is allowed to select one favorite candy bar from the bag. When they make the selection, the students from your class clip off the end of the wrapper and slide the candy bar onto a napkin. Your students must retain the wrapper for the activity, whereas the students in the other class get to eat the candy bar. Your students return to your classroom with the empty wrappers. You class project is to make a bar graph for displaying the five candy bars preferences for your grade. The unique part of this activity is that you can use the wrappers of candy bars to make a giant bar graph. This graph can be displayed outside your classroom for all students to see. When completed, take a picture of your class in front of the graph. Have your students write an essay describing the process they went through to complete the activity. Also, have the students draw some conclusions about their graphs. Finally, have the class write letters to the headquarters of the candy bar companies describing their project. Be sure to include the photograph. Who knows what they may send back!

TAG 6.3

This activity requires a microwave and microwave popcorn packages from several different brands. Begin this activity by having each student in the class answer the following questions:

1. Which brand of popcorn will have the most popped pieces? Why?
2. Which brand of popcorn will have the most unpopped kernels? Why?

3. Which brand of popcorn does your family eat at home if any? Why?

Divide your class so that each group gets one bag of popcorn. For example, if you have six brands and 24 students, each group will have four children. Pop each bag in the microwave. Keep a close eye on the time so the popcorn does not burn. Once that burned popcorn smell gets out, it will permeate the school! Be sure to allow the popcorn to cool before you give the bags to the respective groups. One person in each group should make a data sheet with two columns: popped popcorn and unpopped kernels. One person should be in charge of recording the data. Have the rest of the group begin counting the popped and unpopped popcorn. Have each group construct a pie chart to represent the data. Be sure to have the students include the percentages on the pie chart. This will allow the students to see which brand had the greatest percentage of popped popcorn, the greatest percentage of unpopped kernels, the smallest percentage of popped popcorn, and the smallest percentage of unpopped kernels. Have the students compare each other's pie charts. Have the students answer the following questions after they review all of the pie charts in the class:

1. Which is the first brand of popcorn you would buy and why?
2. Which is the last brand of popcorn you would buy and why?
3. If the brand had the most pieces of popped popcorn in it, does that make it the best popcorn to buy? Why or why not?

Add a few of your own questions as well. The students will love this activity because they get to eat the data at the end! Once again, you might have your stu-dents write letters to the companies including copies of all the pie charts and results from the class activity.

TAG 6.4

Have students bring in newspapers from home. Give each student a section of the newspaper. Ask each student to find an example of the use of a measure of central tendency. Have the student highlight the use with a marker. Post on an interactive bulletin board in the room.

Answers will vary. Try the sports page. For example, in basketball, a player's statistics usually shows their average points per game, which is the mean.

TAG 6.5

Give each student a die. Ask the student to roll it 100 times and record the value on the top face each time. What is the mode value? Are most of the values close to being equal? Why do you think that is so?

Answers will vary. Ideally, the number of times a 1, 2, 3, 4, 5, or 6 shows should be about the same. However, this is a relatively small sample, which could cause the results to be different from what would normally be expected.

TAG 6.6

Combine all the results for the whole class from the TAG 6.5 activity. Do the results change? Why would there be an expected change?

Answers will vary. The results should be closer to being the same for each possible value since the number of trials in the sample is so much larger.

TAG 6.7

Supply each student with a paper drink cup (getting some for a variety of fast

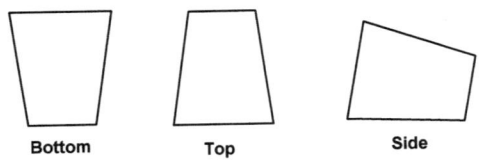

TAG FIG. 6.2.

food restaurants can provide some added interest). Each student should drop the cup 25 times, recording whether it lands on its top, side, or bottom as shown in TAG Fig. 6.2. Ask the students to predict which of the three options they feel will be the most prevalent, and ask them to defend their position in writing. Have them do a frequency distribution of the three possibilities. Would the results vary if all the data were compiled? Why or why not?

Answers will vary, but not much. The cups will almost always land on their sides. Compiling all the data will not alter the results much.

TAG 6.8

Have each student flip a coin 50 times, recording the number of heads and tails. What is the class average for heads?

Answers will vary. The expectation would be 25 heads and 25 tails, but the sample is small so that probably will not happen.

TAG 6.9

Each student should list their top five preferred records, tapes, CDs, movies, TV shows, and so on. Have them compile the results, making a frequency distribution for the class information and list the most popular title. Ask the class which measure of central tendency represents the most popular title? Would the other measures of central tendency be appropriate in this situation?

Answers will vary.

TAG 6.10

Have each student record the amount of rain or snow at their home over a given period of time. Compile the results and determine the different measures of central tendency. Why could it be that different students would have different data for the same time period?

Answers will vary. We have all seen situations where it rains harder in one location than another when the locations are relatively close together. This type thing could impact the results here.

TAG 6.11

Have the students use the sports section of a paper to determine the batting average, average goals per game, yardage gained per carry, points scored per game, and so on of their favorite player in some sport. Find the salary figures for these individuals, and determine how much they make per hit, goal, point, yard, and so on. What is the average income of professional athletes? Is it reasonable for children to aspire to become professional athletes? Why or why not?

Answers will vary. It is important that students not be discouraged from aspiring to become professional athletes. At the same time, they need to be made aware that the number who actually attain that goal is extremely small when compared with all who try. For example, lots of youngsters dream of becoming a professional basketball player. If there are 50 professional basketball teams (men and women leagues) and each team carries 15 players, that is a total of 750 professional basketball players. Some players participate at a professional level for several years, so there are not many openings for rookies each year.

TAG 6.12

What is the probability of 2 students in a class of 30 having the same birthday (month and day only)? What would the chance be if there were 40 students in the class?

The probability is 70% that 2 students will have the same birthday with a group of 30 students. The probability is 89% that 2 students will have the same birthday with a group of 40 students and 97% with 50 students (Brumbaugh et al. 2001, p. 221).

TAG 7.1

What is the sum of the first 100 consecutive counting numbers?

Answer: It has to be $\dfrac{100 \times 101}{2} = 5050$.

TAG 7.2

Take an ordinary sheet of paper and fold it in half. Fold it in half a second time. Fold it in half a third time. If you could continue folding it in half 50 times, how high would the stack of paper be? Take an ordinary sheet of paper and fold it in half. Fold it in half a second time. Fold it in half a third time. If you could continue folding it in half 50 times, how high would the stack of paper be?

Answer: 2^{50} times the paper thickness = 1125899906842624 times the thickness of the paper. If the paper is 0.003 of an inch thick, the stack is $\dfrac{422212465065984}{125}$ inches thick $= \dfrac{35184372088832}{125}$ feet thick $= \dfrac{1099511627776}{20625}$ miles high = 53,309,654.64 miles which is about $\dfrac{2}{3}$ of

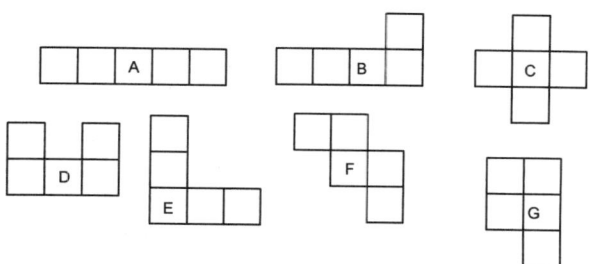

TAG FIG. 7.1.

the distance to the sun. That is a fair sized stack!

TAG 7.3

Suppose the class is given the set of shapes shown in TAG Fig. 7.1. Each shape is made up of five congruent squares. What possible questions could be generated from these shapes?

Answer: What is the area of each figure? What is the perimeter of each figure? What is the maximum perimeter generated by five congruent squares? What is the minimum perimeter generated by five congruent squares? How many different ways can five congruent squares be arranged? How many of the shapes in TAG Fig. 7.1 can be folded to form a box without a lid? There may be other responses.

TAG 7.4

A farmer had 26 cows. All but 9 died. How many lived?

Answer: 9.

TAG 7.5

A uniform log can be cut into three pieces in 12 seconds. Assuming the same rate of cutting, how long would it take a similar log to be cut into four pieces?

Answer: 18 seconds.

TAG 7.6

How many different ways can you add four odd counting numbers to get a sum of 10?
Answer: 1 + 1 + 1 + 7, 1 + 1 + 3 + 5, 1 + 3 + 3 + 3

TAG 7.7

How many cubic inches of dirt are there in a hole that is 1 foot deep, 2 feet wide, and 6 feet long?
None. It is a hole. If you wanted to know how many cubic inches of dirt had been taken out of the hole, 1 ft × 2 ft × 6 ft × 1728 cu in /cu ft = 20,736 cu in.

TAG 7.8

How many squares are there in a 4 × 4 grid?

30. There is one 4 × 4 square, four 3 × 3 squares, nine 2 × 2 squares, and sixteen 1 × 1 squares giving a total of 1 + 4 + 9 + 16 = 30. Place a 3 × 3 square at the top left corner of the 4 × 4 square. That 3 × 3 can also be slid right to occupy a different position, then down one square and finally left one square giving a total of four different locations of 3 × 3 squares on a 4 × 4 grid.

TAG 7.9

A little green frog is sitting at the bottom of the stairs. She wants to get to the 10th step, so she leaps up two steps and then back one. Then she leaps another two steps and back one. How many leaps will she have to take if she follows this same pattern until she reaches the 10th step?

Nine leaps. Up to 2, back to 1; up to 3, back to 2; up to 4, back to 3; up to 5, back to 4; up to 6, back to 5; up to 7, back to 6; up to 8, back to 7; up to 9, back to 8; up to 10 and FINISHED.

TAG 7.10

If there are 7 months that have 31 days in them and 11 months that have 30 days in them, how many months have 28 days in them?

12 months have 28 days in them. This problem can cause an interesting discussion about whether we mean 28 or more (giving the answer of all) or exactly 28 (giving the answer of one) when we say 28 days. Responding different from what the majority of the students select provides an opportunity for some good discussion.

TAG 7.11

There are exactly 11 people in a room, and each person shakes hands with every other person in the room. When A shakes with B, B is also shaking with A. That counts as *one* handshake. How many handshakes will there be when everyone is finished?

55. Two people have 1 shake; 3 people have 3 shakes (AB, AC, BC); 4 people have 6 shakes (AB, AC, AD, BC, BD, CD); 5 have 10; 6 have 15; 7 have 21; 8 have 28; 9 have 36; 10 have 45; 11 have 55. OR, if N = the number of people shaking hands, the formula $\frac{(N)(N-1)}{2}$ gives the total (in this example, $\frac{(11)(11-1)}{2} = \frac{(11)(10)}{2} = 55$ —remember Gauss?).

TAG 7.12

TTTTTTT9 What number does this represent?

79   There are seven Ts for 70, followed by 9 for 79.

TAG 7.13

There are nine stalls in a barn. Each stall fits only one horse. If there are 10 horses and only 9 stalls, how can all the horses fit into the 9 stalls without placing more than 1 horse in each stall? Explain how you got your answer.

"T e n h o r s e s" has nine letters in it. Spell the words, putting one letter per stall. This trick question has generated a lot of discussion and stimulates divergent thinking. The objective of this problem is more than finding the answer.

TAG 7.14

You are given five beans and four bowls. Place an odd number of beans in each bowl. Use all beans.

Put all the bowls inside each other and all the beans in the top bowl. There are variations of this that could be used. For example, put one bean in the smallest bowl two in the next smallest and two in the largest, still putting all the bowls inside each other. The smallest bowl would have one bean in it. The next smallest would have three in it (2 directly and 1 inside the smallest bowl which is inside the second smallest bowl). And so on.

TAG 7.15

You are to take a pill every half hour. You have 18 pills to take. How long will the pills last?

$8\frac{1}{2}$ hours. The tendency is to divide 18 by 2, getting 9. However, the first pill is taken at the beginning of the time period

or at time zero. So the second one is taken at the first half hour, the third at the first hour, and so on. There are no pills left to be taken at the ninth hour.

TAG 7.16

If you got a 40% discount on a $150 pair of sport shoes and 20% of a $200 set of roller blades, what was the percent discount on the total purchase (assuming no taxes are involved)?

28.57142% You pay $90 for the shoes and $160 for the skates for a total of $250 spent instead of $350. $\frac{100}{350} = 0.2857142$ or 28.57142%

TAG 7.17

How old would you be in years if you lived 1,000,000 hours?

114.07712 years.

TAG 7.18

A kid has $3.15 in U.S. coins, but only dimes and quarters. There are more quarters than dimes. How many of each coin does the kid have? Explain how you got your answer.

11 quarters and 4 dimes. Could be guess and check. Easiest way is to start at $3.15 and back down to $2.75, which is the first odd batch of quarters from the top.

TAG 7.19

There are three children in a family. The oldest is 15. The average of their ages is 11. The median age is 10. How old is the youngest child?

8.   Because the average age is 11, the total age has to be 33. Take out the 15 year oldest and the 10 year median and you are left with 8.

TAG 7.20

A famous mathematician was born on March 14, which could be written 3.14. This date is the start of a representation for pi. It is interesting that this mathematician was born on "pi day." Give his name.

Albert Einstein.

TAG 7.21

What is the next number in this sequence and why?

10, 4, 3, 11, 15, ?
   A) 14, B) 1 C) 17 D) 12
   14. Count the letters in each of the ones given. The number of letters increases one each time.